Second Edition

THE STRATEGY AND TACTICS OF PRICING

A guide to profitable decision making

THOMAS T. NAGLE

Strategic Pricing Group, Inc.
  and
School of Management, Boston University

REED K. HOLDEN

Strategic Pricing Group, Inc.
  and
School of Management, Boston University

PRENTICE HALL
Englewood Cliffs, New Jersey 07632

Library of Congress Cataloging-in-Publication Data

Nagle, Thomas T.
    The strategy and tactics of pricing : a guide to profitable
decision making / Thomas T. Nagle, Reed K. Holden. -- 2nd ed.
        p.   cm.
    Includes bibliographical references and index.
    ISBN 0-13-669376-8   -- ISBN 0-13-669060-2 (pbk.)
    1. Pricing. 2. Marketing--Decision making.   I. Holden, Reed K.
II. Title.
HF5416.5.N34 1994
658.8'16--dc20   94-15812
                                                        CIP

To Barbara Fenn Haller,
for six years of devotion and perseverance
through development of our business
and production of this second edition

Acquisitions editor   Sandra Steiner
Production editor   Maureen Wilson
Cover designer   Tweet Design
Buyer   Patrice Fraccio
Editorial Assistant   Cathi Profitko

 © 1995, 1987 by Prentice-Hall, Inc.
A Simon & Schuster Company
Englewood Cliffs, New Jersey 07632

Printed in the United States of America

10

ISBN 0-13-669376-8

Prentice-Hall International (UK) Limited, *London*
Prentice-Hall of Australia Pty. Limited, *Sydney*
Prentice-Hall Canada Inc., *Toronto*
Prentice-Hall Hispanoamericana, S.A., *Mexico*
Prentice-Hall of India Private Limited, *New Delhi*
Prentice-Hall of Japan, Inc., *Tokyo*
Simon & Schuster Asia Pte. Ltd., *Singapore*
Editora Prentice Hall do Brasil, Ltda., *Rio de Janeiro*

CONTENTS

PREFACE xi

ACKNOWLEDGMENTS xiii

Chapter 1

STRATEGIC PRICING

The harvest of your profit potential 1

WHY PRICING IS OFTEN INEFFECTIVE 1

The cost-plus delusion 3 *Customer-driven pricing* 7
Competition-driven pricing 8

PLANNING FOR EFFECTIVE PRICING 9

Learning effective pricing: the plan of this book 12

SUMMARY 14

NOTES 15

Chapter 2

COSTS

How should they affect pricing decisions? 17

DETERMINING RELEVANT COSTS 18

Why incremental costs? 19 *Why avoidable costs?* 23

ESTIMATING RELEVANT COSTS 28

PERCENT CONTRIBUTION MARGIN AND PRICING
STRATEGY 31

SUMMARY 33

NOTES 34

Chapter 3

FINANCIAL ANALYSIS

Market-based pricing for profit   36

BREAKEVEN SALES ANALYSIS: THE BASIC CASE   38

BREAKEVEN SALES INCORPORATING A CHANGE IN VARIABLE COST   41

BREAKEVEN SALES WITH INCREMENTAL FIXED COSTS   43

BREAKEVEN SALES ANALYSIS FOR REACTIVE PRICING   46

CALCULATING POTENTIAL FINANCIAL IMPLICATIONS   48

BREAKEVEN SALES CURVES   50

Watching your baseline   54
Covering nonincremental fixed and sunk costs   55

SUMMARY   57

NOTES   57

Appendix 3A   Derivation of the breakeven formula   58

Appendix 3B   Breakeven analysis of price changes   61

DEVELOPING A BREAKEVEN CHART   61

BREAKEVEN ANALYSIS WITH MORE THAN ONE INCREMENTAL FIXED COST   63

BREAKEVEN GRAPHS   66

SUMMARY   71

Chapter 4

CUSTOMERS

Understanding and influencing the purchase decision   72

ROLE OF VALUE IN PRICING   73

FACTORS AFFECTING PRICE SENSITIVITY   77

Perceived substitutes effect   78   Unique value effect   79
Switching cost effect   80   Difficult comparison effect   81
Price-quality effect   83   Expenditure effect   86
End-benefit effect   87   Shared-cost effect   89
Fairness effect   91   Inventory effect   93

MANAGERIAL ANALYSIS OF PRICE SENSITIVITY   94

PREPARING A MANAGERIAL ANALYSIS   95

ECONOMICS OF PRICE SENSITIVITY   100

GENERALIZATIONS ABOUT PRICE ELASTICITIES   101

SUMMARY   103

NOTES   104

Appendix 4A   Economic value analysis: an illustration   107

ECONOMIC VALUE ANALYSIS   107

INTERPRETING ECONOMIC VALUE   110

ECONOMIC VALUE PROFILE   111

NOTES   114

Chapter 5

COMPETITION

Managing your market proactively   115

UNDERSTANDING THE PRICING GAME   117

PLAN FOR PROFITABLE PRICING   118

Anticipate and manage competition   119
Establish pricing policies consistent with the plans   121

MANAGING COMPETITIVE INFORMATION   123

Collect and evaluate information   124
Selectively communicate information   126

ALLOCATING COMPETITIVE RESOURCES   129

Seek competitive advantage, not market share   130
Select your confrontations   132

SUMMARY   136

NOTES   137

Appendix 5A   Market-share myth   139

NOTES   140

Chapter 6

STRATEGY

Integrating the elements of profitable pricing   141

A FRAMEWORK FOR PRICING   141

Data collection   142   Strategic analyses   143
An illustration   145

GENERIC PRICING STRATEGIES   **152**
Skim pricing   *154*   *Penetration pricing*   *158*
Neutral pricing   *160*
STRATEGIC PRICE SEGMENTATION   **161**
SUMMARY   **166**
NOTES   **166**

Chapter 7

LIFE CYCLE PRICING
Adapting strategy in a changing environment   **167**

PRICING THE INNOVATION FOR MARKET DEVELOPMENT   **168**
Marketing innovations through price-induced sampling   *170*
Marketing innovations through direct sales   *171*
Marketing innovations through distribution channels   *172*
PRICING THE NEW PRODUCT FOR GROWTH   **172**
Pricing the differentiated product   *173*
Pricing the low-cost product   *174*
Choosing a growth strategy   *175*
Price reductions in growth   *178*
PRICING THE ESTABLISHED PRODUCT IN MATURITY   **178**
PRICING A PRODUCT IN MARKET DECLINE   **182**
Alternative strategies in decline   *182*
SUMMARY   **185**
NOTES   **186**

Chapter 8

CUSTOMER NEGOTIATION
Pricing in the trenches   **189**

NEGOTIATED VERSUS FIXED-PRICE POLICIES   **189**
Reasons for negotiating price   *190*
Undoing the damage   *191*
Understanding the buying center   *192*
Negotiation Strategies   *193*
Negotiating with price buyers   *193*
Negotiating with loyal buyers   *195*
Negotiating with value buyers   *196*
Avoiding the price trap   *198*

PREPARING COMPETITIVE BIDS   199

Quantitative analysis   *199*   *Probability of success*   *201*
The winner's curse   *205*

SUMMARY   206

NOTES   206

Appendix 8A   Incentives for selling value, not volume   208

NOTE   209

Chapter 9

SEGMENTED PRICING

Tactics for separating markets   210

SEGMENTING BY BUYER IDENTIFICATION   211

Obtaining information   *212*
Segmenting by salespeople   *212*

SEGMENTING BY PURCHASE LOCATION   213

SEGMENTING BY TIME OF PURCHASE   215

Peak-load pricing   *215*   *Yield management*   *217*

SEGMENTING BY PURCHASE QUANTITY   218

Volume discounts   *219*   *Order discounts*   *220*
Step discounts   *221*   *Two-part pricing*   *222*

SEGMENTING BY PRODUCT DESIGN   223

SEGMENTING BY PRODUCT BUNDLING   225

Optional bundling   *226*   *Value-added bundling*   *227*

SEGMENTING BY TIE-INS AND METERING   228

Tie-in sales   *228*   *Metering*   *229*

IMPORTANCE OF SEGMENTED PRICING   230

SUMMARY   231

NOTES   232

Chapter 10

PRICING IN THE MARKETING MIX

Developing an integrated strategy   235

PRICING AND THE PRODUCT LINE   235

Pricing substitute products   *237*
Pricing complementary products   *238*
Selecting loss leaders   *240*

PRICING AND PROMOTION   241

Pricing and advertising   242
Pricing and personal selling   246
Setting the promotional budget   248

PRICE AS A PROMOTIONAL TOOL   249

Pricing tactics to induce trial   250   Defensive dealing   253
Trade dealing   255

PRICING AND DISTRIBUTION   257

Selecting an appropriate channel   257
Maintaining minimum resale prices   259
Limiting maximum resale prices   260

SUMMARY   264

NOTES   265

Chapter 11

COMPETITIVE ADVANTAGES

Establishing foundations for more profitable pricing   269

COMPETITIVE COST ADVANTAGES   270

Internal cost efficiencies   270
External cost efficiencies   281
Temporary cost advantages   289

COMPETITIVE PRODUCT ADVANTAGES   289

Product superiority   290   Product augmentation   291
Sustaining product advantages   292

SUMMARY   294

NOTES   295

Chapter 12

PRICING PSYCHOLOGY

Models of purchase behavior   298

PERCEPTION OF PRICE DIFFERENCES   299

Perception of percentage differences   299
Perception of odd endings   300

FORMULATION OF REFERENCE PRICES   302

Current price influences   302   Past price influences   307
Purchase context influences   309

INFLUENCE OF FRAMING ON PRICE PERCEPTION   310

Framing buyers' reference points: the endowment effect   312

Framing gains and losses   *314*
Framing multiple gains or losses   *314*

PRICING PROBABILISTIC GOODS   **316**

SUMMARY   **318**

NOTES   **319**

Chapter 13

MEASURING PRICE SENSITIVITY

Research techniques to supplement judgment   323

TYPES OF MEASUREMENT PROCEDURES   **324**

Uncontrolled studies of actual purchases   *325*
Experimentally controlled studies of actual purchases   *331*
Uncontrolled studies of preferences and intentions   *337*
Experimentally controlled studies of preferences and intentions   *342*

USING MEASUREMENT TECHNIQUES APPROPRIATELY   **349**

Using judgment for better measurement   *350*
Selecting the appropriate measurement technique   *353*

SUMMARY   **355**

NOTES   **356**

Chapter 14

THE LAW AND ETHICS

Determining the constraints on pricing   360

THE LEGAL SANCTIONS   **361**

PRICING AND THE LAW: A BRIEF HISTORY   **363**

THE CASE LAW   **366**

Explicit agreements   *366*   *Nonexplicit agreements*   *371*
Price discrimination   *374*
Tie-in sales and requirement contracts   *379*
Predation   *381*

ETHICAL CONSTRAINTS ON PRICING   **383**

SUMMARY   **386**

NOTES   **388**

INDEXES   399

SUBJECT INDEX   **399**

AUTHOR INDEX   **406**

PREFACE

"Pricing is the moment of truth—all of marketing comes to focus in the pricing decision."[1]

When Raymond Corey wrote these words at the Harvard Business School in the early 1960s, marketing was just coming into its own as the driving force of a business. Unfortunately, few marketing practitioners actually took Corey's words to heart. Enjoying their new prestige and power to influence corporate strategy, they were reluctant to let financial considerations constrain their "strategic" thinking. Instead, they focused on achieving market share and customer satisfaction, believing that high profitability would somehow naturally follow. Marketing academics also slighted pricing, offering little research and few courses on the subject. Whenever the subject of pricing problems did arise, professors assured their students that all could be solved indirectly by redoubling efforts to differentiate the products and services.

These attitudes toward pricing changed radically when marketers encountered the challenges of the 1980s. Companies with leading brand names saw brand loyalty and their power over distribution erode from years of price "promotion" to defend market share. Even large companies often found profits unattainable, as smaller firms targeted and lured away their most profitable customers (a practice labeled "cream skimming" by the victims). Then, successful corporate raiders showed that they could increase cash flow and profits, often by raising prices and cutting marketing expenditures. In response, the survivors "restructured" their businesses by applying rigorous financial criteria to all their expenditures, including marketing and sales.

Marketers were challenged to show that their efforts to differentiate products and increase market share could ultimately pay off at the bottom line. To do so, successful marketing executives began incorporating pricing as an integral part of their jobs; leading business schools began making it an integral part of their marketing curricula. Both efforts required information which our seminars and the first edition of this text were designed to satisfy. In the seven years since the first edition, not only has interest in pricing grown but so has our knowledge of the subject. First, research on pricing by marketers, economists, and cost accountants has increased in both quality and quantity, thus expanding our understanding and providing more effective tools for making pricing decisions. Moreover, the intervening years have taught us that it is often better to aim for practical improvement than to cling to the impractical "ideal." These insights are reflected in this new edition.

Since the first edition, the nature of pricing problems has undergone considerable change. In the early 1980s, the most common pricing errors could be traced to cost-based formulas. From Wang Computer to Sears Roebuck, managements tried in vain to solve problems of excessive fixed costs simply by raising their gross margins. The result, of course, was decreasingly competitive products. Today, all but the most naive companies have abandoned purely cost-driven pricing. For many, however, the transition to more market-driven pricing has done little for profitability. Unleashing sales and marketing managers from financial constraints has led to ad hoc price negotiations. Price lists have lost their credibility; customers have become tougher negotiators; the prices charged have lost their connection to value received. Consequently, many companies have lost control of their pricing and, therefore, of their ability to formulate pricing strategies.

The second edition of this text offers specific help to companies struggling with these problems. The completely new chapter on competition (Chapter 5) shows how to manage, rather than simply react to, a difficult competitive environment. The new chapter on customer negotiation (Chapter 8) shows sales representatives and managers how to reestablish a connection between the value they offer and the prices they charge. The chapter on financial analysis (Chapter 3) now explains how to analyze "reactive" price changes to defend sales. And the chapter on strategy (Chapter 6) provides a behavioral segmentation for pricing that reflects different purchase behaviors that effective pricing strategies must accommodate.

As in the first edition, the primary objective of this edition is to develop a practical and readable manager's guide to pricing, not a textbook. Our references are not necessarily to the seminal articles on the subject, but to those that are most managerially relevant and accessible. For reviews of the academic pricing literature, we recommend the texts by Kent Monroe[2] and Hermann Simon.[3] Professors will be happy to learn that an expanded Instructor's Manual for this edition includes substantially more classroom exercises, minicases, and examination questions. We expect that the combination of clear writing and current, relevant examples will continue to make this the most popular text in the classroom.

NOTES

1. E. Raymond Corey, *Industrial Marketing: Cases and Concepts* (Englewood Cliffs, N.J.: Prentice Hall, 1962).
2. Kent Monroe, *Pricing: Making Profitable Decisions*, 2nd ed. (New York: McGraw-Hill, 1990).
3. Hermann Simon, *Price Management* (Amsterdam: Elsevier Science Publishers, 1989).

ACKNOWLEDGMENTS

We cannot practically enumerate all those people to whom we owe a debt of gratitude but collectively they have contributed substantially to the content of this work. We wish to renew our thanks to all who contributed to the first edition and whose specific contributions were acknowledged there. The success of that edition not only created the demand for a second edition, but also gave us access to client companies and managers from whom we have learned much more about pricing strategy and implementation than would have been possible from purely academic research. Many thanks to our students and seminar participants at Boston University, the University of Chicago Center for Continuing Studies, Management Center Europe, the Singapore Institute of Management, the RAYMA Management Institute, and at numerous companies. Their probing questions and challenging problems continue to keep our work interesting and relevant.

We gratefully acknowledge the advice of numerous experts in marketing, pricing, and business management whose published and unpublished insights we have incorporated into this text. While we could never enumerate them all, we wish to acknowledge our special debt to Kevin Clancy, Richard Harmer, Jay Klopmeker, Milind Lele, Mike Marn, and Gerald Smith. Our research assistants conducted extensive literature reviews and wrote drafts incorporating those reviews with material from the first edition and with notes from our seminars and consulting. Of special note are the contributions of Jim Muth (Chapter 5 on Competition), Cathy Grafton (Chapter 9 on Price Segmentation), and David Kreidberg (Chapter 7 on Life Cycle Pricing and Chapter 8 on Customer Negotiation). We also wish to acknowledge those contributors to the book whose precise contributions are cited in the text: Gerald Smith (Chapters 3 and 12), John Martin (Chapter 13), Craig Harkins and Donna Hamlin (Chapter 13), and Neil E. Graham and William E. Kovacic (Chapter 14).

Much of the success of the first edition, and the promise of the second, comes from the exceptional clarity and style of the writing. All too often the excitement, if not the content, of marketing gets lost in the written word. To the extent that we have avoided this pitfall, some of the credit goes to others. Rena Henderson and Barbara Haller extensively edited drafts of the new chapters, in which our literary sins were most numerous and appalling. Their exceptional abilities to criticize constructively were greatly appreciated. In addition, we had the good fortune to work with very thorough and exceptionally patient editors at Prentice Hall. The copy editor, Terry Seng, and the production editor, Kristin E. Dackow, took the time to understand what we were doing, thus enabling them to correct errors and confusions of content as well as of style. Sandra Steiner, marketing editor at Prentice Hall, deserves credit for convincing us to complete a second edition and getting us what we needed to do so.

Finally, Tom Nagle thanks his wife, Leslie, for her tolerance and patience while he neglected their life together to finally complete this second edition. Reed Holden thanks his wife, Annie; his children, Rebecca and Mark; his parents, Carl and Dottie Holden; and close friends, Ray and Ramona Nichols, for their unwavering support and encouragement during the final stages of the writing and development of the book.

STRATEGIC PRICING

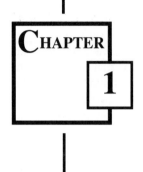

CHAPTER 1

THE HARVEST OF YOUR PROFIT POTENTIAL

Marketing consists of four coequal elements—(1) the product, (2) its promotion, (3) its distribution, and (4) its pricing. The first three elements—product, promotion, and distribution—are a firm's attempt to *create* value in the marketplace. The last element—pricing—differs essentially from the other three: It is the firm's attempt to *capture* some of that value in the profits it earns. If effective product development, promotion, and distribution sow the seeds of business success, effective pricing is the harvest. Although effective pricing can never compensate for poor execution of the first three elements, ineffective pricing can surely prevent those efforts from resulting in financial success. Regrettably, that is a common occurrence.

WHY PRICING IS OFTEN INEFFECTIVE

Philips leads the world in consumer electronics innovation; Citicorp has achieved a commanding share of the credit card business; a handful of airlines dominates the airports of America. Yet, in every case, smaller, less visibly successful competitors in the same industries are substantially and consistently more profitable.[1] Why do these large companies and many others that clearly create great value for their customers fail to capture that value in their earnings? The reason, we believe, is their failure to integrate their value-creating activities with their pricing decisions.

Consequently, whatever profitability they do achieve is less by design than as a byproduct.

The difference between successful and unsuccessful pricers lies in how they approach the process. To achieve superior, sustainable profitability, pricing must become an integral part of strategy, not merely an afterthought. Strategic pricers do not ask, "What prices do we need to cover our costs and earn a profit?" Rather, they ask, "What costs can we afford to incur, given the prices achievable in the market, and still earn a profit?" Strategic pricers do not ask, "What price is this customer willing to pay?" but "What is our product worth to this customer and how can we better communicate that value, thus justifying the price?" When value doesn't justify price to some customers, strategic pricers don't surreptitiously discount. Instead, they consider how they can segment the market with different products or distribution channels to serve these customers without undermining the perceived value to other customers. And strategic pricers never ask, "What prices do we need to meet our sales or market-share objectives?" Instead, they ask, "What level of sales or market share can we most profitably achieve?"

Strategic pricing often requires more than just a change in attitude; it requires a change in when, how, and who makes pricing decisions. For example, strategic pricing requires anticipating price levels before beginning product development. The only way to ensure profitable pricing is to reject those ideas early for which adequate value cannot be captured to justify the cost. Strategic pricing also requires that management take responsibility for establishing a coherent set of pricing policies and procedures, consistent with its strategic goals for the company. Abdicating responsibility for pricing to the sales force or to the distribution channel is abdicating responsibility for the strategic direction of the business. Perhaps most important, strategic pricing requires a new relationship between marketing and finance.

Strategic pricing is actually the interface between marketing and finance. It involves finding a balance between the customers' desire to obtain good value and the firm's need to cover costs and earn profits. Unfortunately, pricing at most companies is characterized more by conflict than by balance between these objectives. If pricing is to reflect value to the customer, specific prices must be set by those best able to anticipate that value—presumably marketing and sales managers. But their efforts will not generate sustainable profits unless constrained by appropriate financial objectives. Rather than attempting to "cover costs," finance must learn how costs change with changes in sales and use that knowledge to develop appropriate incentives for marketing and sales to achieve their objectives profitably.

With their respective roles appropriately defined, marketing and finance can work together toward a common goal—to achieve profitability through strategic pricing.

Before marketing and finance can attain this goal, however, they must discard the flawed thinking about pricing that leads them into conflict and that drives them to make unprofitable decisions. Let's look at these flawed paradigms and destroy them once and for all.

The cost-plus delusion

Cost-plus pricing is, historically, the most common pricing procedure because it carries an aura of financial prudence. Financial prudence according to this view, is achieved by pricing every product or service to yield a fair return over all costs, fully and fairly allocated. In theory, it is a simple guide to profitability; in practice, it is a blueprint for mediocre financial performance.

The problem with cost-driven pricing is fundamental. In most industries it is impossible to determine a product's unit cost before determining its price. Why? Because unit costs change with volume. This cost change occurs because a significant portion of costs are "fixed" and must somehow be "allocated" to determine the full unit cost. Unfortunately, since these allocations depend on volume, which changes with changes in price, unit cost is a moving target.

To "solve" the problem of determining unit cost, cost-based pricers are forced to make the absurd assumption that they can set price without affecting volume. The failure to account for the effects of price on volume, and of volume on costs, leads managers directly into pricing decisions that undermine profits. One particularly tragic example, for the company and its customers, was Wang Laboratory's experience in pricing the world's first word processor. Introduced in 1976, the product was an instant success, enabling Wang to grow rapidly and dominate the market. By the mid-1980s, however, personal computers with word processing software were becoming credible competitors. As competition increased and growth slowed, the company's cost-driven pricing philosophy began killing its market advantage. Unit costs were repeatedly recalculated and prices raised to reflect the rising overhead allocation. As a result, sales declined even further. Before long, even Wang's most loyal customers began making the switch to cheaper alternatives.

A price increase to "cover" higher fixed costs reduces sales further and causes unit cost to rise even higher. The result is often that price increases actually reduce profits. On the other hand, if a price cut causes sales to increase, fixed costs are spread over more units, making unit costs decline. The result is often increased profit. Instead of pricing *reactively* to cover costs and profit objectives, managers need to price *proactively*. They need to acknowledge that pricing affects sales volume, and that volume affects costs.

The dangers of cost-based pricing are not limited to products facing increasing competition and declining volume. In fact, cost-based pricing is even more insidious when applied to strong products since there are no signals (such as declining market share) to warn of the potential damage. For example, an international telecommunications company with many leading technologies uses cost-based pricing only as a "starting point" for pricing. Product and sales managers review the cost-based "target prices" for consistency with market conditions and then argue for adjustments to reflect market conditions. Everyone in the organization finds this system fair and reasonable.

But does the system foster profitability? During the three years it has been in place, marketing has frequently requested and received permission to charge prices less than the cost-based "target" in order to reflect market conditions. Now, how many times during those three years do you think marketing argued that a target price should be raised to reflect market conditions? Never, despite the fact that the company often has large backlogs of orders on some of its most popular products. At this company, as at many others, cost-based target prices have become cost-based "caps" on profitability for the most valuable products.

Cost-driven pricing leads to overpricing in weak markets and underpricing in strong ones—exactly the opposite direction of a prudent strategy. The financial questions that should drive proactive pricing are "How much more sales volume must we achieve to earn additional profit from a lower price?" and "How much sales volume can we lose and still earn additional profit from a higher price?" The answers to these questions depend on how the cost of the product changes with volume. They do not depend on whether the current price of a product, at current volume, covers the cost and profit objectives.

How, then, should managers deal with the problem of pricing to cover costs and achieve profit objectives? They shouldn't. The question itself reflects an erroneous perception of the role of pricing, a perception based on the belief that one can first determine sales levels, then calculate unit cost and profit objectives, and then set a price. Once managers realize that sales volume (the beginning assumption) depends on the price (the end of the process), the flawed circularity of cost-based pricing is obvious. The only way to ensure profitable pricing is to let anticipated pricing determine the costs incurred rather than the other way around. Value-based pricing must begin *before* investments are made.

Exhibit 1.1 illustrates the flawed progression of cost-based pricing and the necessary progression for value-based pricing. Cost-based pricing is product driven. Engineering and manufacturing departments design and make what they consider a "good"product. In the process, they make investments and incur costs to add features and related services. Finance then totals these costs to determine a "target" price. Only at this stage does

---

EXHIBIT 1.1

Role of Pricing Product Development

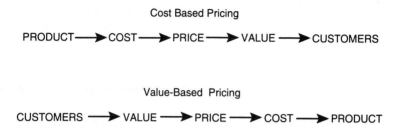

Cost Based Pricing

PRODUCT ⟶ COST ⟶ PRICE ⟶ VALUE ⟶ CUSTOMERS

Value-Based Pricing

CUSTOMERS ⟶ VALUE ⟶ PRICE ⟶ COST ⟶ PRODUCT

---

marketing enter the process, charged with the task of demonstrating enough value in the product to justify the price to customers.

If the cost-based price proves unjustifiable, managers may try to fix the process by allowing "flexibility" in the markups. Although this tactic may prevent the unnecessary loss of market share in the short run, it is not fundamentally a solution. The problem will arise again as the features and costs of new products continue to mismatch the needs and values of customers. Moreover, when customers are rewarded with discounts for their price resistance, this resistance becomes more frequent even when the product has value to them. Solving the problems of cost-based pricing requires more than a quick fix. It requires completely reversing the process. For value pricing, the target price is based on an estimate of value, not costs. The target price then drives decisions about what costs to incur, rather than the other way around.

Examples of purely value-based pricing are infrequent, but the successes they illustrate are usually dramatic. In 1992, Compaq converted itself from a company with declining share and profitability into the industry price leader. How? By designing a new line of computers to meet the particular cost-performance target that customers most frequently demanded. Thirty years earlier, Lee Iacocca saved Ford from extinction by building a sports car that middle-class people could afford. From an engineering perspective, it was hardly a good sports car. But from the customers perspective, it represented a better value than they ever thought they could afford. From a sales and profit perspective, it was the most successful car in history (see Exhibit 1.2).

EXHIBIT 1.2

The Story of the Mustang

In the early 1960s, America was young, confident, and in love with sports cars. Many popular songs of the era were odes to those cars. Unfortunately for Ford, the cars arousing the greatest passion were products of General Motors and European manufacturers. Hoping to remedy this situation, Ford set out to build a sports car that would woo buyers to its showrooms. Had Ford followed the traditional approach for developing a new car, management would have begun the process by sending a memo to the design department, instructing it to develop a sports car that would top the competition. Each designer would then have drawn on individual preconceptions of what makes a good sports car in order to design bodies, suspensions, and engines that would be better. In a few weeks, management would have reviewed the designs and picked out the best prospects. Next, management would have turned those designs over to the marketing research department. Researchers would have asked potential customers which they preferred and whether they liked Ford's designs better than the competition's, given prices that would cover their costs and yield the desired rate of return. The best choice would ultimately have been built and would have evoked the adoration of many, but would have been purchased by only the few who could have afforded it.

Fortunately, Ford's general manager had a better idea. Unlike most top auto executives, he was not an expert in finance, accounting, or production. He was Lee Iacocca, a marketer. He did not begin looking for a new car in the design department. He began by researching what customers wanted. Iacocca found that a large and growing share of the auto market longed for a sports car, but that most people could not afford one. He also learned that most buyers did not really need much of what makes a "good" sports car to satisfy their desires. What they craved was not sports car performance—a costly engine, drive train, and suspension—but sports car excitement—styling, bucket seats, vinyl trim, and fancy wheel covers. Nobody at the time was selling excitement at a price most customers could afford: less than $2,500.

The challenge for Ford was to design a car that looked sufficiently sporty to satisfy most buyers, but without the usual mechanical elements of a sports car that drove its price out of reach. To meet that challenge, Ford built its sports car with the mechanical workings of an existing economy car, the Falcon. Many hard-core sports car enthusiasts, including some at Ford, were appalled. The car was obviously no match for GM's Corvette. But it was what many people seemed to want, at a price they could afford.

In April 1964, Ford introduced its Mustang sports car, at a base price of $2,368. More Mustangs were sold in the first year than any other car Ford ever built. In just the first two years, net profits from the Mustang were $1.1 billion, in 1964 dollars.[1] That was far more than any of Ford's competitors made selling their "good" sports cars, priced to cover costs and achieve a target rate of return.

Ford began with the customers, asking what they wanted and what they were willing to pay for it. Their response determined the price that a car would have to sell for. Only then did Ford attempt to develop a product that could satisfy potential customers at a price they were willing to pay, while still permitting a substantial profit.

Notice that costs played an essentially important role in Ford's strategy; they determined what Ford's product would look like. Cost considerations determined what attributes of a sports car the Mustang could include and what it could not, and still leave Ford with a profit. For what customers would pay, they could not afford everything they might have liked. At $2,368 however what they got in the Mustang was a good value.

---

[1] Lee Iacocca (with William Novak), *Iacocca: An Autobiography* (Toronto: Bantam Books, 1984), p. 74.

Customer-driven pricing

Many companies now recognize the fallacy of cost-based pricing and its adverse effect on profit. They realize the need for pricing to reflect market conditions. Consequently, they have taken pricing authority away from financial managers and given it to sales or product managers. In theory, this trend is clearly consistent with value-based pricing, since marketing and sales are that part of the organization best positioned to understand value to the customer. In practice, however, companies' misuse of pricing to achieve short-term sales objectives often undermines perceived value and depresses their profits even further.

The purpose of value-based pricing is not simply to create satisfied customers. Customer satisfaction can usually be bought by discounting sufficiently, but marketers delude themselves if they believe that the resulting sales represent marketing successes. The purpose of value-based pricing is to price more profitably by capturing more value, not necessarily by making more sales. When marketers confuse the first objective with the second, they fall into the trap of pricing at whatever buyers are willing to pay, rather than at what the product is really worth. Although that decision enables them to meet their sales objectives, it invariably undermines long-term profitability.

Two problems arise when prices reflect the amount buyers seem willing to pay. First, sophisticated buyers are rarely honest about how much they are actually willing to pay for a product. Professional purchasing agents are adept at concealing the true value of the product to their organizations. Once buyers learn that sellers' prices are flexible, the former have a financial incentive to conceal information from, and even actively mislead, the latter. Obviously, this tactic undermines the salesperson's ability to establish close relationships with customers and to understand their needs.

Second, there is an even more fundamental problem with pricing to reflect the customers' willingness to pay. The job of sales and marketing is not simply to process orders at whatever price customers are currently willing to pay. It is to raise customers' willingness to pay a price that better reflects the product's true value. Many companies underprice truly innovative products because they ask potential customers, who are ignorant of the product's value, what they would be willing to pay. But we know from studies of innovations that the "regular" price has little impact on customers' willingness to try them. For example, most customers initially perceived that photocopiers, mainframe computers, and food processors lacked adequate value to justify their prices. Only after extensive marketing to communicate and guarantee value did these products achieve market acceptance. *Forget what customers who have never used your product are initially willing to pay!* Instead, understand the value of the product to satisfied customers and communicate that value to others. Low pricing is never a substitute for an adequate marketing and sales effort.

Competition-driven pricing

Lastly, consider the policy of letting pricing be dictated by competitive conditions. In this view, pricing is a tool to achieve sales objectives. In the minds of some managers, this method is "pricing strategically". Actually, it is more analogous to "letting the tail wag the dog." Why should an organization want to achieve market-share goals? Because more market share usually produces greater profit. Priorities are confused, however, when managers reduce the profitability of prices simply to achieve the market-share goal. Prices should be lowered only when they are no longer justified by the value offered in comparison to the valued offered by the competition.

Although price cutting is probably the quickest, most effective way to achieve sales objectives, it is usually a poor decision financially. Since a price cut can be so easily matched, it offers only a short-term competitive advantage at the expense of permanently lower margins. Consequently, unless a company has good reason to believe that its competitors cannot match a price cut, the long-term cost of using price as a competitive weapon usually exceeds any short-term benefit. Although product differentiation, advertising, and improved distribution do not increase sales as quickly as price cuts, their benefit is more sustainable and thus is usually more cost-effective.

The goal of pricing should be to find the combination of margin and market share that maximizes profitability over the long term. Often, the most profitable price is one that substantially restricts market share relative to the competition. Godiva chocolates, BMW cars, Peterbilt trucks, and Snap-On tools would no doubt all gain substantial market share if priced closer to the competition. It is doubtful, however, that the added share would be worth forgoing their profitable and successful positioning as high-priced brands.

Although the fallacy of competition-driven pricing is most obvious for high-priced products, the principle can be more generally applied. Many companies that were recapitalized in the 1980s learned that they could substantially increase cash flow simply by scaling back their market-share objectives. One industrial company increased price by 9 percent and suffered a 20 percent loss of market share. Even though some capacity was idled, its contribution to profit increased by more than 70 percent! This company learned that four out of five of its customers valued the product by at least 9 percent more than they had been paying. The company had been prevented from capturing that value by an excessive market-share goal.

The goal of value-based strategy is to maximize the difference between the value created for the customer and the cost incurred by the company. The goal of pricing in that strategy is to capture a substantial share of the value created in the earnings of the firm. The marketing revolution that took place from the 1960s through the 1970s has taken many companies far in achieving the first goal. The purpose of this text is to show them how to achieve the second goal—reaping their just rewards.

PLANNING FOR EFFECTIVE PRICING

Like most marketing decisions, pricing is an art. It depends as much on good judgment as on precise calculation. But the fact that pricing depends on judgment is no justification for pricing decisions based on hunches or intuition. Good judgment requires understanding. One must comprehend the factors that make some pricing strategies succeed and others fail. Exhibit 1.3 illustrates what a manager needs to understand and accommodate in order to plan an effective pricing strategy.

First, the manager must understand how costs, customers, and competition determine a product's pricing environment. In some companies, when the time arrives to make a pricing decision, managers simply meet at a specified time and make a decision. They do not study how the firm's costs are affected by changes in sales. They do not talk first to potential buyers to learn what role price will play in their purchase decisions, nor do they analyze the past behavior and likely actions of competitors. Consequently, the pricing process becomes nothing more than an exercise in the blind leading the blind.

EXHIBIT 1.3

Developing an Effective Pricing Strategy

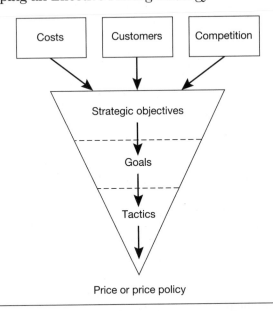

Only after understanding the environment is management ready to formulate strategy. Strategy formulation begins with setting objectives. Strategic objectives are general aspirations toward which all activities in the firm, not only pricing, are directed. They are open-ended and timeless in that they are never achieved with finality. For example, Texas Instruments' strategic objective has been to achieve a substantial cost advantage by maintaining a dominant market share in technologies offering substantial economies of experience. That objective was sufficiently general so that it could continue to guide the firm's pricing policies year after year. It was also the objective for production, promotion, and sales decisions. Objectives are a firm's general aspirations for the product, which price may sometimes be used actively to achieve. Under different circumstances, the same objectives may be actively achieved in other ways, with price set only to avoid impeding that progress.

Once objectives are formulated, goals are considered. For the specialist in pricing, setting goals is the more important aspect of strategy formulation. Unlike objectives, strategic goals are concrete and have deadlines. They apply to specific activities, although some goals may be shared by more than one marketing activity (for example, pricing and advertising) or by a marketing and a nonmarketing activity (for example, pricing and production). When the Apple Macintosh computer was introduced in 1984, some pricing goals might have been (1) to make the product affordable and a good value for most college students, (2) to get certain target market segments to see the Macintosh as a better value than the IBM PCjr, (3) to encourage at least 90 percent of all Apple retailers to carry the Macintosh while providing a strong selling effort, and (4) to accomplish all this within eighteen months. Those pricing goals complemented goals for other activities. For example, the goals for advertising may have been to make the product known to at least three-fourths of all college students within one year and for production to reduce costs by 15 percent annually. The general objective of all the specific goals, however, was to establish the Macintosh system as a viable competitor that would continue Apple's historical growth in sales and profits.

There are many objectives and goals that management can pursue, but only a subset of these is profitably attainable in any particular environment. Unfortunately, some companies set pricing objectives based on wishful thinking, which makes the objectives useless at best. Objectives and their corresponding goals cannot be judged solely by the desirability of achieving them; they must also be judged by the probability that they can be profitably achieved. A substantial increase in market share is a reasonable pricing goal in some cases, but it is clearly impractical when the firm has opportunistic competitors with lower incremental costs. Unless the firm can reduce its costs, it must find a segment that it can attract with a better product or distribution; it cannot afford to compete on price. Even for products without competition, it is foolish to set market share goals for pricing when most potential customers are not price sensitive. In this environment, market-share goals should perhaps be part of the distribution and promotional strategies rather than the pricing strategy.

Tactics are considered next. They are specific actions a firm takes to implement its strategy, hoping to achieve its goals and objectives. If one objective is to maintain a dominant market share, and a pricing goal is to never let market share fall below the previous year's level, then the firm's tactic might be to meet all competitive price cuts. If one objective is to expand sales to college students, and the pricing goal is a 50 percent increase in the share of that market within the next two years, the tactic might be student discounts. If one objective is to utilize production capacity, and the goal is to average 80 percent utilization while avoiding the need for extra capacity to meet temporary demand peaks, the tactic might be to charge lower prices at nonpeak times and higher prices at peak times. Some pricing tactics are straightforward, involving simple increases or decreases in the list prices. Frequently, however, effective pricing tactics become quite complicated and involve much more than manipulation of the price itself.

For example, the selective communication of information to influence competitors' pricing (discussed in Chap. 5) must be done well to effectively execute strategy in highly competitive industries. Product bundling, the selling of different products in combination for a single price, is another important tactic when introducing new innovations and when segmenting markets. Moreover, pricing tactics also involve coordinating pricing with promotion and distribution to achieve the maximum effect. Should a product manager with a limited budget alternate between spending on advertising campaigns and price promotions, or would advertising and price promotions be more effective if done simultaneously? And how can a product manager ensure that a promotional price cut at the wholesale level will ultimately be passed on to consumers? Tactical implementation also requires a basic understanding of the law. There are times when it is illegal to discount prices, and there are serious legal constraints on communication about pricing (or terms of sale) among competitors. Tactical implementation is as challenging and as important for success as is setting appropriate objectives and goals.

Learning effective pricing: the plan of this book

The organization of this book is intended to serve the interests of students studying effective pricing and practitioners applying it. Theorists will need to use the index at the end of the book because principles are not organized to show their theoretical generality but to aid their practical application. The first eight chapters give a complete overview of the strategy and tactics of pricing and a basic structure that can be applied immediately to improve pricing decisions. The last six chapters develop certain issues in greater depth to make the basic structure more useful.

Because understanding the pricing environment is a precondition to effective strategy formulation, the following chapters are devoted to each aspect of that environment. The purpose is to teach you what to look for when attempting to understand a product's pricing environment. Chapter 2 explains why some costs are relevant for pricing decisions whereas others are simply misleading. It provides a set of criteria for distinguishing among them. Chapter 3 shows how to conduct financial analysis for pricing decisions without letting costs drive those decisions. Chapter 4 identifies the major factors that influence buyers' price sensitivity and explains how those factors can be used to segment customers and to influence the role of price in their purchase decisions. Chapter 5 explains the process of price competition and how to manage it proactively.

Chapter 6 explains how to integrate your understanding of costs, customers, and competition into an effective pricing strategy. It explains the various types of pricing strategies that a company might pursue and the environmental conditions that make them appropriate. It illustrates the principles of effective pricing by looking at both pricing mistakes, where management failed to set prices consistent with the environment, and successes, where management used effective pricing techniques to make better decisions.

An effective pricing strategy, once formulated, cannot be static. Pricing strategy must be consistent with an environment that is constantly changing. Part of that change is due to natural evolution over a product's life cycle and can therefore be anticipated. Chapter 7 explains how the pricing environment changes over a product's life cycle and how an effective pricing strategy will evolve with it. Chapter 8 describes tactics for implementing strategies when prices are negotiated or when they are determined via competitive bidding.

Chapter 9 is devoted entirely to tactics for segmented pricing which enable a company to charge different prices for the same product attributes. In almost all markets, various groups of buyers value the same product attributes differently, making some degree of segmented pricing essential for capturing a product's value. Moreover, in a competitive environment, segmented pricing to reflect cost differences is often essential for the maintenance of a strong market position. Market leaders who fail to segment for pricing eventually face smaller competitors who undercut their prices by focusing on customers who can be served at lower cost.

Finally, an effective pricing strategy requires coordination between pricing and other marketing activities. A product's price affects the market's perception of its attributes, the effectiveness of its advertising, and the attention it receives in channels of distribution. These factors, in turn, affect the price at which the product can profitably sell. While pricing is a specialized marketing activity, it is an integral part of a total marketing plan. A pricing strategy can be fully effective only if it is coordinated with the product, promotion, and distribution strategies that it complements. Chapter 10 explains specifically how pricing interacts with other elements in the marketing mix and how marketers can use those interactions to improve pricing effectiveness.

Since pricing can only capture value, not create it, sustainable profitability is limited by a firm's competitive advantages. Chapter 11 explains how companies in all types of businesses (1) have developed product advantages that reduce price sensitivity, enabling them to earn higher margins without losing sales to aggressive competitors, and (2) have developed cost advantages, allowing them to price aggressively without forgoing profit.

Chapter 12 describes in more detail the implications of consumer psychology in pricing. Of course, long before you reach this chapter you will see that buyer psychology plays an essential role in pricing. Chapter 4 explains how and why price sometimes affects consumer perceptions of a product's quality, and how the end benefit affects consumer perceptions about the importance of a price differential. These established principles of psychology should be considered in any pricing decision. At the moment, however, the most interesting research in pricing having important implications for practice is at the frontiers of psychology, where controversy abounds. For example, conflicting studies show that ending prices with the number 9 (for example, $39.99) rather than with a round number ending in zero has either no effect or a huge effect on consumers' inclination to buy. The marketing manager who is aware of such potential psychological effects can determine whether those effects are applicable to his or her products and adjust the pricing accordingly.

Chapter 13 shows how to use research techniques to measure price sensitivity. It explains how and when you can use sales data and survey data to improve your understanding of buyers. Some readers may be surprised to find this chapter near the end of the book. How can one presume to set prices before having measured buyers' price sensitivity? For most pricing decisions, precise estimates of price sensitivity are impractical because they would cost too much time and money, or because the estimates would be unreliable. Consequently, most pricing decisions rest solely on managerial judgments about price sensitivity made after studying the buying habits and decision processes of buyers as discussed in chapters 4 and 6. Still, there are products for which direct measurement of price sensitivity are a cost-effective complement to managerial judgments. In particular, frequently-purchased products in mature markets often enjoy the kind of market stability necessary for accurate measurement and can generate enough additional revenue to justify the expense.

Chapter 14 deals with the legal and ethical constraints on pricing. Previous chapters discuss legal constraints on specific pricing tactics, whereas this chapter provides a more integrated overview of the complex and sometimes contradictory judicial interpretations of the laws. It identifies the penalties for pricing practices found to violate the law and reviews judicial rulings to help the reader gauge the probability that a given pricing practice would be found unacceptable if challenged in court. It also describes a topology for determining ethical standards before potentially compromising situations arise.

SUMMARY

The importance of pricing to successful marketing was unappreciated for many years. Surveys conducted in the 1950s indicated that most firms either mechanically set prices based on their costs or imitated the pricing of competitors. Only half the practitioners surveyed in a 1964 study rated pricing as an important policy decision.[2] Since then, the views of marketing managers have radically changed. A 1984 survey revealed that top marketing executives considered pricing the most critical issue with which they had to contend.[3] *Business Week* described these changes as "little short of a revolution" and went on to predict that "an ability to adapt to the new pricing environment will characterize those companies that succeed in competing over the next decade."[4]

Progressive companies have begun doing more than just worrying about pricing. To increase profitability, they are abandoning traditional reactive pricing procedures in favor of new proactive strategies. In the 1990s, companies are applying activity-based costing techniques to manufacturing activities, learning the true cost of different product lines, and to marketing activities, learning the true cost of serving different customer segments. Some firms are also using market research techniques to better understand the motivations of customers, and are studying "game theory" to better anticipate their competitors. Many are replacing sales goals with profit goals, as they manage for competitive advantage rather than market share.

It is not surprising that pricing has taken its place as a major element in marketing strategy in the last decade. After all, marketing itself has been in the midst of a revolution. The meaning of marketing has been transformed from "selling what the company produces" to "producing what the customer wants to buy." Marketing has become the means by which firms identify unmet needs in the marketplace, develop products to satisfy those needs, promote them honestly, and follow with post-purchase support to ensure customer satisfaction. But, as selfless as all this may sound, the ultimate goal of marketing is not to convert the firm into a charitable organization for the sole benefit of consumers. The ultimate goal is profits for the stockholders, jobs for the employees and growth for the organization.

The justification for marketing's consumer focus is the belief that serving the customer is the most efficient and effective way for a firm to achieve its goals. In case after case, from Hewlett Packard's laser printers and Caterpillar's tractors to Toyota's automobiles and McDonald's hamburgers, we have learned that one can create greater and more enduring value by listening to the market and by satisfying real needs than by trying to convince the market to make do with whatever the company produces. But efficacy in creating value is not enough. Firms successful at product development, promotion, and distribution still fail unless they can capture some of the value they create in the prices they earn.

Perhaps it is reasonable that marketers have only recently begun to focus seriously on effective pricing. Only after managers have mastered the techniques of creating value do the techniques of capturing value become important. As one marketing expert aptly stated. "For marketing strategists, [pricing] is the moment of truth—all of marketing comes to focus in the pricing decision."[5] The purpose of this book is to make sure that when you reach that moment, you know what to do.

NOTES

1. Matsushita earns twice Philips' return on sales; Advanta (a division of Colonial National Bank) earns many times more than Citicorp's return on assets; Southwest Airlines is one of the few airlines that consistently earns profits; and Cooper Tire is the most profitable and fastest growing tire company.

2. Jon G. Udal, "How Important is Pricing in Competitive Strategy," *Journal of Marketing*, 28 (January 1964), 44–48.

3. Fleming Associates, *1984 Key Pressure Points for Top Marketing Executives* (Sarasota, Florida: Fleming Associates, 1984). Pricing was again the most important issue for marketing executives when this study was repeated two years later. See Fleming Associates, *1986 Key Pressure Points for Top Marketing Executives* (Sarasota, Florida: Fleming Associates, 1986). See also Barbara Coe, "Perceptions on the Role of Pricing in the 1980's Among Industrial Marketers," *1983 AMA Educators' Proceedings*, series no. 49 (Chicago, American Marketing Assoc., 1983), pp. 235–40; Robert J. Dolan "The Panic of the 1980's: It's Pricing," *Sales and Marketing Management* (June 19, 1980), pp. 47–49.

4. "Flexible Pricing," *Business Week*, December 12, 1977, pp. 78–81, 84, 88.

5. Raymond Corey, *Industrial Marketing: Cases and Concepts*, 3rd ed. (Englewood Cliffs, N.J.: Prentice-Hall, Inc., 1983), p. 311.

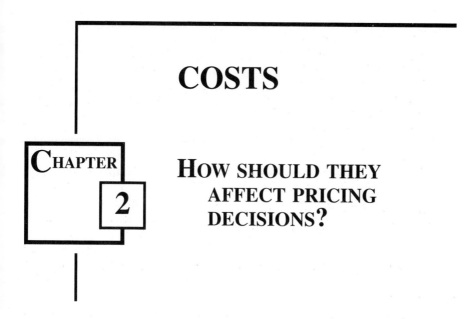

COSTS

HOW SHOULD THEY AFFECT PRICING DECISIONS?

Costs should never determine price, but costs do play a critical role in formulating a pricing strategy. Pricing decisions are inexorably tied to decisions about sales levels, and sales involve costs of production, marketing, and administration. It is true that how much buyers will pay is unrelated to the seller's cost. But it is also true that a seller's decisions about which products to produce and in what quantities depend critically on their cost of production.

The mistake that cost-plus pricers make is not that they consider costs in their pricing, but that they select the quantities they will sell and the buyers they will serve before identifying the prices they can charge. They then try to impose cost-based prices that may be either more or less than what the buyers will pay. In contrast, effective pricers make their decisions in exactly the opposite order. They first evaluate what buyers will pay and only then choose quantities to produce and markets to serve.

Firms that price effectively decide what to produce and to whom to sell it by comparing the prices they can charge with the costs they must incur. Consequently, costs affect the prices they charge. A low-cost firm can charge lower prices and sell more because it can profitably use low prices to attract more price-sensitive buyers. A higher-cost firm, on the other hand, cannot afford to underbid low-cost producers for the patronage of the more price-sensitive buyers. It must target those buyers willing to pay a premium price.

Similarly, changes in costs should cause firms to change their prices, not because that changes what buyers will pay, but because it changes the quantities that the firm can profitably supply and the buyers it can profitably serve. When the cost of jet fuel rises, most airlines are not naive enough to try passing on the fuel cost through a cost-plus formula while maintaining their previous schedules. But some airlines do raise their average revenue per mile. They do so by reducing the number of flights they offer in order to fill the remaining planes with more full-fare passengers. To make room for those passengers, they eliminate or reduce some discount fares. Thus the cost increase for jet fuel affects the mix of prices offered and, therefore, increases the average price charged. But that is the result of a strategic decision to reduce the number of flights and change the mix of passengers served, not of an attempt to charge higher prices for the same service to the same people.

Such decisions about quantities to sell and buyers to serve are an important part of pricing strategy for all firms and the most important part for many. In this chapter, we discuss how a proper understanding of costs enables one to make those decisions correctly. First, however, a word of encouragement. Understanding costs is probably the most challenging aspect of pricing. You will probably not master these concepts on first reading this chapter. Your goal should be simply to understand the issues involved and the techniques for dealing with them. Mastery of the techniques will come with practice.

DETERMINING RELEVANT COSTS

One cannot price effectively without understanding costs. To understand one's costs is not simply to know their amounts. Even the least effective pricers, those who mechanically apply cost-plus formulas, know how much they spend on labor, raw materials, and overhead. Managers who really understand their costs know more than their levels; they know how their costs will change with the changes in sales that result from pricing decisions.

Not all costs are relevant for every pricing decision. A first step in pricing is to identify the relevant costs: those that actually determine the profit impact of the pricing decision. Our purpose in this section is to set forth the guidelines for identifying the relevant costs once they are measured. In principle, identifying the relevant costs for pricing decisions is actually fairly straightforward. They are the costs that are incremental (not average), and avoidable (not sunk). In practice, identifying costs that meet those criteria can be difficult. Consequently, we will explain each distinction in detail and illustrate it in the context of a practical pricing problem.

Why incremental costs?

Pricing decisions affect whether a company will sell less of the product at a higher price or more of the product at a lower price. In either scenario, some costs remain the same (in total). Consequently, those costs do not affect the relative profitability of one price versus the other. Only costs that rise or fall (in total) when prices change affect the relative profitability of different pricing strategies. We call these costs *incremental* because they represent the increment to costs (positive or negative) that results from the pricing decision.

Incremental costs are the costs associated with *changes* in pricing and sales. The distinction between incremental and nonincremental costs parallels closely, but not exactly, the more familiar distinction between variable and fixed costs. *Variable costs*, such as the costs of raw materials in a manufacturing process, are costs of doing business. Since pricing decisions affect the amount of business that a company does, variable costs are always incremental for pricing. In contrast, *fixed costs*, such as those of product design, advertising, and overhead, are costs of being in business.[1] They are incremental when deciding whether a price will generate enough revenue to justify being in the business of selling a particular type of product or serving a particular type of customer. Since fixed costs are not affected by how much of the product a company actually sells, most are not incremental when management must decide whether to adopt a simple price change.

Some fixed costs, however, are incremental for pricing decisions, and they must be appropriately identified. Incremental fixed costs are those that directly result from implementing a price change or from offering a version of the product at a different price level. For example, the fixed cost for a restaurant to print menus with new prices or for a public utility to gain regulatory approval of a rate increase would be incremental when deciding whether to make those changes. The fixed cost for an airline to advertise a new discount service or to upgrade its planes' interiors to offer a premium-priced service would be incremental when deciding whether to offer products at those price levels.

To further complicate matters, many costs are neither purely fixed nor purely variable. They are fixed over a range of sales but vary when sales go outside that range. The determination of whether such *semifixed costs* are incremental for a particular pricing decision is necessary to make that decision correctly. Consider, for example, the role of capital equipment costs when deciding whether to expand output. A manufacturer may be able to fill orders for up to 100 additional units each month without purchasing any new equipment simply by using the available equipment more extensively. Consequently, equipment costs are nonincremental when figuring the cost of producing up to 100 additional units. But if the quantity of additional orders increased by 150 units each month, the factory would have to purchase additional equipment. The added cost of new equipment would then become incremental and relevant in deciding whether the company can profitably price low enough to attract additional business.

To illustrate the importance of properly identifying the incremental costs when making a pricing decision, consider the problem faced by the business manager of a symphony orchestra. The orchestra usually performs two Saturday evenings each month during the season with a new program for each performance. It incurs the following costs for each performance:

Fixed overhead costs	$1,500
Rehearsal costs	$4,500
Performance costs	$2,000
Variable costs (e.g., programs, tickets)	$1 per patron

The orchestra's business manager is concerned about her very thin profit margin. She has currently set ticket prices at $10. If she could sell out the entire 1,100-seat hall, total revenues would be $11,000 and total costs $9,100, leaving a healthy $1,900 profit per performance.[2] Unfortunately, the usual attendance is only 900 patrons, resulting in an average cost per ticket sold of $9.89, which is precariously close to the $10.00 admission price. With revenues of just $9,000 per performance and costs of $8,900, total profit per performance is a dismal $100.

The orchestra's business manager does not believe that a simple price increase would solve the problem. A higher price would simply reduce attendance more, leaving less revenue per performance than the orchestra earns now. Consequently, she is considering three proposals designed to increase profits by reaching out to new markets. Two of the proposals involve selling seats at discount prices. The three options are:

1. *A "student rush" ticket priced at $4 and sold to college students one-half hour before the performance on a first-come, first-served basis.* The manager estimates she could sell 200 such tickets to people who otherwise would not attend. Clearly, however, the price of these tickets would not cover even half the average cost per ticket.

2. *A Sunday matinee repeat of the Saturday evening performance with tickets priced at $6.* The manager expects she could sell 700 matinee tickets, but 150 of those would be to people who would otherwise have attended the higher-priced Saturday performance. Thus net patronage would increase by 550, but again the price of these tickets would not cover average cost.

3. *A new series of concerts to be performed on the alternate Saturdays.* The tickets would be priced at $10, and the manager expects that she

would sell 800 tickets but that 100 tickets would be sold to people who would attend the new series instead of the old one. Thus net patronage would increase by 700.

Which, if any, of these proposals should the orchestra adopt? An analysis of the alternatives is shown in Exhibit 2.1. The revenue gain is clearly smallest for the student rush, the lowest-priced alternative designed to attract a fringe market, while the revenue gain is greatest for the new series, which attracts many more full-price patrons. But profitability depends on the incremental costs as well as the revenues of each proposal. For the student rush, neither rehearsal costs nor performance costs are incremental. They are irrelevant to the profitability of that proposal since they do not change regardless of whether this proposal is implemented. Only the variable per-patron costs are incremental, and therefore relevant, for the student-rush proposal. For the Sunday matinee, however, the performance cost and the per-patron cost are incremental and affect the profitability of that option. For the totally new series, all costs except overhead are incremental.

To evaluate the profitability of each option, we subtract from revenues only those costs incremental to it. For the student rush, that means subtracting only the $200 of per-patron costs from the revenues, yielding a contribution to profit of $600. For the Sunday matinee, it means subtracting

EXHIBIT 2.1

Analysis of Three Proposals for the Symphony Orchestra

	I Student Rush	II Sunday Matinee	III New Series
Price	$ 4	$ 6	$ 10
× Unit sales	200	700	800
= Revenue	$800	$4,200	$8,000
– Other sales forgone	(0)	($1,500)	($1,000)
Revenue gain	$800	$2,700	$7,000
Incremental rehearsal cost	0	0	$4,500
Incremental performance cost	0	$2,000	2,000
Variable costs	$200	550	700
Incremental costs	$200	$2,550	$7,200
Net profit contribution	$600	$ 150	($ 200)

the performance cost and the variable per-patron costs for those additional patrons (550) who would not otherwise have attended any performance, yielding a profit contribution of $150. For the new series, it means subtracting the incremental rehearsal, performance, and per-patron costs, yielding a net loss of $200. Thus, the lowest priced option which yields the least amount of additional revenue is, in fact, the most profitable.

The setting out of alternatives as in Exhibit 2.1 clearly highlights the best option. In practice, opportunities are often missed because managers do not look at incremental costs, focusing instead on the average costs that are more readily available from accounting data. Note again that the orchestra's current average cost (total cost divided by the number of tickets sold) is $9.89 per patron and would drop to $8.27 per patron if the student-rush proposal were adopted. The student-rush tickets, priced at $4.00 each, *cover less than half the average cost per ticket*. The manager who focuses on average cost would be misled into rejecting a profitable proposal in the mistaken belief that the price would be inadequate. Average cost includes costs that are not incremental and therefore irrelevant to evaluating the proposed opportunity. The adequacy of any price can be ascertained only by looking at the incremental cost of sales and ignoring those costs that would be incurred anyway.

Although the orchestra example is hypothetical, the problem it illustrates is highly realistic. Scores of companies profit from products that they price below average cost when average cost includes fixed costs that are not true costs of sales.

- ■ Packaged goods manufacturers supply generic versions of their branded products often at prices below average cost. They can do so profitably because they can produce them with little or no incremental costs of capital, shipping, and selling beyond those already incurred to produce their branded versions.

- ■ A leading manufacturer of industrial cranes also does milling work for other companies whenever the firm's vertical turret lathes would not otherwise be used. The price for such work does not cover a proportionate share of the equipment cost. It is, however, profitable work since the equipment must be available to produce the firm's primary product. The equipment cost is therefore not incremental to the additional milling work.

- ■ Airlines fly night coaches at fares that do not cover proportionate share of capital costs for the plane and ground facilities. Those costs must be incurred to provide daytime service and so are irrelevant when judging whether night coach fares are adequate to justify this service. In fact, night coach fares often add incrementally more to profits precisely because they require no additional capital.

In each of these cases, the key to getting the business is having a low price. Yet one should never be deceived into thinking that low-price sales are necessarily low-profit sales. In some cases, they make a disproportionately large contribution to profit because they make a small incremental addition to costs.

Why avoidable costs?

The hardest principle for many business decision makers to accept is that only avoidable costs are relevant for pricing. *Avoidable costs* are those that either have not yet been incurred or that can be reversed. The costs of selling a product, delivering it to the customer, and replacing the sold item in inventory are avoidable, as is the rental cost of buildings and equipment that are not covered by a long-term lease. The opposite of avoidable costs are *sunk costs*—those costs that a company is irreversibly committed to bear. For example, a company's past expenditures on research and development are sunk costs since they cannot be changed regardless of any decisions it makes in the present. The rent on buildings and equipment within the term of a current lease is sunk, except to the extent that the firm can avoid the expense by subletting the property.[3]

The cost of assets that a firm owns may or may not be sunk. If an asset can be sold for an amount equal to its purchase price times the percentage of its remaining useful life, then none of its cost is sunk since the cost can be entirely recovered through resale. Popular models of commercial airplanes often retain their value in this way, making avoidable the entire cost of their continued use. If an asset has no resale value, then its cost is entirely sunk even though it may have much useful life remaining. A neon sign depicting a company's corporate logo may have much useful life remaining, but its cost is entirely sunk since no other company would care to buy it. Frequently, the cost of assets is partially avoidable and partially sunk. For example, a new truck could be resold for a substantial portion of its purchase price but would lose some market value immediately after purchase. The portion of the new price that could not be recaptured is sunk and should not be considered in pricing decisions. Only depreciation of the resale value of the truck is an avoidable cost of using it.

From a practical standpoint, the easiest way to identify the avoidable cost is to recognize that it is the *future*, not the historical, cost associated with making a sale. What, for example, is the cost for an oil company to sell a gallon of gasoline at one of its company-owned stations? One might be inclined to say that it is the cost of the oil used to make the gasoline plus the cost of refining and distribution. Unfortunately, that view could lead refiners to make some costly pricing mistakes. Most oil company managers realize that the relevant cost for pricing gasoline is not the historical cost of producing a gallon of gasoline, but the future cost of replacing the inventory when sales are made. Even LIFO (last-in, first-out) accounting can be misleading for companies that are drawing down large inventories. To account accurately for the effect of a sale on profitability, managers need to adopt NIFO (next-in, first-out) accounting for managerial decision making.[4]

The distinction between the historical cost of aquisition and the future cost of replacement is merely academic when supply costs are stable. It becomes very practical when costs rise or fall.[5] When the price of crude oil rises, companies quickly raise prices, long before any gasoline made from the more expensive crude reaches the pump. Politicians and consumer advocates label this practice *price gouging*, since companies with large inventories of gasoline increase their reported profits by selling their gasoline at higher prices than they paid to produce it. But what is the real incremental cost to the company of selling a gallon of gasoline?

Each gallon of gasoline sold requires the purchase of oil at the new, higher price for the company to maintain its gasoline inventory. If that price is not covered by revenue from sales of gasoline, the company suffers from a reduced cash flow from every sale. Even though the sales appear profitable from an historical cost standpoint, the company must add to its working capital (by borrowing money or by retaining a larger portion of its earnings) to pay the new, higher cost of crude oil. Consequently the real "cash" cost of making a sale rises immediately by an amount equal to the increase in the replacement cost of crude oil.

Now what happens when crude oil prices decline? If a company with large inventories held its prices high until all inventories were sold, it would be undercut by anyone with smaller inventories who could profitably take advantage of the lower cost of crude to gain market share. The company would see its sales, profits, and cash flow decline. The intelligent company again bases its prices on the replacement cost, not the historical cost, of its inventory. In historical terms, it reports a loss. However, that loss corresponds to an equal reduction in the cost of replacing its inventories with cheaper crude oil. Since the company simply reduces its operating capital by the amount of the reported loss, its cash flow remains unaffected.

Unfortunately, even level-headed businesspeople often let sunk costs sneak into their decision making, resulting in pricing mistakes that squander profits. The case of a small midwestern publisher of esoteric books illustrates this risk. The publisher customarily priced a book at $20 per copy, which included a $4 contribution to overhead and profit. The firm printed 2,000 of each book on the first run and normally sold less than half of them in the first year. The remaining copies were added to inventory. The company was moderately profitable until 1980 when, due to a substantial increase in interest rates, the $4 contribution per book could no longer fully cover the interest cost of its working capital.

Recognizing that they had a problem, the managers called in a pricing consultant to show them how to improve the profitability of their prices in order to cover their increased costs. They were, however, quite resistant to the consultant's suggestion that they run a half-price sale on all their slow-moving titles. The publisher's business manager pointed out immediately that half price would not even cover the cost of goods sold. He explained to the consultant, "Our problem is that our prices are not currently adequate to cover our overhead. I fail to see how cutting our prices even lower, eliminating the gross margin we now have so that we cannot even cover the cost of production, is a solution to our problem."

The business manager's logic was quite compelling, and the other managers found it convincing. But his argument was based on the fallacy of looking at sunk costs of production as a guide to pricing rather than at the avoidable cost of holding inventory, which he incorrectly classified as part of overhead. No doubt, the firm regretted having printed many of the books in its warehouse. But since the production cost of those books was no longer avoidable regardless of the pricing strategy adopted, and since the firm did not plan to replace them, historical production costs were irrelevant to a pricing decision.[6] What was relevant was the avoidable cost of working capital required to hold the books in inventory.

If, by cutting prices and selling the books sooner instead of later, the publisher could save more in interest than he lost from a price cut, then price cutting clearly would increase profit although reducing revenue below the cost of goods sold. In this case, the publisher could ultimately sell all of his books for $20 if he held them long enough. By selling some books immediately for $10, however, he could avoid the interest cost of holding them until he could get the higher price. Exhibit 2.2 shows the cumulative interest cost of holding a book in inventory, given that it could be sold immediately for $10 and that the firm's cost of capital is 18 percent.

EXHIBIT 2.2

The Cumulative Interest Cost of Holding a Book in Inventory

				Years Inventory Held				
	1	2	3	4	5	6	7	8
Interest cost to hold inventory[1]	$1.80	3.90	6.43	9.39	12.88	16.99	21.85	27.59

[1] Interest cost to year $n = \$10(1.18^n - 1)$.

Since the interest cost of holding a book longer than four years exceeds the proposed $10 price cut, any book for which the firm held more than four years of inventory could be sold more profitably now at half price than later at full price.[7]

The error made by the business manager was understandable. It is a common one among people who think about pricing problems in terms of a traditional income statement.

Avoiding Misleading Accounting   Unfortunately, accounting statements can often be misleading. One must approach them with care when making pricing decisions. Let us further examine the publisher's error, and others, to better understand the pitfalls in accounting data and how to deal with them. By accounting convention, an income statement follows the form:

> Sales revenue
>
> −Cost of goods sold
> ────────────────
> = Gross profit
>
> −Selling expenses
> −Depreciation
> −Administrative overhead
> ────────────────
> = Operating profit
>
> −Interest expense
> ────────────────
> = Pretax profit
>
> −Taxes
> ────────────────
> = Net profit

This can naturally lead managers to think about pricing sequentially, as a set of hurdles to be overcome in order. First they try to get over the *gross profit* hurdle by maximizing their sales revenue and minimizing the cost of goods sold. Then they navigate the second hurdle by minimizing selling expenses, depreciation, and overhead to maximize the *operating profit*. Similarly, they minimize their interest expense to clear the *pretax profit* hurdle and finally minimize their taxes to reach their ultimate goal of a large, positive *net profit*. They imagine that by doing their best to maximize income at each step they will surely then reach their goal of a maximum bottom line.

Unfortunately, the road to a profitable bottom line is not so straight. Profitable pricing often calls for sacrificing gross profit in order to reduce expenses further down the line. The publisher in our last example could report a much healthier gross profit by refusing to sell any book for less than $20, but only by bearing interest expenses that would exceed the extra gross profit, leaving an even smaller pretax profit. Moreover, interest is not the only cost that can profitably be reduced by trading off sales revenue. Discount sales through direct mail often save selling expenses that substantially exceed the reduction in sales revenue. While such discounts depress gross profit, the greater savings in selling expenses produce a net increase in the operating profit. Discounting for a sale prior to the date of an inventory tax may also save more on tax payments than the revenue loss.

Effective pricing cannot be done in steps. It requires that one approach the problem holistically, looking for each tradeoff between higher prices and higher costs, cutting gross profit whenever necessary to cut expenses by even more. The best way to avoid being misled by a traditional income statement is to develop a managerial costing system independent of the system used for financial reporting,[8] as follows:

Sales revenue

−Incremental, avoidable variable costs
= Total contribution (in dollars)

−Incremental, avoidable fixed costs
= Net contribution

−Other fixed or sunk costs
= Pretax profit

−Income taxes
= Net profit

The value of reorganization is that it first focuses attention on costs that are incremental and avoidable and only later looks at costs that are nonincremental and sunk for the pricing decision. In this analysis, maximizing the *profit contribution* of a pricing decision is the same as maximizing the net profit, since the fixed or sunk costs subtracted from the profit contribution are not influenced by the pricing decisions and since income taxes are determined by the pretax profit rather than by unit sales.

One could not do such a cost analysis simply by reorganizing the numbers on a traditional income statement. The traditional income statement reports quarterly or annual totals. For pricing, we are not concerned about the cost of all units produced in a period; we are concerned only with the cost of the units that will be affected by the decision to be made. Thus, the relevant cost to consider when evaluating a price reduction is the cost of the additional units that the firm expects to sell because of the price cut. The relevant cost to consider when evaluating a price increase is the avoided cost of units that the firm will not produce because sales will be reduced by the price rise. For any managerial decision, including pricing decisions, it is important to isolate and consider only the costs that affect the profitability of that decision.

ESTIMATING RELEVANT COSTS

The essence of incremental costing is to measure the cost incurred because a product is sold, or not incurred because it is not sold. We cannot here delve into all the details of setting up a useful managerial accounting system. That task occupies an entire literature on "activity-based costing," to which we refer the reader interested in the details of cost management.[9] For our purposes, it will suffice to caution that there are four common errors that managers frequently make when attempting to develop useful estimates of true costs.

1. *Beware of averaging total variable costs to estimate the cost of a single unit.* The average of variable costs is often an adequate indicator of the incremental cost per unit, but it can be dangerously misleading in those cases where the incremental cost per unit is not constant. The relevant incremental cost for pricing is the actual incremental cost of the particular units affected by a pricing decision, which is not necessarily equal to average variable cost. Consider the following example:

A company is currently producing 1,100 units per day, incurring a total materials cost of $4,400 per day and labor costs of $9,200 per day. The labor costs consist of $8,000 in regular pay and $1,200 in overtime pay per day. Labor and materials are the only two costs that change when this firm makes small changes in output. What then is its relevant cost for pricing? One might be tempted to answer that the relevant cost is the sum of the labor and materials costs ($13,600) divided by total output (1,100 units), or approximately $12.36 per unit. Such calculation would lead to serious underpricing, since the *average* variable cost is not the *incremental* cost of producing units affected by a price change. A price increase, for example, might eliminate only sales that are now produced on overtime at a cost substantially above the average.

What is the cost of producing the last units, those that might not be sold if the product's price was raised? It may be reasonable to assume that materials costs are approximately the same for all units, so that average materials cost is a good measure of the incremental materials cost for the last units. Thus a good estimate of the relevant materials cost is $4.00 per unit ($4,400/1,100). We know, however, that labor costs are not the same for all units. The company must pay time-and-a-half for overtime, which are the labor hours that could be eliminated if price is increased and if less of the product is sold. Even if workers are equally productive during over-

time and regular hours, producing approximately 100 units per day during
overtime hours, the labor cost is $12.00 per unit ($1,200/100), resulting in a
labor and materials cost for the last 100 units of $16.00 each, substantially
above the $12.36 average cost.[10]

   2. *Beware of accounting depreciation formulas.* The relevant depreciation expense that should be used for all managerial decision making
is the change in the current value of assets. Depreciation of assets is
usually calculated in a number of different ways depending upon the
intended use of the data. For reporting to the Internal Revenue
Service, depreciation is accelerated to minimize tax liability. For standard financial reporting, rates of depreciation are estimated as accurately as possible but are applied to historical costs.[11] For pricing and
any other managerial decision making, however, depreciation expenses should be based on forecasts of the actual decline in the current market value of assets as a result of their use.

   Failure to accurately measure depreciation expenses can severely dis-
tort an analysis of pricing options. For example, the author of one marketing textbook wrote that a particular airline could price low on routes where
its older planes were fully depreciated, but had to price high on routes
where new planes were generating large depreciation charges. Such pricing would be quite senseless. Old planes obviously have a market value regardless of their book value. The decline in that market value should either
be paid for by passengers who fly on those planes or the planes should be
sold. Similarly, if the market value of new planes does not really depreciate
as quickly as the financial statements indicate, excessive depreciation expenses could make revenues appear inadequate to justify what are actually
profitable new investments. The relevant depreciation expense for pricing
is the true decline in an asset's resale value.

   3. *Beware of treating a single cost as either all relevant or all irrelevant for
pricing.* A single cost on the firm's books may have two separate components—one incremental and the other not, or one avoidable and the
other sunk—that must be distinguished. Such a cost must be divided
into the portion that is relevant for pricing and the portion that is not.
Even incremental labor costs are often not entirely unavoidable.

   During the recession of 1981–1982, some steel producers found when
they considered laying off high-seniority employees that the avoidable portion of their labor costs were only a small part of their total labor costs. Their
union contracts committed them to paying senior employees much of their
wages even when laid off. Consequently, those companies found that the
prices they needed to cover their incremental, avoidable costs were actually
quite low, justifying continued operations at some mills even though those
operations produced substantial losses when all costs were considered.

   4. *Beware of overlooking opportunity costs.* Opportunity cost is the contribution that a firm forgoes when it uses assets for one purpose

rather than another. They are relevant costs for pricing even though they do not appear on financial statements. They should be assigned hard numbers in any managerial accounting system, and pricers should incorporate them into their analyses as they would any other cost. In the example of the book publisher, the cost of capital required to maintain the firm's inventory was the cost of borrowed funds (18 percent). It therefore generated an explicit interest expense on the firm's income statement. A proper analysis of the publisher's problem would have been no different had we assumed that the inventory was financed entirely with internally generated funds. Those internally generated funds do not create an interest expense on the publisher's income statement, but they do have alternative uses. Internally generated funds that are used to finance inventories could have been used to purchase an interest-bearing note or could have been invested in some profitable sideline business such as printing stationery. The interest income that could have been earned from the best of these alternatives is an incremental, avoidable cost of using internally generated funds, just as the interest paid explicitly is an incremental, avoidable cost of using borrowed funds.

The same argument would apply when costing the use of a manufacturing or retailing facility. The historical cost of building a facility is irrelevant to pricing. The current cost of using the facility is relevant, however, if the current capacity can be sold or used to sell more of an alternative product. The relevant cost of using sunk manufacturing or retailing capacity is zero only when the amount of capacity exceeds what can be profitably put to some use. When a plant or store can be fully used to generate positive incremental contribution, the incremental, variable (or semifixed) cost of using the capacity to sell more of the product is not zero. It is the contribution lost from having to sell less of another product. That opportunity cost can easily exceed not only the historical cost but even the replacement cost of the capacity.

Even if a company has current excess capacity but there is some probability that future business might have to be turned away, the capacity should be assigned an opportunity cost for pricing. Airlines, for example, first raise prices and then stop selling discounted seats for a particular flight long before the flight is full. The opportunity cost of selling a discounted seat is near zero only if that seat would otherwise certainly be empty at flight time. As a plane's capacity fills, however, the probability increases that selling a discounted seat will require turning away a passenger who would have paid full fare on the day of the flight. The probability of such a passenger wanting the seat, times the contribution that would be earned at full price, is the opportunity cost of selling a discounted seat.

Obviously, moving from costing principles to estimating the true cost of a sale is not easy. Determining which costs are incremental and avoidable requires making uncertain judgments that are debatable. This is not, however, a reason to avoid making such judgments, even in the absence of a good managerial costing system. *It is better to make pricing decisions based on an approximation of the true unit cost of a product or service than on a precise accounting of costs that are, at best, irrelevant to its profitability!*

PERCENT CONTRIBUTION MARGIN AND PRICING STRATEGY

There are three benefits to determining the true unit cost of a product or service for pricing. First, it is a necessary first step toward controlling costs. The best way to control variable costs is not necessarily appropriate for controlling fixed costs. Second, it enables management to determine the minimum price at which the firm can profitably accept incremental business that will not affect the pricing of its other sales. Third, and most important for our purposes, it enables management to determine the contribution margin for each product sold, which, as will be seen in the next chapter on financial analysis, is essential for making informed, profitable pricing decisions.

The size of the contribution as a percent of the price has important strategic implications. It is the share of price that adds to profit or reduces losses. It is not the return on sales, which is used by financial analysts to compare the performance of different companies in the same industry. The return on sales indicates the average profit as a percentage of the price after accounting for all costs. Our concern, however, is not with the average, but with the added profit resulting from an additional sale. Even when variable costs are constant, the added profit from a sale exceeds the average profit because some costs are fixed or sunk. The share of the price that adds to profit, the contribution margin, is everything above the share required to cover the incremental, variable cost of the sale.

When variable cost is constant for all units affected by a particular pricing decision, it is proper to calculate the percent contribution margin from aggregate sales data. After calculating the sales revenue and total contribution margin resulting from a change in sales, one can calculate the percent contribution margin, or %CM, as follows:

$$\%CM = \frac{\text{Total contribution margin}}{\text{Sales revenue}} \times 100$$

When variable costs are not constant for all units (for example, when the units affected by a price change are produced on overtime), it is important to calculate a dollar contribution margin per unit for just the units affected by the price change. The dollar contribution margin per unit, $\$CM$, is simply

$$\$CM = \text{Price} - \text{Variable cost}$$

where variable cost is the cost per unit of only those units affected by the price change and includes only those costs that are avoidable. With the dollar contribution margin, one can calculate the percent contribution margin without being misled when variable costs are not constant. The formula for this calculation of the percent contribution margin is

$$\%CM = \frac{\$CM}{\text{Price}}$$

which gives the percent contribution margin in decimal form.

The percent contribution margin is a measure of the leverage between a firm's sales volume and its profit. It indicates the importance of sales volume as a marketing objective. To illustrate, look at Exhibit 2.3. A company sells two products, each with the same net profit on sales, but with substantially different contribution margins. A company using full-cost pricing would, therefore, treat them the same. But the actual effect of a price change for these two products would be radically different because of their varying cost structures.

Product A has high variable costs equal to 80 percent of its price. Its percent contribution margin is therefore 20 percent. Product B has low

EXHIBIT 2.3

Effect of Contribution Margin on Breakeven Sales Changes

	Product A	Product B
Percentage of selling price accounted for by:		
Variable costs	80.0	20.0
Fixed or sunk costs	10.0	70.0
Net profit margin	10.0	10.0
Contribution margin	20.0	80.0
Break-even sales change (%) for a:		
5% Price reduction/advantage	+33.3	+6.7
10% Price reduction/advantage	+100.0	+14.3
20% Price reduction/advantage	∞	+33.3
5% Price increase/premium	−20.0	−5.9
10% Price increase/premium	−33.3	−11.1
20% Price increase/premium	−50.0	−20.0

variable costs equal to 20 percent of its product's price. Its percent contribution margin is therefore 80 percent. Although at current sales volumes each product earns the same net profit, the effect on each of a change in sales volume is dramatically different. For product A, only $0.20 of every additional sales dollar increases profit or reduces losses. For product B that figure is $0.80.

The lower part of Exhibit 2.3 illustrates the impact of this difference on pricing decisions. In order for product A with its relatively small percent contribution margin to profit from a 5 percent price cut, its sales must increase by more than 33 percent, compared with only 6.7 percent for product B with its larger percent contribution margin. To profit from a 10 percent price cut, product A's sales must increase by more than 100 percent, compared with only 14.3 percent for product B. Clearly, this company cannot justify a strategy of low pricing to build volume for product A nearly as easily as it can for product B. The opposite conclusion follows for price increases. Product A can afford to lose much more sales than product B and still profit from higher prices. Consequently, it is much easier to justify a premium price strategy for product A than for product B.

SUMMARY

Costs are central considerations in pricing. Without understanding which costs are incremental and avoidable, a firm cannot accurately determine at what price, if any, a market can profitably be served. By erroneously looking at historical costs, a firm could sell its inventory too cheaply. By mistakenly looking at nonincremental fixed costs, a firm could overlook highly profitable opportunities where price is adequate to more than cover the incremental costs. By overlooking opportunity costs, successful companies frequently underprice their products. In short, when managers do not understand the true cost of a sale, their companies unnecessarily forgo significant profit opportunities.

Having identified the right costs, one must also understand how to use them. The most important reason to identify costs correctly is to be able to calculate an accurate contribution margin. The contribution margin is a measure of the leverage between a product's profitability and its sales volume. An accurate contribution margin enables management to determine the amount by which sales must increase following a price cut or by how little they must decline following a price increase to make the price change profitable. Understanding how changes in sales will affect a product's profitability is the first step in pricing the product effectively.

It is, however, just the first step. Next, one must learn how to judge the likely impact of a price change on sales. That requires understanding how buyers are likely to perceive a price change and how competitors are likely to react to it. We take up these subjects in the next two chapters.

NOTES

1. Beware of costs classified as "overhead." Often costs end up in that classification, even though they are clearly variable, simply because "overhead" is a convenient dumping ground for costs that one has not associated with the products that caused them to be incurred. A clue to the existence of such a misclassification is the incongruous term *variable overhead*.

2. Revenue = $1,100 \times \$10$; Cost = $\$1,500 + \$4,500 + \$2,000 + (\$1 \times 1,100)$.

3. Most economics and accounting texts equate avoidable costs with variable costs, and sunk costs with fixed costs for theoretical convenience. Unfortunately, those texts usually fail to explain adequately that this is an assumption rather than a necessarily true statement. Consequently, many students come away from such a course with the idea that a firm should always continue producing if price at least covers variable costs. That rule is correct only when the variable costs are entirely avoidable and the fixed costs are entirely sunk. In many industries (for example, airlines), large fixed costs are mostly avoidable since the assets can be readily resold. Consequently, they should always be considered in deciding whether a price is adequate to serve a market.

4. LIFO and NIFO costs are the same in any accounting period when a firm makes a net addition to its inventory. In periods when the firm draws down its inventory, LIFO will understate costs after the firm uses up the portion of its inventory valued at current prices and begins "dipping into old layers" of inventory valued at unrealistic past prices.

5. Neil Churchill, "Don't Let Inflation Get the Best of You," *Harvard Business Review*, March–April 1982.

6. The forward-looking production cost of replacing the book in inventory would have been relevant if the firm intended to maintain its current inventory levels.

7. We are assuming here that the half-price sale will not reduce the rate of sales after the sale is over. When it will, then one must add the discounted value of those lost sales to the price discount and compare that figure with the interest cost of holding the inventory. In other industries (for example, hotels, theaters), the cost of capacity is variable (you can build a hotel with any number of rooms or a theater with any number of seats), but this cost becomes sunk after capacity is built.

8. Robert S. Kaplan, "One Cost System Isn't Enough," *Harvard Business Review*, 66 (January–February 1988), 61–66.

9. Robin Cooper and Robert S. Kaplan, "Profit Priorities from Activity-Based Costing," *Harvard Business Review*, 69 (May–June 1991), 130–135; James P. Borden, "Review of Literature on Activity-Based Costing," *Cost Management*, 4 (Spring 1990), 5–12; Peter B. B. Turney, "Ten Myths About Implementing an Activity-Based Cost System," *Cost Management*, 4 (Spring 1990), 24–32: George J. Beaujon, and Vinod R. Singhal, "Understanding the Activity Costs in an Activity-Based Cost System," *Cost Management*, 4 (Spring 1990), 51–72.

10. The calculation of the portion of output produced on overtime (assuming equal productivity) is as follows: $1,200 overtime is the equivalent in hours of

$800 regular time ($1,200/1.5) and is 9 percent of the total hours worked ($800/[$8,000 + $800]). Multiplying 9 percent times 1,100 units shows that 100 units are produced on overtime if production is at a constant rate.

11. Since 1979, however, the Financial Accounting Standards Board has required that large, publicly held corporations also report supplemental information on increases or decreases in current costs of inventory, property, plant, and equipment, net of inflation. See FASB *Statement of Financial Standards No. 33*, "Financial Reporting and Changing Prices," 1979.

FINANCIAL ANALYSIS

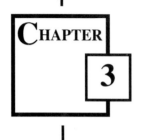

CHAPTER 3

MARKET-BASED PRICING FOR PROFIT

This chapter is coauthored by Professor Gerald E. Smith of Boston College with Dr. Thomas Nagle.

Internal financial considerations and external market considerations are, at most companies, antagonistic forces in pricing decisions. Financial managers allocate costs to determine how *high* prices must be to cover costs and achieve their profit objectives. Marketing and salespeople analyze buyers to determine how *low* prices must be to achieve their sales objectives. The pricing decisions that result are politically charged compromises, not thoughtful implementations of a coherent strategy. Although common, such pricing policies are neither necessary nor desirable. An effective pricing decision should involve an optimal blending of, not a compromise between, internal financial constraints and external market conditions.

Unfortunately, few managers have any idea how to facilitate such a cross-functional blending of these two legitimate concerns. From traditional cost accounting, they learn to take sales goals as "given" before allocating costs, thus precluding the ability to incorporate market forces into pricing decisions. From marketing, they are told that effective pricing should be entirely "customer-driven," ignoring costs except as a minimum constraint below which the sale would become unprofitable. Perhaps along the way, these managers study economics and learn that, in theory, optimal pricing is a blending of cost and demand considerations. In practice, however, they find the economist's assumption of a known demand curve hopelessly unrealistic.

Consequently, pricing at most companies remains trapped between cost- and customer-driven procedures that are inherently incompatible.

The purpose of this chapter is to suggest how managers can break this tactical pricing deadlock and infuse strategic balance into pricing decisions. Many marketers argue that costs should play no role in market-based pricing. This is clearly wrong. Without perfect segmentation (the ability to negotiate independently a unique price for every customer), pricers must make trade-offs between charging higher margins to fewer customers and lower margins to more customers. Once we understand the true cost and contribution of a sale, managers can appropriately integrate costs into what is otherwise a market-driven approach to pricing strategy.

This chapter describes a simple, logically intuitive procedure for quantitatively evaluating the potential profitability of a price change. First, managers develop a baseline, or standard of comparison to measure the effects of a price change. For example, they might compare the effects of a pending price change with the product's current level of profitability, or with a budgeted level of profitability, or perhaps with a hypothetical scenario that management is particularly interested in exploring. Second, they calculate an incremental "breakeven" for the price change to determine under what market conditions the change will prove profitable. Marketing managers must then determine whether they can actually meet those conditions.

The key to integrating costs and quantitatively assessing the consequences of a price change is the incremental breakeven analysis. Although similar in form to the common breakevens that managers use to evaluate investments, incremental breakeven analysis for pricing is quite different in practice. Rather than evaluating the product's overall profitability, which depends on many factors other than price, incremental breakeven analysis focuses on the incremental profitability of price changes. Consequently, managers start from a baseline reflecting current or projected sales and profitability *at the current price*. Then they ask whether a change in price could improve the situation. More precisely, they ask:

> How much would the sales volume have to increase to profit from a price reduction?
> How much could the sales volume decline before a price increase becomes unprofitable?

Answers to these questions depend on the product's contribution margin.

The sample problems in this chapter introduce the four equations involved in performing such an analysis and illustrate how to use them. They are based on the experience of Westside Manufacturing, a small company manufacturing pillows for sale through specialty bedding and dry cleaning stores. Although the examples are, for simplicity, based on a small manufacturing business, the equations are equally applicable for analyzing any size or type of business that cannot negotiate a unique price for each customer.[1] If customers can be somewhat segmented for pricing, the formulas apply to pricing within a segment.

Westside Manufacturing's income and costs for a typical month are:

Sales	4,000 units
Wholesale price	$10.00 per unit
Revenue	$40,000
Variable costs	$5.50 per unit
Fixed costs	$15,000

Westside is considering a 5 percent price cut, which it believes would make it more competitive with alternative suppliers, enabling it to further increase its sales. Management believes that the company would need to incur no additional fixed costs as a result of this pricing decision. How much would sales have to increase for this company to profit from a 5 percent cut in price?

BREAKEVEN SALES ANALYSIS: THE BASIC CASE

To answer Westside's question, we calculate the breakeven sales change. This, for a price cut, is the minimum increase in sales volume necessary for the price cut to produce an increase in contribution relative to the baseline. Fortunately, making this calculation is simple, as will be shown shortly. First, however, it may be more intuitive to illustrate the analysis graphically in Exhibit 3.1.

In this exhibit it is easy to visualize the financial trade-offs involved in the proposed price change. Before the price change, Westside receives a price of $10.00 per unit and sells 4,000 units, resulting in total revenues of $40,000 (the total area of boxes a and b). From this Westside pays variable costs of $5.50 per unit, for a total of $22,000 (box b). Therefore, *before* the price change, total contribution is $40,000 minus $22,000, or $18,000 (box a). In order for the proposed price cut to be profitable, contribution *after* the price cut must exceed $18,000.

After the 5 percent price reduction, Westside receives a price of only $9.50 per unit, or $0.50 less contribution per unit. Since it normally sells 4,000 units, Westside would expect to lose $2,000 in total contribution (box c) on sales that it could have made at a higher price. This is called the *price effect*. Fortunately, the price cut can be expected to increase sales volume.

Exhibit 3.1

Finding the Breakeven Sales Change

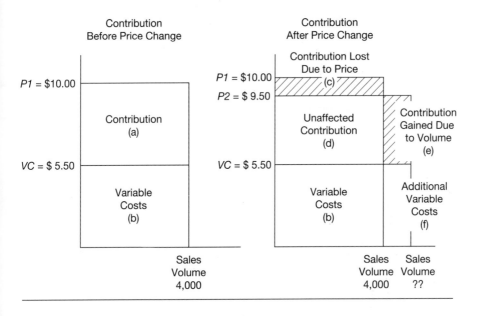

The contribution earned from that increased volume, the *volume effect* (box e), is unknown. The price reduction will be profitable, however, when the volume effect (the area of box e) exceeds the price effect (the area of box c). That is, in order for the price change to be profitable the gain in contribution resulting from the change in sales volume must be greater than the loss in contribution resulting from the change in price. The purpose of breakeven analysis is to calculate the *minimum* sales volume necessary for the volume effect (box e) to balance the price effect (box c). When sales exceed that amount, the price cut is profitable.

So how do we determine the breakeven sales change? We know that the lost contribution due to the price effect (box c) is $2,000, which means that the gain in contribution due to the volume effect (box e) must be at least $2,000 for the price cut to be profitable. Since each new unit sold following the price cut results in $4.00 in contribution ($9.50 – $5.50 = $4.00), Westside must sell at least an additional 500 units ($2,000 divided by $4.00 per unit) to make the price cut profitable.

The minimum sales change necessary to maintain at least the same contribution can be directly calculated by using the following simple formula (see Appendix 3A for derivation):

$$\% \text{ Breakeven sales change } = \frac{-\text{Price change}}{CM + \text{Price change}}$$

$$= \frac{-\Delta P}{CM + \Delta P}$$

In this equation, the price change and contribution margin may be stated in dollars, percents, or decimals, (as long as their use is consistent). The result of this equation is a decimal ratio that, when multiplied by 100, is the percent change in unit sales necessary to maintain the same level of contribution after the price change. The minus sign in the numerator indicates a trade-off between price and volume: Price cuts increase the volume and price increases reduce the volume necessary to achieve any particular level of profitability. The larger the price change—or the smaller the contribution margin—the greater the volume change necessary to generate at least as much contribution as before.

Assume for the moment that there are no incremental fixed costs in implementing Westside's proposed 5 percent price cut. For convenience we make our calculations in dollars (rather than in percents or decimals). Using the contribution margin equation (Chapter 2), we can write:

$$\$CM = \$10.00 - \$5.50 = \$4.50$$

Given this, we can easily calculate the breakeven sales change as follows:

$$\% \text{ Breakeven sales change } = \frac{-(-\$0.50)}{\$4.50 + (-\$0.50)} = 0.125 \text{ } or \text{ } 12.5\%$$

Thus, the price cut is profitable only if sales volume increases more than 12.5 percent. Relative to its current level of sales volume, Westside would have to sell at least 500 units more to maintain the same level of profitability it had prior to the price cut, as shown below:

$$\text{Unit breakeven sales change} = 0.125 \times 4,000 = 500 \text{ units}$$

If the actual increase in sales volume exceeds the breakeven sales change, the price cut will be profitable. If the actual increase in sales vol-

ume falls short of the breakeven sales change, the price change will be unprofitable. Assuming that Westside's goal is to increase its current profits,
management should initiate the price reduction only if it believes that sales
will increase by more than 12.5 percent, or 500 units, as a result.

If Westside's sales increase as a result of the price change by more
than the breakeven amount—say, by an additional 550 units—Westside
will realize a gain in profit contribution. If, however, Westside sells only an
additional 450 units as a result of the price cut, it will suffer a loss in contribution. Once we have the breakeven sales change and the profit contribution, calculating the precise change in contribution associated with any
change in volume is quite simple: It is simply the difference between the
actual sales volume and the breakeven sales volume, times the new contribution margin (calculated *after* the price change). For Westside's 550-unit
and 450-unit volume changes, the change in contribution equals:

$$(550 - 500) \times \$4.00 = \$200$$

$$(450 - 500) \times \$4.00 = -\$200$$

The $4.00 in these equations is the new contribution margin ($9.50 – $5.50).
Alternatively, you might have noticed that the denominator of the percent
breakeven formula is also the new contribution margin.

We have illustrated breakeven analysis using Westside's proposed 5
percent price cut. The logic is exactly the same for a price increase. Since a
price increase results in a gain in unit contribution, Westside can "absorb"
some reduction in sales volume and still increase its profitability. How
much of a reduction in sales volume can Westside tolerate before the price
increase becomes unprofitable? The answer is, until the loss in contribution
due to reduced sales volume is exactly offset by the gain in contribution
due to the price increase. As an exercise, calculate how much sales
Westside could afford to lose before a 5 percent price increase becomes unprofitable.[2]

BREAKEVEN SALES INCORPORATING A CHANGE IN VARIABLE COST

Thus far we have dealt only with price changes that involve no changes in
unit variable costs or in fixed costs. Often, however, price changes are
made as part of a marketing plan involving cost changes as well. A price
increase may be made along with product improvements that increase
variable cost, or a price cut might be made to push the product with lower
variable selling costs. Expenditures that represent fixed costs might also
change along with a price change. We need to consider these two types of

incremental costs when calculating the price-volume trade-off necessary for making pricing decisions profitable. We begin this section by integrating changes in variable cost into the financial analysis. In the next section, we do the same with changes in fixed costs.

Fortunately, dealing with a change in variable cost involves only a simple generalization of the breakeven sales change formula already introduced. To illustrate, we return to Westside Manufacturing's proposed 5 percent price cut. Suppose that Westside's price cut is accompanied by a reduction in variable cost of $0.22 per pillow, resulting from Westside's decision to use a new synthetic filler to replace the goose feathers it currently uses. Variable costs are $5.50 before the price change and $5.28 after the price change. By how much would sales volume have to increase to assure that the proposed price cut is profitable?

When variable costs change along with the price change, managers simply need to subtract the cost change from the price change before doing the breakeven sales change calculation. Unlike the case of a simple price change, managers *must* state the terms on the right-hand side of the equation in currency units (dollars, pounds, french francs, and so forth) rather than in percentage changes:

$$\% \text{ Breakeven sales change} = \frac{-(\$\Delta P - \$\Delta C)}{\$CM + (\$\Delta P - \$\Delta C)}$$

where Δ indicates "change in," P = price, and C = cost. Note that when the change in variable cost ($\$\Delta C$) is zero, this equation is identical to the breakeven formula previously presented. Note also that the term ($\$\Delta P - \$\Delta C$) is the change in the contribution margin and that the denominator (the original contribution margin plus the change) is the new contribution margin. Thus, the general form of the break-even pricing equation is simply written as follows:

$$\% \text{ Breakeven sales change} = \frac{-\$\Delta CM}{\text{New } \$CM}$$

For Westside, the next step in using this equation to evaluate the proposed price change is to calculate the change in contribution margin. Recall that the change in price is $9.50 – $10.00 or –$0.50. The change in variable costs is –$0.22. Thus, the change in contribution can be calculated as follows:

$$\$\Delta CM = (\$\Delta P - \$\Delta C) = -\$0.50 - (-\$0.22) = -\$0.28$$

Previous calculations illustrated that the contribution margin before the price change is $4.50. We can therefore calculate the breakeven sales change as follows:

$$\% \text{ Breakeven sales change } = \frac{-(-\$0.28)}{\$4.50 + (\$0.28)} = 0.066, \text{ or } +6.6\%$$

In units, the breakeven sales change is $0.066 \times 4{,}000$ units, or 265.

Given management's projection of a $0.22 reduction in variable costs, the price cut can be profitable only if management believes that sales volume will increase by more than 6.6 percent, or 265 units. Note that this increase is substantially less than the required sales increase (12.5 percent) calculated before assuming a reduction in variable cost. Why does a variable cost reduction lower the necessary breakeven sales change? Because it increases the contribution margin earned on each sale, making it possible to recover the contribution lost due to the price effect with less additional volume. This relationship is illustrated graphically for Westside Manufacturing in Exhibit 3.2. Westside can realize a gain in contribution due to the change in variable costs (box f), in addition to a gain in contribution due to any increase in sales volume.

BREAKEVEN SALES WITH INCREMENTAL FIXED COSTS

Although most fixed costs do not impact the incremental profitability of a pricing decision (because they do not change), some pricing decisions necessarily involve changes in fixed costs, even though these costs do not otherwise change with small changes in volume. The management of a discount airline considering whether to reposition as a higher-priced business-travelers' airline, would probably choose to refurbish its lounges and planes. A regulated utility would need to cover the fixed cost of regulatory hearings to gain approval for a higher price. A fast-food restaurant would need to advertise its promotionally priced "special-value" meals to potential customers. These are incremental fixed costs, necessary for the success of a new pricing strategy but unrelated to the sales volume actually gained at those prices. Recall also that semifixed costs remain fixed only within certain ranges of sales. If a price change causes sales to move outside that range, the level of semifixed costs increases or decreases. Such changes in fixed and semifixed costs need to be covered for a price change to be justified, since without the price change these incremental costs can be avoided.

Fortunately, calculating the sales volume necessary to cover an incremental fixed cost is already a familiar exercise for many managers evaluating investments independent of price changes. For example, suppose a

---

EXHIBIT 3.2

Finding the Breakeven Sales Change Given a Change in
Variable Costs

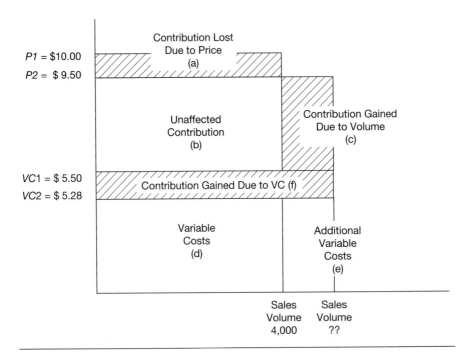

---

product manager is evaluating a $150,000 fixed expenditure to redesign a
product's packaging. The product's unit price is $10, and unit variable
costs total $5. How many units must be sold for the firm to recover the
$150,000 incremental investment? The answer as found in most managerial
economics texts, is given by the following equation:

$$\text{Breakeven sales volume} = \frac{\$ \text{Change in fixed costs}}{\$CM}$$

Remembering that the CM equals price – variable cost, the breakeven
sales volume for this example is:

$$\text{Breakeven sales volume} = \frac{\$150,000}{\$10 - \$5} = 30,000 \text{ units}$$

How can the manager do breakeven analysis for a change in pricing strategy that involves both a price change and a change in fixed cost? He simply adds the calculations for (a) the breakeven sales change for a price change and (b) the breakeven sales volume for the related fixed investment.

The breakeven sales change for a price change with incremental fixed costs is the basic breakeven sales change plus the sales change necessary to cover the incremental fixed costs. Since we normally analyze the breakeven for a price change as a *percent*, and the breakeven for an investment in *units*, we need to multiply or divide by initial unit sales to make them consistent. Consequently, the *unit* breakeven sales change with a change in fixed costs is

$$\text{Unit breakeven sales change} = \frac{-\$\Delta CM}{\text{New }\$CM} \times \text{Initial unit sales} + \frac{\$ \text{Change in fixed costs}}{\text{New }\$CM}$$

The calculation for the *percent* breakeven sales change is

$$\text{\% Breakeven sales change} = \frac{-\$\Delta CM}{\text{New }\$CM} + \frac{\$ \text{Change in fixed costs}}{\text{New }\$CM \times \text{Initial unit sales}}$$

In both cases, if the "$ change in fixed costs" is zero, we have the breakeven sales change equation for a simple price change.

To illustrate the equations for a price cut, return again to the pricing decision faced by Westside Manufacturing. Westside is considering a 5 percent price cut. We already calculated that it can profit if sales increase by more than 12.5 percent. Now suppose that Westside cannot increase its output without incurring additional semifixed costs. At the company's current rate of sales—4,000 units per month—it is fully utilizing the capacity of the equipment at its four work stations. To increase capacity enough to handle 12.5 percent more sales, the company must install equipment for another work station, at a monthly cost of $800. The new station raises plant capacity by 1,000 units beyond the current capacity of 4,000 units. What is the minimum sales increase required to justify a 5 percent price reduction, given that it involves an $800 increase in monthly fixed costs? The answer is determined as follows:

$$\text{Unit breakeven sales change} = 0.125 \times 4{,}000 \text{ units} + \frac{\$800}{\$4} = 700 \text{ units}$$

$$\text{\% Breakeven sales change} = 0.125 + \frac{\$800}{\$4 \times 4{,}000 \text{ units}} = 0.175, \text{ or } 17.5\%$$

The company could profit from a 5 percent price reduction if sales increased by more than 700 units (17.5 percent), which is less than the 1,000 units of added capacity provided by the new work station. Whether a prudent manager should actually implement such a price decrease depends on other factors as well: How likely is it that sales will increase substantially more than the breakeven minimum, thus adding to profit? How likely is it that sales will increase by less, thus reducing profit? How soon could the decision be reversed, if at all, if sales do not increase adequately?

Even if management considers it likely that orders will increase by more than the breakeven quantity, it should hesitate before making the decision. If orders increase by significantly less than the breakeven minimum, this company could lose substantially, especially if the cost of the new work station is largely sunk once the expenditure has been made. On the other hand, if orders increase by significantly more, the most the company could increase its sales without bearing the semifixed cost for further expansion is 25 percent, or 1,000 units. Consequently, management must be quite confident of a large sales increase before implementing the 5 percent price reduction.

Consider, however, if the company has already invested in the additional capacity and if the semifixed costs are already sunk. The monthly cost of the fifth work station is then entirely irrelevant to pricing, since that cost would have to be borne whether or not the capacity is used. Thus, the decision to cut price rests entirely on management's judgment of whether the price cut will stimulate unit sales by more than 12.5 percent. If the actual sales increase is more than 12.5 percent but less than 17.5 percent, management will regret having invested in the fifth work station. Given that this cost can no longer be avoided, however, the most profitable course of action is to price low enough to use the station, even though that price will not fully cover its cost.

BREAKEVEN SALES ANALYSIS FOR REACTIVE PRICING

So far we have restricted our discussion to *proactive price changes*, where the firm contemplates initiating a price change ahead of its competitors. The goal of such a change is to enhance profitability. Often, however, a company initiates *reactive price changes* when it is confronted with a competitor's price change that will impact the former's sales unless it responds. The key uncertainty involved in analyzing a reactive price change is the sales loss the company will suffer if it fails to meet a competitor's price cut, or the sales gain the company will achieve if it fails to follow a competitor's price increase. Is the potential sales loss sufficient to justify cutting price to protect the sales volume? Or is the potential sales gain enough to justify forgoing the opportunity for a cooperative price increase? A slightly different form of the breakeven sales formula is used to analyze such situations.

To calculate the breakeven sales changes for a reactive price change, we need to address the following key questions: (1) What is the minimum potential sales loss that justifies meeting a lower competitive price? And (2) what is the minimum potential sales gain that justifies *not* following a competitive price increase? The basic formula for these calculation is

$$\text{\% Breakeven sales change for reactive price change} = \frac{\text{Change in price}}{\text{Contribution margin}} = \frac{\Delta P}{CM}$$

To illustrate, suppose that Westside's principal competitor, Eastside, has just reduced its prices by 15 percent. If Westside's customers are highly loyal, it probably would not pay for Westside to match this cut. If, on the other hand, customers are quite price sensitive, Westside may have to match this price cut to minimize the damage. What is the minimum potential loss in sales volume that justifies meeting Eastside's price cut? The answer (calculated in percentage terms) is as follows[3]

$$\text{\% Breakeven sales change for reactive price change} = \frac{-15\%}{45\%} = -0.333, \text{ or } 33.3\%$$

Thus, if Westside expects sales volume to fall by more than 33 percent as a result of Eastside's new price, it would be less damaging to Westside's profitability to match the price cut than to lose sales. On the other hand, if Westside expects that sales volume will fall by less than 33 percent, it would be less damaging to Westside's profitability to let Eastside take the sales than it would be to cut price to meet this challenge.

This analysis has focused on minimizing losses in the face of a competitor's proactive price reduction. However, the procedure for analysis is the same when a competitor suddenly raises its prices. Suppose, for example, that Eastside raises its price by 15 percent. Westside might be tempted to match Eastside's price increase. If, however, Westside does not respond to Eastside's new price, Westside will likely gain additional sales volume as Eastside's customers switch to Westside. How much of a gain in sales volume must be realized in order for no price reaction to be more profitable than a reactive price increase? The answer is similarly found using the breakeven sales change formula with a reactive price change. If Westside is confident that sales volume will increase by more than 33.3 percent if it does not react, a nonreactive price policy would be more profitable. If Westside's management does not expect sales volume to increase by 33.3 percent, a reactive price increase would be more profitable.

Of course, the competitive analysis we have done is, by itself, overly simplistic. Eastside might be tempted to attack Westside's other markets if Westside does not respond to Eastside's price cut. And Westside's not matching Eastside's price increase might force Eastside to roll back its prices. These long-run strategic concerns might outweigh the short-term profit implications of a decision to react. In order to make such a judgment, however, the company must first determine the short-term profit implications. Sometimes long-term competitive strategies are not worth the short-term cost.

CALCULATING POTENTIAL FINANCIAL IMPLICATIONS

To grasp fully the potential impact of a price change, especially when the decision involves incremental changes in fixed costs, it is useful to calculate the profit impact for a range of potential sales changes and to summarize them with a breakeven table and chart. Doing so is relatively simple after having calculated the basic breakeven sales change. Using this calculation, one can then simulate what-if scenarios that include different levels of actual sales volume following the price change.

The top half of Exhibit 3.3 is a summary of the basic breakeven sales change analysis for Westside's 5 percent price cut, with one column summarizing the level of contribution before the price change (the column labeled Baseline) and one column summarizing the contribution after the price change (the column labeled Proposed Price Change). The bottom half of Exhibit 3.3 summarizes nine what-if scenarios showing the profitability associated with changes in sales volume ranging from 0 percent to 40 percent given incremental semifixed costs of $800 per 1,000 units. Columns 1 and 2 show the actual change in volume for each scenario. Columns 3 through 5 calculate the change in profit that results from each change in sales.

To illustrate how these breakeven sales-change scenarios are calculated, let us focus for a moment on scenario 6, where actual sales volume is projected to increase 20 percent. A 20 percent change in actual sales volume is equivalent to an 800-unit change in actual sales volume, since 800 units is 20 percent of the baseline sales volume of 4,000 units. How does this increase in sales translate into changes in profitability? Column 3 shows that a 20 percent (or an 800-unit) increase in sales volume results in a change in contribution after the price change of $1,200. This is calculated by taking the difference between the actual unit sales change (800 units) and the breakeven sales change shown in the top half of the exhibit (500 units), and multiplying by the new contribution margin after the price change ($4). However, the calculations made in column 3 do not take into account the incremental fixed costs required to implement the price change (shown in column 4). Column 5 shows the change in profit after subtracting the change in fixed costs from the incremental contribution generated. Where there is inadequate incremental contribution to cover the incremental fixed costs, as in scenarios 1 through 4, the change in profit is negative. Scenario 5 illustrates the breakeven sales change. Scenarios 6 through 9 are all profitable scenarios since they result in greater profit after the price change than before.

EXHIBIT 3.3

Breakeven Sales Analysis and Breakeven Sales Simulated Scenarios: Westside Manufacturing Proposed 5% Price Reduction

Breakeven Sales Change Summary	Baseline	Proposed Price Change
Price/unit	$10.00	$9.50
% price change		-5%
$ Contribution/unit	$4.50	$4.00
% Contribution	45%	42%
Breakeven sales change (%)		12.5%
Breakeven sales change (units)		500
Total sales volume (units)	4,000	4,500
Total contribution	$18,000	$18,000

Breakeven Sales Change Simulated Scenarios

		% Change in Actual Sales Volume	Unit Change in Actual Sales Volume	Change in Contribution After Price Change	Incremental Fixed Costs	Total Change in Profit After Price Change
Simulated Scenarios	1	0.0	0	-2,000	800	-2,800
	2	5.0	200	-1,200	800	-2000
	3	10.0	400	-400	800	-1,200
	4	12.5	500	0	800	-800
	5	17.5	700	800	800	0
	6	20.0	800	1,200	800	400
	7	25.0	1,000	2,000	800	1,200
	8	30.0	1,200	2,800	1,600	1,200
	9	40.0	1,600	4,400	1,600	2,800

Exhibit 3.4

Breakeven Analysis of a Price Change

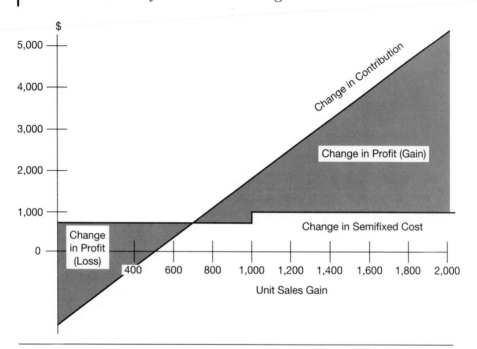

The interrelationships among contribution, incremental fixed costs, and the sales change that results from a price change are often easier to comprehend with a graph. Exhibit 3.4 illustrates the relationships among the data in Exhibit 3.3. Appendix 3B, at the end of this chapter, explains how to produce breakeven graphs. They are especially useful in comprehending the implications of price changes when many fixed costs become incremental at different sales volumes.

Breakeven Sales Curves

So far we have discussed breakeven sales analysis in terms of a single change in price and its resultant breakeven sales change. In the example above, Westside Manufacturing considered a 5 percent price reduction, which we calculated would require a 17.5 percent increase in sales volume to achieve enough incremental contribution to cover the incremental fixed cost. However, what if the company wants to consider a range of potential price changes? How can we use breakeven sales analysis to consider alternative price changes simultaneously? The answer is by charting a breakeven sales curve, which summarizes the results of a series of breakeven sales analyses for different price changes.

Constructing breakeven sales curves requires doing a series of what-if analyses, similar to the simulated scenarios discussed in the last section. Exhibits 3.5 and 3.6 show numerically and graphically a breakeven sales curve for Westside Manufacturing, with simulated scenarios of price changes ranging from +25 to –20 percent. Note in Exhibit 3.6 that the vertical axis shows different price levels for the product, and the horizontal axis shows a volume level associated with each price level. Each point on the curve represents the sales volume necessary to achieve as much profit after the price change as would be earned at the baseline price. For example, Westside's baseline price is $10.00 per unit, and baseline sales volume is 4,000 units. If, however, Westside cuts the price by 15 percent to $8.50, its sales volume would have to increase 70 percent to 6,800 units to achieve the same profitability. Conversely, if Westside increases its price by 15 percent to $11.50, its sales volume could decrease 25 percent to 3,000 units and still allow Westside to achieve equal profitability.

EXHIBIT 3.5

Breakeven Sales Curve Calculations (with Incremental Fixed Costs)*

Price Change	Price	% Breakeven Sales Change	Unit Breakeven Sales Change	Unit Breakeven Sales Volume	Incremental Fixed Costs
25%	$12.50	-35.7%	-1,429	2,571	$0
20%	$12.00	-30.8%	-1,231	2,769	$0
15%	$11.50	-25.0%	-1,000	3,000	$0
10%	$11.00	-18.2%	-727	3,273	$0
5%	$10.50	-10.0%	-400	3,600	$0
0%	$10.00	0.0%	0	4,000	$0
-5%	$9.50	17.5%	700	4,700	$800
-10%	$9.00	40.0%	1,600	5,600	$1,600
-15%	$8.50	70.0%	2,800	6,800	$2,400
-20%	$8.00	20.0%	4,800	8,800	$4,000

* Increases in sales volume require investment in one new machine for each additional 1,000 units produced, or fraction thereof, at a cost of $800 per machine.

EXHIBIT 3.6

Breakeven Sales Curve Tradeoff Between Price and Sales
Volume Required for Constant Profitability

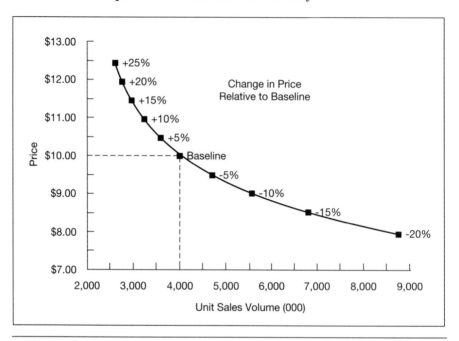

The breakeven sales curve is a simple, yet powerful tool to synthesize
and evaluate the dynamics behind the profitability of potential price
changes. It presents succinctly and visually the dividing line that separates
profitable price decisions from unprofitable ones. Profitable price decisions
are those that result in sales volumes in the area to the right of the curve.
Unprofitable price decisions are those that result in sales volumes in the
area to the left of the curve. What is the logic behind this? Recall the previous discussion of what happens before and after a price change. The
breakeven sales curve represents those sales volume levels associated with
their respective levels of price, where the company will make just as much
net contribution *after* the price change as it made *before* the price change. If
the company's sales volume after the price change is greater than the
breakeven sales volume (that is, actual sales volume is to the right of the
curve), the price change will add to profitability. If the company's sales volume after the price change is less than the breakeven sales volume (that is,
the area to the left of the curve), the price change will be unprofitable. For

example, for Westside a price of $8.50 requires a sales volume of at least 6,800 units to achieve a net gain in profitability. If, after reducing its price to $8.50, management believes it will sell more than 6,800 units (a point to the right of the curve), then a decision to implement a price of $8.50 per unit would be profitable.

The breakeven sales curve also clearly illustrates the relationship between the breakeven approach to pricing and the economic concept of price elasticity. Note that the breakeven sales curve looks suspiciously like the traditional downward-sloping demand curve in economic theory, in which different levels of price (on the vertical axis) are associated with different levels of quantity demanded (on the horizontal axis). On a traditional demand curve, the slope between any two points on the curve determines the elasticity of demand, a measure of price sensitivity expressed as the percent change in quantity demanded for a given percent change in price. An economist who knew the shape of such a curve could calculate the profit-maximizing price.

Unfortunately, few firms use economic theory to set price because of the unrealistic expectation that they first have to know their demand curve, or at least the demand elasticity around the current price level. To overcome this shortcoming, we have addressed the problem in reverse order. Rather than asking, "What is the firm's demand elasticity?" we ask instead, "What is the minimum demand elasticity required?" to justify a particular strategic pricing decision. Breakeven sales analysis calculates the minimum or maximum demand elasticity required to profit from a particular pricing decision. The breakeven sales curve illustrates a set of minimum elasticities necessary to make a price cut profitable, or the maximum elasticity tolerable to make a price increase profitable. One is then led to ask whether the level of price sensitivity in the market is greater or less than the level of price sensitivity required by the firm's cost and margin structure.

This relationship between the breakeven sales curve and the demand curve is illustrated in Exhibits 3.7 and 3.8, where hypothetical demand curves are shown with Westside's break-even sales curve. If demand is more elastic as in Exhibit 3.7, price reductions relative to the baseline price result in gains in profitability, and price increases result in losses in profitability. If demand is less elastic, as in Exhibit 3.8, price increases relative to the baseline price result in gains in profitability, and price reductions result in losses in profitability. Although few, if any, managers actually know the demand curve for their product, we have encountered many who can comfortably make judgments about whether it is more or less elastic than is required by the breakeven sales curve. Moreover, although we have not found any market research technique that can estimate a demand curve with great precision, we have seen many (described in Chapter 13) that could enable management to confidently accept or reject a particular breakeven sales level as achievable.

Exhibit 3.7

Breakeven Sales Curve Relationship Between Price Elasticity of Demand and Profitability

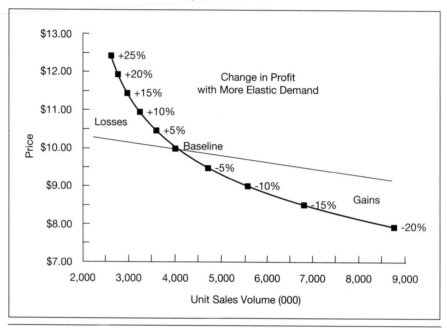

Watching your baseline

In the preceding examples, the baseline sales from which we calculated breakeven sales changes was assumed to be the current level. For simplicity, we assume a static market. In many cases, however, sales grow or decline even if price remains constant. As a result, the baseline for calculating breakeven sales changes is not necessarily the current level of sales. Rather, it is the level that would occur if no price change is made.

Consider, for example, a company in a high-growth industry with current sales of 2,000 units on which it earns a contribution margin of 55 percent. If the company does not change its price, management expects that sales will increase by 20 percent (the projected growth of total industry sales) to 2,400 units. However, management is considering a 5 percent price cut in an attempt to increase the company's market share. The price cut would be accompanied by an advertising campaign intended to heighten consumer awareness of the change. The campaign would take time to design, delaying implementation of the price change until next year. The initial sales level for the constant contribution analysis, therefore, would be

EXHIBIT 3.8

Breakeven Sales Curve Relationship Between Price Elasticity of Demand and Profitability: Changes in Profit with More Inelastic Demand

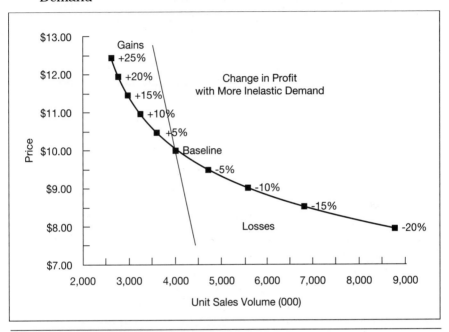

the projected sales in the future, or 2,400 units. Consequently the breakeven sales change would be:

$$\% \text{ Breakeven sales change} = \frac{-(-5\%)}{55\% + (-5\%)} = 0.10, \text{ or } 10\%$$

or

$$0.10 \times 2,400 = 240 \text{ units}$$

If the current sales level is used in the calculation, the unit breakeven sales change is calculated as 200 units, understating the change required by 40 units.

Covering nonincremental fixed and sunk costs

By this point, one might be wondering about the nonincremental fixed and sunk costs that have been ignored when analyzing pricing decisions. A company's goal must surely be to cover all of its costs, including all fixed and sunk costs, or it will soon go bankrupt. This concern is justified and is central to the issue of customer-driven pricing.

Note that the goal in calculating a contribution margin and in using it to evaluate price changes and differentials is to set prices to maximize a product's profit contribution. Profit contribution, you will recall, is the income remaining after all incremental, avoidable costs have been covered. It is money available to cover nonincremental fixed and sunk costs and to contribute to profit. When managers consider only the incremental, avoidable costs in making pricing decisions, they are not saying that other costs are unimportant. They realize, however, that the level of those costs is irrelevant to decisions about which price will generate the most money to cover them and to earn a profit. Since nonincremental fixed and sunk costs do not change with a pricing decision, they do not affect the relative profitability of one price versus an alternative. Consequently, consideration of them simply clouds the issue of which price changes and levels will generate the most profit to cover them.

Some managers still get nervous about ignoring some costs, and they should. All costs are important to profitability since they all, regardless of how they are classified, have to be covered before profits are earned. At some point, all costs must be considered. What distinguishes value-based pricing from cost-driven pricing is *when* they are considered. A major reason that this approach to pricing is more profitable than cost-driven pricing is that it encourages managers to think about costs when they can still do something about them. *Every cost is incremental and avoidable at some time.* For example, even the cost of product development and design, although it is fixed and sunk by the time the first unit is sold, is incremental and avoidable before the design process begins. The same is true for other costs. The key to profitable pricing is to recognize that customers in the marketplace, not costs, determine what a product can sell for. Consequently, before incurring any costs, managers need to estimate what customers will pay for the intended product. Then they decide what costs they can profitably incur, given the expected revenue.

Of course, no one has perfect foresight. Managers must make decisions to incur costs without knowing for certain how the market will respond. When their expectations are accurate, the market rewards them with sales at the prices they expected, enabling them to cover all costs and to earn a profit. When they overestimate a product's value, profit contribution may prove inadequate to cover all the costs incurred. In that case, a good manager seeks to minimize the loss. This can be done only by maximizing profit contribution (revenue minus incremental, avoidable costs). Short-sighted efforts to build nonincremental fixed and sunk costs into a price that will justify past mistakes will only reduce volume further, making the losses worse.

SUMMARY

The profitability of pricing decisions depends largely on the product's cost structure and contribution margin and on market sensitivity to changes in price. In Chapter 2 we discussed the importance of identifying the costs that are most relevant to the profitability of a pricing decision, namely, incremental and avoidable costs. Having identified the right costs, one must also understand how to use them. The most important reason to identify costs correctly is to be able to calculate an accurate contribution margin. An accurate contribution margin enables management to determine the amount by which sales must increase following a price cut, or by how little they may decline following a price increase to make the price change profitable. Understanding how changes in sales will affect a product's profitability is the first step in pricing the product effectively.

It is, however, just the first step. Next one must learn how to judge the likely impact of a price change on sales, which requires understanding how buyers are likely to perceive a price change and how competitors are likely to react to it. We consider these subjects in the next two chapters.

NOTES

1. The rule for analyzing the profitability of independently negotiated prices is simple: A price is profitable as long as it covers incremental costs. Unfortunately, many managers make the mistake of applying that rule when prices are not independent across customers. They assume, mistakenly, that because they negotiate prices individually they are negotiating them *independently*. In fact, because customers talk to one other and learn the prices that others pay, prices are rarely independent. The low price you charge to one customer will eventually depress the prices that you can charge to others.

2. $$\frac{-\$0.50}{\$4.50 + \$0.50} = -0.10, \text{ or } -10\%$$

3. This equation can also accommodate a change in variable cost by simply replacing the "change in price" with the "change in price minus the change in variable cost." One can also add to it the breakeven necessary to cover a change in fixed costs.

Appendix 3A
Derivation of the breakeven formula

A price change can either increase or reduce a company's profits, depending on how it affects sales. The breakeven formula is a simple way to discover at what point the change in sales becomes large enough to make a price reduction profitable, or a price increase unprofitable.

Exhibit 3A.1 illustrates the breakeven problem. At the initial price P, a company can sell the quantity Q. Its total revenue is P times Q, which graphically is the area of the rectangle bordered by the lines $0P$ and $0Q$. If C is the product's variable cost then the total profit contribution earned at price P is $(P - C)Q$. Total profit contribution is shown graphically as the rectangle bordered by the lines CP and $0Q$.

If this company reduces its price from P to P', its profits will change. First, it will lose an amount equal to the change in price, ΔP, times the amount that it could sell without the price change, Q. Graphically, that loss is the rectangle labeled A. Somewhat offsetting that loss, however, the company will enjoy a gain from the additional sales it can make because of the lower price. The amount of the gain is the profit that the company will earn

---

EXHIBIT 3A.1

Breakeven Sales Change Relationships

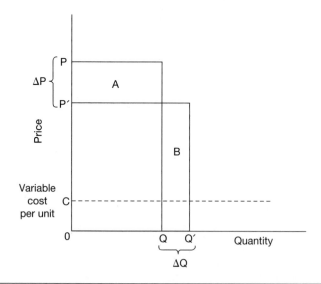

from each additional sale, $P' - C$, times the change in sales, ΔQ. Graphically, that gain is the rectangle labeled B. Whether or not the price reduction is profitable depends on whether or not rectangle B is greater than rectangle A, and that depends on the size of ΔQ.

The logic of a price increase is similar. If P' were the initial price and Q' the initial quantity, then the profitability of a price increase to P would again depend on the size of ΔQ. If ΔQ were small, rectangle A, the gain on sales made at the higher price, would exceed rectangle B, the loss on sales that would not be made because of the higher price. However, ΔQ might be large enough to make B larger than A, in which case the price increase would be unprofitable.

To calculate the formula for the breakeven ΔQ (at which the gain from a price reduction just outweighs the loss or the loss from a price increase just outweighs the gain), we need to state the problem algebraically. Before the price change, the profit earned was $(P - C)Q$. After the change, the profit was $(P' - C)Q'$. Noting, however, that $P' = P + \Delta P$ (we write $+ \Delta P$ since ΔP is a negative number) and that $Q' = Q + \Delta Q$, we can write the profit after the price change as $(P + \Delta P - C)(Q + \Delta Q)$. Since our goal is to find the ΔQ at which profits would be just equal before and after the price change, we can begin by setting those profits equal algebraically:

$$(P - C)Q = (P + \Delta P - C)(Q + \Delta Q)$$

Multiplying this equation through yields

$$PQ - CQ = PQ + \Delta PQ - CQ + P\Delta Q + \Delta P\Delta Q - C\Delta Q$$

We can simplify this equation by subtracting PQ and adding CQ to both sides to obtain

$$0 = \Delta PQ + P\Delta Q + \Delta P\Delta Q - C\Delta Q$$

Note that all the remaining terms in the equation contain the "change sign" Δ. This is because only the changes are relevant for evaluating a price change. If we solve this equation for ΔQ, we obtain the new equation

$$\frac{\Delta Q}{Q} = \frac{-\Delta P}{P + \Delta P - C}$$

which, in words, is

$$\% \text{ Breakeven sales change} = \frac{-\text{Price change}}{CM + \text{Price change}}$$

To express the right side in percentages, multiply the right side by

$$\frac{\left(\dfrac{1}{P}\right)}{\left(\dfrac{1}{P}\right)}$$

Appendix 3B
Breakeven analysis of price changes

Breakeven analysis is a common tool in managerial accounting, particularly useful for evaluating potential investments. Unfortunately, the traditional forms of breakeven analysis appropriate for evaluating investment decisions are often misleading when applied to pricing decisions. Individual investments (Should the company buy a new computer? Should it develop a new product? Should it field a salesforce to enter a new market?) can often be evaluated apart from other investments. Consequently, it is appropriate to use traditional breakeven analysis, which compares the total revenue from the investment with its total cost.

Usually, however, one cannot set a price for each individual sale independent of other sales. To gain an additional sale by charging one customer a lower price normally requires charging other customers, at least others in that same market segment, the lower price as well. Consequently, it is usually misleading to evaluate the profitability of an additional sale by comparing only the price earned from that sale to the cost of that sale. To comprehend the profit implications of a price change, one must compare the change in revenue from all sales with the change in costs.

The need to focus attention on the changes in revenues and costs rather than on their totals requires a different kind of breakeven analysis for pricing decisions. Where traditional breakeven analysis of investments deals with total revenue and all costs, breakeven analysis of pricing decisions deals with the *change* in revenue in excess of variable cost (the dollar contribution margin) and with the *change* in incremental fixed costs. In the body of this chapter, you learned a number of formulas for breakeven analysis of pricing decisions and saw how to use them in the Westside Manufacturing example. In this appendix, you will learn how to use those equations to develop breakeven graphs and to analyze more complex pricing problems involving multiple sources of fixed costs that become incremental at different quantities.

DEVELOPING A BREAKEVEN CHART

A breakeven chart, such as Exhibit 3.4 is useful in determining the possible effects of a price change. It plots both the change in the dollar contribution margin and the changes in relevant costs, enabling the pricing analyst to see the change in net profit that a change in sales volume would generate. To develop such a chart, it is useful to begin by preparing a table, such as Exhibit 3.5, organizing all relevant data in a concise form.

As an illustration, let us examine the case of PQR Industries. PQR manufactures and markets home video equipment. One of the most popular items in the company's product line is a video tape player with current sales of 4,000 units at $250.00 each. Sales have been growing rapidly and are expected to reach 4,800 units in the next year if the price remains unchanged. Variable costs are $112.50 per unit, resulting in a percent contribution margin of:

$$\%CM = \frac{\$250.00 - \$112.50}{\$250.00} = .55 = 55\%$$

Despite its projected growth in sales at the current price, PQR is considering a 5 percent price cut to remain competitive and retain its share in this rapidly growing market. Since the cut would be implemented in the next year, the initial sales level, or baseline is next year's projected sales (4,800 units). Calculation of the breakeven sales change is as follows:

$$\% \text{ breakeven sales change} = \frac{-(-5.0)}{55.0 + (-5.0)} = \frac{5}{50} = .10 = 10\%$$

$$\text{Unit breakeven sales change} = .10 \times 4,800 \text{ units} = 480 \text{ units}$$

Production capacity is currently limited to 5,000 units but can be increased by purchasing equipment which costs $15,000 for each additional 1,000 units of capacity. The breakeven sales change, considering this change in fixed costs, is:

$$\begin{array}{c} \% \text{ breakeven sales change} \\ \text{(with incremental fixed costs)} \end{array} = 10 + \frac{\$15,000}{\$125.00 \times 4,800} = 12.5\%$$

$$\text{Unit breakeven sales} = .125 \times 4,8000 \text{ units} = 600 \text{ units}$$

Note that the price cut brings the price down to $237.50, resulting in a new dollar contribution margin of $125.00 per unit.

Since the actual sales change that would result from the price cut is unknown, a breakeven table and chart should be prepared to show the profitability of the price change at various possible sales changes.

Exhibit 3B.1 shows a breakeven table for PQR's proposed 5 percent price cut. The first two columns show the potential levels of sales changes. Column 3 shows the change in total contribution margin that would result

---

EXHIBIT 3B.1

Breakeven Table for PQR Industries' Proposed 5% Price Cut

(1)	(2)	Change in (3)	(4)	(5)
Sales				
(%)	(Units)	Contribution Margin	Fixed Costs	Profit Contribution
0.0	0	-$ 60,000	0	-$ 60,000
5.0	240	-$ 30,000	$15,000	-$ 45,000
10.0	480	0	$15,000	-$ 15,000
12.5	600	$ 15,000	$15,000	0
15.0	720	$ 30,000	$15,000	$ 15,000
20.0	960	$ 60,000	$15,000	$ 45,000
25.0	1200	$ 90,000	$15,000	$ 75,000
30.0	1440	$120,000	$30,000	$ 90,000
40.0	1920	$180,000	$30,000	$150,000

Note: Proposed change −5% or $12,50/unit; initial price = $250; %CM = 45%; semifixed cost = $15,000 per 1,000 units capacity over 5,000 units

---

at each level using the change in profit formula. In the case of a 5 percent change in sales, the result would be:

Change in profit = (240 units − 480 units) × $125.00/unit = −$30,000

Subtracting the change in fixed costs shown in column 4 from column 3 results in column 5, the change in profit contribution. Alternatively, we could have generated column 5 more directly by calculating the breakeven sales change including the change in fixed costs and substituting that number in the change in profit equation.

When plotted on a graph, the data from this table form a breakeven chart (Exhibit 3B.2). The horizontal axis represents the change in unit sales and the vertical axis represents dollars of change. The line labeled "change in fixed costs" shows the increase in costs due to added capacity, as taken from column 4 of the table. The data in column 3 were used to plot the "change in contribution margin" line. The distance between the two lines represents the change in profit contribution (column 5). At the points where the "change in contribution margin" line is above the "change in fixed costs" line, the change in profit contribution (and net profit) is positive. The price cut would be profitable if sales changed by those amounts.

Exhibit 3B.2

Breakeven Analysis of PQR Industries' 5% Price Cut

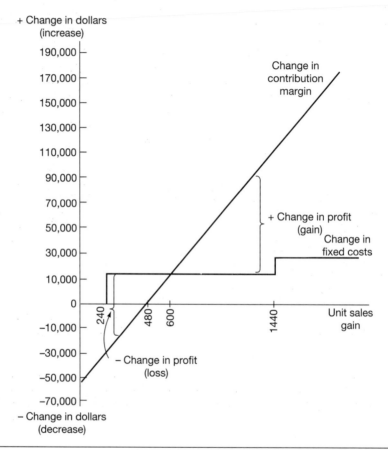

Breakeven Analysis with More Than One Incremental Fixed Cost

To this point, we have always assumed that a company has only one fixed cost that changes with a price change. Frequently, however, a company will have several semifixed costs that change at different levels of volume. This makes analysis of a price change more complicated and the use of breakeven analysis more essential to the management of that complexity.

Let us return to PQR Industries. Because of the cost of adding a machine, management investigated alternative methods of increasing production. It was determined that the addition of one machine operator could delay purchase of a machine until sales exceeded 5,400 units (or 600 units more than the baseline initial sales). Although labor costs are normally variable with production, machine operators are skilled laborers who, according to union rules, can only be hired as full-time employees working only at their specialties. The result is that a machine operator's salary is a semifixed cost. It was also discovered that the union contract required one skilled worker be added for each 1,000 units of increased production. Finally, the plant engineer informed management that there was space for only one additional machine. If more equipment were purchased, more space would have to be rented, at a cost of $105,000 per year. The situation is summarized as follows:

Sales	4,800 units
Wholesale price	$250.00/unit
Variable cost	$112.50/unit
Semi-fixed costs	
Machine operators	$7,500 per 1,000 units of added production
Equipment	$15,000 per 1,000 units of added production beyond a 600 unit gain
Space	$105,000 per year for rental if more than one machine is added

Due to the complexity of these costs, there is more than one breakeven sales change and a single calculation is not sufficient. For example, any increase in sales will require the hiring of a machine operator. The breakeven sales change for a 5 percent price cut becomes:

% breakeven sales change (with cost of machine operator)

$$= 10\% + \frac{\$7,500}{\$125 \times 4,800} = 11.25\%$$

Unit breakeven sales change

$$= 0.1125 \times 4,800 \text{ units} = 540 \text{ units}$$

If, however, the total sales exceed 5,400 units and equipment must be purchased, a new calculation is required as follows:

% breakeven sales change (with cost of equipment)

$$= 11.25\% + \frac{\$15,000}{\$125 \times 4,800} = 13.75\%$$

Unit breakeven sales change

$$= 0.1375 \times 4,800 \text{ units} = 660 \text{ units}$$

If more space would have to be rented, still another breakeven calculation would be required.

It seems obvious that when there are multiple sources of incremental fixed costs, analysis via calculation of breakeven sales changes could become both tedious and confusing. A breakeven table and chart are usually essential to the clear sorting out of these problems. Organizing the data into a table (Exhibit 3B.3) and plotting it on a graph (Exhibit 3B.4) makes the options much clearer. At changes in sales of between 540 and 600 units, the price change is slightly profitable. Once the change in sales exceeds 600 units, however, fixed costs must rise again due to the need for more equipment, and profits will become negative. They will not return to positive again until the change in sales exceeds 660 units, causing the change in contribution to rise above the change in fixed costs.

Note that 12.5 percent, or 600 units, is the maximum sales change possible before additional costs must be incurred. To determine whether the investment in additional equipment is worthwhile, management must decide whether the possibility that sales will grow enough to achieve a profit contribution of more than $7,500 (that is, by more than 15 percent) after the equipment is purchased would be enough to justify foregoing the more certain profit to be gained from reaching only a 12.5 percent increase in sales.

This type of situation arises whenever there is a change in fixed costs, most dramatically when the second machine is bought and space must be rented. It seems unlikely that sales growth due to the price change would be sufficient to justify renting more space. In fact, sales would have to increase by more than 53 percent before such an increase in fixed costs would produce a positive net profit. Moreover, the investment would not be justified if the profit that could be earned by not meeting the entire sales gain were higher.

BREAKEVEN GRAPHS

The calculations for determining breakeven sales changes for a price increase are the same as those for a price cut. For price increases, however, sales volumes decline rather than increase. Consequently, the direction of the horizontal axis measures declines in sales volumes rather than increases.

To illustrate, let us consider again the case of PQR Industries. In addition to VCRs, PQR sells projection televisions for $3,000. Variable costs of $1,650 per unit leave the company with a contribution margin of $1,350 per unit, or 45 percent. The company is considering a price increase next year on this item. The initial sales level for evaluating the increase (next year's projected sales) is 4,000 units, which exceeds the company's current capacity of 3,600 units.

Concern about capacity constraints and the slowing growth of the market for this product have caused management to consider instituting a

Exhibit 3B.3

Revised Breakeven Table for PQR Industries' Proposed 5% Price Cut

Changes in

Sales (%)	Sales (Units)	Contribution Margin ($)	Cost of Operators ($)	Cost of Equipment ($)	Cost of Space ($)	Total Fixed Costs ($)	Profit Contribution ($)
0.00	0	-60,000	0	0	0	0	-60,000
5.00	240	-30,000	7,500	0	0	7,500	-37,500
10.00	480	0	7,500	0	0	7,500	-7,500
11.25	540	7,500	7,500	0	0	7,500	0
12.50	600	15,000	7,500	0	0	7,500	7,500
13.75	660	22,500	7,500	15,000	0	22,500	0
15.00	720	30,000	7,500	15,000	0	22,500	7,500
20.00	960	60,000	7,500	15,000	0	22,500	37,500
25.00	1,200	90,000	15,000	15,000	0	30,000	60,000
30.00	1,440	120,000	15,000	15,000	0	30,000	90,000
35.00	1,680	150,000	15,000	30,000	105,000	150,000	0
40.00	1,920	180,000	15,000	30,000	105,000	150,000	30,000

Note: Proposed change: -5%, or $12.50/unit; initial price = $250; %CM = 45%; semifixed costs = $7,500/1,000 units for machine operators $15,000/1000 units over 5,400 units for equipment $90,000/year for space rental if more than one piece of equipment is added.

Exhibit 3B.4

Revised Breakeven Analysis of PQR Industries' 5% Cut

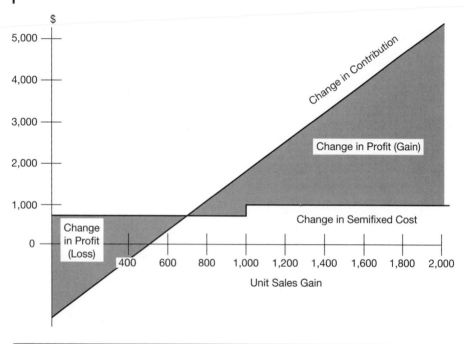

---

price increase in order to maximize profits. The breakeven sales change for the proposed 5 percent price increase is:

$$\% \text{ breakeven sales change} = \frac{-(5)}{45 + 5} = -10\%$$

Unit breakeven sales change $= -0.10 \times 4{,}000 \text{ units} = -400 \text{ units}$

As long as the price increase causes sales to decline by less than 10 percent or 400 units, the price increase will cause the total dollar contribution from this product to increase.

To increase production beyond the current 3,600-unit capacity, additional equipment must be bought at a cost of $150,000. If, however, as a result of the price increase, sales decrease to the point that current capacity is sufficient, purchase of new equipment would not be necessary. The expenditure avoided is a negative change in fixed costs from the level required to achieve the 4,000-unit baseline sales level. A new breakeven sales change is calculated as follows:

$$\begin{array}{l} \text{\% breakeven sales change} \\ \text{(including change in fixed costs)} \end{array} = -10\% + \frac{-\$150.000}{\$1,500 \times 4,000}$$

$$= -12.5\%$$

On the basis of the data in Exhibit 3B.5, we can produce a breakeven graph for this price change (Exhibit 3B.6). The lines representing changes in contribution margin and fixed costs run opposite to the directions we are accustomed to seeing for price cuts, but the change in profit contribution,

EXHIBIT 3B.5

Breakeven Table for PQR Industries' Proposed 5% Price Increase

Change in

(1)	(2)	(3)	(4)	(5)
Sales				
		Contribution	Fixed	Profit
(%)	(Units)	Margin ($)	Costs ($)	Contribution ($)
0.0	0	600,000	0	600,000
5.0	200	800,000	0	300,000
10.0	400	0	−150,000	150,000
12.5	500	−150,000	−150,000	0
15.0	600	−300,000	−150,000	−150,000
20.0	800	−600,000	−150,000	−450,000
25.0	1000	−900,000	−150,000	−750,000
30.0	1200	−1,200,000	−150,000	−1,050,000

Note: Proposed change −5% or $150/unit initial price = $3,000; %CM = 45%; semifixed cost = $150,000 for capacity over 3,600 units

EXHIBIT 3B.6

Breakeven Analysis for PQR Industries' 5% Price Increase

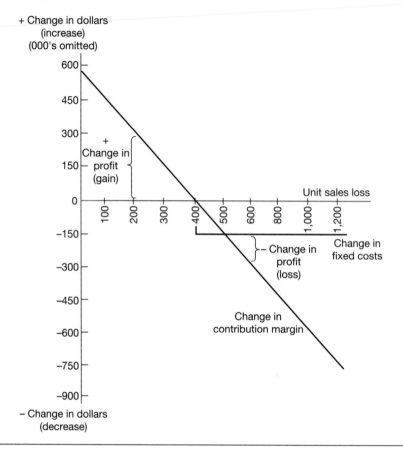

as indicated by the relative positions of these lines, is still interpreted as in earlier examples.

To verify this, let us refer to the graph and examine the results of a 5 percent, or 200-unit, sales decrease. At this point, there has been no change in fixed costs. Therefore, the change in profitability should equal a positive $300,000, the distance between the line indicating change in contribution margin and the horizontal axis. Reference to the related table will show that this is indeed true.

SUMMARY

Predicting the outcome of a price change is not an exact science as later chapters will show. A manager should, therefore, consider all possible outcomes of such a change in order to choose the wisest course of action. Tables and graphs of breakeven analyses are useful, easily produced tools for this purpose.

CUSTOMERS

CHAPTER

4

UNDERSTANDING AND INFLUENCING THE PURCHASE DECISION

In the last chapter, we learned how to prepare an appropriate financial analysis for a pricing decision. In contrast to financial techniques for cost-driven pricing, financial analysis for profit-driven pricing cannot by itself determine a price. This is not a flaw, but a virtue, of the approach that we have developed.

Pricing is not a decision that can be driven solely by the numbers. Managers who perceive it as such have usually deceived themselves into believing that neither customers nor competitors will react to their pricing decisions. Even managers who realize the importance of market reactions for profitable pricing are sometimes taken in by financial analyses that purport to identify *the* right decision based on precise, numerical estimates of customer and competitive responses. Rather than aiding the process of strategic management, however, such analyses usually muddle it by obscuring the essential uncertainty of the market.[1]

The goal of strategic planning is to understand and manage market uncertainty, not to obscure it. Financial analysis can set out the necessary conditions for a profitable pricing decision (a minimum gain or maximum loss in sales), but management must understand customers and competitors well enough to evaluate and influence the probabilities that those conditions will be met. Ultimately, good pricing decisions must be based on managerial judgment about uncertain customer and competitor reactions.

To say that pricing is a matter of judgment about market conditions is not to imply that one can successfully make decisions on a "hunch" or "intuition." On the contrary, *informed* judgment is arguably what distinguishes good managers from those who wield power blindly. In this chapter we discuss guidelines for understanding how customers use price in their purchase decisions. This understanding enables managers to anticipate and influence customers' reactions to pricing decisions and to segment customers by differences in their probable reactions.

ROLE OF VALUE IN PRICING

Among the most useful techniques for pricing are those that help managers determine the "economic value" of their products or services. Marketers have long admonished companies to set prices that reflect value. Unfortunately, because *value* is often poorly defined, value-based pricing is sometimes rejected as impractical. Consequently, let's begin by explaining what we mean by *value*.

In common usuage, the term *value* refers to the total savings or satisfaction that the customer receives from the product. Economists refer to this as *use value*, or the *utility* gained from the product. On a hot summer day at the beach, the "use value" of something cold to drink is extremely high for most people—perhaps as high as $5 for 12 ounces of cold cola or a favorite brand of beer. That information is of little help, however, to a vendor trying to price cold drinks for thirsty sun worshipers, since few potential customers would be willing to pay such a price.

Why not? Because potential customers know that, except in rare situations, they don't have to pay a seller all that a product is really worth to them. They know that competing sellers will give them a better deal, leaving them with "consumer surplus." Perhaps they believe from prior experience that, if they wait a while, another vendor will come along selling cold beverages at prices closer to what they have come to expect from their past experience, say, $1.50. Or they may know that about half a mile up the beach is a snack shop where beverages cost just $1.00. As a last resort, they could drive to a convenience store where they could buy an entire six-pack of cold cola for only $3.49. Consequently, thirsty sun-worshipers will usually reject an unusually high price as "outrageous," even though the product is worth much more to them than that price.

So what do marketers mean when they propose pricing to reflect value? The value that is key to developing effective pricing strategy is not use value, but is what economists call *exchange value* and what marketers call *economic value-to-the-customer*. This value is determined first and foremost by what the customers' alternatives are. Few people will pay even $2 for a cola, even when they value it at $5, if they think the market offers alternatives at substantially lower prices.

Still, only a small segment of customers insists on buying the lowest priced alternative. It is quite likely that many people would buy a cola at the beach for $1.50, despite the availability of the same product for less at a snack shop or convenience store. By offering the product *at the beach* the vendor is pricing a "differentiated product offering" worth more than the available alternatives to some segments of the market. How much more depends on the value customers place on not having to walk up the beach to the snack shop or not having to drive to the convenience store. For some, that value is very high. They are willing to pay a lot for the convenience of not having to exert themselves. For more athletic types who wouldn't mind an excuse to jog along the beach, the premium for convenience may be much less. To ensure the patronage of that segment, the beach vendor would be wise to differentiate his or her offering in some other way that this segment values highly.

A product's "economic value," then, is the price of the customer's best alternative (called the *reference value*) *plus the value of whatever differentiates the offering from the alternative* (called the *differentiation value*). Exhibit 4.1 illustrates these relationships. *Total economic value* is the maximum price that a "smart shopper," fully informed about the market and seeking the best value, would pay. In fact, sophisticated business buyers often demand an economic value analysis that quantifies the benefits of high-priced brands or that shows how low-priced brands can save more than the value of the benefits given up.

Economic value analysis is an especially good sales tool when buyers are facing extreme cost pressures and are, therefore, very price sensitive. Since health-care reimbursement systems were changed to give hospitals and doctors a financial incentive to practice cost-effective medicine, pharmaceutical companies have been forced to go beyond their traditional claims that a product is more clinically effective. Some now offer purchasers elaborate tests to show that differentials in effectiveness are worth the differentials in price. For example, Amgen Inc.'s Neuprogen®, a drug to prevent infections in chemotherapy patients, initally appeared expensive at $1,000 per course of treatment. Amgen successfully countered strong customer resistance by demonstrating that preventing infection was worth at least $6,000 per treatment in avoided hospital costs.

Exhibit 4.2 summarizes the steps necessary to determine economic value. In business markets, where the value of the product translates directly into financial savings or increased revenues for the purchaser, it is often possible to calculate economic value directly. Establishing test sites with customers and documenting value are useful both for setting prices and justifying those prices to potential customers. (See Appendix 4A for an illustration.) In consumer and business markets where the values are less tangible, quantifying value is more difficult. One must frequently rely on market research techniques—such as conjoint or trade-off analysis and sim-

---

EXHIBIT 4.1

Economic Value Analysis

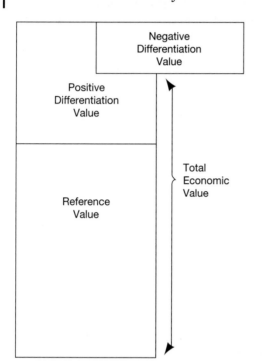

Differentiation Value is the value to the customer (both positive and negative) of any differences between your offering and the reference product.

Reference Value is the cost (adjusted for differences in units) of the competing product that the customer views as the best alternative for this one.

If all customers were "economic men and women," that is, fully informed consumers who completely and rationally analyze all purchase decisions, the economic value would then be the maximum price they would pay for any purchase.

---

ulated test markets—or on inferences made from the pricing of other products offering similar differential benefits.

There are no shortcuts to studying customers' use of the product, whether formally or informally. Many companies shortchange themselves by assuming that if their differentiated product is "x" percent more effective than the competition then the product should be worth exactly "x" percent more in price. If you had cancer and knew of a drug that was 50 percent more effective than the competition's in curing the cancer, would you refuse to pay more than a 50 percent higher price? Suppose you are planning to paint your house and discover a tool that will enable you to finish the job in half the usual time—a 100% increase in technical efficiency. Unless you enjoy the drudgery of painting or place little value on your time, you would no doubt happily pay more than twice the price of a brush to buy this tool. As these examples illustrate, the price premium associated with the economic value of a product is often much greater than the percentage increase in technical efficiency. The value of a differentiated product is proportional to its higher technical efficiency only when a buyer can receive the higher benefit simply by using the undifferentiated product in larger quantities (for example, when using 50% more of the competitive cancer drug or using two brushes at the same time would produce the same increase in efficiency).

Exhibit 4.2

Steps in Economic Value Analysis

Step 1: Identify the cost of the competitive product or process that the customer views as the best alternative.
Restate the cost of the alternative in terms of units of the product for which you are calculating economic value. This is the product's *reference value*, or value if it were functionally identical to the current product. For example, if one unit of your product replaces two of theirs, then the reference value for your product is the cost of two units of their product.

Step 2: Identify all factors that differentiate your product from the competitive product or process. For example,

- Superior (inferior) performance
- Better (poorer) reliability
- Additional (reduced) features
- Lower (higher) maintenance cost
- Superior (inferior) reliability
- Higher (lower) startup costs
- Faster (slower) service

Step 3: Determine the value to the customer of these differentiating factors. Sources of value may be subjective (for example, greater pleasure in consuming the product) or objective (for example, cost savings, profit gains). The positive and negative values associated with the product's differentiating attributes comprise the *differentiation value*.

Warnings:

Consider only the value of the *difference* between this product and the alternative. For example, both products may be highly effective, but only the difference in their effectiveness is differentiation value. The economic value of anything that is the same is already captured in reference value.

Measure the value of the difference as *either* costs saved to achieve a particular benefit *or* as extra benefits achieved for a given cost. Don't add both, that's double counting!

Do not assume that the percentage increase in value is simply proportional to the percentage increase in effectiveness of your product. That usually produces a gross underestimation of the actual value to the customer.

Step 4: Sum the reference value and the differentiation value to determine the *total economic value*, the value that someone would pay who was fully informed and economically rational when making the purchase decision.

Determine the selling price, recognizing that new products must usually be priced below economic value as an inducement to purchase. The prices of established products that already have the customer's business can include a "reputation premium," analogous to the inducement that the newcomer must offer. When buyers have little ability or interest to determine economic value, or when the cost of switching suppliers is high, the factors affecting the "inducement" or "premium" may, in fact, be more important for pricing than the economic value.

FACTORS AFFECTING PRICE SENSITIVITY

Estimating economic value to the customer is fundamental to marketing in general and to pricing in particular, but it is just one facet of the role of price in customer decision making. When dealing with knowledgable and highly sophisticated purchasers (such as a specialized purchasing agent or a dedicated bargain-hunter), economic value analysis can describe and predict buyer behavior quite adequately. However, most customers do not make purchase decisions exactly as economic value analysis would predict. Although getting a good value is often one important purchase consideration, customers will not always choose the very best value for the price they pay.

Sometimes, when the expenditure is small or when someone else is paying the bill, the effort to diligently evaluate all the alternatives is simply not worth the reward. Other times, being unaware of alternatives or unable to evaluate them before purchase makes finding the best deal too difficult or risky. Occasionally, the desire to impress others causes buyers to choose high-priced alternatives. These considerations in purchasing decisions often mitigate the importance of economic value relative to the importance of other factors such as purchase simplicity, safety, prestige, or fairness. Unless we understand these other factors, we cannot hope to predict and, even more important, to influence customers' purchase decisions.

Most market research on price sensitivity relies heavily on the assumption that purchase decisions are motivated by considerations of economic value. What distinguishes useful from misleading research is the extent to which the researcher accounts for differences between the assumptions of this basic model and the way customers in a particular market actually make decisions. Unfortunately, many researchers design a study assuming full knowledge of the prices and features of the common substitutes without first determining how much customers actually know about the substitutes when making a purchase. More often, researchers ask potential customers how they value features of innovative products before those customers have been exposed to a marketing program aimed at transforming those features into perceived benefits.

These and other factors affect the extent to which actual purchase decisions correspond to the model of economic value. Before even attempting to determine the price a customer could be expected to pay for a product, managers need to understand these factors. They are necessary if management is to segment the market by types of customers, to influence the way customers make their decisions, and to anticipate responses to alternative price scenarios. Following is a summary of the most common effects and their influence on customer price sensitivity.

Perceived substitutes effect

Economic value is the value that would be perceived by a customer who is fully informed about the alternatives. In the real world, customers are rarely so informed, they often flounder in a sea of information.[2] This reality has important implications for both segmenting customers and for influencing their price sensitivity. The *perceived substitutes effect* states that buyers are more price sensitive the higher the product's price relative to the prices of the buyers' perceived substitutes.[3]

The key word here is *perceived*. Perception of the available substitutes differs widely among customers and across purchase situations. Customers new to a market are usually less aware of the discount brands than are people with more experience. Consequently, they usually pay relatively high prices and buy from the most visible suppliers. In a similar vein, restauranteurs in resort areas face far less pressure to compete on price, despite the greater concentration of restaurants in those locations, because their transient clientel is usually unaware of better alternatives. Local residents view restaurants near resort hotels as "tourist traps," precisely because they can charge higher prices than restaurants less visible to tourists but patronized by a more informed clientel.

Effective marketing efforts can position a brand as a good value by targeting customers with a high reference for comparison. Chesebrough-Ponds can price its petroleum jelly 1,400 percent higher per ounce when packaged and sold as Vaseline Lip Therapy® because the perceived substitute for that positioning, Chapstick®, has a similar price. Woolite®, although expensive for a detergent, has successfully positioned itself as an inexpensive alternative to dry cleaning. Loctite Corp. positioned its powerful industrial adhesive as a substitute for nuts and bolts, enabling the company to charge a high price by the standards of its product category and still promise substantial savings for purchasers.

The method of product distribution can influence the buyers' perception of substitutes. When products are sold to buyers in their homes, as are some cosmetics, encyclopedias, and household products, or via telephone solicitation, buyers are generally much less aware of the cost and availability of alternatives. A seller can even influence buyers' knowledge of substitutes by the method of display. For example, when generic grocery products first became available, some stores placed them beside the corresponding branded products, whereas others placed the generics in a separate section. The sales of low-priced generic products were much greater—and sales of higher-priced branded items correspondingly less—in stores where the generic and branded products were placed side by side for easy comparison.

A customer's perception of the available substitutes is not necessarily based on awareness of specific brands and exact prices. Given the number of product categories and brands from which most people make purchases, maintaining awareness of such a vast amount of information would be impossible, even for the most educated and diligent customer. Consequently, for many product categories, a customer simply maintains a general expectation of a price level that seems reasonable. Psychologists call this expectation the customer's *reference price* expectation for the category.

We know from managerial experience and controlled experiments that these reference price expectations are manageable at the point of sale. For example, a business machine company with three models in its line found the sales of the top-end model disappointing. The company believed that many customers who should have valued the extra features of this high-production machine were instead buying the mid-priced model. Management's initial assumption was that the high-end model must be overpriced. After talking with customers in the appropriate segment, however, they learned that most did not think that the product was overpriced. They simply could not overcome the objections of the financial officer that the company did not need "the most expensive model." The solution: The company added a fourth, even more expensive model to its line. The new model sold very poorly, but sales of what was previously the top-end model increased dramatically.

Unique value effect

Since the customer's perception of substitutes is such an important determinant of price sensitivity, much of the marketer's effort is directed toward reducing the effect of substitutes (the reference value) on the total economic value. The goal is to offer something unique, a "differentiation," that buyers will pay for despite the existence of lower-priced alternatives.

Buyers are less sensitive to a product's price the more they value any unique attributes that differentiate the offering from competing products. This *unique value effect* is the rationale behind the ongoing efforts to differentiate the products and services of marketing-driven companies. Companies devote enormous expenditures to redesigning and reformulating products with the hope of creating unique attributes that consumers will value. Companies are motivated to do so because the more buyers value a product's unique style, flavor, or performance, the less importance they will place on its price premium when deciding whether to buy it. Heinz, for example, developed a secret formula for making its ketchup thicker than the competitors' and was able to increase its market share from 27 to 48 percent, despite establishing a 15 percent wholesale price premium.[4]

We should note, however, that differentiation alone does not produce this effect. Customers must first recognize a differentiation and then be convinced of its value. Heinz's advertising campaign, which convinced customers that thicker ketchup is better ketchup, was essential to converting its differentiation into a unique value. Marketers affect the value of their products by "positioning" them in ways that emphasize their positive differentiation and deemphasize their negative differentiation vis-a-vis the competition.[5] The Volvo, for example, is physically differentiated in part by its heavy-duty, utilitarian construction, but that did not automatically create differentiation value in the minds of customers. Converting the product's features into perceived value required advertising to explicitly emphasize the extra safety and durability that Volvo's construction makes possible, while implicitly deemphasizing the fact that its construction also results in relatively poor gas mileage. Sellers of products that offer little positive differentiation attempt to undermine the unique value effect by belittling the importance of the differences claimed by their competitors' higher-priced products. Discount motel chains, long-distance telephone companies, and airlines have used advertising that belittles the differentiation offered by higher-priced competitors to reassure potential customers that their lower prices really do represent a better value.

Switching cost effect

Buyers are less sensitive to the price of a product the greater the added cost (both monetary and nonmonetary) of switching suppliers. The reason for this effect is that many products require that the buyer make product-specific investments to use them. If those investments do not need to be repeated when buying from the current supplier, but do when buying from a new supplier, that difference is a switching cost that limits interbrand price sensitivity. For example, airlines are reluctant to change suppliers, from, say, Boeing to Airbus planes, because of the added cost to retrain their mechanics and to invest in a stock of new spare parts. Once an airline begins buying from a supplier, it takes a very attractive offer from a competitor to induce them to switch. Similarly, even personal relationships can represent a significant intangible investment that limits the attractiveness of a competing offer. For example, busy executives must invest considerable time in developing a rapport with their accountants, lawyers, and childcare providers. Once these "investments" are made, they are reluctant to repeat them simply because otherwise equally qualified suppliers offer a lower price.

This is the *switching cost effect*: The greater the product-specific investment that a buyer must make to switch suppliers, the less price sensitive that buyer is when choosing between alternatives.[6] Since this effect is often attributed simply to consumer "inertia," it is easy to underestimate its predictability and manageability. In fact, even highly rational, value-seeking consumers are influenced by it. During the 1980s, many companies developed objectively superior business spreadsheet programs and priced them substantially below the market leader, Lotus 1-2-3. Most of those companies failed and none ever came close to the sales of Lotus. The reason: Once people had learned how to use the Lotus program, they simply were unwilling to learn how to use another one. Recognizing this effect, Borland tailored both its product and its pricing to overcome it. Borland's QuattroPro® spreadsheet enabled Lotus 1-2-3 users to use the 1-2-3 commands with which they were already familiar. In addition, Borland offered a deeply discounted price to customers who already had the 1-2-3 software. Thus, Borland was able to partially overcome the switching cost effect and capture about 20 percent of the market.[7]

Finally, we should note that whenever complementary investments become obsolete and must be replaced, price sensitivity will increase just as if they had never been made. Initially, when gasoline prices increased in the 1970s, consumers were willing to pay higher prices rather than cut back their gasoline consumption. Having already invested in big "gas guzzlers," they felt they had little choice but to use them. As those cars wore out, however, consumers willingly replaced them with more fuel-efficient models and so reduced their total gasoline consumption substantially.[8]

Difficult comparison effect

The concept of economic value assumes that customers can actually compare what the alternative suppliers have to offer. In fact, it is often quite difficult to determine the true attributes of a product or service prior to purchase. For example, consumers suffering from a headache may be aware of many alternative pain relievers that are cheaper than their usual brand (the perceived substitute) and that claim to be equally effective. But if they are unsure that these cheaper brands are chemically identical to the one they usually buy, or if they doubt that the cheaper brand will be as effective, they will not consider them perfect substitutes. Consequently, they may continue paying a higher price for the assurance that their regular brand offers that the substitutes do not: the confidence accumulated from past experience that their brand *can* do what the others only *promise* to do.

Even price itself is often difficult to compare across brands, thus reducing price sensitivity. Full-service stockbrokers have developed unique pricing schedules that make comparison among them very difficult. Some price a transaction based on the number of shares traded, some on the value of the shares traded, some on the total value of the transaction. Similarly, branded grocery products are often packaged in odd shapes and sizes, making price comparisons with cheaper brands difficult. When, however, stores offer unit pricing (showing the price of all products by the ounce or gallon), grocery shoppers can readily identify the cheaper brands. In one study of unit pricing, the market shares of cheaper brands increased substantially after stores ranked brands by their unit prices.[9]

These examples illustrate the *difficult comparison effect*: Buyers are less sensitive to the price of a known or reputable supplier when they have difficulty comparing alternatives. Rather than attempting to find the best value in the market and risk getting a poor value in the process, many buyers simply settle for what they are confident will be a satisfactory purchase. Their confidence in the brand's reputation may be based either on their own experience with the brand or on the experience of other people whose judgment they trust. Examples of suppliers whose profitability rests on the trust that consumers associate with their names are McDonald's, AT&T, Kitchenaid, Marriott, and JCPenney. The trust for which buyers will pay price premiums is not that sellers of these products will necessarily provide the highest quality, but rather that they will consistently provide the good value-for-money that buyers have come to expect from them.

The same principle applies to business markets. Industrial buyers are commonly thought to seek many suppliers whom they play one against the other for lower prices. In fact, industrial buyers usually follow such a policy only for those products whose quality and reliability they can easily evaluate at the time of purchase. When products are difficult to evaluate and the cost of failure is high, industrial purchasers are at least as brand loyal, and as price insensitive, as are household buyers. In fact, for purchases that are particularly risky and difficult to evaluate (such as mainframe computers, new plant construction, and consulting services), industrial buyers will often develop loyal relationships with a list of "approved suppliers" with whom they have had previous satisfactory experience.[10] They will not even consider purchasing from an unknown supplier, even though that supplier claims to offer the same quality at a lower price.

Because the difficult comparison effect causes value to be associated with known brand names, market researchers often treat brand names no differently than any other tangible product attribute. Managers of those brands need to realize, however, that there is rarely any inherent value in a brand name. Its value depends upon the difficulty of making product comparisons and the perceived risk associated with trying an unknown supplier. Consequently, its value is often ephemeral. IBM traditionally enjoyed over a 20 percent price premium because of its enviable reputation. Customers paid the premium because they feared buying a costly mainframe from a competitor and finding its reliability or performance inadequate. The premium predictably declined, however, as customers became more knowledgeable and technological changes reduced the risk of trying competitors' products. Anything that reduces the buyers' cost of evaluating alternatives (for example, objective quality ratings such as those done by *Consumer Reports*, unit price information, or small trial sizes) will minimize the importance of past experience and increase buyers' sensitivity to brands that promise to offer a better value.

Price-quality effect

Generally, price represents nothing more than the money a buyer must give to the seller as part of the purchase agreement. For a few products, however, price means much more. These products fall into three categories: image products, exclusive products, and products without any other cues to their relative quality. In these cases, price is more than just a burden; it is also a signal of the value a buyer can expect to receive. In such cases, price sensitivity is influenced by the *price-quality effect*, which states that buyers are less sensitive to a product's price to the extent that a higher price signals better quality.

A buyer might use price as a quality signal for a number of reasons. Consider what motivates the purchase of an obvious image product, the Rolls Royce automobile. One would be hard-pressed to argue that the Rolls offers a value superior to that of luxury cars costing much less. Because a Rolls is handmade, its parts fit poorly, its finish is uneven, and the cost of maintenance is very high. The problems with the Rolls are the ones that mass production was meant to solve: problems of consistency and cost. But Rolls buyers do not purchase the car for cost-effective transportation any more than they buy a solid gold Rolex to tell time. They buy these items to communicate to others that they can afford them. They pay a premium for the confidence that their Rolls's uniquely expensive method of production ensures its continued value as a symbol of wealth.

People often value such symbols when the product reflects on them personally. Consequently, brands that can offer the consumer *prestige* in addition to the direct benefits of consumption can, and must, command higher prices than similar less prestigious products. For example, the American Express Gold Card costs from 50 to 200 percent more than the less prestigious varieties issued by the same companies. Purchasers' price sensitivity decreases to the degree that they value the recognition or ego gratification the card gives them. Prestige is more influential for some purchases than for others. For example, a store's prestige image is more important when buying a gift than when buying an item for personal use.

A prestige image is only one reason that buyers might find a more expensive purchase more satisfying. The exclusivity that discourages some people from buying at a high price can, in addition to image, add objectively to the value. Many professionals—doctors, dentists, attorneys, and hairdressers—set high prices to reduce their clientele, enabling them to schedule clients farther apart. This ensures that each one will be served without delay at his or her appointed time, a valuable service for busy people. Some business travelers fly first class, not because of the leg room or the food, but because the high price reduces the probability of sitting next to a small child or loquacious vacationer who might interfere with the work they must do in flight. Even public restrooms sometimes have pay stalls alongside free ones. The exclusivity resulting from a high price is itself desirable when consuming these products.

Often, the perception of higher quality at higher prices reduces price sensitivity even when consumers seek neither prestige nor exclusivity. This occurs when potential buyers cannot ascertain the objective quality of a product before purchase *and* lack other cues, such as a known brand name, a country of origin, or a trusted endorsement to guide their decision. For example, the name of a restaurant in a strange location, a folk artist at a fair, or a totally new brand with which the buyer has no prior experience. In these cases, consumers will rely somewhat on relative price as a cue to a product's relative quality, apparently assuming that the higher price is probably justified by corresponding higher value.

As an illustration of how strong this effect can be, researchers have reported cases where a new synthetic car wax faced strong consumer resistance until its price was raised from $0.69 to $1.69.[11] Similarly, sales of new creamy-style cheesecake were poor until the company raised the price to equal that of its heavy (and more costly to produce) regular-style cheesecake. Buyers could not judge the quality of either product before purchase. Consequently, buyers played it safe by avoiding cheap products that they believed were more likely to be inferior.

Extreme cases such as these, where sales respond positively to a higher price, are admittedly rare. They lead one to expect, however, that in other cases sales simply respond less negatively to a higher price than they would if buyers did not associate a higher price with higher expected quality. Numerous studies[12] have shown that, even when the objective quality

of a brand is unaffected by its price, consumers use price as a quality cue to
the degree that:

    1.   They believe qualities differ among brands within the product
class.

    2.   They perceive that low quality imposes the risk of a large loss.

    3.   They lack other information (such as a known brand name) en-
abling them to evaluate quality before purchase.

    The more consumers must rely on price to judge quality, the less price
sensitive they will be. For most purchase decisions, consumers can either
examine a product before purchase or infer its quality from past experience
with the brand (the difficult comparison effect). Studies indicate that under
these conditions, price is not used as a quality cue.[13] Nevertheless, the conditions for using price as a quality cue occur in one very important case:
when new products are first offered to a market.

    Market researchers frequently observe a low level of buyer price sen-
sitivity for new products. Exhibit 4.3 shows the results of a typical pricing
study for a new household product. In the first test, the product was described for buyers who were then asked if they intended to try it when it
became available. There was no significant difference in stated purchase intention between those buyers who were told that the product would cost

---

EXHIBIT 4.3

Effect of Price on Purchase Intention for a Product of Unknown
Quality

	At $1.59 (%)	At $2.29 (%)	Difference (%)
Test 1: Intention to try after concept description			
Definitely would buy	13	13	0
Probably would buy	46	46	0
Might/might not buy	30	30	0
Probably would not buy	9	8	1
Definitely would not buy	2	3	−1
Test 2: Intention to buy after in-home use			
Definitely would buy	34	24	10
Probably would buy	30	24	6
Might/might not buy	10	16	−6
Probably would not buy	14	12	2
Definitely would not buy	12	23	−11

    Source: Courtesy of BASES Division, Burke Marketing Services, Inc.

$1.59 and those who were told it would cost $2.29. In a second test, however, buyers who expressed an interest in the product were given a supply to take home. After using the product, they were asked the same questions regarding their purchase intention when the product became available. In this case, a higher price caused purchase intentions to decline significantly. A more recent study on the effect of discounting shows that while large discounts increase sales of familiar brands, they can actually undermine the sales of brands unfamiliar to the consumer.[14]

Expenditure effect

A buyer's willingness to evaluate alternatives depends also on how large the expenditure is relative to the effort necessary to reduce it. For businesses, this effect is determined by the absolute size of the expenditure; for households, it is determined by the size of the expenditure relative to the available income. The *expenditure effect* states that buyers are more price sensitive when the expenditure is larger, either in dollar terms or as a percentage of household income. The more a buyer spends for a product, the greater the gain from carefully evaluating the expenditure and attempting to find a better deal. This partially explains why heating insulation costs $2 per foot when sold to maintenance men in lots of 25 feet, but only $0.50 per foot when sold to building contractors by truckloads of tens of thousands of feet. For most people, on the other hand, small "impulse purchases" are simply not worth any effort to ensure that the price is a good deal. Consequently, percentage price differences across suppliers are often very large.

The effect of the expenditure size on price sensitivity is confounded in consumer markets by the effect of income. A family with five children may spend substantially more on food than a smaller family, yet still be less price sensitive if the cost of food accounts for a smaller portion of the large family's higher income. This relationship between a buyer's price sensitivity and the percentage of income devoted to the product results from the trade-offs buyers must make between conserving their limited income and conserving the limited time they have to shop. Higher-income buyers can afford a wider variety of goods but cannot always afford more time to shop for them. Consequently, they cannot afford to shop as carefully as lower-income buyers and so they accept higher prices as a substitute for time spent shopping.[15]

The expenditure size relative to income is also a constraint on both a business's and a household's primary demand for a product. A young man may long for a sports car, believing that a Porsche clearly has differentiating attributes that justify its premium price relative to similar cars. An economic value analysis of sports cars would reveal his decided preference and belief that the Porsche offers a "good value" relative to other sports cars. At his low income, however, he is not making purchase decisions among competing sports cars. Expenditures in other purchase categories (housing, food, education) are of higher importance than a sports car and those categories currently consume his income. Until his income rises, or the price of sports cars becomes much less, his brand preference within the category is not relevant.

End-benefit effect

An individual purchase is often one of many that a buyer makes to achieve a single benefit. Cream cheese is one of several products that a cook must buy to make a cheesecake. And a disk drive is one small component that a systems analyst must use to make a computer system. This relationship is the basis of the *end-benefit effect*, which can be divided into two parts: the derived demand and the share of total cost.

Derived demand is the relationship between the ultimate goal of a purchase, the desired end-benefit, and the buyer's price sensitivity for something that contributes toward achieving that end-benefit. The more sensitive buyers are to the cost of the end-benefit, the more sensitive they will be to the price of products that contribute to that end-benefit.

The relationship between the price of a product and the larger end benefit is more tangible in business markets. The more (less) price sensitive the demand for a company's own product, the more (less) price sensitive that company will be when purchasing supplies. A manufacturer of office furniture purchases sheet steel from which it makes desks. The more desks it can sell, the more steel it will buy. If desk buyers are highly price sensitive, any attempt to pass on steel price increases to the price of desks would cause a large reduction in sales. Consequently, the high price sensitivity of desk buyers would force the desk manufacturer to be highly sensitive to the cost of its desks and, therefore, to the price of steel.

Imagine how the manufacturer's purchase behavior would change, however, if booming demand causes an order backlog to lengthen and customers to lose leverage in negotiating desk prices. Since the manufacturer could now more easily pass on added costs to the customer its goal in purchasing would become less to save money on supplies and more to ensure on-time and defect-free deliveries to keep the manufacturing process running smoothly. It is essential for salespeople in business markets to understand the end-benefit that drives a customer's purchase decision (is it cost-minimization, maximum output, quality improvement, civic mindedness, or what?) in order to infer the importance of price in the purchase decision.

The relationship between price sensitivity for a product and for the end-product to which it contributes is strongly mitigated by the second part of the end-benefit effect, the share of total cost. Consider the case of two different buyers of sheet steel, the desk manufacturer and a luggage manufacturer who uses sheet steel to reinforce the luggage. Even if the ultimate buyers of desks and of luggage are equally price sensitive, the manufacturers of these products are not. The price of steel is probably a much larger share of the total cost of desks than of the total cost of luggage. Consequently, any attempt to pass on a steel price increase would drive up the price of desks much more than it would the price of luggage. The desk manufacturer would, therefore, reduce its steel purchases proportionately more for any steel price increase, either because it would sell proportionately fewer desks when passing on the increase, or because it would find some way to use less steel in order to hold down costs.

This part of the end-benefit effect states that customers are more (less) price sensitive whenever the purchase price accounts for a larger (smaller) share of the total cost of the end-benefit. The total cost of the end-benefit may include the cost of purchasing other products as well as the monetary and nonmonetary costs of shopping. This effect points toward opportunities to charge very high prices for products sold to complement much larger expenditures. For example, Zymol "vegetarian" car wax, which produces an exceptional shine, is targeted toward owners of BMWs, Rolls Royces, and classic cars, for whom the total cost of auto ownership is exceptionally high. Consequently, they hardly notice the $40 price per 8-ounce jar.[16]

To fully appreciate the marketing implications of the end-benefit effect, managers need to recognize that it is not just an economic, but also a psychological phenomenon. Consider how a wife would react if, after celebrating a very special occasion at a nice restaurant, her husband paid for it with a 2-for-1 discount coupon. Unless the spouse is an economist, this action would probably be seen as rather unromantic. Most people think it tacky to search for the best deal when an end-benefit is emotionally important to them. Moreover, one must also recognize that the "total cost" of the end-benefit need not be only monetary. Dieters are less sensitive to price than are nondieters when treating themselves to chocolates or ice cream because the dollar expenditure is only a small part of the total cost (both monetary and nonmonetary) that they pay for this treat.

The psychological aspects of this effect make it an excellent target for promotional activity. Once a brand is established in customers' minds as somehow "better," advertisers can increase the value of that perceived difference by relating it to an important end-benefit, such as the safety of one's family (Exhibit 4.4). Promotional campaigns are frequently designed to portray a purchase as just a small part of a larger end-benefit which makes the cost of purchase seem relatively inconsequential. Hammermill ran a long series of advertisements portraying the extra cost of its copier paper as trivial when compared with the cost of the copier, or with the cost of people's time whose productivity depends on it. Similarly, Mobil Oil po-

---

EXHIBIT 4.4

Establishing an Important End-benefit

Source: DDB Needham Worldwide

---

sitions the cost of its premium-priced Mobil 1® motor oil as well-justified considering the price of the car that the oil is intended to protect (Exhibit 4.5).

Shared-cost effect

Although the portion of the benefit accounted for by the product's price is an important determinant of price sensitivity, so also is the portion of that price actually paid by the buyer. People purchase many products that are actually paid for in whole or in part by someone else. Insurance covers a share of the buyer's cost of a doctor's visit or a prescription drug. Tax deductions cover a share of the cost of publications, educational seminars, and travel related to one's profession. Businesses usually compensate their salespeople for all or part of their travel and entertainment expenses.

EXHIBIT 4.5

Establishing a Larger End-benefit

Acura Integra GS $16,685	Ford Escort GT...$10,588	Oldsmobile 98 Regency Brougham ...$21,595
Acura Legend Coupe LS 30,690	Ford Tempo LX...11,422	Peugeot 405 Mi16 21,990
Alfa Romeo Veloce.....................................20,950	Ford Mustang GT.......................................14,803	Plymouth Laser RS..................................12,675
Audi 80 Quattro...22,800	Ford Taurus LX...16,180	Pontiac Sunbird GT.................................12,444
Audi 100...26,900	Ford Probe GT 15,543	Pontiac Grand Am SE.............................15,194
Audi Quattro V-8..47,450	Ford Thunderbird Super Coupe 20,390	Pontiac Firebird Trans Am GTA.........23,320
Bentley Mulsanne S................................133,200	Ford LTD Country Squire.........................17,921	Pontiac 6000 S/E......................................16,909
BMW 325is...28,950	Honda Accord EX 16,595	Pontiac Bonneville SSE..........................23,994
BMW 535i...43,600	Honda Civic..10,920	Pontiac Grand Prix SE............................17,684
BMW 750il..70,000	Jaguar XJ-6 Vanden Plas...........................48,000	Porsche 944...41,900
Buick Skylark Custom LE........................13,145	Lamborghini Countach 145,000	Porsche 911 Targa....................................59,900
Buick Regal Limited..................................15,860	Lexus LS 400...35,000	Porsche 928...74,545
Buick LeSabre Estate Wagon 17,940	Lincoln Town Car.......................................27,986	Rolls-Royce Corniche II.....................215,800
Buick Electra Park Avenue......................21,750	Lincoln Mark VII LSC...............................29,468	Saab 900...17,515
Buick Reatta...28,335	Lotus Esprit...71,500	Saab 9000 CD 32,995
Cadillac DeVille..27,540	Mercedes-Benz 190E 31,600	Sterling 827SL..29,975
Cadillac Allante 50,900	Mercedes-Benz 300CE.................................55,700	Subaru Legacy LS.....................................14,699
Chevrolet Beretta GT 12,500	Mercedes-Benz 500SL.................................83,500	Subaru XT-6..17,111
Chevrolet Camaro IROC-Z 15,360	Mercury Topaz LS.......................................12,360	Suzuki Swift GS...9,264
Chevrolet Lumina.......................................14,240	Mercury Sable LS..16,067	Toyota Camry LE.......................................14,658
Chevrolet Caprice Brougham..................16,325	Mercury Cougar XR-7.................................20,213	Toyota Cressida...21,498
Chevrolet Corvette ZR-1...........................58,995	Mitsubishi Galant GSX...............................17,171	Toyota Corolla LE.....................................11,703
Chevrolet Geo Metro....................................8,465	Mitsubishi Eclipse GSX...............................17,260	Toyota Celica GT-S....................................17,258
Chrysler LeBaron.......................................15,995	Nissan Stanza GXE......................................14,775	Toyota Supra Turbo.................................25,200
Chrysler Fifth Avenue..............................20,860	Nissan Axxess SE..16,749	Volkswagen GTI..10,800
Dodge Daytona ES Turbo.........................13,700	Nissan Maxima SE 18,749	Volkswagen Jetta GLI..............................14,555
Dodge Colt Vista..13,906	Nissan 300ZX Turbo...................................33,000	Volkswagen Corrado................................17,990
Eagle Premier ES..17,845	Oldsmobile Cutlass Calais SL....................14,015	Volkswagen Passat GL.............................14,770
Eagle Talon TSi Turbo...............................15,613	Oldsmobile Cutlass Supreme Intl.............17,995	Volvo 240-DL...18,450
Ferrari Testarossa 150,600	Oldsmobile 88 Royale................................15,995	Volvo 780...38,735

Source: Automotive News 12/18/89. "Pricing the '90 Models."

Isn't your car worth the extra protection?

College-bound students often choose an expensive private school knowing that a scholarship or a generous relative will cover all or part of the tuition. In each case, the smaller the portion of the purchase price buyers must pay themselves, the less price sensitive they are. The effect of partial or complete reimbursement on price sensitivity is called the *shared-cost effect*.

This effect has led to some interesting pricing policies in markets where it is effective. Boots Pharmaceuticals, for example, recognized that low introductory pricing of its antiarthritic prescription drug, Rufen®, would be ineffective because insurance reimbursements cover such a high portion of its price. It successfully circumvented the problem by attaching a coupon to the bottle that a buyer could send in for a $1.50 rebate.[17] Similarly, airlines and hotels offer frequent customer awards which business customers value more highly than a price cut, for which they would be reimbursed anyway.

Fairness effect

The concept of a "fair price" has bedeviled marketers for centuries. In the Dark Ages, merchants were put to death for exceeding public norms regarding the "just price." In the more recent dark history of communism, those who "profiteered" by charging more than the official prices—at which the state was unable to meet demand—were regarded as criminals. Even in modern market economies, "price gougers" are often criticized in the press, hassled by regulators, and boycotted by the public. Consequently, it is well worth our time to understand this phenomenon.

Buyers are more sensitive to a product's price when it is outside the range that they perceive as "fair" or "reasonable" given the purchase context. But what is fair? Managers should note that the concept of fairness has little to do with profitability. Oil companies are frequently accused of gouging, although their profits are below the average of U.S. industry. In contrast, popular forms of entertainment (for example, Disney World, state lotteries) and food (Godiva chocolates and Häagen-Dazs ice cream) are expensive and very profitable, yet their pricing escapes widespread criticism.

Three things appear to determine people's perception of fairness in pricing. The most obvious is how the current price compares to prices previously encountered for the product. Consumers generally consider large price increases unfair even when necessary to equate supply and demand.[18] Gasoline prices are considered "unfair" whenever they increase significantly above what they were in the recent past. Consequently, customers switch from branded to generic brands and from premium to cheaper grades. Oil refiners are initially forced to reduce their margins when oil prices rise. They can restore their higher margins as customers come to accept the higher prices as usual.

Perceptions of what is reasonable are also affected by prices paid for similar products or in similar purchase situations. The clearest cases of this phenomenon are in the pharmaceuticals industry. Patients, and even doctors, consider pills costing $1 or more per dose "outrageous," even when reduced patient suffering and reduced cost of other medical services clearly justify the price in value terms. Since most medications in oral form (aspirin, vitamins) cost only a few cents each, people simply expect that other oral medications should be similarly priced.

Customers also expect to pay less in some purchase locations or situations than in others. In a now famous experiment, people were asked to imagine that they were lying on a beach, thirsty for a favorite brand of beer. A friend was walking to a nearby location and would bring back beer if the price was not too high. Each person was asked to specify the maximum amount that he or she would pay, not knowing that half of them had been told that the friend would patronize a "fancy resort hotel" and the other half that the friend would patronize "a small, run-down grocery store." Although these individuals would not themselves visit (or enjoy the amenities of) the purchase location, the median acceptable price given by those who expected the beer to come from the hotel—$2.65—was dramatically higher than the median acceptable price given by those who expected it to come from the grocery store—$1.50.[19]

Finally, perceptions of fairness seem to be related to whether the product is necessary to maintain a previously enjoyed standard of living (the price is paid to avoid a loss), or is purchased to get something more out of life (the price is paid to achieve a gain). Products that are necessary to maintain one's current living standards are quickly perceived as "necessities," although mankind has probably survived without them for most of its history. Charging a high price for a "necessity" is generally perceived as unfair. People object to prices for medical care since they feel that they shouldn't have to pay to be healthy. After all, they were healthy last year without having to buy prescriptions and medical advice. Why should they have to pay for health now? These same people, however, may buy a new car, jewelry, or a vacation without ever objecting to equally high prices or price increases. What distinguishes these expenditures is that a high price simply reduces the amount of the gain (the quality of the car, the size of the diamond, the length of the vacation) that one can obtain, rather than reducing the quality of life that the buyer has come to perceive as "necessary."[20]

Fortunately, perceptions of fairness can be managed. Companies that must frequently adjust prices to reflect supply and demand or to segment buyers with different price sensitivities are careful to set the "regular" price at the highest possible level, rather than at the average or most common price. This enables them to "discount" to almost everyone, a practice that is seen as more fair than charging premiums above a lower "regular" price.[21] Similarly, when shortages limit supply at "fair" prices (for example, Superbowl tickets), sellers make the price premium seem more palatable by bundling the product, e.g., selling it as part of a larger purchase (for example, a complete Superbowl package including transportation, hotel, and tickets).[22] Pharmaceutical companies attempt to distinguish high-priced oral medicines from cheaper ones by packaging tablets individually in blister packs rather than in bottles, like aspirin. Insurance companies are careful to market their product as offering gains of "security" and "peace of mind" rather than as preventing a loss, which customers are more likely to resent having to pay for.

Inventory effect

There is one more factor that influences price sensitivities, although only in the short run and only with a transitory effect. Buyers' ability to hold an inventory of a product for later use substantially increases their sensitivity to temporary price deviations from what they expect in the long run. This is the inventory effect.

If a supermarket features canned tomatoes among its discounted items for one week, it can reasonably expect that the percentage increase in sales of canned tomatoes will exceed the percentage increase when it features fresh tomatoes with a similar price cut. Consumers can easily stock up on canned tomatoes for use many weeks hence, but cannot do so with the more perishable fresh ones. Of course, this effect may only be short-lived. To the extent that buyers of the canned tomatoes would have bought the same brand in later weeks, the loss of sales as buyers use up their inventories will cancel out most of their extra purchases made when the item was discounted. But, to the extent that buyers of the featured brand switched from other brands to take advantage of the price cut, their large purchases of the featured brand will be at the expense of current and future sales of competing brands.

To fully grasp the extent of this effect, it is useful to think of inventories broadly to include the early purchase of durable goods. When U.S. automobile companies initiated their first rebates (temporary price cuts) to spur lagging sales, they were perceived as phenomenally successful. The press said that car buyers were more price sensitive than anyone had imagined, indicating that the industry would have been better off all along if cars had been priced lower. Unfortunately, as the rebate programs were repeated, becoming a more permanent feature of automobile pricing, buyers showed no enduring sensitivity to price cutting and the rates of sales fell back to its pre-discount level. The rebates prompted few additional new car purchases that would not otherwise have been made. Instead, many families simply bought cars during the initial rebate period that they would otherwise have bought later.

The effect of inventories on price sensitivity depends critically on buyer expectations about future prices. Consequently, in evaluating this effect, a price must be judged high or low relative to prices buyers expect to pay in the future, rather than to prices that prevailed in the recent past. A major processor of smoked meat products noted that grocers learned to order extra quantities at the end of each quarter, after the company instituted a quarterly review of its pricing during a period of high inflation. Since the company usually increased prices after the review, buyers saw the current end-of-quarter prices as bargains relative to the prices they expected in the future. Similarly, U.S. oil refiners actually reduced their oil purchases and drew down their inventories when crude oil prices began to fall in early 1983 and again in late 1985. They did so because they saw these declines as a sign that the power of the OPEC cartel was eroding. The current prices, while lower than those of the recent past, nevertheless looked high compared with the prices they expected in the near future.

MANAGERIAL ANALYSIS OF PRICE SENSITIVITY

The formulation of every pricing strategy should begin with a managerial analysis of price sensitivity. There are three reasons why such an analysis should be conducted, even if one ultimately intends to gauge price sensitivity more quantitatively (techniques for which we discuss in Chapter 13). First, a managerial analysis can identify market segments that are likely to have different price sensitivities. This is necessary, not only to formulate a segmentation strategy (with different products, channels, and purchase options) that captures the different value to each segment, but also to develop valid quantitative measures of their price sensitivity.[23] Second, a managerial analysis indicates the range of prices within which the firm should ultimately price its product, thus enabling one to design surveys or experiments to focus only on price differences within that range. Thus, a good managerial analysis can both increase the accuracy and reduce the cost of more formal market research.

Third, and perhaps most important, managers need to analyze buyer price sensitivity to determine how effectively to influence it in each market. Pricing strategy has too long suffered from the economist's assumption of a fixed demand curve defining the relationship between price and purchase volume. Both marketing researchers and managers treat price sensitivity as if it were a law of nature that they must discover, rather than as a shifting preference that they can influence. If politicians took the same attitude, they would stop campaigning as soon as they learned that they trailed the leader by more than the margin of error in the poll. Instead, what they do is to find out *why* people prefer the leading competitor. They look for both misunderstandings about the candidate's positions and beliefs about what the most important issues are. Then they begin a campaign to change those understandings and beliefs. Marketers should be doing the very same thing.

The fact that customers are not purchasing a product or service is not by itself a reason to cut its price. Instead, it may be a reason to change the marketing program to justify the price. For example, in this chapter we saw how price sensitivity can be reduced when marketers can:

- ■ Position the product relative to a more costly substitute.
- ■ Focus the customer's attention on unique features.
- ■ Increase switching costs.

- Convince customers that cross-brand comparisons are difficult and, therefore, risky.
- Promote the product's high price to give it a "status" image.
- Relate the product to an important end-benefit for which the customer is less cost sensitive, or one to which your price contributes only a small share of cost.
- Manage expectations to minimize the perception of price as "unfair." Simply knowing how customers will respond to a price change, without understanding why, limits one's ability to manage the market environment.

Preparing a Managerial Analysis

The preceding discussion of the factors influencing price sensitivity is aimed at helping managers improve their judgments by indicating what factors to consider and how to evaluate them. A managerial analysis of price sensitivity should be a written document that can be criticized and improved over time. Although the report itself may be compiled by one person, it should reflect the efforts and judgments of all individuals in a firm who are in a position to add useful information or insight. When information from internal resources is inadequate, the evaluation may require market research. Such research, rather than merely measuring price sensitivity directly, should measure the underlying factors that influence it—awareness of alternatives, confidence in making brand comparisons, the price as a portion of the end-benefit's total cost, the share of the cost paid by others, and so forth. A managerial analysis of price sensitivity is complete when it answers questions such as the following about each of the factors described in this chapter:

1. Perceived substitutes effect

- What alternatives are buyers (or segments of buyers) typically aware of when making a purchase?
- To what extent are buyers aware of the prices of those substitutes?
- To what extent can buyers' price expectations be influenced by the positioning of one brand relative to particular alternatives, or by the alternatives offered them?

For a consumer product, finding out what alternatives buyers face usually requires nothing more than a visit or telephone inquiry to a few retailers or distributors. For an industrial product, identifying alternatives may be as easy as simply noting the products displayed at trade shows and asking about their availability in various locations and for various uses. One's sales force, sales agents, or manufacturer representatives are also particularly good sources for identifying buyer awareness of alternatives. For example, a brief form asking the salesperson to note each alternative mentioned by the buyer during a sales presentation can be a cheap, reliable source of information. Finally, survey research which asks a question such as, "How many brands of this product can you name?" can be a source of data on awareness of alternatives.

The second part of this effort involves gauging price awareness. Do buyers know the prices of alternatives? Are some segments of buyers much more, or less, informed than others? What do those who cannot recall specific prices believe is a typical price for this product? At what price level would they consider a brand in this market to be expensive or cheap?

2.   Unique value effect

■   Does the product have any unique (tangible or intangible) attributes that differentiate it from competing products?

■   What attributes do customers believe are important when choosing a supplier?

■   How much do buyers value unique, differentiating attributes? How can one increase the perceived importance of differentiating attributes and/or reduce the importance of those offered by the competition?

If a product's differentiating attributes are tangible, they can be ascertained simply by observation. If differentiating attributes stem from a reputation for post-purchase service or from some other intangible, identifying them requires formal or informal market research. Either way, identifying differentiating attributes is normally not difficult, but placing a value on those attributes is. Two techniques have been developed for doing so. Economic value analysis relies on the researcher's own evaluation of what the differentiating attributes should be worth to a fully informed buyer. It is used extensively and is explained in Appendix 4A. *Trade-off* (or *conjoint*) *analysis* asks consumers to make choices between price and attribute combinations that are then used to predict how they would value the attributes of existing and hypothetical products. This technique is explained in Chapter 11.

3.   Switching cost effect

■   To what extent have buyers already made investments (both monetary and psychological) in dealing with one supplier that they would need to incur again if they switched suppliers?

■ For how long are buyers locked in by those expenditures?

In most cases, a formal or informal questioning of buyers can produce this information without difficulty.

4. Difficult comparison effect

■ How difficult is it for buyers to compare the offers of different suppliers?
■ Can the attributes of a product be determined by observation, or must the product be purchased and consumed to learn what it offers?
■ What portion of the market has positive past experience with your products? With the brands of the competition?
■ Is the product highly complex, requiring costly specialists to evaluate its differentiating attributes?
■ Are the prices of different suppliers easily comparable, or are they stated for different sizes and combinations that make comparisons difficult?

Answers to these questions are generally obvious from simple observation of buyers making purchase decisions within the product class. Unfortunately, ascertaining the added value that buyers place on a product due to prior experience with it is particularly difficult. One method is by reference to similar products. In the pharmaceuticals industry, for example, there is much historical evidence for the price premium that known brands of most drugs can sustain over their generic equivalents. As new drugs are developed, the value of a known brand name can be inferred from other categories of drugs with similar levels of risk. In the absence of historical evidence on similar products, the manager must resort to pure judgment based upon his or her understanding of the difficulty of obtaining information and the risks of product trial when assigning value to past experience associated with a brand name.

5. Price-quality effect

■ Is a prestige image an important attribute of the product?
■ Is the product enhanced in value when its price excludes some consumers?
■ Is the product of unknown quality and are there few reliable cues for ascertaining quality before purchase?

These questions are difficult to answer. Survey research by experienced professionals may reveal answers, but these are questions that buyers will not necessarily answer candidly. In many cases, the firm must rely purely upon judgment based on comparison with similar product categories. Occasionally, experimental research is used to measure the value of price as a quality cue.[24]

6. Expenditure effect

■   How significant are buyers' expenditures for the product in absolute dollar terms (for business buyers) and as a portion of income (for end consumers)?

This effect is normally fairly easy to ascertain. One can purchase detailed data on many consumer products from consumer panels showing the consumption rates of brands by numerous demographic classifications, including income. Government agencies, trade associations, and private companies collect data on purchasers of industrial products. When industrial products are used directly in the production of the buying firms' products, total expenditures can often be inferred from publicly available data. A company can conduct its own direct mail or telephone survey at a reasonable cost. As a last resort, an engineering study could estimate buyers' various costs of manufacturing.

7. End-benefit effect

■   What end-benefits do buyers seek from the product?
■   How price sensitive are buyers to the cost of the end-benefit?
■   What portion of the end-benefit does the price of the product account for?
■   To what extent can the product be repositioned in customers' minds as related to an end-benefit for which the buyer is less cost sensitive or which has a larger total cost?

To evaluate a buyer's sensitivity to the cost of the benefit to which a product contributes, one must analyze the benefit with respect to the factors influencing price sensitivity. Determining the share of the benefit's cost for which the product's cost accounts is generally straightforward. For industrial products, the information is often available directly from buyers, but can also be inferred from public data on final sales and a simple engineering study of the buyer's production process. For consumer products, the information generally requires survey research that asks the consumer to identify other product purchases (for example, airfare, hotel and car rental, equipment rental) made in conjunction with the purchase of the product in question (for example, the ski resort lift ticket) to generate a particular end-product (a ski vacation).

8.   Shared-cost effect

■ Does the buyer pay the full cost of the product?
■ If not, what portion of the cost does the buyer pay?

The answers to these questions are readily available through formal or informal surveys of corporate reimbursement policies, from analyses of insurance coverage available from insurers, and from governmental publications explaining treatment of expenditures for tax deductibility.

9.   Fairness effect

■ How does the product's current price compare with prices people have paid in the past for products in this category?
■ What do buyers expect to pay for similar products in similar purchase contexts?
■ Is the product seen as necessary to maintain a previously enjoyed standard of living, or is it purchased to gain something more out of life?

Answers to these questions are easy to gauge from formal or informal survey research.

10.   Inventory effect

■ Do buyers hold inventories of the product?
■ Do they expect the current price to be temporary?

The size of buyers' inventories can be readily ascertained by survey research. However, their beliefs about the permanence of a price may not be as easy to learn. Usually, when a seller announces a limited-time sale, he or she can reasonably assume that buyers will treat the sale price as temporary. But when buyers are trying to second-guess a seller's regular price increases or decreases, estimating their expectations is extremely difficult. The estimate must normally rely on inferences made from informal research and past buyer behavior.

The fact that answers to these questions are probably different for different customers is not a problem; rather it is an opportunity to increase profitability by using a segmented pricing strategy (discussed in Chapters 6, 7, and 9). Answers also may depend on such factors as how the product is distributed and advertised. Recognition of these effects also offers an important guide to development of the most profitable strategy. Finally, it is necessary to anticipate the likely response to alternative pricing strategies. Will buyers be responsive if prices are lower than the competition's, or would equal prices and alternative marketing tools be more cost effective in attracting them? Are some buyers potentially price insensitive and willing, under the right circumstances, to pay a premium price? Only after answering such general questions and formulating an overall positioning strategy is a manager ready to more precisely estimate price sensitivity. This estimate may be obtained using formal measurement techniques (Chapter 13) or through less formal experimentation in the marketplace.

ECONOMICS OF PRICE SENSITIVITY

Up to this point, we have spoken of price sensitivity without precisely defining it. For individual analysis, defining price sensitivity is relatively easy. Most individual purchase decisions involve an all-or-nothing choice among brands, with price having little effect on the quantity purchased (an individual's demand curve for a brand is simply one point on a graph). Consequently, we can easily define price sensitivity as the highest price (what economists call the *reservation price*) that a consumer would pay to buy the desired quantity of that brand. This approach breaks down, however, when we reach market-level analysis. When we ask, "How much will our customers pay?" the question immediately comes back to "Which customers?" Buyers have different reservation prices which, collectively, define broad ranges of prices that would be necessary to capture their patronage.

A segmentation strategy to divide a large market into subgroups can reduce the range of reservation prices with which one must deal, but, even within a segment, pricing to capture that market segment is rarely an all-or-nothing proposition. Consequently, we require a more operationally useful definition of price sensitivity to analyze price changes on a market or segment level. The definition commonly used by price analysts is called *price elasticity*. It is the percentage change in a product's unit sales resulting from a given percentage change in its price. It is sometimes calculated from actual or hypothetical sales changes using the following formula:

$$E = \frac{\%\ \text{Change in unit sales}}{\%\ \text{Change in price}}$$

E, the demand elasticity, is generally a negative number, since positive price changes (price increases) generally produce sales declines and negative price changes (price cuts) generally produce sales increases. The greater the value of E, the more "elastic" the demand; the smaller its value, the more "inelastic" the demand.

This definition of price elasticity enables one to talk about price sensitivity conceptually, independent of a particular price change. When considering specific price changes, an elasticity can be converted into an expected unit sales change simply by multiplying by the percentage price change under consideration. For example, if one estimates that a product's price elasticity is –2.50, one would expect that a 10 percent price increase would reduce its sales by 25 percent (–2.50 × 10 percent). One should be aware, however, that a product's price sensitivity is not the same at all price levels. Consequently, an elasticity estimated around a price of, say, $3, may be valid for evaluating price changes of 10 percent above or below that amount, but would be of little value in evaluating a price change to $5 or to $1.

This concept relates directly to the procedures for financial analysis developed in Chapter 3, where a formula was used to calculate the "% change in unit sales" necessary to make a "% change in price" profitable (see pp. 3-4–3-10). In effect, a very particular type of demand elasticity—the minimum elasticity necessary to justify a price change—was calculated. This calculation enabled us to analyze the profitability of a price change without expecting managers to "know" their actual demand curve. Instead, the procedure required much less information, that is, a judgment about whether the elasticity for a specific price change would exceed or fall short of a particular necessary level.

GENERALIZATIONS ABOUT PRICE ELASTICITIES

Chapter 13 discusses techniques that have been used to estimate price elasticities. Using those techniques, market researchers have attempted to find empirical regularities between price elasticities and more easily observable variables. Unfortunately, most generalizations appear to be weak at best. Researchers have found that price elasticities often differ widely across different brands in the same product class.[25] Exhibit 4.6 illustrates the typical variation in price elasticities for brands of the same product, in this case, coffee. The elasticities range from a very low short-run estimate of 0.21 to a very high long-run estimate of 10.28. Such differences make sense when we recognize that brands have different attributes that result in different value effects. For example, researchers who estimated price elasticities for breakfast cereals discovered that differences in price elasticities were related to differences in the amount of sugar the brands contain.[26]

Price elasticities are often related to a brand's relative price, but the relationship differs across product classes. The president of one research firm that specializes in estimating price sensitivity reports that "the further a brand's price is from the category average in either direction, the lower its demand elasticity."[27] But in some categories other researchers have found strong positive or strong negative relationships between price levels and price elasticities. For example, higher-priced brands of frozen orange juice

EXHIBIT 4.6

Variations in Price Elasticities among Brands of the Same Product

	Short-Run Elasticity	Long-Run Elasticity
Regular Coffee		
Brand A	–2.32	–3.27
Brand B	–4.26	–6.76
Brand C	–0.21	–1.13
Brand D	–4.23	–4.85
Brand E	–1.63	–2.59
Instant Coffee		
Brand A	–0.47	–1.11
Brand B	–2.62	–10.28
Brand C	–3.05	–4.24
Brand D	–1.03	–5.00

Source: Lester Telser, "The Demand for Branded Goods as Estimated from Consumer Panel Data," *Review of Economics and Statistics*, 4 (August 1962), 321.

have been associated with lower price elasticities, whereas higher-priced brands of cereals have been associated with higher price elasticities.[28]

This trend probably reflects the fact that the high- and low-priced products in these categories are not relevant substitutes for each other. For high-priced frozen orange juice, the best substitute is liquid juice in a carton, not low-priced frozen juice. And in cereals, the high-priced brands are generally children's presweetened cereals that are not close substitutes for lower-priced adult cereals. Most experts seem to believe that among a set of products that are relevant substitutes for one another, sales of the lowest- and highest-priced products respond less to price changes than do products priced closer to the average.

Price elasticities are often related to a brand's relative age, but the relationship differs across product classes. In pharmaceuticals, the price elasticities of established brands are much lower than those of new brands.[29] In that category, there is an understandably high difficult comparison effect associated with knowing from prior experience that a brand works. In cereals, however, the price elasticities of established brands are higher than those of new brands.[30] In that category, people tend to seek variety. Thus they often are willing to try a new brand just because it is new and will repeat the purchase of an old brand only when it becomes price competitive.[31]

Clearly, there are few simple rules of thumb that one can use to predict relative price elasticities without studying the factors that determine price sensitivity in the particular category. There is, however, one rule of thumb that is generally reliable across product categories: Price elasticities are generally related to market share. Within a product class, and after controlling for differences in relative price, the sales of small market-share brands tend to be more price sensitive than those of brands with larger market shares. Intuitively, this relationship makes sense. A company with a large market share, such as AT&T, which has 60 percent of the interstate long-distance telephone market, has little room to gain additional market share by price cutting. On the other hand, a company with a small market share, such as Sprint, which has a 10 percent share of the long-distance market, could increase its sales by 20 percent with a price reduction that would take less than 4 percent of AT&T's customers.

SUMMARY

Although price is often more important to the seller than to the buyer, the buyer can still reject any price offer that is more than he or she is willing to pay. Firms that fail to recognize this fact and base price on their internal needs alone generally fail to attain their full profit potential. An effective pricing strategy requires a good understanding of buyers' price sensitivity. That understanding usually begins with an analysis of the product's economic value. For most products, however, economic value analysis does not fully capture the role of price in individual decision making. Most consumers do not approximate the image of a fully informed "economic individual" who always seeks the best value in the market regardless of the effort required. The analysis must quickly go beyond economic value to an understanding of the role that economic value will play in the purchase decision.

Ten factors influence the role of price in a purchase decision:

1. Perceived substitutes effect
2. Unique value effect
3. Switching cost effect
4. Difficult comparison effect
5. Price-quality effect
6. Expenditure effect
7. End-benefit effect
8. Shared-cost effect
9. Fairness effect
10. Inventory effect

We also reviewed a list of questions managers might ask when evaluating the importance of each factor in the pricing of their products.

Finally, this chapter introduced the concept of price elasticity, a market level summary of consumer reactions to purchase decisions. We reviewed literature that describes how elasticity varies over the short- and long-runs, and discussed possible generalizations that might be accurately inferred about price sensitivities. Although price sensitivities often follow patterns within product classes, those patterns are generally not consistent across product classes. Price elasticities are not reliably correlated with a brand's relative price level or its age. The only safe regularity is that brands with significantly larger market shares generally have lower price elasticities (after controlling for other factors) than do competing brands with lower market shares.

NOTES

1. Decision makers frequently misperceive *concise* estimates of demand elasticity, customer value, or competitive response as *precise* estimates of the stable underlying processes. In fact, concise estimates are often very inaccurate, whereas less concise estimates give the decision maker a more accurate picture of the uncertainty in the data. A method of quantifying decisions without losing sight of the underlying uncertainty in the data is Baysian analysis, definitely the best approach for managers who are comfortable dealing with statistical probabilities.

2. Richard W. Olshavsky and Donald H. Granbois. "Consumer Decision Making—Fact or Fiction?" *Journal of Consumer Research*, 6 (September 1979), 93–100.

3. This is called the "substitute awareness effect" in the first (1987) edition of this text.

4. Betsy Morris, "Thwack! Smack! Sounds Thrill Makers of Hunt's Ketchup," *Wall Street Journal*, April 27, 1984, pp. 1, 23.

5. David A. Aker and J. Gary Shansby, "Position Your Product," *Business Horizons*, 25, no. 3 (May–June 1982), 56–62.

6. This was called the "sunk investment effect" in the first (1987) edition of this text.

7. "Borland the Barbarian," *Business Week*, July 1, 1991, p. 68.

8. Douglas R. Bohi, *Analyzing Demand Behavior: A Study of Energy Elasticities* (Baltimore: Johns Hopkins Press, 1981), p. 126. Shows long-run estimates of price elasticity about 3.5 times the short-run estimates; yet more recent data have proved that even those long-run estimates were too low.

9. J. Edward Russo, "The Value of Unit Price Information," *Journal of Marketing Research*, 14 (May 1977), 193–201.

10. Barbara Jackson, *Winning and Keeping Industrial Customers: The Dynamics of Customer Relationships*: (Lexington, Mass.: D. D. Heath Co.), 1985; and "Build Customer Relationships that Last," *Harvard Business Review*, November–December 1985, pp. 120–28.

11. Andre Gabor and Clive Granger, "The Pricing of New Products," *Scientific Business*, 3 (August 1965), 141–50.

12. Harold Leavitt, "A Note on Some Empirical Findings About the Meaning of Price," *Journal of Business*, 27 (July 1954), 205–10; Donald Tull, R. A. Boring, and M. H. Gonsior, "A Note on the Relationship Between Price and Imputed Quality," *Journal of Business*, 37 (April 1964), 186–91; Benson Shapiro, "Price Reliance: Existence and Sources," *Journal of Marketing Research*, 10 (August 1973), 286–94. For a review of these studies and others on this topic, see Kent Monroe, "Buyers' Subjective Perceptions of Price," *Journal of Marketing Research*, 10 (February 1973), 70–80.

13. Ben Enis and James Stafford, "The Price-Quality Relationship: An Extension," *Journal of Marketing Research*, 6 (November 1969), 256–58; Jacob Jacoby, Jerry Olson, and Rafael Haddock, "Price, Brand Name, and Product Composition Characteristics and Determinants of Perceived Quality," *Journal of Applied Psychology*, 55 (December 1971), 570–78, David Gardner, "An Experimental Investigation of the Price-Quality Relationship," *Journal of Retailing*, 46 (Fall 1970), 25–41, David Gardner, "Is There a Generalized Price-Quality Relationship?" *Journal of Marketing Research*, 8 (May 1971), 241–43; Vithala Rao, "Salience of Price in the Perception of Product Quality: A Multidimensional Measurement Approach," Proceedings, Fall Educators' Conference (Chicago: American Marketing Association, 1971), pp. 571–77. Edward Smith and Charles Broome, "Experimental Determination of the Effect of Price and Market-Standing Information on Consumers' Brand Preferences," Proceedings, Fall Educators' Conference (Chicago: American Marketing Association, 1966), pp. 520–31.

14. David J. Moore and Richard W. Olshavsky, "Brand Choice and Deep Price Discounts," *Psychology & Marketing*, 6, no. 3 (Fall 1989), 181–96. Interestingly, the study indicated that small discounts did not have the same negative effect on sales.

15. Andre Gabor and Clive Granger, "Price as an Index of Quality-Report on an Inquiry," *Economica*, February 1966, pp. 43–70, surveyed 640 housewives and showed that awareness of grocery prices was inversely related to income, except for the poorest and presumably least educated consumers. See also Roger E. Alcaly, "Information and Food Prices," *Bell Journal of Economics*, 7 (Autumn 1976), 658–71.

16. Jerry Flint, "Fruit Salad Car Wax," *Forbes*, April 27, 1992, pp. 126, 129.

17. "Tumult over a Drug Rebate," *Business Week*, February 1, 1982, p. 55.

18. Daniel Kahneman, Jack L. Knetsch, and Richard H. Thaler, "Fairness as a Constraint on Profit Seeking: Entitlements in the Market," *American Economic Review*, 76, no. 4, (September 1986), 728–41.

19. Richard Thaler, "Mental Accounting and Consumer Choice," *Marketing Science*, 4 (Summer 1985), 206.

20. We discuss the rationale for this concept of fairness in Chapter 12.

21. Daniel Kahneman, Jack L. Knetsch, and Richard H. Thaler, "The Endowment Effect, Loss Aversion, and Status Quo Bias," *Journal of Economic Perspectives*, 5(no. 1) (Winter 1991), 203–204.

22. Thayler, "Mental Accounting," p. 211.

23. Identifying market segments with different price sensitivities is extremely important when, as is usually the case, the relative sizes of different segments are not naturally represented in the same proportions in an experimental or survey research population.

24. See Monroe, "Buyers Subjective Perceptions of Price," pp. 70–80.

25. Lester G. Telser, "The Demand for Branded Goods as Estimated from Consumer Panel Data," *Review of Economics and Statistics*, 4 (August 1962), 300–24, William T. Moran, "Insights from Pricing Research," in *Pricing Practices and Strategies*, ed. Earl L. Bailey (New York: The Conference Board, Inc., 1978), p. 9; Auijit Ghosh, Scott A. Neslin, and Robert Shoemaker, "Are There Associations Between Price Elasticity and Brand Characteristics?" Proceedings, Fall Educators' Conference (Chicago: American Marketing Association, 1983), p. 228; Lakshman Krishnamurthi and S. P. Raj, "An Empirical Analysis of the Relationship Between Brand Loyalty and Consumer Price Elasticity," *Marketing Science*, 10, no. 2 (Spring 1991), 172–183.

26. Ghosh, Neslin, and Shoemaker, "Are There Associations Between Price Elasticity and Brand Characteristics?" pp. 228–29.

27. Moran, "Insights from Pricing Research," p. 9.

28. Ghosh, Neslin, and Shoemaker, "Are There Associations Between Price Elasticity and Brand Characteristics?" pp. 228–29.

29. Hermann Simon, "Dynamics of Price Elasticity and Brand Life Cycles: An Empirical Study," *Journal of Marketing Research*, 16 (November 1979), 439–52.

30. Ghosh, Neslin, and Shoemaker, "Are There Associations Between Price Elasticity and Brand Characteristics?" p. 229.

31. Although there is no general pattern relating price sensitivity to the age of an individual brand, the price sensitivity of all brands in a product class is related to the age of that class. See Chapter 8.

Appendix 4A
Economic value analysis: an illustration

ECONOMIC VALUE ANALYSIS

A common mistake in formulating pricing strategy is taking competitors' prices as the standard by which to judge one's own. As a result, some companies incorrectly assume that they must price lower than competitors to achieve the goal of gaining or maintaining market share, whereas other companies incorrectly assume that pricing above competitors will necessarily place them at a competitive disadvantage. But buyers do not judge prices purely in dollar terms. They judge them in terms of the economic values that those prices represent. Consequently, a product that buyers perceive as having a higher economic value than its competitors (for example, the IBM personal computer) can often be priced above competing products and still capture a large market share, whenever one that has a low economic value (for example, generic canned vegetables) may still seem unattractive despite a comparatively low price. To determine the effect that a price has in achieving pricing goals and objectives, a company should first determine the product's economic value.

Du Pont, a company known for its innovation, has often faced the problem of determining economic value for a new, differentiated product. In 1955, for example, Du Pont introduced Alathon 25®, a polyethylene resin designed to compete with other resins in the manufacture of flexible pipe.[1] Alathon had a differentiating advantage in that the pipe made with it was substantially more durable. Tests indicated that Alathon 25® pipe had failure rates of 1 to 3 percent compared with 7 to 8 percent for the competition. What, then, was the product's economic value?

To answer that question, it is useful to think of a product's economic value to a customer as the sum of two parts: its reference value and its differentiation value. The *reference value* is the cost of whatever competing product the customer views as the best substitute for the product being evaluated. The reference value equals the competing product's price, adjusted for any difference in the quantity used.

The *differentiation value* is the value of a product's attributes that are different from those of the best substitute. If the buyer likes the differentiating attributes, the differentiation value is positive. If the buyer dislikes them, the differentiation value is negative.

In the case of Alathon 25®, it would be appropriate to do two economic value analyses: one for pipe extruders who purchase Alathon and one for pipe buyers who purchase pipe made of Alathon. We look at the value analysis for pipe buyers first, since the analysis for pipe extruders depends on it.

The most common substitute for Alathon pipe at the time was a pipe made of an off-grade resin selling for $5 to $7 per hundred feet. That is the reference value from which Du Pont would begin to calculate the total value of Alathon-based pipe. The more difficult part of the analysis involves determining differentiation value. One must study how buyers use the product and the impact of its differentiating attributes to determine their value.

Greater durability means that users have to buy less replacement pipe. That difference alone is worth a 5 to 6 percent price premium. But the differentiation value of Alathon is not simply the savings on expenditures for replacement pipe; it includes also the labor saved from not having to replace ruptured sections and from the cleanups and damages avoided. Those values will vary for different users of flexible pipe. Some buyers of flexible pipe bury it underground; others leave it exposed. The differentiation value to the former buyers will be greater, reflecting the greater cost of pipe replacement. Similarly, some buyers use the pipe to carry water, whereas others use it to carry toxic or offensive wastes. The differentiation value for the latter will be greater, reflecting the higher cost to them of post-failure clean ups. Obviously, then, there is no one economic value for a product unless all buyers use it in the same way. Each buyer segment, defined by its use of the product, has a different economic value, depending upon how the differentiating attributes affect the segment.

Let us, then, for illustration, calculate the differentiation value of Alathon 25® for one market segment: farmers who use it as part of below-ground irrigation systems. Exhibit 4A.1 illustrates the economic value of Alathon pipe for them. For that purpose, farmers use a pipe thickness that sells for $6.50 per hundred feet when it is made of off-grade resins. They save $0.31 to $0.39 per hundred feet by not having to purchase as much pipe for replacement. The labor cost of replacing a failed pipe is about $60.00, so a 5 to 6 percent lower failure rate raises Alathon's differentiation value by $3.00 to $3.60 per hundred feet. Pipe failures, if not detected quickly, can also damage crops. Crop damage per failure might range from nothing, if the failure occurred after plants were mature and well rooted, to $40.00 if vulnerable seedlings were washed out. Since young, poorly rooted crops are in place approximately 20 percent of the time that the irrigation system is in use, reduced crop damage would add at least $0.40 to the differentiation value of Alathon pipe ($40.00 × 0.20 × 0.05). Thus, for this segment, the total economic value of Alathon pipe would be in the range of from $10.21 to $10.96 per hundred feet.

Du Pont does not sell flexible pipe; it sells the Alathon 25® from which pipe is made. Thus, the next step is to calculate the economic value of Alathon to extruders who make such pipe for farmers. The calculation is illustrated in Exhibit 4A.2. The reference value is the cost of the less durable commodity resin, which was $0.28 per pound. That resin enabled an ex-

EXHIBIT 4A.1

Economic Value of Alathon 25® Pipe for Below-ground Irrigation (Per Hundred Feet)

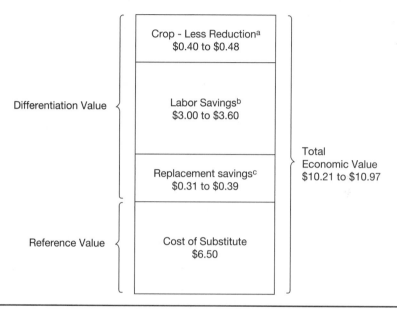

a $40.00 × .20 × 5% to 6% = $0.40 to $.48.
b 5% to 6% × $60.00 = $3.00 to $3.60.
c New value per 100 feet = ($6.50 × 1.08)/1.03 = $6.81.
Differentiation value of failure rate reduction from 8% to 3% = $6.81 – 6.50 - $0.31, or
New value per 100 feet = ($6.50 × 1.07)/1.01 – $6.89.
Differentiation value of failure rate reduction from 7% to 1% = $6.89 - $6.50 = $0.39.

truder to make a $6.50 pipe for a resin cost of about $4.55. By making the same pipe with Alathon 25®, however, the extruder could produce a product with a value to buyers of $10.21 to $10.96. That adds $0.228 to $0.275 per pound to the differentiation value of Alathon. For extruders, however, there are also some drawbacks to selling Alathon. Because buyers must buy less of it for replacement of failures, an extruder may suffer reduced profits from lost sales. Given the extruder's contribution of $1.95 per hundred feed of pipe, that corresponds to a negative differentiation value of about $0.01 per pound. Extruders might also expect to be compensated for the risks of having to deal with a single source of supply, reducing differentiation value by another $0.02 per pound. Finally, they will encounter higher selling costs for the new pipe, representing about $0.08 per pound.[2]

EXHIBIT 4A.2

Economic Value of Alathon 25® for Pipe Extruders (Per Pound)

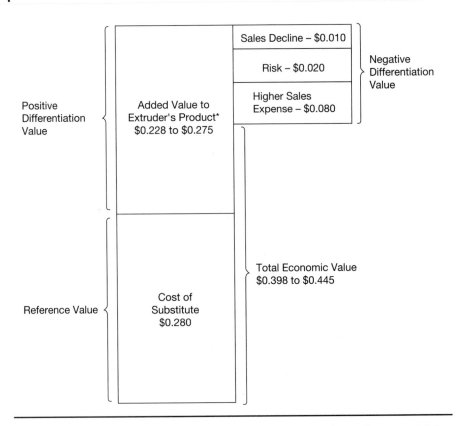

* It takes 16.25 pounds of Alathon to make 100 feet of pipe ($4.55/$0.28 = 16.25). Thus, the added value of Alathon pipe per pound of Alathon is (at minimum) ($10.21 − $6.50)/16.25 = $0.228 per pound.

Consequently, the economic value of Alathon for extruders of farm irrigation pipe is $0.384 to $0.480 per pound.

INTERPRETING ECONOMIC VALUE

It is important to note that the economic value derived from this procedure is not necessarily the perceived value that a buyer would actually place on the product. A buyer may be unaware of a product and thus remain influenced by its price (the perceived substitute effect). A buyer may be unsure of a product's differentiating attributes and may be unwilling to invest the time and expense to learn about them (the difficult comparison effect). If the product's price is small, the buyer may make an impulse purchase without really thinking about its economic value (the expenditure effect). Similarly, other effects can influence price sensitivity in ways that undermine the influence that economic value has on the purchase decision. A product's market value is determined not only by the product's economic value, but also by the accuracy with which buyers perceive that value and by how much importance they place on getting the most for their money.

This limitation of economic value analysis is both a weakness and a strength. It is a weakness in that economic value cannot indicate the appropriate price to charge but only the maximum price that a segment of buyers would pay if they were perfectly cognizant of the product's economic value and motivated by that value in making their purchase decisions. It is also a strength, however, in that it enables a firm to determine whether a product is selling poorly because it is overpriced relative to its true value or because it is underpromoted and thus unappreciated by the market. The only solution to the former problem is to cut price. A better solution to the latter problem is often to maintain or even increase price while aggressively educating the market. That is precisely what Du Pont did with Alathon 25®. After years of cutting Alathon's price to build sales with little success, du Pont raised its price from \$0.355 to \$0.380 per pound while at the same time beginning an aggressive marketing campaign. Sales doubled in the following year as buyers became aware of Alathon's superior economic value to them.

Economic value analysis has additional uses as well.[3] The analysis can indicate which attribute improvements would give a new product the largest gain in economic value, thus serving to direct new product research efforts. Moreover, the same analysis can aid sales representatives in demonstrating to buyers why a superior product is really worth the premium price it carries. But, most important, economic value analysis can help a firm identify different market segments that do not necessarily value the product's various attributes in the same way. The identification of segments and the economic value of a product to them are essential elements in formulating pricing strategy.

ECONOMIC VALUE PROFILE

The analysis of economic value shown above was for one segment in Du Pont's total market for Alathon. However, an understanding of only one segment is no basis for formulating a pricing strategy. To determine the role that price should play in a product's marketing, one must determine the economic value of all the segments that comprise the market, as well as the size of each segment. With that information, one can develop an *economic value profile* of the market and determine what market segments can be served most profitably.

Exhibit 4A.3 illustrates a hypothetical economic value profile for Alathon 25®. The profile is built from economic value analyses for each of the potential market segments to which the product might be sold. It en-

---

EXHIBIT 4A.3

Economic Value Profile for Alathon 25®

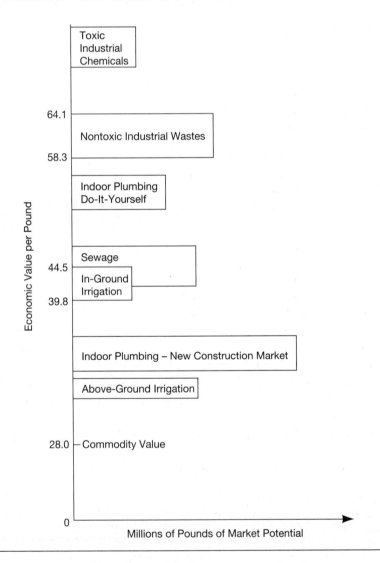

ables a manager to determine at what price level the product is price competitive for each market segment. The segments are identified by the factors that determine the different ways potential buyers value the product. In this case, the type of buyer (industrial, farming, plumbing), as well as the use for which the buyer purchases the product (in-ground versus above-ground irrigation, toxic versus nontoxic chemical transmission), affects the value of the product's differentiating attributes.

By observing how a price change would affect the product's price competitiveness for each segment, a manager can observe how the value effect will influence price sensitivity. A natural next step is to derive a demand curve from the value profile, assuming that at each price the firm can capture the sales potential of each market segment with an economic value for the product that is above the price. Although such an excercise is often done by marketing research companies that measure the value effect, it can be dangerously misleading unless properly interpreted. A manager must remember that such a curve shows only the effect that economic value has on the purchase decision. Although economic value is arguably the most important determinant of price sensitivity for most products, it is not the most important for all products and is almost never of sole importance for any product. There is more to good marketing than the product and its price, and more to marketing success than price competitiveness. Promotional and distributional competitiveness are also important, sometimes the most important, factors determining a product's ability to capture the sales potential in a market segment.

For example, MCI is certainly very competitive with AT&T in pricing of its long-distance telephone calls. Yet, as of this writing, MCI still holds a substantially smaller market share. It lags behind because, despite years of aggressive advertising and telephone sales, many people still remain unaware that MCI offers an alternative to AT&T and that its attributes are comparable (the substitute awareness and difficult comparison effects). Many people also consider the potential savings too small to justify the effort of changing to MCI (the total expenditure effect). And many business users can either bill someone else for the calls (the shared-cost effect) or are very concerned that "cheaper" may imply lower quality (the price-quality effect). MCI is quite price competitive for most economic value segments of the market, but for those segments that are hard to reach promotionally or distributionally, MCI's prices are not enough to overcome buyers' generally low price sensitivity. This market serves as a stark reminder that there is more to price sensitivity than economic value.

An economic value profile is still a useful input in formulating a pricing strategy, especially in those markets where economic value is the dominant factor driving the purchase decision. Along with analysis of the other factors affecting price sensitivity, it can help the manager to anticipate and influence buyers' responses to price changes.

NOTES

1. This illustration is developed from information in E. Raymond Corey, "E.I. Du Pont de Nemours & Co," *Industrial Marketing: Cases and Concepts*, 2nd ed. (Englewood Cliffs, N.J.: Prentice-Hall, Inc., 1976), pp. 179–87; and Benson P. Shapiro and Barbara B. Jackson, "Industrial Pricing to Meet Customer Needs," *Harvard Business Review*, 56 (November–December 1978), 119–27. The numbers are illustrative, not necessarily those actually arrived at by Du Pont.

2. If Alathon were easier or more difficult to extrude, its differentiation value would also be affected. If more or less Alathon were required to replace a pound of commodity resin, then the analysis would have to reflect the cost of whatever amount of the substitute would be required in lieu of one pound of Alathon. Since Alathon is extruded in the same way as commodity-grade resin, and in the same quantities, these factors do not affect the economic value analysis in this case.

3. See John L. Forbis and Nitin T. Mehta, "Value-Based Strategies for Industrial Products," *Business Horizons*, 24, no. 3 (May–June 1981), 32–42; and Irwin Gross, "Insights from Pricing Research," in *Pricing Practices and Strategies*, ed. Earl L. Bailey (New York: The Conference Board, 1978), pp. 34–39.

COMPETITION

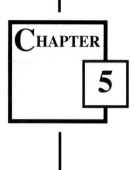

CHAPTER
5

MANAGING YOUR MARKET PROACTIVELY

Pricing against competition is more challenging and hazardous than pricing a unique product.[1] In the absence of competition, managers can anticipate the effect of a price change entirely by analyzing buyers' price sensitivity. When a product is just one among many, however, competitors can wreak havoc with such predictions. Price discounting in competitive markets—whether explicit or disguised with rebates, coupons, or generous payment terms—is almost a sure bet to enhance immediate sales and profits. It is easy to become seduced by these quick highs and fail to recognize the longer-term consequences. The price cut that boosts your sales today will invariably change the industry you compete in tomorrow. Frequently, that change is for the worse.

The recent experience of a large building products manufacturer illustrates just such a problem. This company had been consistently profitable as a market-share leader. Despite the commodity-like nature of its product, the company enjoyed a small price premium reflecting its perceived technical superiority and exceptional customer service. Still, the company had long been losing market share due to aggressive price competition from smaller competitors. New management, which took control following a leveraged buyout, was determined to reverse this trend.

Although this company offered standard discounts for volume, quick payment, and so forth, the company had historically been reluctant to negotiate prices with any but its largest customers. Consequently, smaller competitors could predictably set their prices just beneath the leader's price umbrella. To thwart the competition, the new management decided to close the umbrella. Whenever an account seemed seriously threatened by a lower-cost bid, sales managers were authorized to negotiate "special deals" that would retain the business at lower, but still profitable prices. The effect of this policy was dramatic; the company effectively stopped the erosion of established customers, while continuing to gain new business based on quality and service. Over the next few quarters, market share not only stopped declining, but actually rose by a few points.

Was this a wise strategic move? The company won more pricing battles and, consequently, gained volume and profits. But how would the market change as a result of this company's new pricing policy? What was the predictable long-run impact of this strategy on the nature of competition in the industry? At first, the market changed very little because the company took pains to limit public knowledge of the new policy. Over time, however, customers talked with one another. The company's traditional customers, who had been willingly paying a price premium for the company's product quality and service, began learning that others got the same quality and service for less. Moreover, they learned that others got lower prices because they were tougher negotiators who had threatened to give their business to other suppliers.

It is not difficult to imagine what happened next. Previously loyal buyers resolved to no longer "get taken" simply because they hadn't investigated their alternatives. Purchasing authority was moved from users to purchasing departments; doors opened to competitors that had previously been closed; and, instead of giving this company their business, previously loyal customers began giving it only the last look. With more competitors involved in each sale, the sales cycle grew longer and the number of requests for "special deals" grew exponentially. In fact, within two years, management was looking for a way to automate the process of preparing them.

This company created a financial incentive for its buyers to become more informed and less loyal, and they responded. Although the policy reversed a decline in market share, both industry prices and the company's price premium declined. Management complained about declining profits and loss of customer loyalty, but made no connection between those changes and its own policies. Management eventually responded to buyers' reluctance to pay the traditional price premium for quality and service by looking for ways to cut costs in those areas.

The lesson here is not that management should avoid defending market share or should never initiate price cuts. The lesson is that, before taking such actions, management must determine the long-run strategic consequences and weigh them against the short-term benefits. A pricing decision should never be made simply to make the next sale or to meet some short-term sales objective, but rather to enhance the firm's long-term ability to operate profitably. Although this company achieved immediate benefits from its policy to thwart the competition, it unwittingly undermined the industry price level and customers' willingness to pay for the advantages they perceived in its product.

Successful price competitors must learn to anticipate the longer-term consequences of their actions so that they can balance them against the short-term benefits. Pricing is like playing chess. Those who make moves one at a time—seeking to minimize immediate losses or to exploit immediate opportunities—will invariably be beaten by those who can envision the game a few moves ahead. One should never cut price simply to get a particular customer's business or to meet a current sales objective.

Because price changes affect sales more quickly than other marketing decisions, they are often used as a quick-fix solution to short-term problems. Profitable pricing requires, however, that managers also consider how each decision will affect future competitive behavior and profitability. Procter & Gamble, for example, abandoned a decade-long policy of chronic "price promotion," despite the short-term benefits, after realizing that it caused large retailers to adopt purchasing patterns that substantially raised its costs of manufacturing and distribution.

Pricing decisions should always be made as part of a longer-term marketing strategy to capture value. Otherwise, it is possible to win many individual battles for market share and still end up losing the war for profitability. This is not to argue that underpricing the competition is never a successful strategy in the long run, but the conditions necessary to make it successful depend critically upon how customers and competitors react to it. The goal of this chapter is to provide guidelines for anticipating those reactions, influencing them, and integrating them into a long-term strategic plan.

UNDERSTANDING THE PRICING GAME

Pricing is a "game," as defined by game theorists, because success depends not only on a company's own pricing decisions, but also on how customers and competitors respond to them. Unfortunately, pricing strategically for sustainable profitability is a type of game requiring skills foreign to many marketing and sales managers. What most of us know about competition we learned from sports, academics, and perhaps from intracompany sales contests. The rules for success in these types of competition are quite different from those for success in pricing. The reason, in technical jargon, is that the former are all examples of "positive-sum" games whereas pricing is a "negative-sum" game. Understanding the difference is crucial to playing the pricing game successfully.[2]

Positive-sum games are those in which the very process of competition creates benefits. Consequently, the more prolonged and intense the game—in sports, academics, or sales—the greater the rewards to the players. The winner always finds playing such games worthwhile, and even the loser may gain enough from the experience so as not to regret having played. In fact, people with a healthy attitude toward these activities often seek opportunities to challenge themselves simply to benefit from the experience. Such a strong competitive spirit is a criterion commonly used to identify job candidates with potential for success in sales.

Unfortunately, that same gung-ho attraction to competition is quite unhealthy when applied to negative-sum games: those in which the process of competition imposes costs on the players. Warfare, labor actions, and dueling are negative-sum games because the loser never benefits from participation. The longer the conflict drags on, the more likely it is that even the winner will find that playing was not worth the cost. Price competition is usually a negative-sum game since the more intense price competition is, the more it undermines the value of the market over which one is competing.[3] Price competitors do well, therefore, to forget what they learned about competing from sports and other positive-sum games, and to try instead to draw lessons from less familiar competitions like warfare or dueling.

Contrary to common analogies equating marketing with warfare, the most valuable skill for managing in a negative-sum environment is not the art of the general, whose job is to win battles, but the art of the diplomat, whose job is to minimize their frequency and intensity. Diplomacy is not capitulation. It is, rather, the art of dispassionately weighing the costs and benefits of competition, while managing that process to achieve objectives *without unnecessary or prolonged conflict*.

Unfortunately, all too many managers—and the experts who advise them—know more about winning pricing battles than about preventing those that are not worth fighting. After lifetimes of success at sports, academics, and sales, they find old habits hard to break. The remainder of this chapter is about the diplomacy of price competition: an essential skill for managers who gauge their success not only by their ability to win sales and market share, but also by their ability to do so profitably over the long haul.

Diplomacy is a process of making plans, manipulating information, and choosing confrontations wisely. Competitive pricing, when managed strategically for sustainable profitability, involves the same elements.

PLAN FOR PROFITABLE PRICING

Management cannot make thoughtful trade-offs between the immediate gains from price competition and the longer-term rewards of a profitable industry without a plan for making such trade-offs. Unfortunately, companies in competitive industries often operate without one. They have, of course, lofty corporate objectives for sales and profit, but they lack realistic plans for achieving them. To quote the marketing vice president of one such company, "We don't have time to waste planning for the future; we're too busy dealing with the problems of today." Of course, many managers are overwhelmed by the competitive "problems of today" precisely because they failed to anticipate those problems when they still had time to prevent them.

Anticipate and manage competition

A realistic strategic plan explicitly recognizes that the firm's results are determined not just by its own decisions, but by the interaction of its decisions with the decisions of its competitors and customers. Marketing plans at most companies address only that company's own plans for each product and the expected result in sales and profits. They ignore equally important information: the plans and aspirations of customers and competitors. Exhibit 5.1 illustrates the interrelationship of information required for realistic strategic planning. Unfortunately, typical marketing plans cover only the elements of the first row labeled "our company." Planners at those companies make assumptions without having to justify market conditions that would support their rosy scenarios. A realistic plan for managing competition is two-dimensional. Each decision must not only be rationalized internally (horizontally) with what the company hopes to achieve, but also externally (vertically) with what competitive conditions will permit it to achieve.[4]

If companies did two-dimensional planning for competition, they could avoid, or at least prepare for, the price wars necessary to resolve inconsistencies. In the early 1980s, major U.S. accounting firms targeted the for-profit health-care market as an opportunity for increased growth and

---

EXHIBIT 5.1

Plan for Managing Competition (Two Dimensional)

	Segment A	Segment B	Segment C	Overall Strategy
Our company				
Competitor A				
Competitor B				
Fringe competitors				
Customers				
Segment's attractiveness				

profitability. Privately managed hospitals and nursing homes were expected to grow rapidly due both to the aging of the U.S. population and the trend toward privatizing the management of health-care institutions. Many of the major accounting firms rapidly expanded the resources devoted to accounting services for this market segment.

As it turned out, the market for health-care accounting services did grow rapidly, just as these companies had predicted. Profitability, however, did not. Contrary to the expectations of the major players, audit prices did not remain stable but, to nearly everyone's surprise, plunged by 30 percent. Business that everyone thought would increase profitability had to be performed at a loss, even to retain previously established accounts. The companies bravely hoped to make up these losses with follow-up consulting.

Here was a classic case of inadequate strategic planning. From public directories, each firm could have counted the number of people hired by each of its competitors for their health-care divisions. Knowing how many people are required for auditing and the expected growth in this market, any firm could have calculated the amount of market share needed to keep each firm's auditors employed. Had any companies done this exercise in advance, they would have discovered that the market size required for all firms to achieve their apparent objectives vastly exceeded what was likely to be available. Consequently, any company that had realistically evaluated this opportunity, taking into account its competitors' goals as well as its own, would have planned for intense price competition.

A company that had anticipated the forthcoming competition could have taken a number of steps to minimize its consequences. If new to this market segment, without any competitive advantages, the firm might wisely have reconsidered the decision to invest in it. If the firm already had a customer base in this segment, it might have preemptively offered small discounts for signing multiyear contracts, precluding the need for larger discounts in the future. The firm might have then proactively begun warding off its weaker competitors. A statement to the business press about its predictions of excess capacity and its preemptive moves to block competition for its current base could well have caused weaker, and less prepared, competitors to withdraw without a fight. Unfortunately, the failure of anyone to anticipate and manage the forthcoming conflict led to an unexpected and unnecessarily costly price war.

In a similar situation, a price war was avoided by the more careful planning of a European industrial products company. This company and its major European competitor had independently achieved sustainable profits by limiting their capacity, thus enabling both of them to operate at high levels of utilization. Consequently, during periods of peak demand, customers in all three market segments were forced to plan orders far in advance and had little leverage to negotiate prices. The company's enviable position was threatened, however, when a foreign competitor, previously an importer, began building domestic production capacity. Management was challenged to formulate an appropriate response.

The natural reaction of those trained to compete in positive-sum games is to fight to defend every point of market share ("Hold that line!"). In industries that have done so (for example, plasterboard in the United Kingdom, compressed gases in Spain, disposable diapers and air travel in the United States, and disk drives and DRAM chips worldwide), the result has been ruinous price warfare that destroyed profits for everyone. This company, however, took a more diplomatic approach. After realizing that there was no way to convince the foreign competitor to withdraw its plans, the company devised a plan to accommodate the newcomer, but on its own terms.

After analyzing its three market segments, the company figured out where the newcomer's sales would cause the least damage. In that low-growth "commodity" segment, the company raised its prices to create an umbrella for the newcomer to enter. In the other segments, the company proposed faster service, guaranteed supply, and protection against near-term price increases in return for signing longer-term contracts.

By the time the new competitor's salespeople began soliciting orders to fill their capacity, they found that they could do so without slashing prices in the commodity segment, but found the other segments difficult to penetrate. Although the two established firms found that the new competition did hurt their overall sales, the damage was much less than if they had engaged in even limited price warfare on their own territory. Moreover, they positioned themselves in segments that were much more defensible (due to demands for service and technical support), while positioning their new competitor in a price-sensitive, low-margin segment that made it especially vulnerable to the effects of price competition. Consequently, the established firms preserved the stability and profitability of pricing in their industry.

This does *not* imply that one should always accommodate new competition. If this new competitor had been poorly financed and suffering from higher costs due to more limited economies of scale, a quick price war resulting in its ultimate bankruptcy, followed by purchase of its capacity by an established firm, might have been a better strategy. The lesson is not that there is any one right competitive strategy, but that any successful strategy requires balancing both long- and short-term effects. In price-competitive industries, one can choose to adapt to competition, to change it, or to eliminate it to minimize its adverse effects on long-term profits. To make that choice, however, one must first anticipate what that impact is likely to be.

Establish pricing policies consistent with the plans

It is one thing for management to articulate a competitive strategy; it is quite another for the organization to implement it. Few people in the organization have the vision or adequate information to understand the overall plan. Moreover, keeping key elements of your strategy proprietary requires limiting such information even within your organization. This creates a problem. How can you make an organization implement a competitive strategy which, at best, it understands to only a limited extent? The answer is by establishing policies. Policies are particularly important for pricing, since the long-run consequences of a pricing decision are usually more important, but much less obvious, than the immediate impact.

For example, a company that seeks to increase sales by getting the organization to offer exceptional levels of service, and customers to see the value of that service, might well establish a fixed-price policy.[5] Having no discretion over the price charged, salespeople would have no choice but to sell value, and the organization no choice but to deliver it. In the short run, such a policy makes everyone's job more difficult, but in the long run it makes the company more efficient in meeting customer needs. A fixed-price policy also enables the salesperson to get closer to customers, since they need not fear that the information they reveal will be used against them in adversarial price negotiations. Such a policy can still be complemented by segmented pricing, offering discounts to specifically identifiable customer groups (for example, large purchasers, government, members of buying organizations), but the criteria and size of the discount available to a particular customer would be out of the hands of the salesperson.

In contrast, a company that sells products in mature, competitive markets where the differentiating factors are not difficult to compare, may be forced to negotiate prices. Various customers may value the product differently, reflecting different values they associate with features, different awareness of the alternatives, and the different importance of the expenditure to them. In this case, one might conclude that the company should have fewer policies regarding pricing, simply letting the sales force price at whatever is necessary to make the sale. In fact, because negotiated pricing risks aggravating price competition (and enables salespeople to use price to compensate for their failures to sell value), one must control the process even more tightly. To prevent purchasing agents from just squeezing a lower price from inexperienced salespeople or playing salespeople off against one another, useful policies to guide price negotiation might include the following:

- Requiring that a negotiated discount be tied to the elimination of the service (for example, training, quick delivery) or feature (for example, choice of color) that the customer claims not to value.
- Requiring that the customer sign the order for a negotiated price requiring them to accept it if approved by the salesperson's management.
- Requiring that the customer commit to a long-term purchase agreement (for example, requirements for the year) in return for gaining a discount.

Obviously, all these restrictions make winning the sale more difficult. They are quite different from the usual policy of "discount only as much as necessary to get the business." Can you see how they are different? Although anyone can achieve sales goals by giving away value, achieving sales *and* profitability requires imposing some cost on the customer who seeks a discount, thus limiting his or her ability to play suppliers off against one another. In contrast, the "discount as necessary" strategy directly rewards a customer for stimulating price warfare among suppliers.

Finally, even policies restricting negotiations are not enough if those who are supposed to implement them have perverse incentives to undermine them. Literally thousands of companies have a strategic objective to sell differentiated products at premium prices, but then have incentive systems for their salespeople, independent representatives, and even sales managers that punish them for pursuing that objective. Selling value requires time and energy. It is much more difficult than selling price. Consequently, a salesperson can almost invariably generate more revenue, and therefore more praise and rewards, by discounting than by convincing customers to buy the product or service on its merits. The key to managing the sales force where prices are negotiated is to reward salespeople not for achieving sales, but for achieving profitable sales. Details for establishing such an incentive system are explained in the appendix to Chapter 8.

MANAGING COMPETITIVE INFORMATION

The key to managing price competition is diplomacy, not generalship. This does not necessarily mean being "Mr. Nice Guy", as diplomats are not always nice. They simply manage to achieve their goals without the necessity of costly confrontation. Their tactics involve not the use of force, but the use of information. In price competition, the meaning that competitors ascribe to a move is often far more important than the move itself.

The decision to cut price to gain a customer may have radically different long-term effects depending upon how the competitor interprets the move. Without any other information, the competitor would probably interpret the move as an opportunistic grab for market share and respond with defensive cuts of its own. If, however, the discount is structured to mimic exactly an offer that the same competitor made recently to one of this company's customers, the competitor may interpret the cut as reflecting the company's resolve to defend its market share. As such, the cut may actually reduce future opportunism and help stabilize industry prices.

Now consider how the competitor might interpret one more alternative: the price cut is totally unprovoked but is exceptionally large, more than the company has ever offered before and probably more than is necessary to take the business. Moreover, it is preceded by an announcement that the company's new, patented manufacturing process not only added to capacity, but also substantially reduced the company's incremental manufacturing costs. In this case, an intelligent competitor might well interpret the price cut as fair warning that resistance to this company's grab for market share will be futile.

Managing information to influence a competitor's expectations is the key to achieving goals without unnecessary negative-sum confrontation.

Managing information requires collecting and evaluating information about the competition, as well as communicating information to the competition that may influence its moves in ways desirable to one's firm.

Collect and evaluate information

Recall the previous discussion describing how public accounting firms failed to use publicly available information to anticipate price competition in the health-care segment. As a consequence, they missed the opportunity to position themselves for that competition and to influence their competitors to avoid it. Such an oversight almost never happens in highly competitive industries that have learned how to manage the competitive process. At the deep-discount end of the retailing market, for example, competitors monitor one another's expansion plans carefully, comparing them with expected growth in the market, before building stores. Sam's Warehouse Clubs, a division of Wal-Mart, is the largest player, both nationally and in Texas. Upon learning that the other discount warehouse retailers were looking for sites to build stores in its fast-growing Texas markets, Sam's preemptively expanded some stores, relocated others, and added more locations in an attempt to preclude that entry. As a result, Costco, the third largest retailer nationally, abandoned all its plans to enter, while others may have scaled back.[6]

Unfortunately, many companies operate not only ignorant of competitors' future plans, but even of their prices! Consequently, they cannot respond quickly to changes. In highly competitive markets, such ignorance creates conditions that invite price warfare. Why would an opportunist ever cut price if it believed that other companies were willing to retaliate? The answer is that the opportunist's management believes that, by quietly negotiating or concealing its price cuts, it can gain sufficient sales volume to justify the move before the competitors find out. This is especially likely in industries with high fixed costs (high %CMs) and during peak seasons when disproportionate amounts of business are at stake.

To minimize such opportunistic behavior, competitors must identify and react to it as quickly as possible.[7] If competitors can react in one week rather than three, the opportunist's potential benefit from price cutting is reduced by two-thirds. At the extreme, if competitors could somehow react instantly, nearly all benefit from being the first to cut price could be eliminated. In highly competitive markets, managers "shop" the competitors' stores and monitor their advertising on a daily basis to adjust their pricing,[8] and the large chains maintain communication systems enabling them to make price changes quickly in response to a competitive threat.[9] As a consequence, by the time most customers even learn what the competition is promoting in a given week, the major competitors have already matched the price.

Knowledge of competitors' prices also helps minimize a purchasing agents' ability to manipulate prices. Frequently in business-to-business markets, price wars begin without the intention of any competitor involved. They are caused by a purchasing agent's manipulation of information. A purchasing agent, frustrated by the inability to get a better price from a favored supplier, may falsely claim that he or she has been offered a better deal from a competitor. If the salesperson doesn't respond, a smart purchasing agent may give the threat more credibility by giving the next order to a competitor even without a price concession. Now the first company believes that its competitor is out "buying business." Perhaps it will match the claimed "lower price" on future orders to this customer, rewarding this customer's duplicitous behavior. If the company is more skilled in price competition, it will not match, but will retaliate by offering the same discount to other good customers of the competitor. The competitor will now justly see this company as a threat and begin its own cuts to defend its share. Without either competitor intending to undermine the industry price level, each has unwittingly been led to do so. The only way to minimize such manipulation is to monitor competitors' prices closely enough so that you can confidently predict when a customer is lying.[10]

There are many potential sources of data about competitors' prices, but collecting that data and converting it into useful information usually requires a formalized process. Many companies require that the sales-force regularly include information on competitors' pricing in their call reports. Having such current information can substantially reduce the time necessary to respond to opportunism since someone collecting information from multiple salespeople and regions can spot a trend much more quickly than can an individual salesperson or sales manager. Favored customers can also be a good source of information. Those who are loyal to the company, perhaps because of its quality or good service, do not want their competitors to get lower prices from anyone else. Consequently, they will warn the company when competitors issue new price sheets or when they hear that someone is discounting to someone else. A partnership with such a customer is very valuable and should be treated as such by the seller.

Trade associations, independent organizations that monitor the industry, and even securities analysts who follow the industry are often good sources of information about competitors' intentions and their pricing moves in selected markets. Sometimes trade associations will collect information on prices charged in the prior week and disseminate it to members who have submitted their own prices. The airlines' computerized reservation systems give the owners of those systems an advance look at all price changes, enabling them to respond even before travel agents see the change. Monitoring price discussions at trade shows can also be another early tip-off. In retail businesses, one can simply "shop" the competitive retailers on a regular basis. In the hotel industry, nearby competitors regularly check their competitors' prices and room availability on particular nights simply by calling to make an unguaranteed reservation. If price competition is an important enough determinant of profit in an industry, managers can easily justify the cost to monitor it.[11]

Selectively communicate information

It is usually much easier for managers to see the value of collecting competitive information than it is for them to see the value in knowingly revealing similar information to the competition. After all, information is power. Why should anyone want to reveal a competitive advantage? The answer: so that you can avoid having to use your advantage in a negative-sum confrontation.

The value of sharing information was obvious, after the fact, to a company supplying the construction industry. Unlike most of its competitors as well as most economists, the company accurately predicted the recession and construction slowdown in the early 1980s. To prepare, the company wisely pared back its inventories and shelved expansion plans just as its competitors were continuing to expand. The company's only mistake was to keep its insight a secret. Management correctly felt that by retrenching more quickly than its competitors, it could weather the hard times more successfully. But when competitors desperately cut prices to clear bloated inventories, the entire industry suffered. Had the company shared its insight and discouraged everyone from overexpansion, its own financial performance, while perhaps *relatively* less outstanding, would have been *absolutely* more profitable. It is usually better to earn just an average return in a profitable industry than to earn an exceptional return in an unprofitable one.

Even company-specific information—about intentions, capabilities, and future plans—can be useful to reveal selectively. Such information, and the information contained in competitors' responses, enables a company to establish plans "on paper" that are consistent with competitors' intentions rather than having to reach consistency through the painful process of confrontation.

Preannounce Price Increases   One of the most important times to communicate intentions is when planning a price increase. Even when a price increase is in the interest of all suppliers, an attempt to raise prices will often fail. All may not immediately recognize that an increase is in their interest, and some may hope to gain sales at the expense of the price leaders by lagging in meeting the increase. Other times, an increase may not be in the firm's interest (perhaps because its costs are lower), meaning that any attempt to raise prices will ultimately fail. Consequently, before initiating a price increase that it expects competitors to follow, a firm's management should publicly explain the industry's need for higher prices and announce its own increase far in advance of the effective date.

This move to "test the waters before diving in" has two purposes: First, it gives competitors time to analyze whether a general price increase is in their interest, and second, it gives the firm an opportunity to back off from the increase if some competitors fail to join in. Even when a general price increase is in the interest of all firms, it may be necessary to announce and then withdraw it a number of times until potentially opportunistic competitors get the message that no price increase will go through without them. It may also be necessary to scale back a price increase if some competitors remain unconvinced that an increase as large as the one proposed is in their interest.

Show Willingness and Ability to Defend   When threatened by the potential opportunism of others, a firm may deter the threat by clearly signaling its commitment and ability to defend its market. For example, Chrysler had the largest U.S. market share for minivans in 1990. Because of the popularity and profitability of this line of automobiles, an onslaught of rivals planned to launch new models for 1991. Chrysler was worried about how they might price them, since it depended heavily on profits from its minivans. In a speech to its dealers covered by the business press, Chrysler sent a clear message to the competitors. Chrysler's president announced that the company had a plan to build a very low-priced version of its minivan. He explained, however, that "it's something we have in the desk drawer if we need it," and he added, lest anyone should miss the point, "If it ever comes to a price war in minivans, I'm convinced we can win it."[12] Chrysler was saying to its competitors: Don't destabilize the market by undercutting our prices, because if you do, we have the capability to meet your challenge and beat it!

Such communications can also be useful even after competitors have started the attack. Such posturing is common in the airline industry. When America West Airline undercut the fare for Northwest Airline's busy Minneapolis–Los Angeles route by $50, Northwest declined to match the cut. Instead, Northwest struck at America West's Phoenix hub by cutting fares a similar amount on the competitor's profitable Phoenix–New York route. Northwest's response fare was initially available for only a limited time, signaling that this was not a price that Northwest wished to sustain any longer than necessary. It could, however, be extended as long as necessary—if America West failed to back off in Minneapolis.[13]

Sometimes, simply publicizing a competitor's opportunism is sufficient to stop it. A client of ours in a nationwide service business dominated the most profitable regions of the country, the Northeast and Midwest. These regions had most of the largest customers. The major competitor had its profitable accounts in the South and West, where its reputation was stronger. In its drive to expand, the competitor began targeting some of our client's best customers with very low pricing. At first, our client attempted to meet these threats selectively, but was gradually losing control of its pricing as a result. Other customers were learning about these deals and demanding them too. Moreover, since low offers cost the competition very little, matching them did not diminish the competitor's enthusiasm to offer them.

What to do? At first one might suggest going to their best customers and offering the same kinds of deals. We, however, felt that was not the best idea in this case because it undermined the integrity of the company's pricing. In fact, we encouraged them to develop a fixed-price policy across customers and to promote it as a fairer way to deal with everyone. We felt that, at least initially, they should neither match the competitors' prices nor attack the competitor. Instead, we suggested a better alternative.

We proposed that they ask for an opportunity to make presentations to their competitor's best customers. During those presentations, they explained their "fair price" policy and why they felt that those prices were well-justified by the value offered. During the presentation, they made a low estimate of what the customer was probably paying for the service from the competitor, based on the low-ball offers that the competitor had been making selectively. When quizzed by the customers, they explained how they used other bids that the competitor had recently won to determine a comparable price for the competitor's product for this customer. Needless to say, within minutes of the completion of the presentation, these customers were on the phone to the competitor, demanding the discounts that were their due as the company's best customers. As we predicted, once the competitor learned that its low-price forays would become the basis of negotiations with its profitable current customers, it stopped selective discounting.

Back up Opportunism with Information   While an opportunistic price cut to buy market share is usually shortsighted, it is sometimes an element of a thoughtful strategy. This is most often the case when a company uses pricing to leverage or to enhance a durable cost advantage. Even companies with competitive advantages, however, often win only pyrrhic victories in battles for market share. Although they ultimately can force competitors to cede market share, the costs of battle frequently exceed the ultimate value of the reward. This is especially true when the war reduces customer price expectations and undermines loyal buyer-seller relationships.

The key to profitably using price as a weapon is to convince competitors to capitulate quickly. When Goodyear grabbed for a larger share of the radial tire market, its CEO gave numerous interviews explaining the size of the company's incremental cost advantage resulting from its construction of a highly automated tire plant in a nonunion state. To make the claim believable, Goodyear conducted guided tours of its new, state-of-the-art tire plant. Finally, the company identified specific financially weak competitors and explained to securities analysts how it could afford to price below the levels that they required to stave off bankruptcy. Within months, many smart but weaker competitors withdrew from the market, recognizing that they could not win a price war against a financially stronger rival with superior technology.[14]

Although the information disclosures discussed here are the most common, they are hardly comprehensive. Almost every public decision a company makes will be gleaned for information by astute competitors. Consequently, companies in price-competitive industries should take steps to manage how their moves are seen by competitors, just as they manage the perceptions of stockholders and securities analysts. For example, will competitors in a highly price-competitive industry interpret closure of a plant as a sign of financial weakness or as a sign that the company is taking steps to end an industry-wide overcapacity problem? How they interpret such a move will probably affect how they react to it. Consequently, it is in the company's interest to supply information that helps them make a favorable interpretation. Think twice, however, before disseminating misleading information that competitors will ultimately discover is incorrect. You may gain in the short run; however, you will undermine your ability to influence competitors decisions and, therefore, to manage price competition in the long run.

ALLOCATING COMPETITIVE RESOURCES

We have been discussing the benefits of avoiding competitive confrontation. But some companies clearly benefit from underpricing their competitors. Under what conditions are the rewards of aggressive pricing large enough to justify such a move? There are three:

1. If managers enjoy a substantial incremental cost advantage or can achieve one with a low-price strategy, their competitors may be unable to match their price cuts. Wal-Mart's unbeatable cost advantage in distribution justified undercutting the prices of traditional department and drug stores. Why? Because even though Wal-Mart's prices were lower, its net operating margins were higher than those of its major competitors.

Consequently, Wal-Mart could attract customers with price differences less than its cost advantage. This strategy is not a negative-sum game, but a transfer of market share to a more efficient competitor. Similarly, Dell convinced computer buyers to purchase by mail, and Southwest convinced airline passengers to bypass travel agents and call the airline directly. In both cases, low prices were the lure for customers to accept a marketing program that cut the seller's cost.

2.   If managers' product offerings are attractive to only a relatively small share of the market, they may rightly assume that their competitors cannot afford to respond to their threat. Small long-distance telephone carriers like Sprint knew that AT&T would not cut its prices to everyone in order to defend the small share that they threatened.

3.   If managers can better afford to sustain a price war than their competition can—because once having captured a customer, they are better able to sell related products profitably—they may financially justify aggressively pricing a product as a loss-leader.[15] Microsoft, for example, initially priced its Windows software very low to increase sales of other Microsoft software that runs on it.

Moreover, sometimes price competition expands a market sufficiently that, despite lower margins and competitors' refusals to allow another company to undercut them, industry profitability can still increase. This sometimes happens in the early stage of market growth.

In too many cases, however—where competitors are operating with similar costs and viable shares in mature markets—price competition is initiated only by short-sighted managers who fail to comprehend the long-run consequences of their actions. For any business that expects to exist beyond the very short run, there are better ways to manage competition.

Seek competitive advantage, not market share

How can companies become more profitable competitors? Unfortunately, many managers believe that the key to profitability is to achieve a dominant market share. That may be a successful strategy if only one firm attempts to pursue it. When many competitors pursue this same strategy, at which only one can succeed, they engage in negative-sum competition which actually destroys profitability for everyone (see Appendix 5A). Fortunately, there are strategies that promote positive-sum competition. Rather than attracting customers by taking less in profit, these strategies attract customers by creating more value or more operating efficiency. They involve either adding to the value of what is offered without adding as much to cost or reducing costs without equally reducing the value offered.

The success of Premier Industrial, a supplier of commodity-like small parts (for example, fasteners, sliders, tubing) used in electrical manufactur-

ing, illustrates the value-added strategy. Premier's prices are typically between 10 and 15 percent more than competitors' prices—and sometimes as
much as 200 percent higher. How does Premier do it? By targeting customers that no one else wants to bother serving. Premier's customers are
those who want to place a small order (Premier's average order is only
$150) and/or who need the product quickly (Premier stocks everything
and ships within 24 hours). In contrast, its larger competitors require a $400
or $500 *minimum* order and can take weeks to ship. Needless to say, the
cost of Premier's operation is way out of line and its growth is below industry average. Moreover, because its customers are not the dominant
market segment, it runs a distant third in market share. But its profits?
Premier's return on equity is 32.2 percent, three times the industry average,
and its return on assets is 25 percent, or four times the average.[16] Contrary
to theory, Premier in not an anomaly. The most profitable U.S. tire company, Cooper, is also relatively small. It avoids the original equipment market, a segment dominated by large, price-sensitive auto companies; it
focuses instead on the replacement market where differentiation is easier.[17]

Warehouse retail stores (Sam's, Costco, B.J.'s, and Price Club) illustrate
the opposite strategy—targeting customers who can be served at lower cost.
These stores offer no decor, limited selection, and almost no service. They are
usually less convenient to get to, and they charge an annual fee just to shop
there. This strategy discourages shoppers who are not small businesses, institutions, or large families that buy a lot on each shopping occasion. These targeted customers are willing to accept the inconvenience of warehouse
shopping because their large expenditures make any percentage savings
worthwhile. Warehouse store markups are only 8 to 10 percent, compared
with 20 to 30 percent for regular discount retailers.[18] These stores nevertheless earn big profits because their high-volume customers produce high sales
per square foot and low costs of service per dollar of sales. The cost of serving a customer who spends $500 is not much more than the cost of serving
one who spends $50 but the cost is spread over ten times as much sales.

As in these examples, the key to achieving a sustainable competitive
advantage is to *target a segment of customers* whose needs can be met more
effectively or efficiently by *focusing* on them. For some companies, the target might be the smaller customers; for others, the larger ones. The lesson
here is not that successful companies should focus on any one type of customer, but that all should focus on serving particular segments particularly
well. When competitors thrive in different segments, each develops opera-
tional advantages to serve its segments, which simultaneously create oper-
ational disadvantages to serving other segments. As a result, profitability
increases while price competition declines, even as consumers are served
better and at lower cost.

Unfortunately, most companies in competitive markets pursue neither of these strategies. They are driven by market share, which they pur-

sue by trying to be all things to all people, rather than capturing and sustaining competitive advantage in serving particular segments. Michael Porter, the Harvard competition guru, calls this "getting stuck in the middle." A firm can survive and even prosper without a focus as long as patents or unique resources protect its business from competition. But when exposed to competitors, some of whom offer higher quality or service while others offer lower costs, the firm's profitability usually gets squeezed.[19]

Select your confrontations

Perhaps the most damaging misconception that many managers hold about competition is that the ultimate winner is the one who is committed to meet every challenge. For many, the idea of choosing some confrontations while avoiding others is foreign, even cowardly. Adhering to the John Wayne model of competition, they instinctively stand their ground to defend market share, despite the adverse impact of that move on profitability. They forget that, even though John Wayne could die valiantly at the Alamo and still go on to make more movies, those who fight real-world negative-sum games are not so fortunate. The real-world competitor who insists on fighting every battle will soon become so exhausted that the company will be unable to strike when the odds are most favorable. The key to surviving a negative-sum pricing game is to fight only those battles for which the likely benefit exceeds the likely cost.

A far better model than John Wayne for dealing with negative-sum competition is Indiana Jones. Unlike John, Indiana acknowledges his vulnerability and doesn't pretend to be bigger or tougher than all competitors—just smarter. He thoughtfully manages the process of competition, choosing his battles carefully. If dominated by superior skill, strength, or numbers, he changes the nature of the confrontation to leverage his advantages. (Remember how Indiana dealt with being confronted by a larger, superior swordsman in a North African bazaar? He avoided fighting honorably on his competitor's terms. Instead, he just shot him.) If Indiana cannot dominate the competition, he runs away to fight another day when the odds are more favorable.

These guidelines are useful for businesses threatened by hostile price competitors; managers must choose their confrontations carefully and structure them to enhance their strengths. The key to surviving a negative-sum pricing game is to avoid even those confrontations that you could win, unless the likely benefit from winning exceeds the likely cost. Do not initiate price discounts unless the short-term gain is worth it *after taking account of competitors' long-term reactions.* Do not react to competitor's price discounts except with price and nonprice tactics that cost *less than accommodating the competitor's behavior would cost.* If managers in general were to follow these two simple rules, far fewer industries would be ravaged by destructive price competition.

Avoid Confrontations That Are Not Cost-effective   The battles for the long-distance telephone market illustrate the careful and judicious use of price in a market where price competition could be very destructive. For MCI, Sprint, and the other new carriers, deep discounting initially made sense for two reasons:

   1.   Having little market share to begin with, they had little to lose from undercutting industry prices.

   2.   They could reasonably predict that AT&T would not react to their price cutting as long as they remained small. Having a large market share, AT&T had a lot to lose by cutting prices to prevent customers' defections.

   AT&T prudently declined to be drawn into price competition. Instead, the company competed with advertising and service levels, meeting competitors' prices only for specific segments in which they had gained substantial market share and so had themselves become vulnerable to price competition.[20]

   Partisans of pricing to defend market share would no doubt contend that AT&T, and other market leaders who fail to defend their market share, are shortsighted. Large market share companies, they would argue, are often better capitalized and thus better able to finance a price war than are their lower-priced competitors. Although price cutting might be more costly for the larger firm in the short run, it can bankrupt smaller competitors and, in the long run, re-establish the leader's market share and its freedom to control market prices. Although such a "predatory" response to competition sounds good in theory, there are two reasons why it rarely works in practice.

   First, predatory pricing is a violation of U.S. antitrust laws if the predatory price is below the predator's variable cost. Such a pricing tactic may in some cases be a violation when the price is below the average of all costs.[21] Consequently, even if a large competitor can afford to price low enough to bankrupt its smaller competitors, it often cannot do so legally. Second, and more important, predation is cost effective only if the predator can later raise prices without attracting a new competitor who replaces the one destroyed. If the vanquished competitor's assets can be sold to new investors at bankrupt-sale prices, predation will simply change the face of the competition, not its intensity.[22]

   The vulnerability represented by a relatively large market share is not the only thing that should prevent management from retaliating against smaller, low-priced competition. Anything that puts the firm at a competitive disadvantage is a legitimate reason to avoid a fight that will cost more than it is worth. U.S. auto companies have often been criticized for not responding to low-priced Japanese competition in the 1960s and 1970s, enabling those newcomers to gain a foothold in the market. In fact, a predatory response would have been very unwise. The Japanese companies enjoyed, at that time, a substantial cost advantage in serving a price-sensitive segment. Meeting their prices would have cost Detroit huge sums that could have been better spent restructuring the U.S. firms to reduce their competitive cost disadvantage and increase their competitive technological and style advantages. Similarly, it would be foolish for convenient local drug stores to meet the prices of Wal-Mart, with its less costly distribution system. Instead, they are better off directing those funds toward reducing their own costs of distribution and increasing the value of convenient local service to their customers.[23]

Compete from Higher Ground   Of course, legitimate price responses can be structured to avoid undermining a firm's profitability or to increase the cost of price competition for the competitor. If managers can "level the playing field" or, better still, can tilt it in their favor, a price retaliation can become cost effective, even for a company with large market share or higher costs. For example, one large company faced a significant loss of share when challenged by a foreign competitor with a 30 percent lower price. Given the defender's large market share, meeting this price would have been too costly, and, since margins in this industry were high, the company also risked the possibility that the newcomer could simply cut price further to maintain its advantage. The defender in this case "tilted the field" with an imaginative price retaliation aimed at the distributors. The company offered a 5 percent price rebate on annual sales to all distributors who bought at least as much as they had in the prior year. Since selling the newcomer's product would jeopardize their rebates, distributors gained a strong incentive not to carry and promote it.

Another way to "level the playing field" is to change the venue for part of the game. Kodak, with its dominant market share in the United States, was highly vulnerable to Fuji's price-competitive entry into many segments of the U.S. film market. Meeting Fuji's price cuts in the United States would have been both prohibitively costly and probably futile considering Fuji's high margins. But in Japan, a country with a passion for cameras, it is Fuji that has the large market share and vulnerable profits. In 1986, Kodak created more leverage against Fuji by acquiring Nagase, a large Japanese film distributor. With control of distribution, Kodak gained the ability to more fully control the price of its products to Japanese end-users. Thus, when Fuji attacks in the U.S. market, Kodak can respond in the Japanese market. This same principle can be applied by moving the competition to another product category. When the French firm, Bic, introduced the cheap disposable razor that increased price competition in Gillette's traditional market, Gillette retaliated not only by introducing its own disposable razor, by also by introducing a cheap disposable pen to compete against the Bic pen. Gillette could hurt Bic much more cost effectively by retaliating in the pen market than in the razor market.

Of course, sometimes one must retaliate simply because the market share at stake is so large that the cost of not retaliating (the volume effect) exceeds the cost of lower margins (the price effect). The natural reaction, however, is often to jump to this conclusion without adequate analysis. Before cutting price, managers should calculate what the price cut will cost each period from lower margins on a given market share. Then they should consider whether there is perhaps some other way to spend that same amount of money each period—on more advertising, more sales support, promotions to the trade—that would have at least as great an impact on long-term sales. Only if the answer to that question is negative should a rational competitor resort to a price defense.

Use a Nonprice Defense That Leverages Your Strengths Although a company should neither initiate nor match price cuts when it has more to lose from lower prices than the competitor, the defender should not simply capitulate. Price is only one dimension of market competition. If the defending firm can retaliate from a position of strength using product, promotion, or distribution as a competitive weapon, it can stem a loss of market share, at least in part, without destroying industry profitability. Fortunately, for companies with large market shares, these nonprice forms of competition usually involve fixed costs, which they can spread over more volume. Consequently, the advantage gained by increasing nonprice competition can overcome, at least in part, the price advantage of smaller and lower-cost competitors.

Few firms understand the principles outlined here; however, companies that manage pricing for long-run profitability are exceptions. A notable example of a company that has done so, and that has been well rewarded for its patience, is Anheuser-Busch. Since the early 1970s, Anheuser-Busch has prospered as the largest U.S. brewer despite intense price competition from regional rivals trying to expand their markets. Anheuser-Busch managed the process intelligently from the start. In the face of discounting from Schlitz, Pabst, and others seeking a larger market share, Anheuser-Busch held its prices but tripled its advertising budget. Since its price-cutting competitors were not national brands, it would have cost them at least 30 percent more to match Anheuser-Busch's national advertising at regional rates. The company also began to segment the market more finely, increasing the numbers of its brands from three to eight within five years, thus separating more of the market from the low-end pricing fray. The company also invested heavily in reducing its incremental costs, and those of its distributors, to get itself in fighting trim should such battles become necessary. It also monitors its distributors closely to ensure that they don't slip up, precluding any need for discounting to move excess volume.

Although Anheuser-Busch eschews price competition, it certainly does not ignore it. The company manages its responses strategically. If just one brand slips in just one area, the company rolls in with extra marketing muscle. Management freely informs the market about the size of its operating margins (now three times those of its competitors) and its market-share goals. When challenged on price by Miller Brewing, its only competitor with equal advertising muscle and segmentation, the company matches the cuts quickly, but (according to public statements) reluctantly, signaling the strategists at Miller that a price war will be costly but avoidable. In this case, managing price competition with diplomacy has even paid off in market share. As Anheuser-Busch's smaller competitors bled themselves to death with self-inflicted price cuts, Anheuser-Busch's market share increased from 25 percent to over 43 percent with a corresponding growth in profits.

Anheuser-Busch's experience is, of course, exceptional. More often than not, market leaders cannot grow profitably in mature, price-competitive markets; they can at least minimize the damage. In principle, however, the appropriate strategy is the same; manage to maximize competitive advantage and the value of the market share already achieved, while avoiding and discouraging negative-sum competition. For example, SMH, the Swiss watch company, profitably established a defense against cheap digital watches by developing its Swatch line of fashion watches, while others in the same industry went upscale to develop the market for status timepieces. Giddings and Lewis recaptured profitability in the machine tool industry by abandoning its share of the price-competitive tool market and recasting itself as a supplier of large, integrated systems. Rather than wasting resources to fight losing battles, these companies used their resources to open new fronts on which they could compete from higher ground.

Summary

No other weapon in a marketer's arsenal can boost sales more quickly or effectively than price. Price discounting—whether explicit or disguised with rebates, coupons, or generous terms—is usually a sure way to enhance immediate profitability. But gaining sales with price is consistent with long-term profitability only when managed as part of a marketing strategy for achieving, exploiting, or sustaining a longer-term competitive advantage. No price cut should ever be initiated simply to make the next sale or to meet some short-term sales objective without being balanced against the likely reactions of competitors and customers. Such a balance cannot be struck on an ad hoc basis. It requires thoughtful planning, information management, and coordination with other marketing resources.

NOTES

1. Sections of this chapter were first published as an article entitled "Managing Price Competition," *Marketing Management*, 2, no. 1 (Spring 1993), 36–45.

2. For more on the practical applications of game theory, see Avinash Dixit and Barry Nalebuff, *Thinking Strategically: A Competitive Edge in Business, Politics, and Everyday Life* (New York: W.W. Norton, 1991); and Rita Koselka, "Evolutionary Economics: Nice Guys Don't Finish Last," *Fortune* (October 11, 1993), pp. 110–114. Kenichi Ohmae, "Getting Back to Strategy," *Harvard Business Review* (November/December 1988), pp. 149–156.

3. Price competition is a positive-sum game only when market demand is sufficiently stimulated by the price cuts and when a firm's costs are sufficiently reduced by a gain in market share that total industry profits can increase even as prices fall.

4. In some industries (for example, telecommunications, pharmaceuticals), an equally important determinant of market attractiveness that should be included on a separate line is "government/regulators."

5. Such a policy is usually appropriate early in the product life cycle, where there are many new customers in the market who need to be "sold" on the product's value.

6. "Shopping Clubs Ready for Battle in Texas Market," *Wall Street Journal*, October 24, 1991, p. B1.

7. Note that this principle applies in the other direction as well. If competitors quickly follow price increases, the cost of leading such increases is vastly reduced. Consequently, companies that wish to encourage responsible leadership by other firms would do well to follow their moves quickly, whether up or down.

8. See Francine Schwadel, "Ferocious Competition Tests the Pricing Skills of a Retail Manager," *Wall Street Journal*, December 11, 1989, p. 1.

9. Even before modern telecommunications, retailers used systems for quick reaction to control opportunistic price cutting. J. Sainsbury, the leading British grocery retailer, is renowned in the industry for its "cascade" telephone alert system in which each store calls five others to alert them to price changes. Within one hour, system-wide price changes can be implemented in response to competitive moves.

10. Another useful tactic that can control such duplicitous behavior in U.S. markets is to require the customer, in order to get the lower price, to initial a clause on the order form which states that the customer understands that this is "a discriminatorily low price offered solely to meet the price offered by a competitor." Since falsely soliciting a discriminatorily low price is a Robinson-Patman Act violation, the purchasing agent is discouraged from using leverage unless he or she actually has it.

11. For more guidance on collecting competitive information, see "These Guys Aren't Spooks. They're 'Competitive Analysts' ", *Business Week*, October 14, 1991, p. 97; and Leonard M. Fuld, *Competitor Intelligence: How to Get It—How to Use it* (New York: Wiley & Sons, 1985).

12. "Chrysler Mulls Cut-Rate Minivan," *USA Today*, April 26, 1990, p. 6B.

13. "Fair Game: Airlines May Be Using a Price-Data Network to Lessen Competition," *Wall Street Journal*, June 28, 1990, p. 1. Despite a U.S. Justice Department investigation into the airline industry's pricing during the late 1980s, of which this is an example, U.S. federal courts have in the past upheld a company's right to consider competitors' independent reactions in making price decisions.

14. "No Retreat, No Surrender," *Forbes*, September 15, 1980, pp. 160–61.

15. See Chapter 10 on Pricing and the Product Line for guidelines to prepare a financial analysis for related sales.

16. Dana Milbank, "Service Enables Nuts-and-Bolts Supplier to Be More Than the Sum of Its Parts," *Wall Street Journal*, November 16, 1990, pp. B1, B9.

17. "Cooper Tire & Rubber: Now Hear This, Jack Welch," *Fortune*, 125, (no. 7) (April 6, 1992), 94–95.

18. "Bargains by the Forklift," *Business Week*, July 15, 1991, p. 152.

19. Michael E. Porter, *Competitive Strategy* (New York: The Free Press, 1980), pp. 41–43. A firm can become large without getting "stuck in the middle" simply by taking on multiple segments. The segments must be managed, however, as a conglomerate of focused businesses rather than as a one-size-fits-all marketing organization. Procter & Gamble is an excellent example of a large company that nevertheless carefully targets each product to meet the needs of a particular focused segment.

20. AT&T did eventually cut its prices across the board on long-distance service in response to a regulatory requirement that it do so to reduce its profitability.

21. See discussion on predatory pricing in Chapter 14.

22. Even where legal, a predatory pricing strategy can pay in the long run in only two cases: when eliminating a competitor destroys an important differentiating asset (for example, its accumulated goodwill with customers), or when it enables the predator to gain such a cost advantage (for example, economies of experience or scale) that it can profitably keep its prices low enough to discourage new entrants.

23. Limited retaliation against a lower-cost competitor can be effective if the competitor has a viable market share and has lowered prices by *more* than its incremental cost advantage. In such a case, the value of each sale to the retaliating company becomes greater than the value of it to the lower-cost competitor, despite its cost advantage.

Appendix 5A
Market-share myth

A common myth among marketers is that market share is the key to profitability. If that were true, of course, recent history would have shown General Motors to be the world's most profitable automobile company; Sears Roebuck, the most profitable retailer; and Philips, the most profitable manufacturer of electrical products ranging from light bulbs to color televisions. In fact, all of these companies, while sales leaders, are financial alsorans. The source of this myth, these examples notwithstanding, is a demonstrable correlation between market share and profitability. As any student of statistics should know, however, correlation does not necessarily imply a causal relationship.

A far more plausible explanation for the correlation is that both profitability and market share are caused by the same underlying source of business success: a sustainable competitive advantage in meeting customer needs more effectively or in doing so more efficiently. When a company has a competitive advantage, it can earn higher margins due either to a price premium or a lower cost of production. That advantage, if sustainable, also discourages competitors from targeting the company's customers or from effectively resisting its attempts to expand. Consequently, although a less fortunate company would face equally efficient competitors who could take market shares with margin-destroying price competition, a company with a competitive advantage can sustain higher market share even as it earns higher profits. Market share, rather than being the key to profitability, is, like profitability, simply another symptom of a fundamentally well-run company.

Unfortunately, when management misperceives the symptom (insufficient market share) as a cause and seeks it by some inappropriate means, such as price cutting, the expected profitability doesn't materialize. On the contrary, a grab for market share unjustified by an underlying competitive advantage can often reduce the company's own and its industry's profitability. The ultimate objective of any strategic plan should not be to achieve or even sustain sales volume, but to build and sustain competitive advantage. Profitability and, in many cases, market share, will follow. In fact, contrary to the myth that a higher market share causes higher profitability, changes in profitability usually *precede* changes in market share, not the other way around. For example, Wal-Mart's competitive advantages made it the most profitable retailer in the United States long before it became the largest, whereas Sears' poor profitability preceded by many years its loss of the dominant market share. This pattern of profitability leading, not following, market share is currently visible in the automobile, steel, and banking industries.

A strategic plan based on building volume, rather than on creating a competitive advantage, is essentially a beggar-thy-neighbor strategy—a negative-sum game that ultimately can only undermine industry profitability. Every point of market share won by reducing margins (either by offering a lower price or by incurring higher costs) invariably reduces the value of the sales gained. Since competitors can effectively retaliate, they probably will, at least partially eliminating any gain in sales while reducing the value of a sale even further.[1] The only sustainable way to increase relative profitability is by achieving a competitive advantage that will enable you to increase sales *and* margins. In short, the goal of a strategic plan should not be to become bigger than the competition (although that may happen), but to become *better*. Such positive-sum competition, rather than undermining the profitability of an industry, constantly renews it.[2]

NOTES

1. This elimination of profitability is viewed as good in the classical economic model of "perfect competition." Unfortunately, this is a model of stagnant technology, no growth, and unchanging consumer desires. The dynamism of capitalism benefits consumers in the real world by creating better technology, rapid growth, and new ways to satisfy consumer needs. For the classic description of such dynamic capitalism, see Frederick Hayek, "The Meaning of Competition," *Individualism and Economic Order* (Chicago: University of Chicago Press, 1980), pp. 92–106.
2. For evidence that there are profit leaders in the bottom and middle ranges of market share almost as frequently as in the top range, see William L. Shanklin, "Market Share Is Not Destiny," *Journal of Business & Industrial Marketing*, 4 (Winter–Spring 1989), 5–16.

STRATEGY

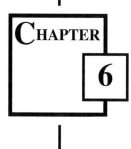

CHAPTER

6

INTEGRATING THE ELEMENTS OF PROFITABLE PRICING

Effective marketing is never limited to pricing alone. However, if long-term profitability is the goal, then the pricing decision provides the unifying focus and rationale for all of the firm's other marketing decisions. In Chapter 1, we saw how managers often make reactive price changes to deal with short-term problems. Effective pricing requires a *proactive* marketing strategy to enhance the firm's relative competitive position and improve its return on investment. The purpose of this chapter is to integrate the principles of cost management, customer behavior, and competition into a more proactive, strategic approach to pricing. We will continue to develop these interrelationships in the next four chapters, showing how market segmentation, negotiation, life-cycle management, and the other elements of product management can support more profitable pricing.

A FRAMEWORK FOR PRICING

Successful pricing is not an end result, but a continual process. The next several pages contain a general framework that managers can use both to set prices for new products and to adapt established prices to changing market conditions. Exhibit 6.1 illustrates the steps of this process, from top to bottom, in chronological order. The first row involves data collection; the second involves analysis of the data; and the third involves integration of that analysis into optimal strategic decisions. The balance of this chapter describes each of these steps and their implementation.

EXHIBIT 6.1

Steps to More Profitable Pricing

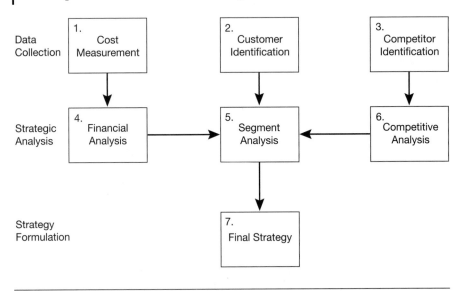

Data collection

Frequently, pricing strategies do not succeed because they fail to reflect all of the key elements. Marketers who are ignorant of costs make pricing decisions that maximize market share rather than profitability. Financial managers who are ignorant of customer value and purchase motivations make pricing decisions that undermine opportunities to spread fixed costs. Marketers and financial managers who fail to collect enough information about the personalities and capabilities of competitors make short-run decisions that look good only until competitors react to them in unanticipated ways. Good pricing decisions require information about all three factors—costs, customers, and competitors—that determine the success of a pricing strategy. Consequently, any pricing analysis should begin with the following:

1. Cost measurement: What are the incremental, avoidable costs relevant to this particular pricing decision?

■   What is the incremental (not average) variable cost of sales, including manufacturing, customer service, and technical support?

- At what levels of output will additional expenditures on semi-fixed costs be required, and how much will they be?
- What are the avoidable (not yet sunk) fixed costs involved to offer this product at the proposed price?

2. Customer identification: Who are the potential customers, and why would they buy this product?

- What is the economic value of this product or service to customers?
- What other factors (such as difficulty in comparing alternatives, prestige associated with the purchase, budget constraints, the ability to shift all or part of the cost to someone else) influence the customers' sensitivity to price?
- How do differences in both perceived value and nonvalue factors influencing price sensitivity divide customers into market segments?
- How could an effective marketing and positioning strategy influence the customers' willingness to pay?

3. Competitor identification: Who are the current and potential competitors whose behavior may constrain the profitability in this market?

- Who are the key current and potential competitors?
- If competitors are currently in this market, what actual transaction prices (as opposed to list prices) do they charge?
- Given competitors' past behavior, personalities, and organizational structures, what is their goal in pricing? Do they seek to maximize profitability or sales?
- What are competitors' strengths and weaknesses relative to the firm? Do they have higher or lower contribution margins, better or poorer reputations, superior or inferior products, more or less diversified product lines?

These three steps in the data-collection phase should be accomplished independently of one another. For example, if the individuals collecting customer information (step 2) believe that incremental costs are low relative to value (step 1), they will be inclined to estimate economic value more conservatively. If those estimating costs (step 1) believe that customer value is high (step 2), they may be inclined to shift more costs to the product. If those collecting competitive information (step 3) know which products customers currently prefer (step 2), they may dismiss the competitive threat represented by a superior new technology that has not yet been widely accepted.

Strategic analyses

The analysis stage, like the data-collection process, involves costs, customers, and competition. At this point, however, the information becomes interrelated. Financial analysis is driven by price, product, and market selection proposals intended to better meet customer needs or to gain competitive advantage. The firm chooses to target customer segments based, in part, on an analysis of the incremental cost of serving them or of the firm's ability to serve them more efficiently and at less cost than competitors can. Competitor analysis is driven partly by the desire to anticipate competitive reactions to specific proposed price changes designed to penetrate customer segments. Integrating the information into a coherent strategy requires the next three steps.

4. *Financial analysis:* What volume trade-offs are necessary for potential price, product, or promotional changes to increase profits? For new products or new markets, what sales volume is required to justify the incremental fixed expenditures?

- What is the contribution margin for the product at the initial baseline price?
- How much additional sales volume is required to make a lower price generate more contribution?
- What is the maximum tolerable loss of sales before a higher price fails to generate more contribution?
- How much additional sales volume is necessary to cover any incremental fixed costs (such as advertising, regulatory approvals) associated with the decision?
- What sales level is necessary to justify selling a new product or moving an established product into a new market, given the incremental fixed costs associated with that sales level?

5. *Segmentation analysis and implementation:* How can the firm price differently to customer segments to reflect differences (a) in price sensitivity and (b) in the incremental cost of serving them? How can the firm most effectively communicate value to these customer segments, given their different purchase motivations?

- How can members of different segments be identified prior to purchase?
- How can "fences" between segments be established so that low-price sales do not undermine value in high-price markets?
- How can the firm avoid violating legal constraints on price segmentations?

6. Competitive analysis: How might competitors react to the firm's proposed pricing moves, and what moves are they likely to initiate? How will competitors' actions and reactions affect the profitability and long-term viability of the firm's proposed strategy?

- ■ What goals can the firm profitably achieve, given its competitors' capabilities and intentions?
- ■ How might the firm use information to influence its competitors' behavior in ways that would make its goals more achievable or profitable?
- ■ How can the firm insulate its profitability from competitive threats by targeting segments where it can achieve a competitive advantage?
- ■ From what markets should the firm strategically withdraw resources when it cannot profit from the inevitable competitive confrontations?

7. Strategy formulation: The end result of the financial analysis phase is a price-value strategy, a plan for conducting future business. As this book has already illustrated, no one "right" strategy exists for every situation. Some of the worst strategic mistakes have been made by managers who tried to superimpose strategies that work in one industry onto another industry with entirely different cost, customer, or competitive conditions. To be effective, the process of strategy formulation should begin with these three elements in order to formulate a price-value strategy that optimally balances them.

The purpose of the schematic illustrated in Exhibit 6.1 is not necessarily to formalize decisions, although formalizing the process is advisable in large companies where different people possess the relevant information about costs, customers, and competition. Only a formalized decision-making process can ensure management of large companies that all information is incorporated into the pricing decision. In small companies, however, this procedure is often successfully implemented informally. To succeed, whoever manages the process must simply understand what he or she is trying to achieve and what information and analyses are necessary to reach a successful conclusion. The following example illustrates how one company used the pricing process informally to make more profitable decisions.

An illustration

Ritter & Sons is a wholesale producer of potted plants and cut flowers.[1] Ritter's most popular product is potted chrysanthemums (mums), which are particularly in demand around certain holidays, especially

Mother's Day, Easter, and Memorial Day, but maintain a high level of sales throughout the year. Exhibit 6.2 shows Ritter's revenues, costs, and sales from mums for a recent fiscal year. After attending a seminar on pricing, the company's chief financial officer, Don Ritter, began to wonder whether this product might somehow be priced more profitably. A serious examination of the effect of raising and lowering the wholesale price of mums from the current price of $3.85 per unit was then begun.

Don's first step was to identify the relevant cost and contribution margin for mums. Looking only at the data in Exhibit 6.2, Don was somewhat uncertain how to proceed. He reasoned that the costs of the cuttings, shipping, packaging, and pottery were clearly incremental and avoidable and that the cost of administrative overhead was fixed. He was far less certain about labor and the capital cost of the greenhouses. Some of Ritter's work force consisted of long-time employees whose knowledge of planting techniques was highly valuable. It would not be practical to lay them off, even if they were not needed during certain seasons. Most production employees, however, were transient laborers who were hired during peak seasons and who found work elsewhere when less labor was required.

After consulting with the production manager for potted plants, Don concluded that about $7,000 of the labor cost of mums was fixed. The re-

---

Exhibit 6.2

Cost Projection for Proposed Crop of Mums

Crop: 6" Mums Preparer: DR	Total	Per Unit
Unit sales	$ 86,250	1
Revenue	$332,063	$3.85
Cost of cuttings	34,500	0.40
Gross Margin	297,563	3.45
Labor	51,850	0.60
Shipping	26,563	0.31
Pkg. foil	9,056	0.10
Pkg. sleeve	4,312	0.05
Pkg. carton	4,399	0.05
Pottery	14,663	0.17
Capital cost allocation	66,686	0.77
Overhead allocation	73,320	0.85
Operating profit	$ 46,714	$ 0.54

maining $44,850 (or $0.52 per unit) was variable and thus relevant to the pricing decision.

Don also wondered how he should treat the capital cost of the greenhouses. He was sure that Ritter's policy of allocating the capital cost (interest and depreciation) equally to every plant sold was not correct. However, when Don suggested to his brother Paul, the company's president, that since these costs were sunk, they should be entirely ignored in pricing, Paul found the suggestion unsettling. He pointed out that Ritter used all of its greenhouse capacity in the peak season, that it had expanded its capacity in recent years, and that it planned further expansions in the coming year. Unless the price of mums reflected the capital cost of building additional greenhouses, how could Ritter justify such investments?

That argument made sense to Don. Surely the cost of greenhouses is incremental if they are all in use, since additional capacity would then have to be built if Ritter were to sell more mums. But that same cost is clearly not incremental during seasons when there is excess capacity. Ritter's policy of making all mums grown in a year bear a $0.77 capital cost was simply misleading. Additional mums could be grown without bearing any additional capital cost during seasons with excess capacity. Mums grown in peak seasons, however, actually cost much more than Ritter had been assuming, since those mums require the capital additions. Thus, if the annual cost of an additional greenhouse (depreciation, interest, maintenance, heating) is $9,000, and if the greenhouse will hold 5,000 mums for three crops each year, the capital cost per mum would be $0.60 ($9,000/[3 × 5,000]) only if all greenhouses are fully utilized throughout the year. Since the greenhouses are filled to capacity for only one crop per year, the relevant capital cost for pricing that crop is $1.80 per mum ($9,000/5,000), while it is zero for pricing crops at other times.[2]

As a result of his discussions, Don calculated two costs for mums: one to apply when there is excess capacity in the greenhouses and one to apply when greenhouse capacity is fully utilized. His calculations are shown in Exhibit 6.3. These two alternatives do not exhaust the possibilities. For any product, different combinations of costs can be fixed or incremental in different situations. For example, if Ritter found itself with excess mums after they were grown, potted, and ready to sell, the only incremental cost would be the cost of shipping. If Ritter found itself with too little capacity and too little time to make additions before the next peak season, the only way to grow more mums would be to grow fewer types of other flowers. In that case, the cost of greenhouse space for mums would be the opportunity cost (measured by the lost contribution) from not growing and selling those other flowers. The relevant cost for a pricing decision depends on the circumstances. Therefore, one must begin each pricing problem by first determining the relevant cost for that particular decision.

For Ritter, the decision at hand involved planning production quantities and prices for the forthcoming year. There would be three crops of

---

Exhibit 6.3

Relevant Cost of Mums

	With Excess Capacity	At Full Capacity
Price	$ 3.85	$ 3.85
– Cost of cuttings	0.40	0.40
– Incremental labor	0.52	0.52
– Other direct costs	0.68	0.68
= Dollar contribution margin	$ 2.25	$ 2.25
– Incremental capital cost	0	1.80
= Profit contribution	$ 2.25	$ 0.45

---

mums during the year, two during seasons when Ritter would have excess growing capacity and one during the peak season, when capacity would be a constraint. The relevant contribution margin would be $2.25, or 58.5 percent ($2.25/3.85), for all plants. In the peak season, however, the net profit contribution would be considerably less because of the incremental capital cost of the greenhouses.

Don recognized immediately that there was a problem with Ritter's pricing of mums. Since the company had traditionally used cost-plus pricing based on fully allocated average cost, fixed costs were allocated equally to all plants. Consequently, Ritter charged the same price ($3.85) for mums throughout the year. But although mums grown in the off-peak season used the same amount of greenhouse space as those grown during the peak season, the relevant incremental cost of that space was not always the same. Consequently, the profit contribution for mums sold in an off-peak season was much greater than for those sold in the peak season. This difference was not reflected in Ritter's pricing.

Don suspected that Ritter should be charging lower prices during seasons when the contribution margin was large and higher prices when it was small. Using his new understanding of the relevant cost, Don calculated the break-even sales quantities for a 5 percent price cut during the off-peak season, when excess capacity makes capital costs irrelevant, and for a 10 percent price increase during the peak season, when capital costs are incremental to the pricing decision. These calculations are shown in Exhibit 6.4.

Don first calculated the percent break-even quantity for the off-peak season, indicating that Ritter would need at least a 9.3 percent sales in-

---

EXHIBIT 6.4

Breakeven Sales Changes for Proposed Price Changes

5% Off-Peak Season Price Cut

Breakeven sales change $\quad = \dfrac{-(-5.0)}{58.5 - 5.0} = +9.3\%$

10% Peak Season Price Increase

Breakeven sales change $\quad = \dfrac{-10.0}{58.5 + 10.0} = -14.6\%$

Breakeven sales with incremental fixed costs[a] $\quad = -14.6\% + \dfrac{-\$9,000}{\$2.635 \times 45,000}$

$$= -22.2\%$$

[a]The new dollar contribution margin is $2.635 after the 10% price increase. (See Chapter 3 for further explanation of these equations.)

---

crease to justify a 5 percent price cut in the off-peak season. Then he calculated the basic breakeven percentage for a 10 percent price increase during the peak season. If sales declined by less than 14.6 percent as a result of the price increase (equal to 6,570 units given Ritter's expected peak season sales of 45,000 mums), the price increase would be profitable. Don also recognized, however, that if sales declined that much, Ritter could avoid constructing at least one new greenhouse. That capital cost savings could make the price increase profitable even if sales declined by more than the basic breakeven quantity. Assuming that one greenhouse involving a cost of $9,000 per year could be avoided, the break-even decline rises to 22.2 percent (equal to 9,990 units). If a 10 percent price increase caused Ritter to lose less than 22.2 percent of its projected sales for the next peak season, the increase would be profitable.

Judging whether actual sales changes were likely to be greater or smaller than those quantities was beyond Don's expertise. Consequently, he presented his findings to Sue James, Ritter's sales manager. Sue felt certain that sales during the peak season would not decline by 22.2 percent following a 10 percent price increase. She pointed out that the ultimate purchasers in the peak season usually bought the plant as a gift. Consequently, they were much more sensitive to quality than to price (the unique value and price-quality effects). Fortunately, most of Ritter's major competitors could not match Ritter's quality since they had to ship their plants from more distant greenhouses. Ritter's local competition, like Ritter, would not have the capacity to serve more customers during the peak season. The high-quality florists who comprised most of Ritter's customers were, therefore, unlikely to switch suppliers in response to a 10 percent peak-period price increase.

Sue also felt that retailers who currently bought mums from Ritter in the off-peak season could probably not sell in excess of 9.3 percent more, even if they cut their retail prices by the same 5 percent that Ritter contemplated cutting the wholesale price. Thus, the price cut would be profitable only if some retailers who normally bought mums from competitors were to switch and buy from Ritter. This possibility would depend on whether competitors chose to defend their market shares by matching Ritter's price cut. If they did, Ritter would probably gain no more retail accounts. If they did not, Ritter might capture sales to one or more grocery chains whose price-sensitive customers and whose large expenditures on flowers make them diligent in their search for the best price.

Don and Sue needed to identify their competitors and ask, "How does their pricing influence our sales, and how are they likely to respond to any price changes we initiate?" They spent the next two weeks talking with customers and with Ritter employees who had worked for competitors, trying to formulate answers. They learned that they faced two essentially different types of competition. First, they competed with one other large local grower, Mathews Nursery, whose costs are similar to Ritter's. Because Mathews' sales area generally overlapped Ritter's, Mathews would probably be forced to meet any Ritter price cuts. Most of the competition for the largest accounts, however, came from high-volume suppliers that shipped plants into Ritter's sales area as well as into other areas. It would be difficult for them to cut their prices only where they competed with Ritter. Moreover, they already operated on smaller margins because of their higher shipping costs. Consequently, they probably would not match a 5 percent price cut.

Still, Sue thought that even the business of one or two large buyers might not be enough to increase Ritter's total sales in the off-peak season by more than the breakeven quantity. Don recognized that the greater price sensitivity of large buyers might represent an opportunity for segmented pricing. If Ritter could cut prices to the large buyers only, the price cut would be profitable if the percentage increase in sales to that market segment alone exceeded the breakeven increase. Perhaps Ritter could offer a 5 percent quantity discount for which only the large, price-sensitive buyers could qualify.[3] Alternatively, Ritter might sort its mums into "florist quality" and "standard quality," if it could assume that its florists would generally be willing to pay a 5 percent premium to offer the best product to their clientel.

Don decided to make a presentation to the other members of Ritter's management committee, setting out the case for increasing price by 10 percent for the peak season and for reducing price to large buyers by 5 percent for the two off-peak seasons. To illustrate the potential effects of the proposed changes, he calculated the change in Ritter's profits for various possible changes in sales. To illustrate the profit impact for a wide range of sales changes, he presented the results of his calculations graphically. The graph he used to illustrate the effect of a 10 percent price increase at various changes in sales volume is reproduced in Exhibit 6.5. After Don's presentation, Sue James explained why she believed that sales would decline by less than the breakeven quantity if price were raised in the peak season. She also felt sales might increase more than the breakeven percent if price were lowered in the off-peak seasons, especially if the cut could be limited to large buyers.

EXHIBIT 6.5

Profit Impact of a 10 Percent Increase

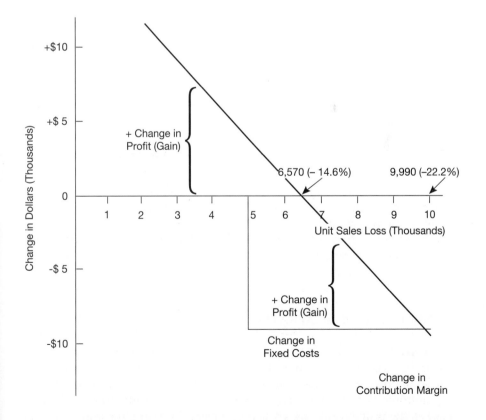

Since Ritter has traditionally set prices based on a full allocation of costs, some managers were initially skeptical of this new approach. They asked probing questions, which Don and Sue's analysis of the market enabled them to answer. The management committee recognized that the decision was not clear-cut. It would ultimately rest on uncertain judgments about sales changes that the proposed price changes would precipitate. If Ritter's regular customers proved to be more price-sensitive than Don and Sue now believed, the proposed 10 percent price increase for the peak season could cause sales to decline by more than the breakeven quantity. If competitors all matched Ritter's 5 percent price cut for large buyers in the off-peak season, sales might not increase by as much as the break-even quantity.

The committee accepted the proposed price changes. In related decisions, they postponed construction of one new greenhouse and established a two-quality approach to pricing mums based on selecting the best for "florist quality" and selling the lower-priced "standard quality" only in lots of 1,000 mums. Finally, they agreed that Don should give a speech at an industry trade show on how this pricing approach can improve capital utilization and efficiency. In the speech, he would reveal Ritter's decision to raise its price in the peak season. (Perhaps the management of Mathews might decide to take such information into account in independently formulating its own pricing decisions.) He would also let it be known that, if Ritter is unable to sell more mums to large local buyers in the off-peak season, it would consider offering the mums at discount prices to florists outside of its local market. This plan, it was hoped, would discourage nonlocal competitors from fighting for local market share, lest the price cutting spread to markets they found more lucrative.

At this point, there was no way to know if these decisions would prove profitable. Management could have requested more formal research into customer motivations or a more detailed analysis of nonlocal competitors' past responses to price cutting. Since past behavior is never a perfect guide to the future, the decision would still have required weighing the risks involved with the benefits promised. Still, Don's analysis ensured that management identified the relevant information for this decision and weighed it appropriately.

GENERIC PRICING STRATEGIES

Before setting a price, a firm must identify the role that price will play in the product's overall marketing strategy. Will price serve to restrict the firm's market to an exclusive segment of buyers, as it does for Nordstrom (retailing), Johnnie Walker Black Label (Scotch), and Peterbilt (trucks)? Will it serve as the primary tool for attracting buyers, as it does for Wal-Mart (retailing), Timex (watches), and Dell (personal computers)? Or will it serve a neutral function, secondary to other aspects of marketing, as it does for JCPenney (retailing) and Buick (automobiles)? There are three generic pricing strategies that a firm might adopt: skim pricing, penetration pricing, and neutral pricing.[4] Each strategy is defined by the role pricing plays in the product's marketing strategy.

Exhibit 6.6 illustrates the relationship between price and economic value as perceived by the "middle market" that constitutes the bulk of potential customers in most product categories.[5] *Skim pricing* involves setting price high relative to the economic value of most potential customers in order to profit from the relative price insensitivity of a small segment. *Penetration pricing* involves setting price low relative to economic value in order to gain from high market share or volume. Note that because we are defining "high" and "low" *relative to value*, a skim price is not necessarily higher, nor is a penetration price necessarily lower, than other prices in the market. For example, Hartmann® and Louis Vuitton® both charge prices at the upper end of the luggage market. Louis Vuitton uses a typical skim

---

EXHIBIT 6.6

Relationship Between Price and Economic Value in Strategy Selection

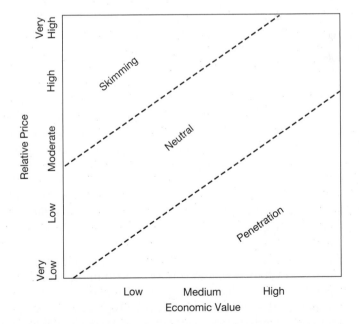

strategy, positioning its luggage as "art" for the discriminating traveler, happy to pay for the prestige and exclusivity that its price, name, and distinctive styling evoke. Its position is *not* that it offers a good value to everyone, but rather that it offers something special for those who can afford it. Hartmann, in contrast, positions its high-priced luggage as an "investment" that justifies its price by extra durability and features. Although Hartmann charges prices comparable to Louis Vuitton, its *neutral strategy* appeals to the buyer looking for a good value, rather than to those for whom value is not the issue.

Although different price-value strategies often coexist in the same market, selection of a strategy is not arbitrary. A firm's cost structure, its customer motivations, and its competitive position will favor one strategy over others in each case. The following section describes the conditions under which each strategy is appropriate. In some industries, particularly those with high fixed costs, profitable growth requires pursuing multiple strategies simultaneously. Consequently, after describing the generic strategies, we will explain the hybrid strategy of segmented pricing.

Skim pricing

Skim pricing (or skimming) is designed to capture high margins at the expense of high sales volume. By definition, skim prices are high in relation to what most buyers are willing to pay. Consequently, this strategy is viable only when the profit from selling to a price-insensitive segment exceeds that from selling to the larger market at a lower price.

Customers   Buyers are often price insensitive because they belong to a market segment that places exceptionally high value on a product's differentiating attributes. Polaroid's ability to give users of its cameras and film instant gratification is worth something to nearly everyone. If Polaroid followed a neutral strategy of pricing its film so that the cost per picture equaled the cost of competitor's film and processing, it would capture most of the market. Instead, Polaroid recognizes that there are some users (real estate agents, insurance claims adjusters, grandparents with lots of discretionary income) who place extremely high value on seeing their pictures immediately. Because these buyers willingly pay more than twice as much for Polaroid film than for regular film and processing, Polaroid can maximize its profits by charging high prices, even though such pricing severely limits its market penetration.

Although unique product attributes can support skim pricing, other factors (discussed in Chapter 4) can support a skimming strategy as well. When an expenditure is small, some buyers purchase on "impulse" without even considering the alternatives. Buyers who travel on business and bill the travel cost to others are another good target for skim pricing.

Restaurants, rental car companies, and hotels often skim price their products when they focus on that market segment. Similarly, the importance attached to the end-benefit blinds proud parents when planning weddings for their children. Photographers, caterers, and florists all profit handsomely from skim pricing to this segment. Buyers who value prestige and exclusivity will pay more simply because they know that others can't buy the product. Stueben Glass increased its cachet and profitability when it reduced the number of retail outlets to one per region and increased its prices.

Costs In addition to a price-insensitive customer segment, successful skim pricing also favors a particular cost environment. When incremental unit costs (variable and incremental "fixed" costs) represent a large share of a product's price, even a small price premium will generate a large percentage increase in the contribution margin. Moreover, since variable costs decline with sales volume, any sales volume lost due to skimming reduces costs substantially. If variable costs are 90 percent of a product's price (yielding a 10 percent contribution margin), a skimming strategy to increase prices by 15 percent would make a product more profitable so long as the firm lost no more than 60 percent of its sales volume!

Marketers often assume that skim pricing is impractical when production economies are large. This is not necessarily the case. If only 15 percent of a market is price insensitive, but many other firms are competing to serve the other 85 percent, the firm that targets the small niche market could become as large, and probably much more profitable, than the largest competitor focusing on the mass market.

Competition Finally, the competitive environment must be right for skimming. A firm must have some source of competitive protection to ensure long-term profitability by precluding competitors from providing lower-priced alternatives. Patents or copyrights are one source of protection against competitive threats. The patent protection that Polaroid enjoys has permitted them to use a skim pricing strategy for instant photography without fear of competition for almost half a century. Other forms of protection include a brand's reputation for quality, access to a scarce resource, preemption of the best distribution channel, and image.[6]

A skim price should not necessarily be avoided even when a firm lacks the ability to prevent competition in the future. When a firm introduces a new product with a high price relative to its manufacturing cost, competitors will be attracted even if the product is priced low relative to its economic value. Pricing low in the face of competition makes sense only when it serves either to establish a competitive advantage or to sustain one that already exists. If it cannot do either, the best rule for pricing is not to worry about the future, but to earn what you can while you can. When competitors enter, duplicating the product's differentiating attributes and thus undermining its economic value, the firm can then choose to reevaluate its strategy.

Sequential Skimming   With some type of competitive protection, a firm selling a repeat-purchase product can maintain a skim price indefinitely. If, however, the product is either (1) a long-lived durable good such as a camera or (2) a product that most buyers would purchase only once, such as a ticket to a stage play, the market can be skimmed for only a limited time at each price. Skimming, in such cases, cannot be maintained indefinitely, but its dynamic variant, *sequential skimming*, may remain profitable for some time.

Sequential skimming, like the more sustainable variety, begins with a price that attracts the least price-sensitive buyers first. After the firm has "skimmed the cream" of buyers, however, that market is gone. Consequently, to maintain its sales, the firm lowers its price enough to sell to the next most lucrative segment. The firm continues this process until it has exhausted all opportunities for skimming, either because it has cut price low enough to attract even the most price-sensitive buyers or because it could not profitably lower the price further.

In theory, a firm could sequentially skim the market for a durable good or a one-time purchase by lowering its price in hundreds of small steps, thus charging every segment the maximum it would pay for the product. In practice, however, potential buyers catch on rather quickly and begin delaying their purchases, anticipating further price reductions. To minimize this problem, the firm can cut price less frequently, thus forcing potential buyers to bear a significant cost of waiting. It can also launch less attractive models as it cuts the price. This is the strategy Polaroid followed, introducing ever-cheaper models of its automatic-developing camera, to bring ever larger segments into the market (see Exhibit 6.7). It is also the strategy that theater companies follow when they perform first in each major city at a high price and return later to perform again at a lower price. Auto dealers can also sequentially cut price on end-of-season models because buyers know that if they wait to purchase at a lower price, the choice of colors and options will be diminished.

Sequential skimming is not always appropriate for durable goods. Often the profit from selling exclusively to price-insensitive buyers is greater than the profit from selling to everyone. Such is the case for products that have added value for some segment because of their limited availability (see the discussion in Chapter 4 concerning the price-quality effect). Much of the value that buyers place on collectors' items (commemorative coins, lithographs, porcelain figurines) stems from the expectation that they will remain rare. To maintain price premiums, sellers often number their products and pledge to produce no more than a certain quantity.

EXHIBIT 6.7

Sequential Skim-Pricing a Patented Product (Polaroid Amateur Cameras)

		Price	
Dates of Sales	Lowest-Priced Model	In Current Dollars	In 1975 Dollars[a]
Black and White Cameras			
1948–1953	Model 95	$ 89.75	$200
1954–1957	Model 95A	89.75	181
1957–1959	Model 80A	72.75	139
1959–1961	Model 80B	72.75	133
1961–1963	Model J33	74.95	134
1965–1970	Model 20	19.95	35
1974–1977	Zip Land	13.95	15
Color Cameras			
1963–1966	Model 100	$164.95	$290
1964–1967	Model 101	134.95	234
1965–1967	Model 104	59.95	103
1969–1972	Color Pack II	29.95	44
1971–1973	Big Shot Portrait[b]	19.95	26
1975–1977	Super Shooter	25.00	25

[a]Current dollars converted to 1975 dollars using Consumer Price Index.

[b]Fixed-focus portrait camera that took only flash pictures at a fixed distance (approximately 39 inches from subject).

Source: *The First Thirty Years, 1948–78: A Chronology of Polaroid Photographic Products* (Cambridge, Mass.: Polaroid Corporation, 1979).

Sometimes, sequential skimming is a good strategy for introducing even nondurable, repeat-purchased products. A firm gains in two ways by only gradually lowering price to expand into new markets. First, if the product has a variety of potential uses, all of which require substantial effort from the seller in technical research and marketing, the company may more efficiently introduce the product by focusing all of its efforts on one use at a time. In fact, it may actually capture the most lucrative markets more quickly than if it spread its resources more thinly. Even if the product's initial growth is slowed, the firm may still benefit in the long run.

Second, sequential skimming enables the firm to build production capacity more gradually. As it expands capacity, it can build new production facilities to incorporate the learning that resulted from production of earlier built facilities and can finance the new facilities with the cash flow that the product is already generating. Moreover, because the firm initially built less capacity, it bears less risk that demand will not be as great as expected. Having begun with a skim price, the firm can easily minimize the effect of overly optimistic forecasts by scaling back its intended expansion and increasing the rate of its price reductions.

Penetration pricing

Penetration pricing involves setting a price far enough below economic value to attract and hold a large base of customers. It is a strategy designed to generate sales volume even at the expense of high margins and, like skim pricing, is favored by a particular environment. Penetration prices are not necessarily cheap, but are low relative to value. Lexus, for example, quickly penetrated the luxury car market, and induced many near-luxury buyers to trade up, because buyers perceived it as representing an exceptionally good value despite being a high-priced car.

Customers   First and foremost, a large share of the market must be willing to change suppliers in response to a price differential. A common misconception is that every market will respond to a price differential, which is why unsuccessful penetration pricing schemes are so common. Low prices will attract few buyers of prestige or exclusive products and can, in fact, undermine the prestige value of their brand names. When Lacoste allowed its "alligator" shirts to be discounted by lower-priced mass merchants, high-image retailers refused to carry the product and consumers migrated to more exclusive brands. Penetration pricing will attract few buyers to products for which the price is a trivial expenditure (chewing gum) or to products for which value is difficult to compare across suppliers (medical care). Penetration prices will not attract buyers whose strong and diverse preferences cause them to value the differentiating attributes of competing brands by more than the price differential.

Of course, not all buyers need be price sensitive for penetration pricing to succeed, but enough of the market must be adequately price sensitive to justify pricing low to capture its patronage. Warehouse clubs (Sam's, Costco, B.J.'s) use penetration pricing successfully to target only buyers willing to purchase in large quantities. Red Roof Inns targets travelers who don't need hotel amenities, such as a pool or lounge, but who just want a good night's sleep in a clean room. Discount clothing stores (Marshalls, T. J. Maxx, Filene's Basement) target those price-sensitive customers willing to shop frequently through limited and rapidly changing stocks to find a bargain. Some wholesalers of sheet steel use penetration prices to attract the high-volume buyers, who require no selling or service and who buy truckload quantities.

Costs   To determine how much volume one must gain to justify penetration pricing, a manager must also consider the cost environment. Costs are more favorable for penetration pricing when incremental costs (variable and incremental fixed) represent a small share of the price, so that each additional sale provides a large contribution to profit. Moreover, because the contribution per sale is already high, a lower price does not represent a large cut in the contribution from each sale. For example, even if a company had to cut its prices 20 percent to attract a large segment of buyers, penetration pricing could still be profitable if the product has a high contribution margin. In order for the strategy to pay with a 90 percent contribution margin, the sales gain would need only exceed 29 percent. The lower the contribution per sale, the larger the sales gain required before penetration pricing is profitable.

Penetration pricing can succeed without a high contribution margin if the strategy creates sufficient variable cost economies, enabling the seller to offer penetration prices without suffering lower margins. The price-sensitivity of their target customers enables warehouse clubs to vary the brands they offer depending upon who gives them the best deal, thus increasing their leverage with suppliers. The penetration prices of warehouse clubs enable them to maintain such high turnover, high sales per square foot, and high sales per employee, that they can in many markets undercut full-service retailers while still earning equal or better profits per sale.

Penetration pricing is often a viable strategy for manufacturers as well. As personal computer users have become more knowledgeable buyers, manufacturers like Dell and Gateway leveraged the economies of mail-order distribution to sell high-quality products using penetration pricing. Competitors who distributed through retail stores could not match their prices, so knowledgeable buyers flocked to them. The problem they now face, however, is how to keep a competitive advantage when competitors, like IBM and Compaq, duplicate their successful distribution strategy and thus match their cost economies.

Competition   For penetration pricing to succeed, competitors must allow a company to set a price that is attractive to a large segment of the market. Competitors always have the option of undercutting a penetration strategy by cutting their own prices, thus preventing the penetration pricer from offering a better value to another segment of the market. Only when competitors lack the ability or incentive to do so is penetration pricing a practical strategy for gaining and holding market share. There are two common situations in which this is likely to occur:

   1.   When the firm has a significant cost advantage and/or a resource advantage so that its competitors believe they would lose if they began a price war.

2. When the firm is currently so small that it can significantly increase its sales without affecting the sales of its competitors enough to prompt a response.

MCI and Sprint successfully used penetration pricing to capture a profitable share of the U.S. telecommunications market. They succeeded because AT&T's ability to respond was constrained by regulators who wanted to increase the number of competitors and by the enormous cost of matching the lower prices for its large installed base.

Occasionally, penetration pricing can succeed in attracting volume without threatening competitors. This can be accomplished in those rare instances where market demand is highly price-sensitive and the company can design a strategy to penetrate market demand without attracting the current customers of competitors. For this strategy to work, it must somehow minimize interbrand price sensitivity at the same time that it attempts to encourage and exploit primary price sensitivity. Charter airline carriers can substantially undercut the prices of scheduled airlines without retaliation because their low service and inflexible schedules make them unattractive to most passengers of scheduled airlines.

Penetration pricing also can prove useful when there is not yet significant competition in a market but when potential entrants are on the horizon. If a firm can rapidly achieve significant cost economies by using penetration pricing, it can in some cases increase its long-run profits while discouraging entry by new competitors that lack such economies. Moreover, penetration pricing in the face of new competition is often a wise strategy even in the absence of such economies. If the product is an infrequently purchased durable good, a penetration price can enable a firm to capture a larger share of the potential market before it must compete for those sales with other firms. If the product is frequently purchased, penetration pricing can enable a firm to attract trial use before buyers have had the opportunity to try a competing brand. It may then later enjoy the low price sensitivity of a known brand competing against the promises of later entrants (the difficult comparison effect).[7]

Neutral pricing

Neutral pricing involves a strategic decision not to use price to gain market share, while not allowing price alone to restrict it. Neutral pricing minimizes the role of price as a marketing tool in favor of other tools that management believes are more powerful or cost-effective for a product's market. A firm generally adopts a neutral pricing strategy by default, because the conditions are not sufficient to support either a skim or penetration strategy. For example, a marketer may be unable to adopt skim pricing because the products in a particular market are so generally viewed as substitutable that no significant segment will pay a premium. That same firm may be unable to adopt a penetration pricing strategy because, as it is a newcomer to the market, customers would be unable to judge its quality before purchase and would infer low quality from low prices (the price-quality effect), or because competitors would respond vigorously to any price that undercut the established price structure. Neutral pricing is especially common in industries where customers are quite value-sensitive, precluding skimming, but competitors are quite volume-sensitive, precluding penetration.

Another reason to adopt a neutral pricing strategy is to maintain a coherent product line pricing strategy. General Motors, for example, traditionally priced its Chevrolet Camaro at a level that would make it affordable to a much broader market than the segment willing to pay a premium for its "sporty" look. This neutral pricing strategy was continued even in years when the car's styling proved so popular that demand exceeded production capacity. Why? Because GM already had one skim-priced product in its product sport line, the Corvette. Another would be viewed as redundant and could take sales away from the higher-priced product. A large number of buyers attracted to showrooms to test drive a Camaro is worth much more than the short-term profit that could have been achieved if GM skim-priced the Camaro.

Although neutral pricing is less proactive than skimming or penetration pricing, its proper execution is no less difficult or important. The neutral price is not necessarily set to equal those of competitors or set near the middle of the range. It can, in principle, be the highest or lowest price in the market and still be neutral. Toshiba laptop computers are consistently priced at the high end of the market, yet they capture large market shares because of the high perceived value associated with their clear screens and reliable performance. Like a skim or penetration price, a neutral price is defined relative to the economic value of the product. A high price is a neutral price when product value seems to justify that price to most potential buyers.

STRATEGIC PRICE SEGMENTATION

An effective managerial analysis of price sensitivity will almost always reveal multiple market segments. Some customers are aware of their alternatives; others are not. Some customers highly value a brand's unique differentiation; others deem it useless at best. Some customers pay all of the cost out-of-pocket; others can shift some of it to a third-party payer. Understanding these differences is key to developing pricing strategies that reflect the way customers value products and services. Unfortunately, many companies think about pricing strategy in terms of "the market" rather than in terms of the individual segments that constitute it. Consequently, they develop strategies that are correct only "on average." A wise, but physically out of shape professor we know surprises his students when he reveals that he and a more athletic friend run an average of five miles every day. Their surprise vanishes when he confesses that his athletic friend runs ten. In marketing, as in athletic accomplishment, differences are much more informative than averages.

A market segmentation based on the price-sensitivity factors described in Chapter 4 reveals more differences among customers, and is therefore more useful, than the simple distinction commonly made between "the price-sensitive segment" and "the quality-sensitive segment." To illustrate, divide the factors influencing price sensitivity into those that affect the perceived value of a product's differentiation (reference value, unique value, difficult comparison, price-quality, and the derived demand of the end-benefit effect) and those that affect the perceived pain of its cost (expenditure-income, shared-cost, fairness, sunk-investment, and the total cost of the end-benefit). The result is Exhibit 6.8, a very useful price-segmentation model developed by Richard Harmer of Boston University.

We can identify at least four price segments on Exhibit 6.8 that are common to many markets. In the upper left-hand corner are buyers who seek to buy at the lowest price consistent with some *minimum* level of acceptable quality that many brands or suppliers could meet. These *price buyers* do not make feature benefit trade-offs and cannot be convinced to pay more for the unique added value of superior features, service, or supplier reputation. In the lower, right-hand corner are the *loyal buyers* who already have a strong preference for one brand, based on its unique reputation, its unique features, or on their past experience with it. If the price of that brand does not exceed what they are willing to pay, they will purchase it without evaluating potential alternatives.

Although these two segments are frequently thought to be two ends of a price-quality continuum, the exhibit clearly reveals two other segments that don't fit with that linear view of markets. Many customers are price-sensitive because they make large expenditures or have limited incomes; yet they are also sensitive to differences offered by various suppliers. Sometimes they may buy a relatively high-priced brand, but will do so only after carefully checking the prices and features of the alternatives and concluding that the added value is worth the added cost. These *value buyers* are represented by the upper right-hand corner of Exhibit 6.8. Their opposites, represented in the lower left-hand corner, are the *convenience buyers*. These buyers are not particularly concerned about the differences among brands—any brand will do—but they also are not particularly concerned about cost. Consequently, they buy whatever is most readily available, minimizing search and evaluation of prices and features.

EXHIBIT 6.8

Price-Segmentation Model

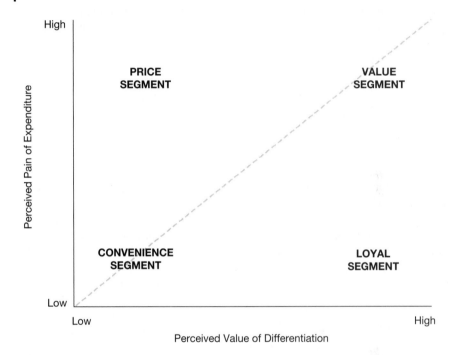

Source: Richard Harmer, Boston University.

For effective pricing, it is important to identify how customers within a market are distributed among these segments, since each segment requires a unique marketing strategy that would be inappropriate for the other segments. In both consumer and business-to-business retailing, there are buyers in all these segments. Discounters, warehouse stores, and industrial jobbers often operate highly profitable businesses targeting the price segment. The key to their success is to minimize cost wherever possible. They offer a very limited choice of brands and sizes that changes based on whatever they can get at the best price. Their customers are those who willingly tolerate this lack of choice in return for what is really important to them—low prices. In contrast, Nordstrom's high-service department store and Caterpillar's high-service dealer network cater to those in the loyal segment. Brand-name discounters, like Service Merchandise, Wal-Mart, and Staples cater to those value buyers who value some aspects of quality but want it at the lowest price possible. Since these buyers are also willing to invest considerable time and inconvenience to achieve that goal, those retailers can offer discounts by minimizing labor and real estate expense. Convenience merchandisers, such as 7-Eleven grocery stores, and high-service industrial distributors, such as Premier Industrial, bear the high cost of offering customers maximum convenience, but enjoy the high prices that they can charge to those who don't have the time or desire to consider alternatives.

To properly evaluate the success of a brand strategy, one must do so with regard to its target segment, not with regard to the market as a whole. Nordstrom has only a small share of the total retail market, whereas Sears has a large share. But it would be silly to argue that Nordstrom's marketing strategy is less successful than Sears'. Nordstrom has done an outstanding job penetrating the relatively small segment that can afford to be loyal to a high-service retailer of the highest quality merchandise, whereas Sears has done a poor job serving its larger target segment of value seekers. Nordstrom's total market share is smaller simply because the size of its target segment is smaller. Nordstrom has been profitable because it has focused on servicing its target segment well. Sears has become unprofitable because it did not understand its target segments and what was required to profitably serve them.

Unfortunately, many companies, particularly those in packaged goods, evaluate brand performance based on its share of total market, rather than on its share of the target market segment. The result is to push brand managers to compromise excellent strategies for their target segments in order to reach into others. Such concerns apparently drove Philip Morris's ill-advised, and terribly costly, decision in 1993 to discount its market-leading Marlboro cigarettes. Discounting the price of Marlboros still left them too expensive for the growing price segment, while it undermined the income earned from the loyal segment. Moreover, competitors found it necessary to match the price cuts to defend the value segment. Philip Morris's decision enabled the company to win back a few points of market share for Marlboro, but it wiped out approximately half of the company's profits from U.S. tobacco sales.

Sears used similar illogic in dropping its traditional price promotions in favor of "everyday low pricing." Consequently, Sears gave away margin unnecessarily to the convenience shoppers, who paid full price to patronize Sears when it was the only retailer in the shopping mall selling appliances, power tools, or other items they wanted to purchase without shopping around. Without deep promotional discounts, however, Sears lost sales to value buyers who would go to the less convenient Wal-Mart or warehouse club before paying even the "everyday low price" at Sears. What the company didn't recognize is that a marketer cannot be everything to everyone with a single price and distribution strategy.

If a company wishes to serve multiple segments profitably, it must do so with multiple strategies, usually involving multiple products, distribution networks, or service distinctions as well as price differences. Philip Morris's problem was not one that required a change in its loyal segment strategy. Marlboro was by far the largest-selling and most profitable cigarette in the world and was not even close to losing that position. Philip Morris's problem was that a small competitor, Ligget, had recognized and developed a price segment for cigarettes when it introduced generics. RJR-Nabisco, its major competitor, more appropriately responded to this challenge by developing and repositioning "flanking" brands to serve both the price and value segments, without undermining its loyal segment. Sears' problem was that the value segment, which has been Sears' major segment, was being drawn away by Wal-Mart, KMart, and similar lower-cost discounters. That problem could not be solved by eliminating its own deep discounts that attracted those customers back to its stores. In fact, it needed either to reach value customers more cost effectively or to reposition itself (as JCPenney did with upgraded merchandise and targeted marketing) to serve a larger share of the convenience and loyal segments.

Price segmentation does not imply that companies must limit their markets and growth to only one segment. Serving multiple segments is necessary to retain customers who are forced to become more frugal buyers during recessions. Pella, a maker of meticulously crafted windows and doors for expensive, custom-designed homes, responded to recession by developing such a multiple segment strategy in the early 1990s. Despite slow sales of its posh "Designer Series" windows, the company did not cut its prices. The company understood that people who build custom houses, still value its product enough to pay for it, even during a recession. Instead, the company launched a new line to appeal to those former loyal buyers who had been forced by economic necessity to become value buyers. Pella's lower-priced "ProLine" series offered value buyers the same quality that they had come to expect with its name, but with a more limited choice of shapes and sizes and without the design services of the Pella distributors, who carry only the Designer Series. In return, value buyers who still want the construction quality of a Pella window can buy one for 12 to 20 percent less. Despite the recession, Pella's 1993 revenues set a record.

The Harmer value-segmentation model in Exhibit 6.8 captures only the most macro of price segments. Within each of the four macro segments, there are still more differences in what constitutes "value," "convenience," "quality/service," or "minimum specifications" to specific customer groups. These examples illustrate, however, that pricing strategy based on even such a limited macro-segmentation scheme can substantially improve on strategy driven by a vague, misleading concept of what is important to the market as a whole.[8]

SUMMARY

This chapter shows how the three elements of price strategy—costs, customers, and competition—interact to prescribe an appropriate strategy. We established an organizational structure for analyzing these elements and showed how the analysis leads to one of three "generic" pricing strategies: skim, penetration, or neutral. Although market segmentation is implicit in these strategies, we described a price-segmentation model as a useful template for explicitly segmenting markets on a macro level. We then illustrated how some well-known pricing failures could have been avoided and how successes have been achieved by using segmentation to formulate pricing strategies. The next four chapters will guide you through implementation of the strategic decisions that these analyses lead you to make.

NOTES

1. Names, numbers, and events have been disguised.
2. We are assuming that a greenhouse depreciates no more rapidly when in use than when idle. If it did depreciate faster when used, the extra depreciation would be an incremental cost even for crops grown during seasons with excess capacity.
3. This option could expose Ritter to the risk of a legal challenge if Ritter's large buyers compete directly with its small buyers in the retailing of mums. Ritter could rebut the challenge if it could justify the 5 percent discount as a cost saving in preparing and shipping larger orders. If not, then Ritter may want to try more complicated methods to segment the market such as offering somewhat different products to the two segments.
4. The following discussion builds on seminal work by Joel Dean in *Managerial Economics* (Englewood Cliffs, N.J.: Prentice-Hall, Inc., 1951), pp. 419–26; and in "Pricing Policies for New Products," *Harvard Business Review*, 18 (November 1950), 45–56, reprinted in vol. 54 (November–December 1976), pp. 141–53.
5. These definitions were created in the context of developed economies with a large middle class, producing a normal distribution of incomes. It is questionable whether these generic labels make sense in undeveloped economies where the income distribution is bipolar. The factors of cost, customer, and competitive trade-offs to optimize strategy are nonetheless valid.
6. See Chapter 11 for a detailed discussion of competitive advantages to defend markets.
7. See Richard Schmalensee, "Product Differentiation Advantages of Pioneering Brands," *American Economic Review*, 72 (June 1982), 349–65.
8. Ronald Henkoff, "Pella: Moving Up by Downscaling," *Fortune* (August 9, 1993), p. 72.

LIFE CYCLE PRICING

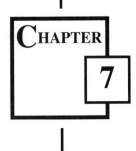

CHAPTER 7

ADAPTING STRATEGY IN A CHANGING ENVIRONMENT

Product concepts, like people, typically pass through predictable phases. There are, of course, exceptions. Death sometimes comes prematurely, dashing expectations before they even begin to materialize; and youth sometimes extends inordinately, deceiving the unwary into thinking it can last forever. Still, the exceptions notwithstanding, the typical life pattern affords one a chance to understand the present, anticipate the future, and prepare to make the most of both. Such understanding, anticipation, and preparation comprise a firm's long-run strategic plan. Profitable pricing is the bottom line measure of that plan's success.

Although different authors have applied the life-cycle idea to individual brands (for example, Ford, Chevrolet) and styles (convertibles, minivans, sports cars), the idea has proven most useful when applied to the general product concept that defines a market (that is, the automobile). A market evolves despite changes in brands and styles. A product concept is born, gradually gains in buyer acceptance, eventually attains full buyer acceptance, and is ultimately discarded for something better. The market defined by that product concept evolves correspondingly through four phases: development, growth, maturity, and decline as Exhibit 7.1 illustrates.[1]

In each of its phases, the market has a unique personality. In preceding chapters, we analyzed the three factors that determine the success or failure of a pricing strategy: the product's relevant costs (Chapter 2), the buyer's price sensitivity (Chapter 4), and the behavior of competitors

EXHIBIT 7.1

Phases of the Market Over the Product Life Cycle

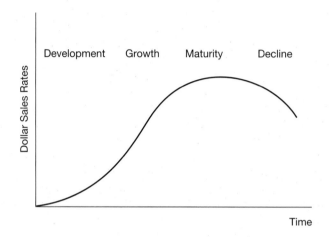

(Chapter 5). These factors vary predictably as the market for a product moves through the phases of its life cycle. Accordingly, one's pricing strategy must vary if it is to remain appropriate, and one's tactics must vary if they are to remain effective. The following sections explain the rationale for these changes in strategy.[2]

PRICING THE INNOVATION FOR MARKET DEVELOPMENT

An *innovation* is a product so new and unique that buyers find the concept somewhat foreign. It does not yet have a place in buyers' life-styles or business practices. Consequently, the market requires substantial education before buyers recognize a product's benefits and accept it as a legitimate way to satisfy their needs. The first automobiles, vacuum cleaners, and prepackaged convenience foods initially had to overcome considerable buyer apathy. The first business computers had to overcome skepticism bordering on hostility. Today, innovations from home banking to video conferencing have encountered similar consumer reluctance, despite their legitimate promise of substantial value. An innovation requires buyers to alter the way they evaluate satisfying their needs. Consequently, before the product can become a success, the market must be developed through the difficult process of buyer education.

Not all new products are innovations, at least from a marketing perspective. Sometimes a new product results from a technological breakthrough that simply lowers the cost of a product concept already well accepted among buyers. In 1909 Ford's Model T was a new product born in the technology of mass production, but its forerunners had already paved the way for its acceptance by consumers. Sometimes a new product simply improves on an already well-established benefit, as was the case with the 3.5-inch computer diskette, the plain paper fax, and the digital watch, all of which required little or no market development.[3] Even when a product provides a completely new benefit, it may not be an innovation from the standpoint of buyers. For example, drugs are so readily accepted as cures in our culture that new ones are generally adopted with little hesitation by both doctors and patients.

A new product that embodies a new concept for fulfilling buyers' needs is an innovation whose success requires buyer education. An important aspect of that educational process is called *information diffusion*. Most of what individuals learn about innovative products comes from seeing and hearing about the experiences of others.[4] The diffusion of that information from person to person has proven especially influential for large-expenditure items, such as consumer durables, where buyers take a significant risk the first time they buy an innovative product. For example, an early study on the diffusion of innovations found that the most important factor influencing a family's first purchase of a window air conditioner was neither an economic factor such as income nor a need factor such as exposure of bedrooms to the sun. The most important factor was social interaction with another family that already had a window air conditioner.[5]

Recognition of the diffusion process is extremely important in formulating a marketing plan for two reasons: First, when information must diffuse through a population of potential buyers, the long-run demand for an innovative product at any time in the future depends on the number of initial buyers. Empirical studies indicate that demand does not begin to accelerate until the first 2 to 5 percent of potential buyers adopt the product.[6] The attainment of those initial sales is often the hardest part of marketing an innovation. Obviously, the sooner the seller can close those first sales, the sooner he or she will secure long-run sales and profit potential.

Second, the "innovators," people who try the new product early, are not generally a random sample of buyers. They are people particularly suited to evaluate the product before purchase. They are also people to whom the later adopters, or "imitators," look for guidance and advice. However, even innovators know little about how attributes or major attribute combinations should be valued. Marketing effects can, therefore, readily influence which attributes drive purchase decisions and how those attributes are valued. Identifying the innovators and making every effort to ensure that their experience is positive is an essential part of marketing an innovation.[7]

What is the appropriate strategy for pricing an innovative new product? To answer that question, it is important to recognize that consumers' price sensitivity when they first encounter an innovation bears little or no relationship to their long-run price sensitivity. Most buyers are relatively price insensitive when facing a new innovation because they tend to use price as a proxy for quality and because there are usually no alternative brands with which to compare. Moreover, until they learn about the product's benefits, they may not even recognize a need for it. They lack a reference for determining value and evaluate what would constitute a fair or bargain price. Consequently, most potential buyers are understandably unimpressed by a low price relative to the product's value, while the innovators are often undeterred by a high one.

Given the problem of buyer ignorance, the firm's primary goal in the market development stage is to educate potential buyers concerning the product's worth. Consequently, the regular or list price for a new innovation should be set to communicate the product's value to the marketplace. It is the price that a seller believes satisfied buyers would pay for a repeat purchase. It gives buyers a reference from which to estimate the product's worth and assess the value of price discounts and future price reductions. If the seller plans a skim-pricing strategy, the list price should be near the relative value that price-insensitive buyers will place on the product. If the seller plans a neutral strategy, the list price should be near the relative value for the more typical potential user. The seller of an innovation should not set a list price for market penetration, however, since the low price sensitivity of uninformed buyers will make that strategy ineffective and may, due to the price-quality effect, damage the product's reputation.

Marketing innovations through price-induced sampling

Whether the list price is the actual price first-time buyers are asked to pay is another question entirely. The answer should depend on the relative cost of different methods for educating buyers about the product's benefits. If the product is frequently purchased, has a low incremental production cost, and its benefits are obvious after just one use, the cheapest and most effective way to educate buyers may be to let them sample the product. For example, on-line service providers like America Online, CompuServe, and Prodigy educate prospective users on the wide variety of valuable resources available through their networks by offering free limited introductory memberships.

Not all innovative products can be economically promoted by price-induced sampling, however. Many innovations are durable goods for which price cutting to induce trial is rarely cost effective. A seller can hardly afford to give the product away and then wait years for a repeat purchase. Moreover, many innovative products, both durables and nondurables, will not immediately reveal their value when sampled once. Few people who sampled smoke alarms, for example, would find them so satisfying that they would yearn to buy more and encourage their friends to do the same. And many innovations (for example, personal computers) require that buyers learn skills before they can realize the product's benefits. Without a program to convince buyers that learning those skills is worth the effort and strong support to ensure that they learn properly, few buyers will sample at any price, and fewer still will find the product worthwhile when they do. In such cases, price-induced sampling does not effectively establish the product's worth in buyers' minds. Instead, market development requires more direct education of buyers before they make their first purchases.

Marketing innovations through direct sales

For innovations that involve a large dollar expenditure per purchase, education usually involves a direct sales force trained to evaluate buyers' needs and to explain how the product will satisfy them. The first refrigerators, for example, were sold to reluctant buyers door-to-door. The salesperson's job was to help buyers imagine the benefits that a refrigerator offered, beyond those that an ice chest was already capable of providing. Only then would those first buyers abandon tradition to make a large capital expenditure on new, risky technology. Business buyers are equally skeptical of the value of new innovations. In the 1950s, most potential users of air freight service thought they had no need for such rapid delivery. American Airlines built the market for this new innovation by offering free logistics consultation. American's sales consultants showed potential buyers how this high-priced innovation in transportation could replace local warehouses, thereby actually saving money.[8] They taught the shippers how to see their distribution problems differently, from a perspective that revealed the previously unrecognized value of rapid delivery by American's planes.

When the innovation is more complicated than refrigeration or air freight, even a convincing evaluation of buyers' needs may leave them too uncertain about the product's benefits to adopt it. For example, a business computer in the 1950s was quite a risky purchase. Even if a buyer was certain about the quality of the computer hardware, he or she had no assurance that a computer system could actually do the billing, payroll, and production scheduling that the salesperson claimed it could do. IBM increased the business adoption rate of computers, quickly overcoming Sperry Rand's three-year lead as a mainframe manufacturer, by mitigating this source of uncertainty. IBM did so by marketing as a single package the hardware, software, systems analysis, and employee training required to guarantee the benefits its salespeople promised.

Neither American nor IBM priced their products cheaply despite their desire for rapid sales growth. Instead, they educated their markets, showing why their products were worth the list price and aided buyers' adoption to minimize the risk of failure. They funded these high levels of education and service with the high prices buyers paid for the perceived value of the products. Du Pont has employed this same high-price, high-promotion strategy in introducing numerous synthetic fabrics and specialty plastics. Apple employed it in developing the market for personal computers. And the most successful marketers of industrial robots are using it today.[9]

Marketing innovations through distribution channels

Not all products have sufficiently large sales per customer to make direct selling practical. This is particularly true of innovative products which are sold indirectly through channels of distribution. However, the problem of educating buyers and minimizing their risk does not go away when the product is handed over to a distributor. It simply makes the need to rely on an independent distribution network problematic. The innovator must somehow convince the distributors who carry the product to promote it vigorously. Consequently, when marketing through distribution channels, an essential part of the market development is low introductory pricing to distributors and retailers.

Low wholesale pricing leaves distributors and retailers with high margins, giving them an incentive to "push" the product with buyer education and service. Cuisinart, Inc., successfully introduced its food processors to the United States by leaving retailers a substantial margin in the suggested retail price. Department and cookware stores responded enthusiastically, spurring sales with in-store demonstrations and classes in Cuisinart-cooking. Millions of consumers then willingly paid the Cuisinart's high retail price once they learned it was justified by the product's benefits. A similar strategy was used by Lotus Development Corporation to introduce its new 1-2-3 spreadsheet product to corporate America. High margin opportunities gave specialty computer dealers an incentive to teach corporate finance and marketing managers how to use spreadsheets.

PRICING THE NEW PRODUCT FOR GROWTH

Once a product concept gains a foothold in the marketplace, the pricing problem begins to change. Repeat purchasers are no longer uncertain of the product's value since they can judge it from their previous experience. First-time buyers can rely on reports from the innovators as the process of information diffusion begins. In growth, therefore, the buyer's concern about the product's utility begins to give way to a more calculating concern about the costs and benefits of alternative brands. Unless a successful innovation is unusually well protected from imitation, the market is ripe for the growth of competition.

As competition begins to break out in the innovative industry, both the original innovator and the later entrants begin to assume competitive positions and prepare to defend them. In doing so, each must decide where it will place its marketing strategy on the continuum between a pure differentiated product strategy and a pure cost leadership strategy.[10]

With a *differentiated product strategy*, the firm directs its marketing efforts toward developing unique attributes (or images) for its product. In growth, the firm must quickly establish a position in research, in production, and in buyer perception as the dominant supplier of those attributes. Then, as competition becomes more intense, the uniqueness of its product creates a value effect that attenuates buyers' price sensitivity, enabling the firm to price profitably despite increasing numbers of competitors.

With a *cost leadership strategy*, the firm directs its marketing efforts toward becoming a low-cost producer. In growth, the firm must focus on developing a product that it can produce at minimum cost, usually by making the product less differentiated. The firm expects that its lower costs will enable it to profit despite competitive pricing.

Pricing the differentiated product

A differentiated product strategy may be focused on a particular buyer segment or directed industry-wide. In either case, the role of pricing is to collect the rewards from producing attributes that buyers find uniquely valuable. If the differentiated product strategy is focused, the firm earns its rewards by skim pricing to the segment that values the product most highly. For example, Godiva (chocolate), BMW (automobiles), and Gucci (apparel) use skim pricing to focus their differentiated product strategies. In contrast, when the differentiated product strategy is industry-wide, the firm sets neutral or penetration prices and earns its rewards from the sales volume that its product can then attract. Kodak (photographic film and paper), Ford (automobiles), and Caterpillar (construction equipment) use neutral pricing to sell their differentiated products to a large share of the market.

Penetration pricing is also possible for a differentiated product, although the penetration price is often at least equal to the dollar prices of less differentiated substitutes. This is common in industrial products where a company may develop a superior piece of equipment, computer software, or service, but price it no more than the competition. The price is used to lock in a large market share before competitors imitate, and therefore eliminate, the product's differential advantage. Although the Windows operating system is clearly a unique product, Microsoft is using penetration pricing to ensure its product remains the dominant architecture and default standard for software application programmers. Penetration pricing is less commonly successful for differentiated consumer products, since buyers who can afford to cater to their desire for the attributes of differentiated products can often also afford to buy them without shopping for bargains.

Pricing the low-cost product

Like the differentiated product strategy, a cost leadership strategy can also be either focused or directed industry-wide. If a firm is seeking industry-wide cost leadership, penetration pricing often plays an active role in the strategy's implementation. For example, when the source of the firm's anticipated cost advantage depends on selling a large volume, it may set low penetration prices during growth to gain a dominant market share. Later, it maintains those penetration prices as a competitive deterrent, while still earning profits due to its superior cost position. Wal-Mart uses this strategy successfully to achieve substantial cost economies in distribution and high sales per square foot. Even when the source of the cost advantage is not a large volume but a more cost-efficient product design, the firm may set low penetration prices to exploit that advantage. Japanese manufacturers used penetration pricing to exploit their cost advantages and dominate world markets for television sets after extensively redesigning the manufacturing production process with automated insertion equipment, modular assembly, and standardized designs.

At this point a definite word of warning is in order. Much of the business literature implies that penetration pricing is the only proper strategy for establishing and exploiting industry-wide cost leadership. That literature is dangerously misleading. If a market is not particularly price sensitive, penetration pricing will not enable a firm to gain enough share to achieve or exploit a cost advantage. In that case, neutral pricing is the most appropriate pricing strategy and can still be quite consistent with the successful pursuit of cost leadership. The marketing histories of many cost leaders (for example, Honda and R. J. Reynolds) confirm that industry-wide cost leadership is attainable without penetration pricing. The battle for the dominant share and cost leadership in those markets and many others is fought and won with weapons such as product variety, advertising, and extensive distribution. In many cases, the battle is won against competitors with lower prices.

Penetration pricing is not always appropriate when a cost leadership strategy is focused. Sometimes the focused firm's cost advantage depends directly on selling to only one or a few large buyers. Since the total expenditure effect makes those buyers price sensitive, penetration pricing may be necessary to hold their patronage. For example, suppliers that sell exclusively to Wal-Mart or to the auto industry enjoy lower costs of selling and distribution but usually have to charge penetration prices to retain that business. When the firm's cost advantage is derived simply from remaining small and flexible, neutral pricing is compatible with focused cost leadership. For example, specialized component assembly is often done by small contract manufacturers that are cost leaders because their small size enables them to maintain nonunion labor, low overhead, and flexibility in accepting and scheduling orders. Since those cost advantages do not depend on maintaining a large volume of orders, and since the buyers that those companies serve are more concerned about quality and reliability than about price, their pricing strategy is usually neutral. When an order requires an especially fast turnaround and the buyer has little time to look for alternatives, those same manufacturers will occasionally even skim price their services.

Choosing a growth strategy

In some growth markets, both the differentiated product and cost leadership strategies are viable concurrently. This is possible when a segment demanding a specialized product for which it will pay a premium, coexists with a market segment that will accept a relatively undifferentiated product for a low price. Hewlett Packard, for example, successfully implemented a differentiated product strategy when the calculator market was in the growth stage, whereas Texas Instruments successfully followed a cost leadership strategy. Unfortunately, not all markets reward and not all firms can implement either strategy. Before selecting a product strategy, with its corresponding pricing strategy, a firm should consider the following questions about its market and its capabilities:

Is there a market segment that desires unique product benefits and is willing to pay premium prices for them? An obvious prerequisite for a focused, differentiated product strategy is to find a market segment that highly values unique product attributes. Contrary to popular misconception, even small firms can be profitable in most industries when they identify such a segment.[11] Two small companies, Harley Davidson (motorcycles) and Premier (industrial distribution), have found niches in an industry dominated by low-cost competitors by serving buyers who desire unique designs and high performance. Jeep (now part of Chrysler) has done well in competing with its lower-cost competitors by serving buyers who want a vehicle that can go where the roads do not.

Does the firm have the requisite distinctive competence to produce and market a differentiated product? The appropriateness of a differentiated product strategy depends not only on the desires of the market, but also on the seller's strengths and weaknesses in production and marketing. Hewlett-Packard was uniquely suited to pursue a differentiated product strategy in laser printers because of its technical knowledge and its reputation in the engineering and scientific markets for producing other high-quality products. Lexus, was uniquely suited to pursue a differentiated product strategy in the luxury/performance segment of the automobile market given its parent company's (Toyota) reputation as a manufacturer of superior quality.

Is the market sufficiently price sensitive to produce significant cost economies? Successful penetration pricing to establish industry-wide cost leadership requires that a large segment of the market be price sensitive. Dell, and later Compaq, recognized that the increased price sensitivity associated with the migration from growth into maturity created a huge opportunity for penetration pricing of high-powered desktop computers. Their high volume enabled them to succeed despite low pricing. If the price-sensitive segment is not substantially larger than the segment willing to pay premium prices for superior quality, a cost leadership strategy based on achieving superior production economies through low prices will not succeed. AGFA, for example, has failed repeatedly to capture a significant share of the U.S. photocopy and x-ray films market using penetration pricing. Apparently, the company still does not realize that the difficult comparison, end-benefit, and price-quality effects mitigate against purchasing film based purely on price even in maturity.

Is the firm willing to commit the resources and bear the risk necessary to see through a cost leadership strategy until it pays off? Attempting to establish a cost advantage, either by penetration pricing or by redesigning the product and manufacturing process, is not for the poor and faint-hearted. The firm must forgo immediate cash flow and commit itself to substantial investment. It does so with only a promise that future profits will be forthcoming. General Electric and RCA both lost fortunes trying to become low-cost computer manufacturers, only to find belatedly that their goal required a much greater commitment of resources than they were willing or able to make.[12] At the same time, Amdahl, Inc. made a fortune producing skimpriced differentiated computers and risked comparatively little capital to do so.

Are there cost advantages that small market-share firms can exploit? Small firms can occasionally be more effective cost leaders than their larger competitors. The closer contact between management and labor in a small firm can often enable it to remain nonunion in an otherwise unionized industry, avoiding costly work rules and strikes as well as higher wages. Moreover, there is considerable evidence that when small firms focus on a narrow, standardized product line, gaining a reputation as a quality producer of that line, they sometimes gain substantial cost advantages in marketing expenditures.[13] In such cases, even a small firm can be profitable as a low price, mass marketer. Intuit, the manufacturer of Quicken® financial management software, leads its market niche without a sales force. Word of mouth and great press save this company millions in marketing expenses.

Then, having chosen a strategy, a firm must also decide just how far to pursue it.

How much product specialization will the market pay for? Firms that pursue differentiated product strategies cannot survive if they completely ignore cost economies to achieve maximum product specialization. Although hundreds of auto manufacturers in the early twentieth century pursued narrowly focused, differentiated product strategies with some success, they ultimately failed as the cost economies of large-scale production overwhelmed the price premium they could charge. The differentiated product marketers who prosper today in the auto industry (for example, Mercedes, Jeep) do so by supplying only those aspects of product specialization that can command a price premium sufficient to cover the extra cost.

How much specialization will the market sacrifice to attain the lowest price? Even if a large segment of the market is primarily price sensitive, these buyers may still be willing to pay for some product specialization. The success of Hunt Club, JCPenney's high-quality brand of men's casual clothing, has effectively shown that traditionally price-sensitive target segments will pay some premium for limited product specialization. Similarly, Presidents Choice, a premium house brand of grocery products, offers value-conscious customers quality higher than store brands at prices still below that of nationally advertised brands.

Rarely is a pure differentiated product strategy or a pure cost leadership strategy viable. What distinguishes the strategies of firms within a given industry is not their purity but their emphasis on price or product differentiation relative to the strategies of competitors. A successful strategy involves a mix of price and product features that corresponds to the demands of some segment of the market. "Our buyers aren't concerned about price" are the famous last words of a differentiated product marketer. At some point, the price premium can always become too large for even the least price-sensitive segment to accept. "We have to compete on price" are the famous last words of a cost leader. Almost any product can be slightly differentiated in some way that will make otherwise price-sensitive buyers willing to pay at least a small price premium.

No doubt some observers will cite evidence that all this strategic positioning is superfluous. They will point to successful firms in growth industries that neither produce distinctive products nor have costs among the industry's lowest. There are such firms in growth industries, but few survive the inevitable transition to maturity when price competition chills the profits of all who have not insulated themselves by developing a distinctive and defensible competitive position.[14] The time to begin developing such a position is in the peak of growth, when high prices and cash flow can support the necessary investment, and before the best positions are preempted by one's competitors.

Price reductions in growth

The best price for the growth stage, regardless of one's product strategy, is normally less than the price set during the market development stage. In most cases, new competition in the growth stage gives buyers more alternatives from which to choose, while their growing familiarity with the product enables them to better evaluate those alternatives. Both factors will increase price sensitivity over what it was in the development stage. Moreover, even if the firm enjoys a patented monopoly, reducing price after the innovation stage speeds the product adoption process and enables the firm to profit from faster market growth.[15] Such price reductions are usually possible without sacrificing profits because of cost economies from an increasing scale of output and accumulating experience.

Pricing in the growth stage is not generally cutthroat. The growth stage is characterized by a rapidly expanding sales base. New firms can generally enter and existing ones expand without forcing their competitors' sales to (correspondingly) contract. For example, the sales of Apple and Radio Shack computers continued to grow rapidly following the 1981 introduction of IBM's PC, despite losses of market share. Because new entrants can grow without forcing established firms to contract, the growth stage normally will not precipitate aggressive price competition. The exceptions occur when:

1. The production economies resulting from producing greater volumes are large and the market is price sensitive. Consequently, each firm sees the battle for volume as a battle for long-run survival (as often occurs in the electronics industry);

2. Sales volume determines which of competing technologies becomes the industry standard (as occurred in the market for video cassette recorders); or

3. The growth of production capacity jumps ahead of the growth in sales (as occurred in the 1970s in the snowmobile market).

In these cases, price competition can become bitter as firms sacrifice short-term profit during growth to ensure their profitability in maturity.

PRICING THE ESTABLISHED PRODUCT IN MATURITY

A typical product spends most of its life in maturity, the phase in which effective pricing is essential for survival, although latitude in decision making is far more limited. Without the rapid sales growth and increasing cost economies that characterize the growth phase, earning a profit in maturity hinges on exploiting whatever latitude one has. Many firms fail to make the transition to market maturity because they failed in growth to achieve strong competitive positions with differentiated products or a cost advantage.[16] Firms that have successfully executed their growth strategies are usually able to price profitably in maturity, although rarely as profitably as at the height of industry growth.

In growth, the source of profit was sales to an expanding market. In maturity that source has been nearly depleted. A maturity strategy predicated on continued expansion of one's customer base will likely be dashed by one's competitors' determination to defend their market shares. In contrast to the growth stage, when competitors could lose share in an expanding market and suffer only a slower rate of sales increase, competitors who lose share in a mature market suffer an absolute sales decline. Having made capacity investments to produce a certain level of output, they will usually defend their market shares to avoid being overwhelmed by sunk costs.[17] Pricing latitude is further reduced by the following factors increasing price competition as the market moves from growth to maturity:

1. The accumulated purchase experience of repeat buyers improves their ability to evaluate and compare competing products, reducing brand loyalty and the value of a brand's reputation.

2. The imitation of the most successful product designs, technologies, and marketing strategies reduces product differentiation, making the various brands of different firms more directly competitive with one another. This homogenizing process is sometimes speeded up when product standards are set by government agencies or by respected independent testing agencies like Underwriters' Laboratories.

3. Buyers' increased price sensitivity and the lower risk that accompanies production of a proven standardized product attract new competitors whose distinctive competence is efficient production and distribution of commodity products. These are often foreign competitors but may also be large domestic firms with years of experience producing or marketing similar products.

All three of these factors worked to reduce prices and margins for photocopiers during the early 1980s and for personal computers and peripherals during the early 1990s, as those markets entered maturity.

Unless a firm can discover a marketing strategy that renews industry growth or a technological breakthrough that enables it to introduce a more differentiated product, it must simply learn to live with these new competitive pressures.[18] Effective pricing in maturity focuses not on valiant efforts to buy market share but on making the most of whatever competitive advantages the firm has. Even before industry growth is exhausted and maturity sets in, a firm does well to seek out opportunities to improve its pricing effectiveness to maintain its profits in maturity, despite increased competition among firms and increased sophistication among buyers. Fertile ground for such opportunities lies in the following areas:

> *Unbundling related products and services.* The goal in the market development stage is to make it easy for potential buyers to try the product and to see its benefits. Consequently, it makes sense to sell everything needed to achieve the benefit for a single price. During the early years of office automation, IBM sold the total office solution, bundling hardware, software, training, and ongoing maintenance contracts. In growth, it make sense for the leading firms to continue bundling products for a different reason: The bundle makes it more difficult for competitors to enter. When all products required for a benefit are priced as a bundle, no new competitor can break in by offering a better version of just one part of that bundle.

As a market moves toward maturity, bundling normally becomes less a competitive defense and more a competitive invitation. As the number of competitors increases, they more closely imitate the differentiating aspects of products in the leading company's bundle. This makes it easier for someone to develop just one superior part, allowing buyers to purchase other parts from the leading company's other competitors. If buyers are forced to purchase from the leading company only as a bundle, the more knowledgeable ones will often abandon it altogether to purchase individual pieces from innovative competitors. Unless the leading company can maintain overall superiority in all products, it is generally better to accommodate competitors in maturity. This is accomplished by selling many buyers most of the products they need for a benefit rather than selling the entire bundle to ever fewer of them. An example of this tactic can be seen in the desktop computer industry where experienced buyers seeking increased performance and customized configurations, choose to satisfy their unique performance need by purchasing options provided by innovative specialized suppliers. To avoid loosing part of the sale, the dominant manufacturers were forced to unbundle the packages they had offered successfully during growth.

> *Improved estimation of price sensitivity.* In the instability of growth when new buyers and sellers are constantly entering the market, formal estimation of buyers' price sensitivity is often a futile exercise. In maturity, when the source of demand is repeat buyers and competition remains more stable, one may better gauge the incremental revenue from a price change and discover that a little fine tuning can significantly improve profits. The techniques for making such estimates of price sensitivity are outlined in Chapter 13.
>
> *Improved control and utilization of costs.* As the number of customers and product variations increases during the growth stage, a firm may

justifiably allocate costs among them arbitrarily. New customers and new products initially require technical, sales, and managerial support that is reasonably allocated to overhead during growth, since it is as much a cost of future sales as of the initial ones. In the transition to maturity, a more accurate allocation of incremental costs to sales may reveal opportunities to significantly increase profit. For example, one may find that sales at certain times of the year, the week, or even the day require capacity that is underutilized during other times. Sales at these times should be priced higher to reflect the cost of capacity.

More important, a careful cost analysis will identify those products and customers that are simply not carrying their own weight. If some products in the line require a disproportionate sales effort, that should be reflected in the incremental cost of their sales and in their prices. If demand cannot support higher prices for them, they are prime candidates for pruning from the line.[19] The same holds true for customers. If some require technical support disproportionate to their contribution, one might well implement a pricing policy of charging separately for such services. While the growth stage provides fertile ground to make long-term investments in product variations and in developing new customer accounts, maturity is the time to cut one's losses on those that have not begun to pay dividends and that cannot be expected to do so.[20]

> *Expansion of the product line.* Although increased competition and buyer sophistication in the maturity phase erode one's pricing latitude for the primary product, the firm may be able to leverage its position (as a differentiated or as a low-cost producer) to sell peripheral goods or services that it can price more profitably. Watterau, Inc., a grocery wholesaler that targets the small, independent supermarkets, has remained profitable in maturity by using its established trade relationships to sell its services in store designing, shelf space utilization, employee training, and financing.[21] The benefits are not only higher profits for Watterau in the short run, but also a customer base more likely to survive and grow in the long run.

> *Reevaluation of distribution channels.* Finally, in the transition to maturity, most manufacturers begin to reevaluate their wholesale prices with an eye to reducing dealer margins. There is no need in maturity to pay dealers to promote the product to new buyers. Repeat purchasers know what they want and are more likely to consider cost rather than the advice and promotion of the distributor or retailer as a guide to purchase. There is also no longer any need to restrict the kind of retailers with whom one deals. The exclusive distribution networks for Apple, Compaq, and even IBM have given way to low-service, low-margin distributors such as discount computer chains, off-price office supply houses, and even warehouse clubs. The discounters who

earlier could destroy one's market development effort can in maturity ensure one's competitiveness among price-sensitive buyers.

PRICING A PRODUCT IN MARKET DECLINE

A downward trend in demand characterizes the market in decline. The trend may be localized, as in the housing markets of shrinking northeastern cities, or general, as in the market for mechanical watches. The decline may be limited, as in the automobile tire market of the late 1970s, or nearly complete, as in the displacement of vinyl records by cassettes and compact discs. The effect of such trends on price depends on the difficulty the industry has in eliminating excess capacity.

When production costs are largely variable, industry capacity tends to adjust quickly to declining demand with little or no effect on prices. Although the demand for haircuts declined precipitously in the late 1960s and early 1970s, prices declined little if at all. Barbers simply left the industry for alternate employment.

When production costs are fixed but easily redirected, the value of the fixed capital in other markets places a lower bound on prices. When political violence reduced the demand for air travel to Beirut, it did not cause a price war between carriers. Airlines simply reallocated their planes to more promising markets.

When production costs are largely fixed and sunk because capital is specialized to the particular market, the effects of market decline are more onerous. Firms in such industries face the prospect of a fatal cash hemorrhage if they cannot maintain a reasonable rate of capacity utilization. Consequently, each firm scrambles for business at the expense of its competitors by cutting prices. Unfortunately, since the price cuts rarely stimulate enough additional market demand to reverse the decline, the inevitable result is reduced profitability industry-wide. The goal of strategy in decline is not to win anything; for some it is to exit with minimum losses. For others the goal is simply to survive the decline with their competitive positions intact and perhaps strengthened by the experience.

Alternative strategies in decline

There are three general strategic approaches that one might take toward a market in decline: retrenchment, harvesting, or consolidation. The tire industry in the 1970s illustrates a market where each of these three alternative competitive strategies was employed.

The tire industry has been a major force in the U.S. economy, with sales in the tens of billions of dollars. In the 1970s, however, the industry was hit with a demand-depressing shock. The increase in oil prices reduced driving and attracted buyers to lighter cars, which cut tire wear and drove up the cost of tire production. Moreover, the steel-belted radial tire, which lasts as long as two or more bias ply tires, became a more cost-effective purchase because of its positive effect on gas mileage. The result of all this was a decline in the tire market to about two-thirds its previous size. At least one company in the industry followed each of the alternative strategies for dealing with the redefined market environment.

Firestone chose retrenchment. A *retrenchment strategy* involves either partial or complete capitulation of some market segments to refocus resources on others where the firm has a stronger position. The firm deliberately forgoes market share but positions itself to be more profitable with the share it retains. Not all firms that forgo market share in a declining market do so as a deliberate strategic decision. Some are forced to sell out to satisfy creditors. Retrenchment, in contrast, is a carefully planned and executed strategy to put the firm in a more viable competitive position, not an immediate necessity to stave off collapse.

By 1979, Firestone realized the error of its earlier belief that it could cheaply adapt old bias-ply tire plants to produce high-quality radials. Before coming to that realization, it lost $400 million and faced the prospect of comparable losses in the future.[22] In that year, Firestone hired a new CEO, John Nevin, whose retrenchment strategy turned the company's fortune around.

Nevin quickly closed seven of Firestone's outmoded plants, slashed inventory, divested the company's plastics subsidiary, and even sold the Firestone Country Club, freeing a total of more than $600 million in working capital. Although plant closings forced a severe trimming of the company's product line, it raised capacity utilization at the remaining plants from 60 to 90 percent, quickly turning Firestone into a low-cost, efficient, and profitable producer. As a result, it could price low to defend its share of these lines without suffering losses. Moreover, the retrenchment freed enough cash for Firestone to strengthen its position as a tire retailer and as a provider of reliable, brand-name auto maintenance. By 1981, Nevin admitted that, "The day has passed when Firestone can say, 'We are a tire company and will participate actively in every element of the tire business throughout America and the world.' " Despite intense price competition from rivals, increased efficiency in production and distribution to its remaining markets enabled Firestone to return to profitability in that year. Firestone's retrenchment strategy continued during 1980s with closure or sale of five more tire plants and divestiture of additional business units in their diversified products group and all or most of their equity positions in tire manufacturing facilities worldwide. Although profits peaked in 1983, sustained profitability eluded Firestone as intense price competition, spurred by domestic overcapacity and aggressive foreign manufacturing, continued to drive per-unit revenues downward. With retrenchment basically completed, in its continuing effort to compete in the worldwide tire market, Firestone rejected its go-it-alone strategy in favor of pursuing an alliance. Negotiations with worldwide manufacturers ultimately resulted in a merger agreement with Bridgestone in 1988.[23]

The essence of a retrenchment strategy is liquidation of those assets and withdrawal from those markets that represent the weakest links in the firm's competitive position, leaving it leaner but more defensible. It involves an explicit strategic decision, not a reaction to crisis. Uniroyal, for example, also sold some assets and abandoned some markets, but only belatedly when forced by the demands of creditors.[24] Such crisis retrenchment is not a strategy designed to strengthen the company in the future but simply to buy it time in the present.

In contrast to Firestone, B. F. Goodrich chose to harvest its tire business. A *harvesting strategy* is a phased withdrawal from the industry. It begins like a retrenchment strategy with abandonment of the weakest links. However, the goal of harvesting is not a smaller, more defensible competitive position but a withdrawal from the industry. The harvesting firm does not price to defend its remaining market share but rather to maximize its income. The harvesting firm may make short-term investments in the industry to keep its position from deteriorating too rapidly, but it avoids fundamental long-term investments, preferring instead to treat its competitive position in the declining market as a "cash cow" for funding more promising ventures in other markets.

Goodrich had the foresight to begin its withdrawal in the mid-1970s, while many of its competitors were still vainly hoping for an industry recovery. By 1980, Goodrich had eliminated all unprofitable tire lines had sold off its European plants, and had divested most of its warehouses and retail outlets.[25] With the resulting $150 million in freed capital as leverage to borrow more, Goodrich sought to move its business to greener pastures, investing most heavily in its profitable polyvinyl chloride operations. In 1981, with more than half of its earnings already coming from nontire sales, the company announced that it would withdraw from the original equipment tire market, effectively completing its harvest. Ultimately Goodrich was acquired by the Michelin Tire Corporation in May of 1990.[26]

Goodyear, the largest and most profitable producer in the industry, decided to take advantage of the decline to consolidate its position. A *consolidation strategy* is an attempt to gain a stronger position in the declining industry. Such a strategy is viable only for a firm that begins the decline in a strong financial position, enabling it to weather the storm that forces its competitors to flee. A successful consolidation leaves a firm poised to profit after the shakeout, with a larger market share in a restructured, less-competitive industry.

With its competitors retrenching and harvesting, Goodyear pursued a consolidation strategy, investing $2 billion on new plant and equipment by the end of the 1970s and expecting to invest close to $400 million per annum more into the 1980s. The goal was not to increase capacity but to position the firm as the lowest-cost producer of high-quality radials. The company closed its inefficient plants in the Northeast and replaced them with automated plants in the South. In each market where its competitors cut back, Goodyear sought to improve its products and lower its costs to capture the sales its competitors abandoned. Throughout the consolidation process, Goodyear (along with Michelin) kept pressure on its weaker rivals by shaving prices, especially in the original equipment market.[27]

Because of its initial position of strength, Goodyear could pursue such a strategy while its competitors could not. It began the decline as a profitable company and stayed in the black during the shakeout. As a result, it could finance the consolidation by borrowing heavily against its earnings. Goodyear already had the largest sales volume, which enabled it to spread more thinly the research and development cost (close to $200 million per year) necessary to take the lead in quality and production efficiency. Although Goodyear's profitability declined during the late 1980s, its adherence to a consolidation strategy lead by nontire asset sales, cost cutting, and expanded product and distribution, has enabled the company to achieve record profits in 1992.

The lesson from this is that there are strategic choices that can improve even the worst phases of life, but the choice is not arbitrary. It depends on a firm's relative ability to pursue a strategy to successful completion, and it requires forethought and planning.

SUMMARY

The factors that influence pricing strategy change over the life of a product concept. The market defined by a product concept passes through four phases: development, growth, maturity, and decline. Briefly, the changes in the strategic environment over those phases are as follows:

Market development. Buyers are price insensitive because they lack knowledge of the product's benefits. Both production and promotional costs are high. Competitors are either nonexistent or few and not a threat since the potential gains from market development exceed those from competitive rivalry. Pricing strategy signals the product's value to potential buyers, but buyer education remains the key to sales growth.

Market growth. Buyers are increasingly informed about product attributes either from personal experience or from communication with innovators. Consequently, they are increasingly responsive to lower prices. If diffusion strongly affects later sales, price reductions can substantially increase the rate of market growth and the product's long-run profitability. Moreover, cost economies accompanying growth usually enable one to cut price while still maintaining profit margins. Although competition increases during this phase, high rates of market growth enable industry-wide expansion, generally precluding the advent of price competition. Price cutting to drive out competitors may occur, however. Cost advantages associated with sales volume are substantial if current market share is expected to determine which competing technology becomes the industry standard, or if capacity outstrips sales growth.

Market maturity. Most buyers are repeat purchasers who are familiar with the product. Increasing homogeneity enables them to better compare competing brands. Consequently, price sensitivity reaches its maximum in this phase. Competition begins to put downward pressure on prices since any firm can grow only by taking sales from its competitors. Despite such competition, profitability depends on having achieved a defensible competitive position through cost leadership or differentiation and on exploiting it effectively. Common opportunities to maintain margins by increasing pricing effectiveness include: unbundling related products, improved demand estimation, improved control and utilization of costs, expansion of the product line, and reevaluation of distribution channels.

Market decline. Reduced buyer demand and excess capacity characterize this phase. If costs are largely variable or if capital can be easily reallocated to more promising markets, prices need fall only slightly to induce some firms to cut capacity. If costs are largely fixed and sunk, average costs soar due to reduced capacity utilization, while price competition increases as firms attempt to increase their capacity utilization by capturing a larger share of a declining market. Three options are available: retrench to one's strongest product lines and price to defend one's share in them, harvest one's entire business by pricing for maximum cashflow, or consolidate one's position by price cutting to drive out weak competitors and capture their markets.

NOTES

1. See Theodore Levitt, "Exploit the Product Life Cycle," *Harvard Business Review*, 43 (November–December 1965), 81–94; John E. Smallwood, "The Product Life Cycle: A Key to Strategic Market Planning," *MSU Business Topics*, Winter 1973, pp. 29–35; and George Day, "The Product Life Cycle: Analysis and Applications," *Journal of Marketing*, 45, no. 4 (Fall 1981), 60–67. For a criticism of the life-cycle concept, especially when applied to individual brands, see Nariman K. Dhalla and Sonia Yosper, "Forget the Product Life Cycle Concept!" *Harvard Business Review*, 54 (January–February 1976), 102–12.

2. For a general overview of marketing strategy over the life cycle, see Michael E. Porter, *Competitive Strategy: Techniques for Analyzing Industries and Competitors* (New York: The Free Press, 1980), Chapter 8.

3. William Qualls, Richard W. Olshavsky, and Ronald E. Michaels, "Shorting of the PLC—An Empirical Test," *Journal of Marketing*, 45, no. 4 (Fall 1981), 76–80.

4. See Everett M. Rogers and F. Floyd Shoemaker, *Communication of Innovations*, 2nd ed. (New York: The Free Press, 1971); Frank M. Bass, "A New Product Growth Model for Consumer Durables," *Management Science*, 15 (January 1969), 215–27.

5. William H. Whyte, "The Web of Word of Mouth," *Fortune*, 50 (November 1954), 140–43, 204–12.

6. Rogers and Shoemaker, *Communication of Innovations*, pp. 180–82.

7. See Everett M. Rogers, *Diffusion of Innovations* (New York: The Free Press, 1962), Chapters 7 and 8; Rogers and Shoemaker, *Communication of Innovations*, Chapter 6; Gregory S. Carpenter and Kent Nakamoto, "Consumer Preference Formation and Pioneering Advantage," *Journal of Marketing Research*, 26 (August 1989), 285–98.

8. Theodore Levitt, *The Marketing Mode* (New York: McGraw-Hill, 1969), pp. 7–8.

9. See Philip Maher, "Coming to Grips with the Robot Market," *Industrial Marketing* (January 1982), pp. 93–98.

10. Porter, *Competitive Strategy*, pp. 34–41.

11. See R. G. Hamermesh, M. J. Anderson, Jr., and J. T. Harris, "Strategies for Low Market Shoe Businesses," *Harvard Business Review*, 56 (May–June 1978), 95–102.

12. William E. Fruhan, Jr., "Pyrrhic Victories in Fights for Market Share," *Harvard Business Review*, 50, no. 5 (September–October 1972), 101–102.

13. See Carolyn Y. Woo and Arnold C. Cooper, "The Surprising Case for Low Market Share," *Harvard Business Review*, 60 (November–December 1982), 106–13; and Porter, *Competitive Strategy*, pp. 38–40.

14. See William Hall, "Survival Strategies in a Hostile Environment," *Harvard Business Review*, 58 (September–October 1980), 75–83.

15. See Abel P. Jeuland, "Parsimonious Models of Diffusion of Innovation, Part B: Incorporating the Variable of Price," University of Chicago working paper (July 1981).

16. See Hall, "Survival Strategies," pp. 75–85.

17. This problem can even result in a period of intensely competitive, unprofitably low pricing in the maturity phase if, as sometimes happens, the industry fails to anticipate the leveling off of sales growth and thus enters maturity having built excess capacity.

18. See Porter, *Competitive Strategy*, pp. 247–49, for a discussion of the problems firms face that do not acknowledge the transition to maturity.

19. See Philip Kotler, "Phasing Out Weak Products," *Harvard Business Review*, 43 (March–April 1965), 107–18.

20. Theodore Levitt, "Marketing When Things Change," *Harvard Business Review*, 55 (November–December 1977), 107–13; Porter, *Competitive Strategy*, pp. 159, 241–249.

21. "A Food Supplier's Bigger Bite," *Business Week*, February 22, 1982, p. 136.

22. "I'm Paid to Be an S.O.B.," *Forbes*, September 15, 1980, pp. 161–62.

23. "Firestone: It worked," *Forbes*, August 17, 1981, pp. 56–57; John J. Nevin, "The Bridgestone Firestone Story," *California Management Review*, Summer 1990, pp. 114–32.

24. "Uniroyal Consolidates to Get into the Black," *Business Week*, February 1, 1980, pp. 40–42.

25. "The Industry Pessimist," *Forbes*, September 15, 1980, pp. 168–69.

26. "Goodrich: Speeding the Switch from Tires to Industrial Chemicals," *Business Week*, March 9, 1981, pp. 48–50.

27. "No Retreat, No Surrender," *Forbes*, September 15, 1980, pp. 160–61.

CUSTOMER NEGOTIATION

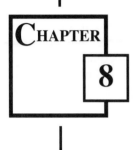

CHAPTER

8

PRICING IN THE TRENCHES

This chapter is coauthored with David Kreidberg of the Strategic Pricing Group, Inc.

It can be said that pricing is the "moment of truth" in marketing. That moment occurs in the offices of purchasing agents and field salespeople, far removed from the marketing departments and executive suites where strategies are created. Consequently, even well-conceived pricing strategies frequently fail due to ineffective implementation. To capture value in pricing, sales managers and salespeople must learn to assess the negotiating positions that customers employ and to respond appropriately. In this chapter, we will

   1.   Analyze and compare the effects of fixed versus negotiable price policies

   2.   Discuss the appropriate negotiation strategy for three types of buyers

   3.   Present an analytical method for preparing closed competitive bids when you have just one chance to make the right price offer

NEGOTIATED VERSUS FIXED-PRICE POLICIES

During recent years, an ever larger share of prices have become negotiable. Companies that for decades enjoyed leading market shares in mainframe computers, office equipment, or pharmaceutical and telecommunications services are today negotiating discounts to retain sales. Hospitals, law firms, and maintenance companies are negotiating prices for services.

Even in consumer markets, substantial discounts are negotiable for high-quality branded products, hotel rooms, annual fees on credit cards, and general merchandise available at local home centers. It seems as though the price of anything and everything is now open to discussion.

Reasons for negotiating price

In many cases price negotiations are both desirable and necessary. When customers purchase unique products (for example, new construction, a telecommunications satellite, or a new home), negotiable prices permit the seller to price based on the buyer's ability and willingness to pay. Moreover, when customers purchase infrequently, they are unlikely to develop the knowledge and expertise to determine the prices that other customers pay. In industries with standardized, frequently purchased products, however, price negotiations undermine a firm's ability to capture the value of its products. Unfortunately, it is in these industries that price negotiation appears to be growing most rapidly.

During the 1970s and 1980s, three forces began pushing companies toward negotiated price policies. First, price controls during the early 1970s left many companies caught between fixed prices for their products and rising costs from external suppliers. To protect themselves, companies raised their published list prices excessively while discounting them surreptitiously. If price controls were imposed again, it would be easy to raise effective prices by reducing the discounts. Second, in the 1980s power in consumer markets shifted toward large retailers such as Safeway grocery stores, Wal-Mart retail stores, and Home Depot home centers. Their tremendous buying volume allowed them to negotiate better deals from even leading-brand manufacturers.

Finally, many markets—from mainframe computers, to home appliances, to legal services—are now experiencing the symptoms of maturity: slower growth; reduced differentiation; and more knowledgeable, value-conscious buyers. Rather than adjust their price policies and margin goals to more accurately reflect the new competitive environment, many companies simply begin negotiating discounts on an individual account basis. Customers learn that the price they pay is related more to negotiating power and ability than to value received. Consequently, selling moves from a cooperative process of finding the best solution for the customer to an adversarial process of dividing the gains. Companies in this situation find that even when they create products of superior value, customers are unwilling to pay a price that reflects that value.

Moreover, negotiable price policies teach salespeople to use price as a tool for closing sales rather than to raise the customers' willingness to pay by selling value. To make matters worse, many companies that negotiate prices actually encourage salespeople to sell on price by rewarding them for achieving sales volume rather than profitability. (See Appendix 8A for a better sales force compensation scheme.)

Managers must recognize that changes in customer value and competitive conditions require ongoing modifications of fixed-price structures to maintain legitimacy in the eyes of customers. Evaluating pricing structures on a continuing basis ensures that companies capture the unique values of individual customer segments and the volume opportunities they represent. Unfortunately, managers unable or unwilling to capture this value cede control over pricing and ultimately over the strategic direction of their businesses. Companies that hope to maintain win-win relationships with their customers by providing exceptional value have little choice but to establish and maintain fixed-price policies that realistically reflect market conditions.

Before you conclude that a fixed-price policy cannot work in your industry, recognize that such a policy need not be a one-price policy. You can and should provide *fixed* discounts for volume, long-term contracts, and bundled purchases. You can also maintain different margins for different products in your line (for example, higher margins for Cadillacs than for Chevrolets) and for objective customer segments (for example, senior citizens). A fixed-price policy means simply that the price for any particular offer (product, quantity, terms, and so forth) sold to someone in a particular customer segment is **nonnegotiable**. If a customer needs a lower price, he or she must be prepared to give up something to qualify for a better discount.

Undoing the damage

For many companies, the problem becomes how to work their way back toward a fixed, value-based pricing policy when customers have come to expect that every price is negotiable. The following guidelines will help you establish a fixed-price policy where account-level negotiation has previously proliferated.

1.   Prices must accurately reflect the unique value of products to different customer segments. If they don't, you must further segment and increase the standard (nonnegotiable) discounts for the most price-sensitive customers. If some price-sensitive customers can't be segmented, then walk away from the business to protect the integrity of your prices to other more profitable segments.

2.   Salespeople must be educated on how to sell product value and be appropriately compensated to do so. (See Appendix 8A.)

3.   Use the switch to a nonnegotiable pricing strategy as a promotional tool. Customers should perceive the fixed-price policy as a fair change for both the buyer and the seller, not as a price increase. This is

done most easily by introducing fixed prices as new products or models are launched.

4.   Use nonprice "closers" as an alternative to price cuts. Added value, in the form of free supplies, extra training, or new services, can help salespeople close sales to value-sensitive customers without so visibly undermining the price level. Make sure you account for the costs of these on a per account basis, just as you would a lower price. Otherwise accounts may appear profitable that actually are not.[1]

Understanding the buying center

Before you can formulate effective negotiation strategy, you must first understand who the buyer is and his or her role within the buying center of the corporation. Sales to organizations is far more complex than sales to individuals because each member of the buying center evaluates alternative products and suppliers based on unique criteria. Buying centers generally consist of individuals who fulfill the following roles:

1.   *Initiators* start the purchasing process. Routine product purchases may be initiated by front-line production workers or supply personnel. In complex purchases, initiators might come from engineering, research and development, or elsewhere in the organization.

2.   *Users* use the product or service. Although easy to identify, users may not have a great deal of power in the purchasing process.

3.   *Buyers* have the formal responsibility for purchasing products and services. Although purchasing agents often fulfill this traditional role, it is not unusual to have other members of the organization perform this task, especially in small organizations or when purchasing capital equipment.

4.   *Gatekeepers* control the flow of information and external contact with the supply firms and are often considered experts in a particular product area. Often this role is fulfilled by a nondecision maker who can only influence the decision process. A common mistake is to assume that the gatekeeper is the decision maker.

5.   *Deciders* possess the final authority to select the vendor(s) who will supply the product. The real decision maker is often shielded by a host of individuals filling other roles.[2]

A common mistake that salespeople make is concentrating on a limited number of people, thus underestimating the impact that other members have on the final decision. A request from engineering might initiate an evaluation based solely on performance and quality; the decision may then move to purchasing, where product attributes are secondary to price. It is imperative that the seller recognize that these changes are taking place and adjust their negotiation strategy accordingly. Selling differentiating attributes to a purchasing agent who does not value them is a useless exercise.

NEGOTIATION STRATEGIES

Effective negotiators must understand the various buying behaviors associated with different types of buyers and their individual purchasing agendas. These behaviors are a function of how buyers value differentiating attributes of products and their willingness to pay for them. Although suppliers often concentrate on selling differentiation value, a buyer's willingness to pay may be based on other criteria (see Chapter 4). Successful sellers must adapt their negotiation strategies accordingly. In this section, we describe sales negotiation strategies for dealing with price buyers, loyal buyers, and value buyers (See Chapter 6 for explanation of this segmentation scheme.) Convenience buyers are excluded because they are not concerned with value or price, but merely availability.

Negotiating with price buyers

Price buyers are usually larger companies and government agencies with the resources and incentives to qualify multiple vendors. They seek to purchase at the lowest cost, subject to the product and supplier meeting minimum specifications. They will not pay for incremental product value beyond their specifications nor for the intrinsic benefits that accompany long-term relationships with suppliers. Their narrow focus on price greatly inhibits the ability of the seller to negotiate based on the value of the product. These buyers may even limit suppliers' contact with other members of the buying center who might acknowledge the product's incremental value and justify paying a higher price. They may even require formal bids and use adversarial negotiation tactics designed to play suppliers off against one another in their search for the lowest price.

There are several strategies for negotiating with price buyers. The first and certainly most difficult option is to refocus their attention on product value and to raise their willingness to pay by proving that added value is cost justified. This is usually not possible for one salesperson to achieve alone. It requires a commitment by the selling company to invest resources to beguile customers into compromising their pure price orientation. For example, American Hospital Supply Company successfully converted hospitals that were traditionally price buyers to value buyers by placing computer terminals in the hospital purchasing departments. These terminals were linked to sophisticated information systems which eliminated the need to manage large inventories. The net result was a more efficient system enabling the customer to save more money from better inventory management than by focusing strictly on supply prices.

Although your long-term objective may be to change price-driven purchasing behavior, many price buyers will never change. In this case, sellers must follow a strategy of *selective participation*, carefully evaluating the short-term profitability and long-term implications of these transactions and accepting them only when they (a) provide incremental contribution and (b) do not undermine more profitable business.

Companies often invest resources to serve price buyers in the vain belief that someday their efforts will prove profitable. Resist the temptation to negotiate for a price buyer's business in anticipation of future profits—they rarely materialize. If you can't participate in their business profitably, acknowledge the futility and walk away. Fortunately, the long-term consequences of walking away from a price buyer's business are minimal. Since, by definition, price buyers react to low prices, you can always go back and participate in their business later by offering a low price *when it is strategically prudent and profitable to do so*! More important, selective participation sends a significant signal to your other customers that you're not going to invest resources where there is no payback. Sales, service, and support personnel focus on servicing value buyers and loyal buyers, since profits are more certain.

The marketer of an electronic commodity had an excellent relationship with Ford and considered the company a loyal customer. Although they also sold to General Motors for many years, GM was strictly a price buyer. Due to their volume and negotiating power, GM received a 15 percent discount on most purchases. The supplier was careful, however, to sell GM only its undifferentiated, older technologies. When the supplier developed a new technology that saved customers money in the production process, Ford was first to receive it. The supplier was reluctant to offer the technology to GM fearing that its adversarial negotiators would force the company to supply the new technology at a lower price or face losing all business with GM. Despite the long-term and persuasive evidence that GM's major competitors' value-driven purchasing policies are successful, GM remains a price buyer by most suppliers, much to its detriment.[3]

The prospect of walking away from price buyers is terrifying to many marketers since price buyers are often their largest customers. By selling to large customers, many firms are focusing on the toughest negotiators with the toughest price buyers and are losing the opportunity to capture additional profits from more profitable segments. The "80/20 rule" states that 80 percent of the volume in a particular industry will come from 20 percent of the largest customers. The net result for suppliers unfortunate enough to win business from this segment is increased sales volume but little or no profit. Hundreds of suppliers to the auto industry are in this situation. A new, more relevant rule for analyzing customer profitability is the 20/225 rule. Recent analysis has shown that some firms are at "break-even" with roughly 70 percent of their customers; 20 percent of the customers provide 225 percent of the profits; and the remaining 10 percent (the larger accounts) are actually costing firms 125 percent of their profits!

Since fixed-cost structures of manufacturing operations are often justified by the volume that large customers represent, it is difficult to totally walk away from all price buyers' business. Fortunately, because large customers often negotiate with multiple suppliers, marketers can look for favorable opportunities for selective participation. When a bidding war occurs, it is best to get in at the end of the process, when sellers are less likely to be emotionally committed to winning the battle (see Chapter 5). When it becomes necessary to bid a lower price, it is just as easy to say to the buyer, "When you're ready to place the purchase order, I'll give you my best price." This limits the damage that a buyer can do by "shopping" the price with competitors and allows the salesperson to take the order "off the street" and thus limit the likelihood that other competitors are considered.

A similar option is the "five minute price" tactic. Here, the low price is not put in writing and is in effect for only a short time. Without documentation, the price buyer has nothing to show competitors to elicit their response. If the seller is the preferred competitor, the buyer may recognize that such a low price might not be offered again and must decide if there is any value in continuing the negotiation process. The risk in employing such a strategy is that customers may determine that the seller is bluffing and ignore the tactic entirely. If this is likely, avoid this tactic.

Negotiating with loyal buyers

Loyal buyers are the polar opposite of price buyers. They value consistent product quality and performance, and they rely on trusted suppliers to continue providing it. Their ongoing loyalty is driven fundamentally by the risk and uncertainty associated with untested suppliers. The critical implications of inadequate performance outweigh for the loyal buyer the benefit of lower price in the short term. Here, confidence in "tried and true" existing solutions from proven vendors sustains ongoing relationships.

Fortify existing relationships by focusing attention on past performance. Stress the impact of inferior product performance on the buyer's firm, the sunk cost of previous investments, and compatibility with future requirements. Utilize unique price and quality metrics to make comparisons between and among vendors more difficult. Above all, make clear your commitment to meeting customers' current and future needs and to eliminate their incentive to look for alternative solutions. Invest sales and management time to thoroughly understand loyal buyers' sources of value. Over time you will be better positioned to react to their needs and reinforce your position as a trusted vendor.

In contrast to adversarial negotiations with price buyers, negotiations with loyal buyers are more amiable and focus on solutions that satisfy both buyer and supplier business goals. Less tangible, more augmented features such as technical expertise, reliability of service, and dedication to customer satisfaction have measurable value in the evaluation process.

Although satisfactory past performance is fundamental, a clear indication of future commitment is also critical.

During the early years of the development of mainframe computers, IBM was competing with another vendor for a large manufacturing firm's accounting business. The customer, aware that it was making an extremely long-term commitment for a mission-critical application, decided to divide its business between the two vendors and let each one run half the payroll and accounting systems for one year. At the end of the year, the results would be evaluated and a long-term contract signed with the premier vendor. Half way through the trial period, a power surge crashed the systems of both vendors, requiring a three-week restart. The competitor assembled a team of 40 engineers and technicians to attack the problem and restart the system. IBM also assigned technicians to restart the system, but in addition IBM recognized that the customer still had a problem. To solve it, IBM assembled a team of 300 clerical workers to process the customer's payroll until the system was restored. IBM won the contract. Implementing such creative solutions shows commitment to total customer satisfaction and helps retain loyal customers for the long run.

Although the loyal segment may be large during the growth stage, it invariably shrinks in maturity, as more competitors develop good reputations and buyers become more knowledgeable repeat purchasers. The loyal segment also contracts during recessions, when even otherwise loyal buyers may be scrambling to cut costs. Thus, a classic dilemma arises: Should the company cut its prices and service levels to focus on loyal customers who are migrating to the value segment, or should it maintain its prices and services to focus on the customers who remain loyal? The answer is both. By unbundling the costs of service (for example, training, installation) and by designing equally reliable but cheaper products, companies can leverage the reputation they developed while buyers were loyal and continue capturing the business of those buyers as they become more value conscious. Thus segmentation pricing strategy is the key to growth in difficult times for such market leaders as General Electric.[4]

Although obtaining business from loyal buyers justifies the investment of a firm's resources, when negotiating with loyal customers already beholden to your competitors the theory of selective participation is once again applicable. By definition, these are loyal customers and the likelihood of them changing suppliers could be extremely low. Intelligent marketers must evaluate their accounts carefully, selecting only those customers who are likely to switch and yield profitable opportunities.

Negotiating with value buyers

Value buyers represent the largest group of buyers in most markets. They seek neither the highest quality nor the cheapest price. Instead, they make their purchase decisions by carefully weighing attributes and analyzing trade-offs, ultimately purchasing the product offering the highest utility per unit price. Unlike price buyers who focus on cost, value buyers both recognize and cost justify the added utility available from more expensive options. This segment, therefore, represents an exceptional opportunity for profits to the firm that can effectively communicate superior value. The difficult challenge with these customers is to retain their business over time since they are constantly reevaluating their alternatives.

The decision to invest resources and develop long-term relationships with value buyers is a difficult one to make. Unlike loyal buyers, who clearly justify investment, or price buyers, whose limited payback is readily apparent, value buyers have no predetermined alliances. Although they may indeed repeatedly purchase your competitively-priced and well-performing product for a while, apparent loyalty quickly erodes when competitors' products imitate your product's features. Given the potential of a short-term relationship, marketers must once again use a strategy of selective participation and carefully analyze whether doing business with this segment represents the most effective allocation of the firm's resources. When negotiating with value buyers your objective is to capture the maximum value of your differentiation on each individual sale.

Successful implementation of a value-based pricing strategy depends upon a salesperson's ability to distinguish between situations in which a lower price is required, and situations in which the customer needs to be better educated on the value of the product. Salespeople must be trained to understand how customers value their products and to use value-based selling techniques and negotiating skills to communicate that value to customers. Finally, salespeople must master techniques used to reduce the damage done when price negotiations do occur.

Salespeople must always keep their emotions out of the negotiations process and must keep sight of their objective of closing the deal. In Chapter 5, we discussed the problem inherent in adopting a "win at all costs" strategy in competitive pricing situations. The same holds true for customer negotiations. It is important for salespeople to maintain a high level of professionalism during the negotiations process, even if the buyer insists on adopting adversarial tactics. In the words of Bob Wolf, a famous lawyer and sports agent, "You don't have to be disagreeable to disagree." Negotiation is not a war to win, but a process to complete to the mutual satisfaction of all those involved.[5]

When conflicts arise, it is important that both parties understand the basis of the conflict, that is, which issues are negotiable and which are not. Fighting over irreconcilable differences clouds the process and inhibits an outcome favorable to both parties. Each side begins to move away from an amicable solution, becoming entrenched in opposing positions from which resolution is virtually impossible. Participants must be willing to compromise in order to come to a satisfactory solution. Suppliers must recognize that cost control is fundamental to customers' competitive pricing, and customers must understand that suppliers are in business to make a profit. Once both parties adopt the objective of "closing the deal" and of being satisfied with the results, the process can focus on how to achieve those objectives.

Avoiding the price trap

Managers often instruct salespeople to "sell on quality, not on price." They are missing the point. Product quality and added features hold no significance until they are valued by customers.[6] Although loyal buyers will buy features, value buyers must be convinced that those features are worth the cost. American Express provides a large number of international offices as a differentiator for people who use their traveler's checks. It was not until they communicated the value of those international offices in replacing lost or stolen checks that their advertising had a positive impact on sales.

Several techniques support selling product value. First, a cost-benefit analysis, such as economic value analysis (See Chapter 4), provides customers with a clear understanding of how your product can save them money or add value to their products. During the sales process, a formal proposal detailing this value analysis should be provided. Many marketers avoid this technique because of the effort required and the risk of documenting specific savings and productivity enhancements. This risk can be minimized if conservative approaches are used in the analysis and if effort is made, up front, to have the critical data verified by the customer. Still, one must "sell" the value to the customer and convince the buying firm that it must pay for value. The following two techniques have been proven to support selling product value:

Subtraction Technique   This technique involves removing product or service attributes from the original package to "justify" the lower price requested by customers. For example, if a buyer objects to the price of a milling machine, the seller could offer the unit at a lower price without some of the value-added features such as training or service. This technique helps distinguish among buyers who are trying to extract a price concession and buyers who do not value specific product attributes. It forces customers to recognize the value of attributes unavailable at the lower price, while refocusing their attention away from the gain of a lower price to the loss of differentiating product attributes. A variant of this technique involves stressing the penalties of doing without your product. This method requires extensive knowledge of competitive products. When used properly, this technique provides salespeople with the opportunity to discuss the "unique benefit" of their products.

Division Technique   This technique breaks down the cost of the product into smaller units relative to the customer's process. For example, if you are selling a $100,000 conveyor belt that is priced 20 percent higher than the competition's, this technique would break down the total cost as follows: (1) The customer's daily production is 10,000 small motors; (2) the motors sell for $40 with a 50 percent contribution margin; (3) assuming a one-year life, the cost of the belt is only four cents per motor; and (4) the difference in price is less than one cent and more than made up in the added sales and profits for the customer if the new belt can save one day of lost production, which is worth $200,000 in contribution. This technique takes advantage of the end-benefit effect and forces the customer to recognize that the price difference is insignificant relative to the risk of failure and other costs of doing business.[7]

PREPARING COMPETITIVE BIDS

Competitive bidding is an alternative to negotiation for price buyers. The buyer develops the specifications and asks for prices. In some cases, such as sales to government, there is no opportunity to sell "value" and the business goes to the lowest bidder. In other cases, you may be able to talk with the buyers and determine what added features might make your bid more attractive despite a higher price. Pricing an order or project for a competitive bid is the ultimate price-buyer situation.[8] It often involves a huge investment on the part of the supplier hoping that its bid will win a *job*. Because competitive bidding is used most often for very large projects, winning or losing can have an exceptional impact on a company's financial health and ultimate survival.

In complex bid situations, every aspect of pricing—costs, price sensitivity, and competition—is uncertain to some degree. No firm is ever entirely certain what each input will be and how it should impact the final pricing strategy. In some cases, the degree of uncertainty is low enough to allow informal judgments to be made. Many companies in industries such as construction, telecommunications, computer and systems integration, are involved in complex, long-term bid situations. Informal judgments do not provide these companies with adequate solutions for developing pricing strategy, which makes pricing in competitive bidding situations particularly risky. Thus companies placing competitive bids are especially willing to use more quantitative techniques to ensure that they make the best possible decisions.

Quantitative analysis

Quantitative analysis brings no new data to the bidding problem. Instead, it helps managers examine the implications of the data. Attempts to make unassisted pricing judgments when facing multiple sources of uncertainty are likely to prove frustrating if not impossible since they require managers to think of more factors simultaneously than is humanly possible. Consequently, managers often disregard data that could improve their decisions. Quantitative bidding analysis enables managers to think about the problem in more tractable pieces, which can then be combined and reviewed. It helps to pinpoint sources of disagreement and to focus on them in discussion. Further, it forces the manager to go to other sources of judgment, and it facilitates evaluating risk-return trade-offs. Finally, since quantitative analysis requires documenting the decision, it helps managers learn from past experiences.

Exhibit 8.1 illustrates a quantitative analysis for a competitive bid. After listing possible bids that it might make, the company calculates the profit contribution associated with each bid.[9] The company then lists the subjective probability of winning, given each possible bid, and multiplies that probability times the profit contribution if it wins the contract with that bid. The last column shows the resulting expected value of each bid.

The bid with the highest expected value (in this case, the bid of $38 million) is the best choice for companies with many bidding opportunities. Others may wish to consider trade-offs between earning the highest expected profit with the assurance of earning at least enough profit contribution to avoid severe financial difficulty. The role of the analysis in the latter case is to identify the trade-off. How much expected profit must be sacrificed for an increase in the probability of winning?

Although simple in theory, competitive bidding is quite challenging in practice, since neither the profit contribution nor the probability of success is ever obvious. The incremental cost of winning a job varies significantly depending on the amount of other business that a company has already won. If a company has excess capacity, the contribution from win-

---

EXHIBIT 8.1

Expected Value of Alternative Competitive Bids

Dollar Amount[a]	Profit Contribution[a]	Probability of Success	Expected Value[a]
$40	$12	.24	$2.9
39	11	.32	3.5
38	10	.44	4.4
37	9	.47	4.2

Note: Expected value of bid (column 4) represents the profit contribution (column 2) multiplied by the probability of success (column 3).
[a] Figures are in millions of dollars.

ning a bid may be quite large since many costs will be sunk. However, if completing a job requires added capacity or costly delays in other jobs, incremental costs will be high and the profit contribution relatively low. Similarly, a bidder should consider the opportunity cost of committing capacity too early. Bidding low enough to win many early bids may preclude bidding on more lucrative jobs later on.

Even more difficult is assigning the probability that a given bid will be successful. Typically, assigning probabilities is a blend of research and judgment. The more a company knows about past bidding behavior in the industry and the current bidding situation, the better are its chances of producing a profitable winning bid. There are two methods for estimating a bid's probability of success: the average opponent approach and the specific opponent approach.[10] The choice between them depends on the amount of information available.

Probability of success

Average Opponent Approach   The average opponent approach is used to establish probability of success when a company has little knowledge about or past experience bidding against any specific competitors. The approach treats all competitors as essentially the same in the aggressiveness of their bidding. The company using this approach begins with an analysis of past bidding behavior. First, it collects as much information as possible about bids on past jobs that were similar to the current job. Then, to facilitate comparison of bids from different jobs, it expresses each bid as a ratio: the bid price divided by the firm's own estimated cost of the job. If the company estimates the cost of a job as $5 million, a bid of $6 million is expressed as 1.2 ($6/$5) and a loss-leader bid of $4.5 million as 0.95 ($4.5/$5). After doing this for as many jobs as possible, the company calculates the percentage of times that competitors' bids exceeded any particular value of the ratio, as follows:

Bids Ratio	Competitive Bids Exceeding Bid Ratio (%)
0.95	100
1.00	98
1.05	92
1.10	80
1.15	67
1.20	55
1.25	42
1.30	20
1.35	8

If management has no other information, the company could use these historical bid frequencies as the probabilities that it would underbid any single competitor on a single bid. For any particular bid ratio, R, we will label the probability (P) of underbidding any single competitor as $P(R)$, that is, $P \times R$. In practice, management usually has additional information about differences between the current bid and previous bids, which it uses to make subjective adjustments to the historical bid frequencies before adopting them as current bid probabilities. For example, if the industry is operating at higher capacity levels now than in the past, management assigns subjective probabilities somewhat higher than the historical bid frequencies. On the other hand, if this job is particularly attractive because of the additional business that winning it might produce in the future, management might expect competitors to bid lower than usual. In the latter case, management assigns subjective probabilities somewhat lower than the historical bid frequencies.

To calculate the probability of winning a particular job, management must next consider the number of bidding competitors. The more bidding competitors, the lower the probability that any one bid will win the job. Since the average opponent approach assumes that management cannot distinguish among its competitors, the probability of underbidding each of them is the same. Consequently, if the number of bidders is N, the probability of winning the job with any particular bid ratio is $P_{win}(R)$; then

$$P_{win}(R) = P(R)^N$$

If the historical bid frequencies shown above equal the subjective probabilities of underbidding a competitor, the probability of winning against two average competitors with a bid ratio of 1.1 is:

$$P_{win}(1.1) = .80^2 = .64 \quad or \quad 64\%$$

Exhibit 8.2 illustrates the probability of winning for each bid ratio, given two, four, or six opponents.

Bidders often do not know how many competitors they will be bidding against, which adds further uncertainty to the problem. Management must formulate subjective probabilities for the number of expected opponents. It then uses those subjective probabilities to weight different calculations of P_{win} that assume different numbers of competitors. For example, if management's subjective probabilities for the number of other bidders are:

2 other bidders .5
3 other bidders .4
4 other bidders .1

the probability of winning with a bid ratio of 1.1 in the example given above is as follows:[11]

$$P_{win}(1.1) = (.5 \times .80^2) + (.4 \times .80^3) + (.1 \times .80^4) = .565 \quad or \quad 56.5\%$$

Specific Opponent Approach The average opponent approach to establishing probability of success is appropriate only when a company knows little about its individual competitors. Usually, however, a company does know who its competitive bidders are and their different motivations. When bidding for government contracts, for example, potential bidders must state an intention to bid some months before the bids are actually due; the list of those firms is available to all competitors. When bidding for specialized construction projects, such as large hydro-electric power plants, the number of qualified bidders is so small that bidding is always against the same three or four competitors. When a company knows who the competitors will be and their prior bidding behavior, the **specific opponent approach** can help them make more successful bids.

The specific opponent approach begins much like the average opponent approach, with an analysis of historical bidding behavior of the competitors. The bidding behavior of each competitor, however, is separately analyzed. For example, if both opponent A and opponent B are frequent bidders, a company using this approach would separate them from other competitors when attempting to estimate the probabilities of underbidding them. For each value of the bid ratio, R, it would calculate the number of times each specific competitor's bid exceeded R. If other bidders, called *peripheral opponents*, are also bidding, they are treated as a separate group using the average opponent approach. An analysis of historical bidding behavior might look like Exhibit 8.3.

Exhibit 8.2

Calculating P_{WIN} Using the Average Opponent Approach

Bid Ratio	Competitive Bids Exceeding Bid Ratio(%)	Probability of Winning Job		
		2 Opponents	4 Opponents	6 Opponents
0.95	100%	1.000	1.000	1.000
1.00	98	.964	.922	.866
1.05	92	.846	.716	.606
1.10	80	.640	.410	.262
1.15	67	.449	.202	.090
1.20	55	.302	.092	.028
1.25	42	.176	.031	.005
1.30	20	.040	.002	*
1.35	8	.006	*	*

* Asterisk denotes a probability of less than .001.

As with the average opponent approach, the company uses any information about differences between this bid and previous bids to adjust the historical frequencies before using them as the probabilities of underbidding competitors on the current job. In addition, it would adjust the historical frequencies for each specific opponent based on whatever information it has about that company. For example, if opponent B recently installed a new president, who announced corporate goals including a substantial increase in market share, one might expect that the probability of B's bid exceeding any given bid ratio would now be lower. Similarly, if opponent A recently won a large contract committing much of its capacity, one might expect the probability that A's bid would exceed any given bid ratio would now be higher.

The probability of winning the job, P_{win}, is the probability of underbidding the specific opponents and the peripheral opponents. Let $P_A(R)$ and $P_B(R)$ be the probability of underbidding specific opponents A and B, respectively, and let $P_O(R)$ be the probability of underbidding one of the peripheral opponents for any particular bid ratio R. If the current job involves bidding against opponents A and B in addition to N peripheral opponents, the probability of winning with any given bid ratio R is as follows:

$$P_{win}(R) = P_A(R) \times P_B(R) \times P_O(R)^N$$

EXHIBIT 8.3

Analysis of Historical Bid Frequencies: Specific Opponent Approach

Opponents' Competitive Bids Exceeding Bid Ratio (%)

Bid Ratio	Opponent A	Opponent B	Peripheral Opponents
0.95	100%	100%	98%
1.00	98	100	95
1.05	90	95	85
1.10	80	78	70
1.15	70	65	58
1.20	55	60	40
1.25	47	55	33
1.30	30	46	20
1.35	24	33	11

If the historical bid frequencies in Exhibit 8.3 are used without adjustment as the probabilities of underbidding the opponents, the probability of winning a job with a bid ratio of 1.2 when bidding against opponents A and B and two peripheral opponents is as follows:

$$P_{\text{win}}(1.2) = .55 \times .60 \times .40^2 = .053 \quad or \quad 5.3\%$$

If management is uncertain whether opponents A or B will bid, it weights the bids of the specific opponents by the subjective probability that each one would bid. If the company is uncertain about the number of peripheral opponents who would bid, it weights the calculation of underbidding exactly as shown for the average opponent approach.

The winner's curse

Competitive bidding is notorious for causing the winning bidders to lose money.[12] In fact, research shows that even bidders who use sophisticated models and formalized techniques often lose money.[13] The reason is the winner's curse. To understand the curse, imagine first that you are one of two bidders and you win a bid with the lower price. You will probably be quite happy. Now imagine that you are one of ten bidders and you believe that your competitors are sophisticated businesspeople who know how to bid a job. Again you win. Are you still as happy? What does it mean that you bid below nine other knowledgeable bidders? Perhaps it means that you were willing to take less profit on the job. On the other hand, it could also mean that you underestimated the cost to complete the work.

The more bidders there are, the more likely you will lose money on every job you win, *even if on average you estimate costs correctly and both you and your competitors set bids that include a reasonable margin of profit.* The reason: The bids you win are not a random sample of the bids you make. You are much more likely to win jobs for which you have underestimated your costs and are unlikely to win those for which you have overestimated your cost. Consequently, the expected profitability of a job, *conditional on the fact that you have won it,* is much less than the expected profitability before winning. The difference between the conditional and unconditional probabilities increases with the number of competitors against whom you must bid.

The only solution to this is, in effect, to formalize the principle of "selective participation" described above. You do that by adding a "fudge factor" to each bid to reflect an estimate of how much you are likely to have underestimated your costs if you actually win a bid. Needless to say, adding this factor will reduce the number of bids you win, but it will ensure that you won't ultimately regret having won them.

SUMMARY

This chapter focused on four issues that arise when salespeople implement pricing strategy. First, we described the long-term problems that companies create when they permit customers to negotiate prices, and we explained how fixed-price policies can limit the damage. Managers often believe that fixed-price policies will not work in their markets. However, once they understand that fixed-price policies need not be one-price policies, most companies can develop segmented pricing policies to charge different prices without undermining the relationship between price and value. Second, we developed strategies for selling to price buyers, loyal buyers, and value buyers. Finally, we presented a formal, analytical model for preparing competitive bids and discussed the problems involved.

In the end, the best tactics can go amiss, and sellers can guess wrong concerning the buyer's intentions and ability to place an order. It is neither possible nor even desirable to win every sale. Still, sellers and buyers should strive to develop trusting relationships guided by positive-sum negotiations. Unfortunately, many buyers focus solely on price, and many sellers use price for short-term gains at the expense of close relationships with buyers. The salesperson's job is not to close every sale, but to selectively participate in those sales that contribute to the company's long-term profitability. The appendix to this chapter describes a compensation system that gives salespeople appropriate incentives to achieve this objective.

NOTES

1. Michael Marn and Robert Rosiella, "Managing Price, Gaining Profit," *Harvard Business Review*, September–October 1992, pp. 84–94.

2. Thomas V. Bonoma, "Major Sales: Who Really Does the Buying?" *Harvard Business Review*, May–June 1982, pp. 111–19.

3. "GM Is Meaner But Hardly Leaner," *Business Week*, October 19, 1992, p. 30.

4. Stratford Sherman, "How to Prosper in the Value Decade," *Fortune*, November 30, 1992, pp. 91–103.

5. Bob Wolf, *Friendly Persuasion* (New York: G. P. Putnam, 1990).

6. Fredric Saunier, *Marketing Strategies for the Online Industry* (Boston: G. K. Hall, 1988).

7. *Dealing with Price Resistance*, A Sales Training Video Tape (Chicago: The Dartnell Corporation, 1985).

8. What buyers sometimes call *bidding* is simply the first step in a negotiation process. After bids are submitted, negotiations continue with the possibility for subsequent changes in features and prices. In this section, we are dealing with bidding as an alternative to price negotiation. The techniques and problems discussed here are applicable when the bidder has only one chance to make a bid.

9. Although a bid may be stated as a fixed dollar amount, bids involving long-term contracts often include clauses to cover cost increases. For a discussion of pricing long-term contracts when costs may change, see Robert J. Dolan, "Pricing Strategies That Adjust to Inflation," *Industrial Marketing Management*, 66 (July 1981), 151–56.

10. See John F. Kottas and Basheer M. Khumawata, "Contract Bid Development for the Small Businessman," *Sloan Management Review*, 14 (Spring 1973), 31–45; Murphy A. Sewall, "A Decision Calculus Model for Contract Bidding," *Journal of Marketing*, 40 (October 1976), 92–98.

11. The general form of the equation, where f_N is the probability that N opponents will bid is $P_{win}(R) = \Sigma_N f_N \times P(R)^N$.

12. Richard H. Thayler, *The Winner's Curse: Paradoxes and Anomalies of Economic Life* (New York: The Free Press, 1992), pp. 50–62.

13. E. C. Capen, R. V. Clapp, and W. M. Campbell, "Competitive Bidding in High-Risk Situations," *Journal of Petroleum Technology*, 23 (June 1971), 641–53.

Appendix 8A
Incentives for selling value, not volume

Selling value is often the key to profitable pricing. Unfortunately, salespeople are usually strong advocates of selling based on price. The tendency of salespeople to seek quick sales to high-volume price buyers, rather than to search out and sell to value buyers, is so common that many people view it as natural. It is not. Salespeople will seek to maximize their performance, however performance is measured. If they are measured and rewarded for achieving sales volume, they will sell volume regardless of value to the customer and profitability to their employers.

Consider the dilemma facing sales representatives (or independent deals or manufacturers' representatives) who are compensated as a percentage of sales. They have a fixed number of hours available for selling. They must choose between selling to high-volume customers who demand a 15 percent price concession or to customers who buy only half the volume but will pay full price. If the time required to make a sales presentation is equal for both, clearly they will target the larger customers. They earn 35 percent more sales in the same amount of time. Also consider the case when they can quickly close a sale by meeting their competitors' 15 percent lower price or invest twice the time to sell the value and avoid the price cut. If their objective is to maximize sales volume, they will sell on price, moving on quickly to the next sale.

But is this volume-maximizing behavior good for the firm? Often not. If the firm has only a 20 percent contribution margin at full price, a 15 percent discount slashes the profitability of a sale by 75 percent! To break even on that 15 percent price cut, the company needs to sell at least three times as much volume to make the same contribution. Consequently, price cutting may benefit salespeople while undermining the profitability of the firm.

The key to inducing the sales force to sell value is to measure their performance and compensate them not just for sales volume, but for sales *profitability*. Although some companies have achieved this by adding Rube Goldberg-like complexity to their compensation scheme, there is a fairly simple, intuitive way to accomplish the same objective. Give salespeople sales goals as before, but tell them that the sales goals are set at "target" prices. If they sell at prices below or above the "target," the sales credit they earn will be adjusted by the profitability of the sale.

The key to this scheme is in calculating the profitability factor. To induce salespeople to maximize their contribution to the firm, sales credit should be multiplied by a profitability factor equal to 1 divided by the percentage contribution margin. This causes the sales credit to vary directly and in the same proportion as the firm's profitability. In the above case, the profitability factor would equal 5 (1 divided by the contribution margin of 20 percent). When the 15 percent price discount is multiplied by the profitability factor of 5, it reduces the sales credit by 75 percent rather than 15 percent. Consequently, when $1,000 worth of product is sold for $850, it produces only $250 of sales credit. When $500 worth of product is sold for $550 (10 percent price premium), the salesperson earns $750 of sales credit ($500 + 5 × $50).[1] In fact, because salespeople are more likely to take a short-term view of profitability (they can always move on to another firm), the optimal profitability factor for the firm is usually *higher* than the factor that maximizes the short-term contribution of an individual salesperson.

This is not merely a theory. As companies have moved toward more negotiated pricing, many have adopted this scheme in markets as diverse as office equipment, market research services, and door-to-door sales. Although a small percentage of salespeople cannot make the transition to value selling and profit-based compensation, most embrace it with enthusiasm. Managers should be prepared for the consequences, however, since salespeople's complaints about the company's competitiveness do not subside. Instead, salespeople who previously complained about the company's high prices begin complaining about slow deliveries, quality defects, lack of innovative product features, and the need for better sales support to demonstrate value. In short, since salespeople cannot sell value that does not exist, they become strong advocates for steps to enhance the value the organization provides.

NOTE

1. The equation for the sales credit earned for an individual sale is

$$\text{Sales Credit} = [TP - F(TP - AP)]Q$$

where TP is the target price, AP is the actual price charged, F is the profitability factor, and Q is the unit sales.

SEGMENTED PRICING

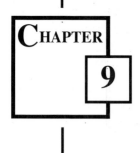

CHAPTER 9

TACTICS FOR SEPARATING MARKETS

Market segmentation is the division of buyers into distinct subsets, or segments, enabling a company to tailor marketing programs more appropriate for the buyers in each segment. Segmentation is important for every aspect of marketing, but especially for pricing. We have seen that an appropriate pricing strategy depends on costs, price sensitivity, and competition. Usually one or more of these factors vary significantly across market segments. When this happens, a pricing strategy based on a single price for all sales is an imperfect compromise. With segmented pricing, management minimizes the need to compromise. Customers who are relatively price insensitive, costly to serve, or poorly served by competitors can be charged more than those who are relatively price sensitive, less costly to serve, or well-served by competitors. Both sales and profitability improve.

If pricing a product differently across segments were easy, everyone would do it. Customers whom management would like to charge a higher price will not identify themselves as members of a relatively price-insensitive segment simply to help the seller charge them a higher price. Distributors can undermine a segmented-pricing strategy as well. If they can figure out how to buy the product cheaply and resell it to segments that will pay more, they can capture the profit from segmented pricing for themselves. Finally, some segmented-pricing tactics violate federal antitrust laws.[1] A company that adopts segmented pricing as a strategic goal still faces the difficult task of developing tactics that overcome all three of these problems. Such tactics are the subject of this chapter.

SEGMENTING BY BUYER IDENTIFICATION

Occasionally pricing differently among segments is easy because buyers in the different segments have obvious characteristics that distinguish them. Barbers charge different prices for short and long hair because long hair is usually more difficult to cut. At times when they have excess capacity, barbers cut children's hair at a substantial discount because many parents view home haircuts as acceptable alternatives to costly barber cuts for their children. For barbers, simple observation of the customers is the key to segmented pricing.

Although observation is the most common method of segmentation, it is often ineffective or counterproductive. The reason? Too often sellers naively think they can segment simply by being responsive to those customers who complain about the price. For example, during the 1980s when overcapacity plagued the lodging industry, some mid- and even upper-level hotel chains instructed their reservation agents to offer customers the "regular" room rate first. If the customer indicated that the price was too high, they were to query the customer about possible ways they might qualify for a small discount (for example, AAA membership). If the customer still resisted and the hotel projected excess capacity for that night, the reservation agent used some excuse to offer a still better rate from a special block of discounted rooms.

Although some hotels still do this, most have learned their lesson. The customers who complain are rarely the most price sensitive. On the contrary, they are the frequent, seasoned business travelers who learn quickly about a hotel's segmentation scheme and love to negotiate. They also love to brag to the other business travelers they meet at the bar about how they paid a lower rate. In contrast, the people who don't complain are more likely to be pleasure travelers who are more price sensitive but don't know the game. Finding the need to economize embarrassing, many will not complain about the price. They will simply hang up or make some excuse about why they cannot book the reservation immediately, and then call Motel 6.

Even less effective is the tactic of some business-to-business salespeople of discounting when customers complain about prices. Large business customers can afford professional actors, called purchasing agents, who have mastered the art of acting price sensitive even when they are not. When constrained by engineering or manufacturing to purchase from a particular supplier, they may still use other bids to extract discounts. Salespeople who don't understand this game end up giving away value unnecessarily to these largest customers. Effective segmentation requires basing discounts on more objective indicators of price sensitivity than mere complaining.

Obtaining information

Rarely is identification of customers in different segments straightforward. Yet, management can sometimes structure a pricing policy that induces the most price-sensitive buyers to volunteer objective information necessary to segment them. Theaters give discounts to college students who are more price sensitive because of their low incomes and their alternative sources of campus entertainment. Students readily volunteer their college identification cards to prove that they are members of the price-sensitive segment. Members of the less price-sensitive segment identify themselves by not producing such identification.

Coupons provided by the seller give price-sensitive shoppers another way to identify themselves.[2] Supermarkets put coupons in their newspaper ads because people who read those ads are part of the segment that compares prices before deciding where to shop. Packaged-goods manufacturers print coupons directly on the packages, expecting that only price-sensitive shoppers will make the effort to clip them out and use them for future purchases. Small-appliance manufacturers use rebates for the same purpose, expecting that only the most price-sensitive shoppers will take the time to fill out a rebate form and mail it in.[3]

Even schools and colleges charge variable tuitions for the same education based on their estimates of their students' price sensitivities. Although the official school catalogs list just one tuition, it is not the one most students pay. Many students receive substantial discounts called *tuition remission scholarships* obtained by revealing personal information on financial-aid applications. By evaluating family income and assets, colleges can set a tuition for each student that makes attendance attractive while still maximizing the school's income.

The key to inducing buyers of any product to reveal their price sensitivities is simply to set prices high and give discounts for information. Those buyers whom the seller wishes to charge the full price need not cooperate; they are identified simply by the process of elimination. Discounts from high prices have the added advantage of making the seller appear charitable to the price-sensitive buyer. Physicians use this argument to justify the higher prices they charge people with comprehensive health insurance.[4] They are not charging more to people with insurance, but rather charging less to people without it. Of course, how you see it depends on your perspective.

Segmenting by salespeople

Often a buyer's relative price sensitivity does not depend on anything immediately observable or on factors a customer freely reveals. It depends instead on how well informed about alternatives a customer is and on the personal values the customer places on the differentiating attributes of the seller's offer.[5] In such cases, the classification of buyers by segment usually requires an expert salesperson trained in soliciting and evaluating the information necessary for segmented pricing.

The retail price of an automobile is typically set by the salesperson who evaluates the buyer's willingness to pay. Notice how the salesperson takes a personal interest in the customer, asking what the customer does for a living (ability to pay), how long he has lived in the area (knowledge of the market), what kinds of cars he has bought before (loyalty to a particular brand), where he lives (value placed on the dealer's location), and whether he has looked at, or is planning to look at, other cars (awareness of alternatives). By the time a deal has been put together, the experienced salesperson has a fairly good idea how sensitive the buyer's purchase decision will be to the product's price.

Since expert salespeople are costly, segmented pricing by a sales force is limited to items that involve large expenditures and is far more prevalent in business than in consumer markets.[6] First time industrial buyers frequently pay higher prices because of their unfamiliarity with alternative suppliers. To become informed they need to seek out alternative suppliers. Their inexperience with the product makes evaluating various suppliers difficult. However, in time new buyers learn what is important in the evaluation of different suppliers. Competing suppliers learn that the new buyers now use the product, and their salespeople are sent to increase awareness of alternatives. Buyers' feelings of obligation to the initial seller wanes after repeated purchases. Industrial salespeople must detect these changes, adjusting price to compensate for buyers' increasing price sensitivity.

SEGMENTING BY PURCHASE LOCATION

If customers in one market segment purchase at different locations, they can be segmented by purchase location. This is common practice for a wide range of products. Dentists, opticians, and other professionals sometimes have multiple offices in different parts of a city, each with a different price schedule reflecting differences in their clients' price sensitivity. Many grocery chains classify their stores by intensity of competition and apply lower markups in those localities where competition is most intense. Ski resorts near Denver use purchase location to segment sales of lift tickets. Tickets purchased at slopeside cost $37 to $39 and are bought by the most affluent skiers who stay in the slopeside hotels and condos. Tickets are cheaper (approximately 10 percent less) at hotels in the nearby town of Dillon, where less-affluent skiers stay in cheaper, off-slope accommodations. In Denver, tickets can be bought at grocery stores and self-serve gas stations for larger discounts (approximately 20 percent less). These discounts attract locals, who know the market well, including the less advertised tourist spots, and who are generally more price sensitive (due to share-of-cost accounted for by the lift ticket in the end-benefit).

Segmentation by location occurs quite often in international marketing. Deutsche Gramaphone historically has sold its records for up to 50 percent more in the European market than in the highly competitive U.S. market. Japanese steel mills are often accused of "dumping" when they charge buyers less than those in Japan. Many industrial manufacturers must charge less to the bargain-conscious Chinese than to the wealthy sheiks of the Mideast. This tactic works when high shipping costs and the need for after-sale service ensure that buyers in low-price countries will not order goods for resale in countries where prices are higher.

A tactic often used to segment markets for pricing bulky industrial products such as steel and wood is *freight absorption*. Freight absorption is the agreement by the seller to bear all or part of shipping costs of the product. This tactic gives buyers who are farther from the seller a larger effective discount. The purpose is to segment buyers to reflect the attractiveness of their alternatives. A steel mill in Pittsburgh, for example, might agree to charge buyers in the Midwest for shipping only from Chicago, even though the product is actually shipped from Pittsburgh. A buyer in Milwaukee would then pay shipping only from Chicago. The seller in Pittsburgh receives only the price the buyer pays less the absorbed portion of the shipping costs. Thus, the seller accepts less for the same product from the more distant buyers than from the buyer next door.

Why should a seller agree to absorb freight charges rather than to employ the more common practice of selling FOB, requiring buyers to bear all freight charges?[7] Competition. Buyers who can purchase from a local supplier and incur less shipping cost will have less value for product of a more distant supplier. The supplier in Pittsburgh who wants to overcome the negative differentiation value associated with its more distant location absorbs the freight cost up to the location of the Chicago competitor. This enables the Pittsburgh supplier to cut price to customers nearer the competitor without having to cut price for more local sales. The Chicago competitor probably uses the same tactic to become more competitive for buyers near Pittsburgh.

With trade barriers coming down, particularly in Europe but also in North America, segmenting by location will become increasingly more difficult for goods easily shipped from one location to another. It will no longer be possible simply to charge less for goods shipped to Athens or Mexico City than those shipped to Paris or New York. Wholesalers will simply buy where the product is cheap and "cross ship" it to where it is dear. Moreover, large multinational companies can quickly detect differences in prices across borders and buy from the cheapest location.

Fortunately, the alternatives to segmenting by location may actually improve profitability. Many companies have used segmenting by location simply because the average buyer in Italy is more price sensitive than the average buyer in Germany. But being right "on average" still leaves a lot of room for costly error. Some Italians are quite wealthy, even by international standards, whereas some Germans are quite poor and price sensitive. Thus, the low average price in Italy is too low for some customers, resulting in lost profits from people who would have paid more, whereas the high price in Germany is too high, resulting in lost profit from people who don't buy. The international companies that will benefit from the integration of previously divided economies will be those that quickly adopt more sophisticated segmentation strategies, enabling them to offer common prices across borders while segmenting buyers by other criteria.

SEGMENTING BY TIME OF PURCHASE

When customers in different market segments purchase at different times, one can segment them for pricing by time of purchase. Theaters segment their markets by offering midday matinees at substantially reduced prices, attracting the price-sensitive retirees, students, and unemployed workers who can most easily attend at such times. Less price-sensitive evening patrons cannot so easily arrange dates or work schedules to take advantage of the cheaper midday ticket prices. Similarly, restaurants usually charge more to their evening patrons, even if they cater primarily to a lunch crowd. There are more numerous inexpensive substitutes for lunches than there are for dinners. A Big Mac or a brown bag, acceptable for lunch, is generally viewed as a poor substitute for a formal dinner as part of an evening's entertainment.

Periodic sales, offering the same merchandise at discounted prices, can also segment markets. This tactic is most successful in markets with a combination of occasional buyers who are relatively unfamiliar with the market, and with more regular buyers who know when the sales are and plan their purchases accordingly. Furniture manufacturers employ this tactic with sales every February and August, months when most people would not naturally think about buying furniture. But people who regularly buy home furnishings, and who are more price sensitive because of the substitute awareness and total expenditure effects, know to plan their purchases to coincide with these sales.

Peak-load pricing

Segmenting by time is also useful when the cost of serving a buyer varies significantly with the time of purchase. This time sensitivity occurs when demand varies at different times but the product is not storable.

Airlines, for example, face greater demand for seats on Mondays, Thursdays, and Fridays than on other days. Early morning and late afternoon departures are also more in demand than departures during the midday and evening. Similar variations in demand are common in practically all industries (autos, clothing), but are usually solved by simply storing excess production when demand is low and selling it when demand exceeds production capacity. An airline, however, cannot store the excess seats it has on Tuesdays in order to meet exceptional demand on Fridays. Seats left unused on Tuesday flights are lost, whereas the ability to serve customers on Friday afternoon is limited by capacity at that time. The same general problem plagues hotels and restaurants, electric utilities, long-distance telephone companies, theaters, computer time-sharing companies, beauty salons, toll bridges, and parking garages. Unable to move supplies of their products from one time to another, their only option is to manage demand. One way of doing so is with *peak-load pricing*.

The principle of peak-load pricing follows from our discussion in Chapter 2 on the distinction between avoidable and sunk costs. Industries with peak-load problems have two different kinds of costs: operating costs and capacity costs. Operating costs are incremental and avoidable regardless of whether demand is at peak or nonpeak levels. The cost of fuel is an operating cost for an electric utility because it is a cost incurred only as needed to meet demand. *Capacity costs*, on the other hand, are the costs of purchasing resources for both peak and nonpeak sales simultaneously. The cost of building generating capacity is a capacity cost because the utility cannot purchase it only for those days or hours when demand is greatest. To have capacity available for hot summer days, the utility must pay for it year-round.

Setting Peak-Load Prices   Setting peak-load prices is often straightforward. Capacity is incremental only for changes in sales during peak periods. Consequently, capacity costs are relevant only for the pricing of peak-period sales when lowering price to serve more customers would require adding more capacity, whereas raising price to serve fewer customers could enable the company to avoid building new capacity. Capacity costs should be ignored when pricing sales in nonpeak periods, since the cost of capacity up to the amount used at peak times is not avoidable. The percent contribution margin for nonpeak sales will, therefore, be greater than for sales at peak times. This will normally result in lower prices being set for nonpeak time periods than for peak time periods.[8]

Peak-load pricing is not always that simple. Consider what happened when the Bell Telephone System first decided to set different prices for calls placed at different times of the day. Bell originally noted that when it charged the same price for all calls the number of calls was greatest during the business day and dropped off substantially in the evenings and on weekends. Concluding that the cost of capacity was relevant only for calls made during the business day, management proceeded to set prices for daytime calls that reflected the entire cost of capacity while setting prices for evenings and weekends that reflected none of the capacity cost. The result was a substantial increase in calls in the evenings and on weekends, an increase so great that more calls were made during less-expensive, non-peak times than during the peak period of the business day.

Ma Bell had encountered a classic problem called *peak reversal*. Clearly, in the quantity of calls placed in the low-priced, nonpeak time period is straining capacity, the cost of building new capacity is relevant for the pricing of those calls. If nonpeak calls were forced to bear all, or even an equal share, of the cost of capacity, the peak calling time would reverse again, reestablishing excess capacity during evenings and weekends. The solution to its peak-reversal problem, as Bell soon discovered, was first to raise the low, nonpeak price just enough so that the number of calls people wanted to make at that time was no greater than the capacity available. In evaluating future decisions to change prices or to add to capacity, Bell needed to consider the contribution generated by both peak and nonpeak calls. Since peak prices were higher, they contributed more to the cost of capacity than did nonpeak calls. Since nonpeak calls still fully used capacity, they also contributed in part.

Peak-load prices are set properly by allocating the cost of capacity to the time period that requires it. Allocating the entire cost of capacity to the peak demand period and pricing accordingly is correct if peak period sales continue to exceed nonpeak sales. If lower pricing in the nonpeak period causes sales to equal or exceed those in the peak period, one must logically conclude that nonpeak sales also partly account for the need to increase capacity. In that case, nonpeak sales should be made to share part of the cost of capacity.[9]

Yield management

A more sophisticated version of peak-load pricing, now widely used in the airline, cruise ship, and lodging industries, is *yield management*. Unlike peak-load pricing, or segmentation based on different costs of serving customers, yield management simultaneously integrates differences both in the cost and in price sensitivity. It is not difficult to see how yield management represents a huge opportunity for increased profitability. Airlines enjoy peak demand from business travelers on Monday mornings and Friday afternoons on many routes, enabling airlines to fill the planes at full coach fares. However, smaller demand at full coach fares would leave many seats unfilled at less popular times. Rather than discounting all seats at those times, as simple peak-load pricing would suggest, the airlines discount only the seats that they cannot sell at full coach fare.

This "selective discounting" is a much superior strategy. After all, business travelers flying midweek do not value getting to the destinations any less than those flying on Mondays or Fridays. The airline's problem is simply that there are not enough midweek business travelers to fill the planes. It makes no sense, therefore, to discount tickets to business travelers since the airline would generate few added sales and would leave a lot of potential revenue "on the table." The goal is to attract new segments when capacity is available without undermining income from segments that would still fly at higher prices. They do this by offering "super saver" fares that are attractive only to price-sensitive segments of customers. Most business travelers don't like the weekend stay requirement and the no-cancellation restrictions that "super saver" fares include.

The purpose of yield-management systems is to help sellers determine how much of their capacity they can afford to sell at discount prices without undermining their ability to serve those customers willing to pay full price. This task presents a problem, because it is usually not possible to sell first to all those customers willing to pay full price and only then to sell the remaining capacity to customers who require a discount. In the airline industry, for example, the normal purchase pattern is exactly the opposite. Business travelers usually do not want to book their seats until near the time of travel, often even the same day, whereas pleasure travelers want to book their vacations at discount fares far in advance. How can an airline decide how many discount seats it can sell weeks before a flight and still have enough seats left to serve its best customers at full fare?

Clearly, one way is to average past sales for a particular flight to estimate how many seats business travelers will buy and then to sell discount tickets to fill the remaining seats. Unfortunately, the average of past sales is only a very rough indicator of the future. It would result in substantial under- and overestimates of seats available for discount sales. A better way is to use past experience to create an "historical booking path" for seat sales beginning 30 days before departure. (See Exhibit 9.1.) If business sales are above the number normally booked 30 days before a flight, then the airline allocates that many fewer seats for discount sales. If business sales fall below the projected booking path, the airline allocates more seats for discount sales. Each day the estimate of actual business sales, and the number of seats available for discount sales, is revised. This practice explains why a pleasure traveler may be told that all discount seats are currently sold, but discover a week later that some have become available. By constantly adjusting the number of seats available at discount, airlines can optimize the total "yield" earned on their investment in their planes, minimizing both the number of full-fare passengers turned away and the number of seats flown empty.[10]

SEGMENTING BY PURCHASE QUANTITY

When customers in different segments buy different quantities, one can sometimes segment them for pricing with quantity discounts. Quantity discount tactics are of four types: *volume discounts, order discounts, step dis-*

EXHIBIT 9.1

Historical Booking Path for One Airline Route

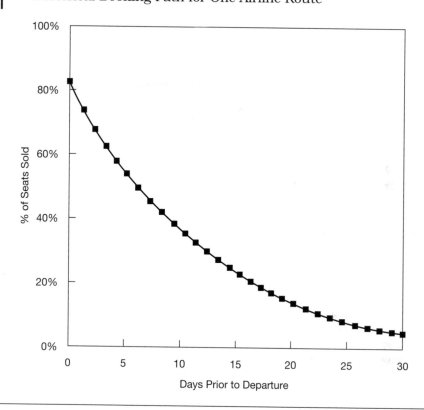

counts, and *two-part prices*. They are common when dealing with differences in price sensitivity, costs, and competition.[11]

Volume discounts

Customers who buy in large volume are usually more price sensitive. They have a larger financial incentive to learn about all alternatives and to negotiate the best possible deal. Moreover, the attractiveness of selling to them generally increases competition for their business. Large buyers are often less costly to serve. Costs of selling and servicing an account generally do not increase proportionately with the volume of purchases. In such cases, volume discounting is a useful tactic for segmented pricing.

Volume discounts are most common when selling products to business customers. Steel manufacturers grant the auto companies substantially lower prices than they offer other industrial buyers. They do so because auto manufacturers use such large volumes they could easily operate their own mills or send negotiators around the world to secure better prices.

Volume discounts are based on the customer's total purchases over a month or year rather than on the amount purchased at any one time. At some companies, the discount is calculated on the volume of all purchases; at others, it is calculated by product or product class. For example, Xerox gives volume discounts based on a buyer's total purchases of copiers, typewriters, or printers. Digital Equipment Corporation gives discounts for multiple purchases of a single model, but in addition, gives discounts based on a buyer's total expenditure on all products from the company.

Although less common, some consumer products are volume discounted as well. Larger packages of most food, health, and cleaning products usually cost less per ounce, and canned beverages cost less in 12-packs than in 6-packs. These differences reflect both cost economies for suppliers and the greater price sensitivity for these products by large families. Similarly, AT&T offers quantity discounts to business users of its long-distance services. For over $25 of service, the discount is 6 percent. For over $200, it is 8 percent. For over $2,000, it is 20 percent.

When offering volume discounts on products sold to business buyers, one must be very careful that quantity discounts do not result in higher costs for small firms than for large ones in the same industry. Volume discounts that make it more difficult for small buyers to compete with larger ones clearly violate the legal prohibition against "discrimination in price . . . where the effect may be substantially to lessen competition," unless the discounts are fully justified by cost differences. (Services are exempt from this restriction). Morton Salt lost a landmark case in which it gave grocery chains a 12.5 percent discount if they bought 5,000 cases a year and a 15 percent discount if they bought 50,000. This policy was found to give larger chains an unfair competitive advantage over smaller grocery retailers and was thus declared illegal.[12]

Order discounts

Often the cost of processing and shipping increases very little with the size of a customer's order. Consequently, the per-unit cost of processing and shipping declines significantly with the quantity ordered. For this reason, sellers generally prefer that buyers place large infrequent orders, rather than small frequent ones. To encourage them to do so, sellers often give discounts based on the quantity purchased in a given order. Such discounts may be offered in addition to volume discounts for total purchases in a year, because volume discounts and order discounts serve separate purposes. The volume discount is to retain the business of large customers. The order discount is to encourage customers to place large orders.

Order discounts are the most common of all quantity discounts. Almost all office supplies are sold with order discounts. Xerox, for example, sells 24-pound laser copier paper at the following prices per carton:

95.80 for 1 carton

82.40 for 2–4 cartons

72.20 for 5–9 cartons

68.05 for 10–19 cartons

65.25 for 20 or more cartons

Step discounts

Step discounts, or *block discounts*, differ from order discounts in that they do not apply to the total quantity purchased, but only to the purchase beyond a specified amount. The rationale is to encourage individual buyers to purchase more of a product without having to cut the price on smaller quantities for which they would pay a higher price. Thus, in contrast to other segmentation tactics, step discounting may segment not only different customers but also different purchases by the same customers. Such pricing is common for public utilities from which customers buy water and electricity for multiple uses and place a different value on it for each use.

Consider, for example, the dilemma that local electric companies face when pricing their product. Most people place a very high value on having some electricity for general use, such as lighting and running appliances. The substitutes (gaslights, oil lamps, and hand-cranked appliances) are not very acceptable. For heating, however, most people use alternative fuels (gas, oil, coal, and kerosene) because of their lower cost. Utilities would like to sell more power for heating and could do so at a price above the cost of generating it. They do not want to cut the price of electricity across the board, however, since that would involve unnecessary discounts on power for higher-valued uses.

One solution to this dilemma is a step-price schedule. Assume that the electric company could charge a typical consumer $.06 per KWH for general electricity usage, but that it must cut its price to $0.04 per KWH to make electricity competitive for heating. If the company charged the lower price to encourage electricity usage for heating, it would forgo a third of the revenue it could earn from supplying power for other uses. By replacing a single price with a block-price schedule, $0.06 per KWH for the first block of 100 KWH and $0.04 for usage thereafter, the company can encourage people to install electric heating without forgoing the higher income it can earn on power for other purposes. To encourage people to use electricity for still more uses, utilities often add still another step discount for quantities in excess of those for general use and heating. Exhibit 9.2 illustrates a step-price schedule for an electric utility.

Exhibit 9.2

Step-Price Schedule for Electricity

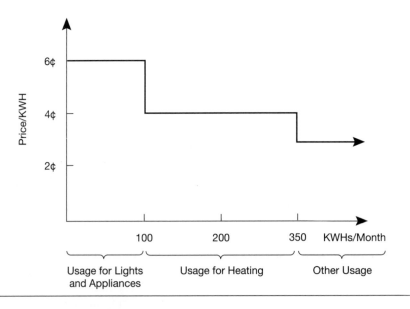

Two-part pricing

Two-part prices involve two separate charges to consume a single product. For example, amusement parks sometimes have an entry fee plus a ticket charge for each ride, car rental companies have a daily rate plus a mileage charge, and health clubs charge an annual membership fee plus additional fees for raquetball and tennis court time. In each of these cases, heavy users pay less than do light users for the same product, since the fixed fee is spread over more units. Sometimes the rationale for two-part pricing is obvious: There are two distinguishable benefits. Nightclubs, for example, offer patrons both entertainment and drinks. They could include the entertainment in the price of the drinks, but then heavy drinkers would pay disproportionately for it and light drinkers would pay little. The heavy drinkers might therefore go elsewhere, while entertainment revenue that could be earned from light drinkers would be lost. To overcome this problem, nightclubs have both a cover charge for the entertainment and a charge for drinks.[13]

The presence of two products is not, however, the reason for most two-part pricing. Car renters, for example, do not obtain value from merely having the car, they want to go somewhere in it. The rationale for two-part pricing in this case is simply that there are significant differences in the incremental cost of serving different types of car renters. Since cars depreciate the more they are driven, it costs more to rent a car to someone who puts more mileage on it. Car rental companies sometimes charge a daily fee based on the average number of miles driven. But, as might be recalled from Chapter 2, there is a danger in averaging costs for different types of buyers: Competitors undercut prices for the most profitable customers. When costs are incurred in two parts, segmentation by two-part pricing enables a company to remain competitive in serving low-cost customers while still profitably serving the high-cost segment.

Given the clear increase in profit using either step discounts or two-part pricing to segment the purchases of each individual customer, why do most companies still charge each individual customer a single price? The answer is that segmenting different purchases by each customer is possible only under limited conditions. It is profitable only when:

Purchase volume by individual buyers is significantly price sensitive. For many products, an individual buyer's demand is an all-or-nothing proposition. Think of some common products (toilet paper, soap, salt, refrigerators, breakfast cereals, umbrellas), and ask yourself whether the quantity bought is really sensitive to even large price variations. Individual customers either buy the product or they do not, but price has very little effect on how much they buy. In this situation, step discounting and two-part pricing are futile.

The product cannot be easily resold or stored for later use. If resale is easy, one buyer could purchase large quantities at a low price (bearing the high prices of initial steps or the fixed fee of a two-part price only once) and resell it to others who want only small amounts and would otherwise have to pay a higher price or a fixed fee to get them. If storage is easy, buyers could obtain discounts by purchasing large quantities at a time without significantly increasing their total use of the product.

Buyers' demands are similar, or it is possible to segment buyers for pricing into groups with similar demands. The more diversity exists among buyers in the quantities that they are willing to purchase at various prices, the less possible it is to effectively segment purchases. The right step-price schedule or fixed fee for one buyer would be wrong for another.

SEGMENTING BY PRODUCT DESIGN

Of the preceding segmentation tactics, only segmenting by buyer identification actually prohibits some buyers from purchasing at the lowest price. Segmenting by location, time, and purchase quantity gives all buyers the option to pay the lowest price if they want it. Marketers use such strategies effectively because they realize that people do not make purchases by evaluating the products alone but by evaluating the entire purchase opportunity. The same narrowly defined product or service may be seen by buyers in different contexts as a substantially different purchase opportunity. A loaf of bread available at a convenience store is not the same purchase opportunity as one available in a crowded supermarket. A movie shown at 1:00 p.m. is not the same purchase opportunity as the same film shown in the evening. Segmentation by location, time, and purchase quantity all involve creating different purchase opportunities designed to induce the price-insensitive or higher-cost buyers to purchase willingly at a higher price.

Although varying such aspects of the purchase opportunity often works, some of the most efficient segmentations involve offering different versions of the product or service itself. The important factor in such a strategy is not differences in production costs: There is frequently little or no cost difference in the different versions. A leading manufacturer of pocket calculators, for example, sold a card-programmable version of one calculator for much more than the nonprogrammable version. The only practical difference between the two was a slot in the plastic case of the programmable version where the cards could be inserted. Similarly, oil companies sell premium gasoline for $0.10 to $0.15 more than regular grade, although the added cost of refining it is only $0.04. To make this tactic work, one must offer a lower-priced version that is in some way inadequate to meet the needs of price-insensitive buyers (such as engineers and owners of high-performance cars in the examples above), but that is still acceptable to price-sensitive buyers.

Airlines have used this tactic quite successfully. Their market consists of both a price-insensitive business traveler and a very price-sensitive vacation traveler. Analysis of these segments revealed that businesspeople place a high value on flexible scheduling. They often do not know in advance exactly when they want to leave or how long they will have to stay. In contrast, vacationers generally plan their trips far in advance. Capitalizing on this difference, airlines set regular ticket prices high and offer discounts only to buyers who purchase their tickets well before departure, or to those who stay at their destination over a weekend, when businesspeople want to be home. By offering lower fares only with inflexible scheduling, airlines have been able to price low enough to attract price-sensitive buyers without making unnecessary concessions to those who are less price sensitive.

Segmenting by product design is easy when selling a service such as air travel because the seller can limit resale of the product. If airline tickets were not issued to specific passengers, firms would soon spring up to buy discounted tickets in advance for resale to businesspeople closer to flight times. When the product is not a service, controlling such arbitrage between the low- and high-priced markets becomes more difficult.

Rohm and Haas Chemical faced this problem with its plastic molding powder, methyl methacrylate. The firm enjoyed a large industrial demand for its product at a price of $0.85 per pound. With only slightly more processing, the firm also sold the product for dental applications at $22.00 per pound. With such a large price difference, distributors soon began buying the industrial grade plastic, doing the additional processing themselves, and selling it to the dental market at prices undercutting Rohm and Haas.

To solve this problem, Rohm and Haas needed to change the low-priced product in some way that made adapting it for sale in the high-priced market impractical. Cooking wines, for example, can sell in grocery stores for less than do drinking wines in liquor stores because the addition of salt to the cooking wine precludes arbitrage. Rohm and Haas considered adding a toxic substance to its industrial grade plastic to make it unusable in the dental market which the company would serve with a higher-priced, nontoxic version. Had they initially sold the pure and the adulterated products under different brand names, this would have been a viable strategy. Unfortunately, the firm's belated recognition of this opportunity precluded such a solution since dental users who had successfully used the industrial grade might fail to heed the warning to stop using it for oral applications. Rohm and Haas was forced instead to adopt the less effective tactic of simply planting a rumor that it had adulterated the industrial-grade plastic.[14]

SEGMENTING BY PRODUCT BUNDLING

Product bundling is a widely used tactic for segmented pricing, although its rationale often goes unnoticed. Retailers bundle free parking with a purchase in their stores. Grocery stores and Fast-Food outlets bundle chances in games with purchase of their products. Newspapers with morning and evening editions bundle advertising space in both of them. Restaurants bundle foods into fixed-price dinners, generally a cheaper alternative to the same items served à la carte. Symphony orchestras bundle diverse concerts into season subscription tickets. These are but a small fraction of the goods sold in bundles, but they illustrate the breadth of the practice—from commodities to services, from necessities to entertainment. What makes bundling a successful segmented-pricing tactic? In each case the products bundled together have a particular relationship to one another in their value to different buyer segments.[15]

Consider how that relationship applies when bundling advertising space for the morning and evening editions in a newspaper. Advertising space in the morning edition is valued more by one segment of advertisers (for example, grocers, retailers) than by another segment (for example, theaters, restaurants), whereas the reverse is true for the evening edition.

EXHIBIT 9.3

Value of Advertising Space by Two Different Segments

Advertiser	Morning Edition	Evening Edition
Segment A (grocers, retailers)	$1,000	$400
Segment B (theaters, restaurants)	$ 700	$600

Exhibit 9.3 shows hypothetical valuations of advertising space by these two types of buyers. Both value advertising space in the morning edition more than in the evening edition. What is important for a bundling strategy, however, is that segment A values space in the morning edition more than does segment B ($1,000 versus $700), whereas the reverse is true for the evening edition ($400 versus $600).

Why would the newspaper want to bundle morning and evening advertising together, requiring buyers to purchase both in order to get either? Without bundling, the paper would have to charge no more than $700 for a morning ad and $400 for an evening ad to attract both segments for both editions. Thus it would collect $1,100 ($700 + $400) from each advertiser. But how much does each segment value the bundle? Segment A values it at $1,400 ($1,000 + $400) whereas segment B values it at $1,300 ($700 + $600). Thus the newspaper can sell a bundle of morning and evening advertising space to both segments for up to $1,300. That is $200 more per buyer than it could earn if it sold the same space separately.

Why is this segmented pricing? Because each segment pays the difference between the separate price of the advertising ($1,100) and the bundled price ($1,300) for a different product. Segment A pays the extra money because of the value it places on morning advertising; segment B pays because of the value it places on the evening edition.[16]

Optional bundling

Generally products are not sold in indivisible bundles only. Most firms follow the tactic of optional bundling where products can be bought separately, but the option is available to buy them in a bundle at prices below their cost if bought separately. Optional bundling is more profitable than indivisible bundling whenever some buyers value one of the items in the bundle very highly but value the other less than it costs to offer it. For such a customer, the extra revenue the firm earns from selling the bundle is less than the extra cost of producing it.

Supermarkets often use optional bundling in the form of special promotions. For example, a supermarket might offer anyone who buys $5 worth of groceries the opportunity to buy one stoneware dish at a very low price. The purpose of this optional bundle is to segment the market. Some customers are loyal shoppers at whatever store is most convenient. They are willing to pay a lot to shop at a particular store but do not value stoneware dishes. In contrast, lower-income customers and those with large families will shop around for the best prices. They are not willing to pay as much for the convenience of shopping at any particular store. Many of those shoppers, however, may value the opportunity to buy a nice set of dishes cheaply. Thus the necessary condition for bundling (a reversal in the relative valuation of the products) is met. Supermarkets make the bundle optional because some shoppers may not want the stoneware dish even at the low price. To force them to purchase it would create unnecessary resentment that could drive them away.

Similarly, giving buyers the option to buy parts separately is common in most cases where bundles are offered. Although tickets to sporting and cultural events are available at a discount in a season ticket bundle, they can be purchased individually as well. Restaurants offer their customers dinner specials (appetizer, entree, dessert, and beverage bundles), but customers can buy just some of the individual parts at higher à la carte prices. For purposes of segmentation, there is never any reason not to give buyers the option of purchasing separately at higher prices. There are, however, psychological reasons for bundling that may justify making the bundles indivisible. We discuss these reasons in Chapter 12 in the section called "Framing."

Value-added bundling

A subtle variation on mixed bundling is value-added bundling. Rather than cutting prices to price-sensitive customers, the value-added bundler instead offers them an additional value of a kind that less price-sensitive buyers do not want. With that strategy, a company can attract price-sensitive buyers without reducing prices to those who are relatively price insensitive. For only $1 extra, Quantas, the Airline of Australia, offers travelers a choice of "land packages" for tourist-class hotels and sightseeing packages in Australia or for a camper-van for 5 days in New Zealand. These options would be unattractive to the typical business traveler but make traveling on Quantas attractive to pleasure travelers whose alternatives would be a charter flight to Australia or a less expensive vacation elsewhere. Alcoa used value-added strategy to encourage the use of aluminum core electrical cable. For most buyers, aluminum's light weight gives it unique and highly valued advantages over competing materials, and Alcoa's prices reflected that value. At those high prices, however, aluminum could not compete with copper in making electrical cable. To overcome this problem, Alcoa began manufacturing aluminum electrical cable itself. It did not, however, pass on the full cost of converting aluminum into cable when pricing cable. In effect, it sold the aluminum in cable for less than it sold virgin aluminum.[17] The combination of the raw aluminum and the processing into cable created an effective bundle since buyers who valued the processing more valued the raw aluminum less.

SEGMENTING BY TIE-INS AND METERING

Segmentation by tie-ins or metering is often extremely important for pricing assets. The reason is that buyers generally place greater value on an asset the more intensely they use it. The buyer of a photocopying machine who makes 20,000 copies a month will value it more than the buyer who makes 5,000 copies. Food processors canning fruit year-round in California value canning machines more than fish packers do in Alaska, who can salmon only a few months each year. In such cases, tactics that segment buyers by use intensity can substantially improve the effectiveness of a pricing strategy.

Tie-in sales

Before the Clayton Antitrust Act of 1914, a common method of monitoring usage intensity was the tie-in sale. Along with the purchase or lease of a machine, a buyer contractually agreed to purchase a commodity used with the machine exclusively from the seller. Thus the Heaton Peninsular Company sold its shoe-making machines with the provision that buyers buy only Heaton Peninsular buttons.[18] The A. B. Dick Company sold its mimeograph equipment with the provision that buyers buy paper, stencils, and ink only from the A. B. Dick Company.[19] American Can leased its canning machines with the provision that they be used to close only American's cans.[20]

In each of these cases, the asset itself sold for a very low explicit price, close to the incremental cost of production. The tied commodity, however, was priced at a premium. Thus the true cost of the asset was its low explicit price, plus the sum of the price premiums paid for the tied commodity. Since buyers who used the asset more intensely bought more of the tied commodity, they effectively paid more for the asset.

Since passage of the Clayton Act, the courts have refused to enforce tying contracts except for service contracts where service is essential to maintain the performance and the reputation of a new product.[21]

Although tying by exclusive sales contracts is generally illegal when used for segmented pricing,[22] opportunities to use this tactic without contracts still exist. No court has ever considered prohibiting theaters from requiring that food consumed on the premises be purchased only from the premium-priced, in-house concession; nor has any court considered pro-hibiting razor manufacturers from creating unique shaving technologies that tie blades to razors. Maintenance and repair services are natural tie-ins to the sale of equipment. Recently, the Supreme Court explicitly confirmed that such noncontractual tie-ins are an acceptable pricing tactic.[23]

The courts have, nevertheless, severely limited tying arrangements in precisely the cases where they are most dramatically effective. Rulings challenge sellers to monitor use without restricting competition. In modern times, that challenge has frequently been met by monitoring with simple metering devices.

Metering

Xerox Corporation developed a metered price policy for its copiers, measuring not only intensity but also type of use. Until the late 1970s, the company leased its machines rather than selling them. Exhibit 9.4 shows the fee schedule for leasing what was a popular Xerox copier. The lessee paid a usage fee for the number of copies made in addition to a monthly minimum charge of $185. Thus, lessees who copied more paid more. Note also, however, that the usage charge fluctuated substantially with the num-ber of copies made per original.

Why would Xerox make the usage charge lower for copying many copies per original? The rationale did not depend on the technology of photocopying. The technology for making ten copies from the same origi-nal was the same as that for making ten copies from ten originals. The ma-chine scanned the original each time in either case. The rationale for this policy was, rather, differences in price sensitivity caused by differences in the available alternatives.

Price sensitivity, recall from Chapter 4, depends critically on the value buyers place on the attributes that differentiate a product from its substi-

---

EXHIBIT 9.4

Metered Pricing (Xerox Copier)

			Meter Rate per Copy from Same Original		
Basic Monthly Use Charge	Monthly Meter Minimum	Total Monthly Minimum	1–3	4–10	11+
$50.00	$135.00	$185.00	4.6¢	3.0¢	2.0¢

Total cost per month for 10,000 copies, 3 copies per original = $510.00; total cost per month for 10,000 copies, 50 copies per original = $279.60.

tutes (the unique value effect). For users who made many copies of each original, photocopiers offered little advantage over offset presses or duplicators. Both these alternative technologies produced clear, high-quality copies at a per-copy cost of labor and materials that declined rapidly with the number of copies made per original. In contrast, for users who made few copies per original, these alternative technologies were poor substitutes for a Xerox machine. The preparation of a master plate or stencil for offsetting or duplicating was prohibitively costly for only a few copies.

Photocopying represented a substantial improvement for making a few copies per original. The other alternatives—retyping or using carbon paper—were either very costly or dismally inferior. Consequently, users who made few copies per original were willing to pay much more per copy than were users who made many copies. The usage charge reflected that difference in value.[24] The monthly cost of the copier in Exhibit 9.4 for users who made eleven or more copies per original was $279.60 for 10,000 copies. For users who made three or fewer copies per original, it was $510.00 for 10,000 copies. The monthly cost for both types of users also varied with use intensity. Xerox used metering to distinguish segments along two different dimensions with obvious success.

The tactic of monitoring use intensity is not limited to machines and may not involve an actual physical counting device. Nationally syndicated newspaper columns are sold to local papers at prices based on use intensity. The monitoring device is simply the papers' circulation figures. Film distributors rent movies at prices based on the number of seats in the theater. And franchisors lease their brand names and reputations to franchisees not for a fixed fee but for a percentage of sales. No matter how intangible the asset, monitoring use can be an important part of its pricing.

IMPORTANCE OF SEGMENTED PRICING

For industries with high fixed costs, segmented pricing is often essential. The U.S. rail system, for example, could never have been built and could not currently be maintained were it not for a strategy of extensively segmented prices. Railroad tariffs are based on the value of the goods hauled. Coal and unprocessed grains, for example, are carried at much lower cost per carload than are manufactured goods. If railroads had to charge all shippers the same tariff charged for unprocessed grain, they would lack sufficient income per shipment to cover their fixed costs. Were they required to charge all shippers the tariff for manufactured goods, they would lose many shippers and so would again lack sufficient revenue. Without segmented pricing, many rail lines could never cover their costs, whereas others would be forced either to raise tariffs above the highest currently charged or suffer the same fate. The railroads survive to serve all their customers at reasonable rates only because the customers can be effectively segmented for pricing.

Segmented pricing also spurs competitive innovation. Companies improve their products because improvement enables them to charge more profitable prices. But such improvements are often valued differently by different buyers. When only a subsegment of a firm's buyers value a potential improvement, the ability to segment them for pricing—to recover costs of development and to earn a profit—provides the sole incentive for such advances. Without segmented pricing, the unique demands of small market segments would more often go unsatisfied.

Segmented pricing is clearly among the most difficult of strategies to implement. While the types of segmentation tactics discussed can serve as a guide to separating markets, finding a basis for a segmentation (that is, a particular buyer characteristic or a particular bundling combination) ultimately requires creative insight. Since each example of segmented pricing is unique in its method of implementation, there can be no simple formula. Finding a basis for segmentation is the key to maintaining a strong competitive position; in some cases, it is essential to remaining viable.

Xerox lost much of its strong competitive position in the copier market precisely because of its reluctance to serve the more price-sensitive segments of the market. The company recognized that the big profits were in serving users who demanded high-quality copies in high volume. Although it served those users well and carefully segmented them for pricing by volume and number of copies per original, it ignored the less profitable market of small offices. It left that market to the Japanese, who could not effectively compete with Xerox because they lacked a comparable distribution and service network. Unfortunately for Xerox, the Japanese used small office copiers to gain enough volume that they ultimately could afford the fixed cost of better distribution and service. Then they could challenge Xerox for a share of more profitable copier segments. The lesson is clear: Ignoring a more price-sensitive segment can leave a dangerous opening for competitors, who eventually can threaten one's competitiveness in the less price-sensitive segment as well.

SUMMARY

Segmented pricing enables a company to develop pricing strategies that are more appropriate for the buyers in each market segment. Buyers who are less price sensitive, more costly to serve, or less well served by competitors can be charged more without the loss of buyers whom the firm can serve more profitably at a lower price. Separating segments for pricing is not easy. It requires creative tactics that keep markets separated while avoiding illegalities. This chapter has explained and illustrated seven general types of segmentation tactics that have proved effective and legal in practice. They are:

- Segmentation by buyer identification
- Segmentation by purchase location
- Segmentation by time of purchase
- Segmentation by purchase quantity
- Segmentation by product design
- Segmentation by product bundling
- Segmentation by tie-ins and metering

Creating a segmented pricing strategy requires a flash of insight. The manager must recognize different segments and separate them with a pricing policy that is unique for each product. The manager is most likely to find such insight when he or she knows where to look. The purpose of this chapter is to guide that search.

NOTES

1. See Chapter 13.
2. See Narasimhan Chakravarthi, "Coupons as Price Discrimination Devices—A Theoretical Perspective and Empirical Analysis," *Marketing Science*, 3 (Spring 1984) 128–47; Naufel J. Vilcassim and Dick R. Wittink, "Supporting a Higher Shelf Price Through Coupon Distributions," *Journal of Consumer Marketing*, 4, no. 2 (Spring 1987), 29–39.
3. See Chapter 12 under Influence of Framing on Price Perceptions for a discussion of why rebates may influence purchases by those customers who do not ultimately redeem them.
4. For a study on segmented pricing of physicians' services by buyer identification, see Reuben Kessel, "Price Discrimination in Medicine," *Journal of Law and Economics*, 2 (October 1958), 20–53.
5. See Walter J. Primeaux Jr., "The Effect of Consumer Knowledge and Bargaining Strength on Final Selling Price: A Case Study," *Journal of Business*, 43 (October 1970), 419–26.
6. In less-developed countries where the services of salespeople are less costly, segmented pricing by salespeople is widely practiced for even small purchases.
7. FOB (free on board) means that the buyer takes possession and thus bears shipping costs from the time the seller loads the goods on board the shipper's vehicle.
8. Exceptions occur when nonpeak demanders are so much less price sensitive than peak demanders that the difference overwhelms the effect of the cost difference. For example, on transatlantic flights between New York and

London, the peak-season demand period is during the summer tourist season, which is also the time when the airlines offer their lowest discount fares. Demand is less price sensitive during the off-peak season when most passengers are traveling on business.

9.   For more on the technical details of peak-load pricing, see Peter O. Steiner, "Peak Loads and Efficient Pricing," *Quarterly Journal of Economics*, 71 (November 1957), 585–610; Jack Hirshleifer, "Peak Loads and Efficient Pricing: Comment," *Quarterly Journal of Economics*, 72 (August 1958), 451–62; "Symposium on Peak-Load Pricing," *Bell Journal of Economics*, 7 (Spring 1976), 197–250.

10. Fred Glover, Randy Glover, Joe Lorenzo, and others, "The Passenger-Mix Problem in the Scheduled Airlines," *Interfaces*, 12 no. 3 (June 1982), 73–79; Eric B. Orkin, "Boosting Your Bottom Line with Yield Management," *Cornell Hotel and Restaurant Administration Quarterly*, February 1988, pp. 52–56.

11. For an in-depth discussion of the motivations for quantity discounting, see Robert J. Dolan, "Pricing Structures with Quantity Discounts: Managerial Issues and Research Opportunities," Harvard Business School Working Paper, 1985.

12. *Federal Trade Commission* v. *Morton Salt*, 334 U.S. 37 (1948).

13. Sometimes charging a single price for a bundle of two separate products is necessary for segmented pricing. It is an effective strategy, however, only when preferences for the two products meet certain conditions. See Segmenting by Product Bundling later in this chapter.

14. G. W. Stocking and M. W. Watkins, *Cartels in Action* (New York: Twentieth Century Fund, 1946), pp. 402–404.

15. This principle was first identified in George Stigler, "*United States* v. *Loew's Inc.*: A Note on Block Booking," *The Supreme Court Law Review* (1965), pp. 152–57; See also Gary D. Eppen, Ward A. Hanson, and R. Kipp Martin, "Bundling—New Products, New Markets, Low Risk," *Sloan Management Review*, 32, no. 4 (Summer 1991), 7–14. The section entitled Framing Multiple Gains or Losses in Chapter 12 gives another rationale for bundling.

16. This is only one of the ways newspapers practice segmented pricing. They also charge higher prices for the same advertising space if the ad is from a national rather than a local advertiser. They charge different prices for different types of advertising, and they give volume discounts. Radio and television stations use similar tactics.

17. Ralph Cassady, Jr., "Techniques and Purposes of Price Discrimination," *Journal of Marketing*, 11, no. 1 (July 1946), 141.

18. *Heaton Peninsular* v. *Eureka Specialty Co.*, 77F288 (6th Cir., 1896).

19. *Henry* v. *A. B. Dick*, 224 U.S. 1 (1912).

20. *United States* v. *American Can Company* (Northern District Court of California, 1949).

21. *United States* v. *Jerrold Electronics Co.*, 187 F.Supp. 545 (E.D. Pa., 1960), affirmed 365 U.S. 567 (1961). *Motion Picture Patents Co.* v. *Universal Film Mfg. Co.*, 243 U.S. 502 (1917). *United Shoe Machinery Corporation* v. *United States* (Supreme Court, 1922). *International Business Machines Corporation* v. *United States* (Supreme Court, 1936).

22. See chapter 14, the section titled "Tie-in Sales and Requirements Contracts," for situations when contractual tie-ins are legal for purposes other than pricing.

23. *Berkey Photo* v. *Eastman Kodak Company* (Second Circuit Court of Appeals, 1979).

24. As an example of how product design must often accommodate a pricing tactic, Xerox was forced to add to its machines covers that had to be closed in order for the user to get the low-usage rate. Before the covers, some nimble users would set the machine to make many copies per original and then quickly change originals between cycles, thus foiling Xerox's strategy.

PRICING IN THE MARKETING MIX

CHAPTER 10

DEVELOPING AN INTEGRATED STRATEGY

Pricing can never be entirely separated from the other elements in a firm's marketing strategy. A product's price affects the market's perception of its attributes and the attributes of other products with which it is sold, the effectiveness of its advertising, and the attention it receives in channels of distribution. Moreover, the interactions go both ways: The product, its advertising, and its distribution affect the success of a particular pricing strategy. Although the process of pricing is a unique and specialized marketing activity, the resulting pricing strategy is an integral part of a larger effort. The success of that effort requires coordination among pricing and the product, promotion, and distribution decisions that together comprise a firm's marketing mix.

To get the most from its various marketing efforts, a firm must coordinate them into a cohesive strategy. In this chapter, we identify the interactions among pricing and other elements of the marketing mix—the product, the promotion, and the distribution—that a firm must manage effectively if its marketing program is to be successful.

PRICING AND THE PRODUCT LINE

The product is management's most powerful tool to influence the pricing environment. It can be designed to appeal to a price-insensitive segment of buyers, thus facilitating a skimming strategy. It can be designed for maximum cost economies, thus facilitating a penetration strategy. Or, as we saw in Chapter 7, it can be designed to facilitate segmented pricing by product design, tying, or bundling. Product-line strategy, using flanking brands or brands that attract more price-sensitive segments to the market, may be the key to effective competitive and segmentation strategies. Moreover, in Chapter 12 on psychological pricing, we explain how product lines affect perceptions of value. Clearly, much of what we discuss elsewhere in this book involves the relationship between a product and its pricing since an effective product strategy is often the key to capturing value. In this section, we expand our discussion of breakeven sales analysis to account for the crossproduct interactions among prices and sales.

Most firms sell multiple products. Auto companies sell different models of cars as well as accessories. Hotels not only rent rooms but also offer meals and cater parties. Supermarkets sell products as diverse as meats, produce, and packaged goods and sometimes offer a limited selection of dinnerware, lawn furniture, toys, and clothing. If one product's sales do not affect the sales of the firm's other products, it can be priced in isolation. Often, however, the sales of different products in a firm's line are interdependent. To maximize profit, prices must reflect that interaction.

The effect of one product's sales on another's can be either adverse or favorable. If adverse, the products are *substitutes*. Most substitutes are different brands in the same product class. For example, generic and branded paper towels are substitutes because increased sales of one reduce sales of the other. Sometimes, however, substitutes appear in completely different product classes. The sales of macaroni products noticeably rise whenever price increases reduce the sales of beef.

If one product's sales favorably affect sales of another, the products are *complements*. Complementarity can arise for either of two reasons: (1) *the products are used together in producing satisfaction*. Tickets to a movie and popcorn are complements because, for many people, each enhances the pleasure they get from the other. Jet engines and spare parts are complements since the higher the sales of engines, the greater the follow-on sales of parts. Consequently, manufacturers compete fiercely for initial sales. (2) *The products are most efficiently purchased together*. Buyers often seek to conserve time by purchasing a set of products from a single seller. For example, consumers who patronize a particular supermarket in order to buy advertised specials are more likely to buy other items at that store, as well as other products of the same manufacturer.[1] An industrial purchasing agent may patronize a vendor for a particular grinding wheel and then simplify his or her purchasing by ordering other abrasives from the same vendor.

Substitutes and complements call for adjustments in pricing when the products are sold by the same company as part of a product line. To correctly evaluate the effect of a price change, management must examine the changes in revenues and costs not only for the product being priced, but also for the other products affected by the price change. To see how this is done, consider the following examples.

Pricing substitute products

A gasoline station offers both a regular and a premium grade of unleaded gasoline. These two products are substitutes; the higher the price of the premium grade, the more people are likely to switch to regular grade. The current prices and costs of the two grades of gasoline are

	Price/Gal.	Variable Cost/ Gal.	Dollar Contribution Margin/Gal.
Regular unleaded	$1.30	$1.10	$0.20
Premium unleaded	1.50	1.20	0.30

How should the station owner evaluate the effect of a 5 percent price increase for premium grade?

If sales of regular and premium are *entirely* independent, the owner simply calculates the percent contribution margin for premium, 20 percent, and proceeds to calculate the breakeven sales change as follows:

$$\frac{-5.0}{20.0 + 5.0} = -20.0\%$$

But in this case, −20% is misleading. A decline greater than 20 percent could still leave the 5 percent price increase profitable. The reason is that some customers who refused to pay 5 percent more for premium would not go to another station but would simply fill up with regular instead. Consequently, each gallon of lost premium sales would not represent a loss of $0.30 contribution, since some of the loss would be recovered in added contribution from sales of regular gasoline.

To properly account for this shifting of profit from one product to another, we need to calculate an adjusted contribution margin for the change in sales of premium. The amount of the adjustment is uncertain because it depends on the share of additional sales of regular that come from reduced sales of premium. From past experience, the manager of this station estimates that approximately half the customers who would decline to buy premium at the higher price would not leave the station but would purchase the regular grade instead. Consequently, the dollar contribution lost from a decline in the sales of premium is really $0.30 per gallon minus the gain in contribution from additional sales of regular.

$$\text{Adjusted } \$CM = \$0.30 - (0.5 \times \$0.20) = \$0.20$$

which represents an adjusted percent contribution margin of

$$\frac{\$0.20}{\$1.50} = 13.3\%$$

As a result, the breakeven sales quantity for a 5 percent price increase on premium is actually

$$\frac{-5.0}{13.3 + 5.0} = -27.3\%$$

This station can actually profit from a price increase on premium despite a decrease in sales greater than 20 percent.

Pricing complementary products

Pricing complementary products is like pricing substitutes except that one must add to, rather than subtract from, the contribution margin to adjust it appropriately. The College Computer Store sells personal computers, software, and printers. These products are complements since the typical computer buyer also purchases two software programs from the same retailer at the time of the computer purchase, and half of all purchasers buy a printer. College Computer's current price on a leading personal computer and the complementary software is

	Unit Price	Unit Variable Cost	Unit Dollar Contribution Margin
Personal computer	$1,500	$1,000	$500
Software program	175	100	75
Printer	1,450	950	500

College Computer is considering dropping the price of the computer by 10 percent to spur sales. If management treats computer sales as independent, it would calculate that the company earns a 33.3 percent contribution margin on the computer. Consequently, the breakeven sales quantity for a 10 percent price cut would be 42.9 percent.

In fact, since additional computer sales will cause an increase in sales of software and printers, the relevant contribution margin for a computer sale is much higher than 33.3 percent. If each computer buyer also buys two software packages, and half buy a printer, the relevant contribution from selling a computer is

$$\text{Adjusted } \$CM = \$500 + (2 \times \$75) + 0.5(500)$$

which represents an adjusted percent contribution margin of

$$\frac{\$900}{\$2,500} = 60\%$$

Recognizing this interaction, College Computer can profitably cut its price even if it expects a percentage increase in sales much less than 42.9 percent. In fact, the breakeven sales change, considering the effect of a sale on the store's total profits from the computer, the software, and the printer, is only

$$\frac{-(-10.0)}{60.0 - 10.0} = 20.0\%$$

When pricing substitutes or complements, managers should evaluate the decision using the adjusted contribution margin which reflects the effect of a sale on the profitability of a company's total product line. The general equation for the *adjustment for a substitute* is

Adjusted $CM = Unadjusted $CM – Change in sales of substitute
$\times$ $CM of substitute

where the change in sales of substitute equals the change per unit of sales of the product being priced. For complements, the adjustment is the same, except that the adjustment is an addition to rather than a subtraction from the unadjusted contribution margin. The equation for the *adjustment for a complement* is:

Adjusted $CM = Unadjusted $CM + Change in sales of complement
$\times$ $CM of complement

where the change in sales of complement equals the expected additional complementary sales for each additional sale of the product being priced.

Complementary sales interactions need not occur at the same point in time. In fact, some of the most important sales follow much later. Pharmaceuticals companies price aggressively for sales in teaching hospitals since physicians trained there are much more likely to prescribe those brands when they enter private practice. Rock stars require that concert promoters keep ticket prices low, even though they could fill the stadium at a higher price, in order to ensure that teenagers are not priced out of the market. They do so because teenage attendance has an especially large effect on subsequent record sales. Complementary products are not necessarily sold even to the same buyers. Singles bars often suspend or reduce their cover charges for women in the belief that when more women patronize their establishments, more men will do so as well.

When there is more than one substitute or complement in a line, it is necessary to make multiple adjustments to the contribution margin to reflect them. Thus, in a grocery store, a low promotional price on strawberries may cause increased sales of both shortcakes and whipped cream, while reducing sales of other fruits. Consequently, the adjusted contribution margin involves both positive and negative adjustments. It is impractical to adjust a contribution margin for every individual interaction with every other product in a broad product line. To overcome this problem, managers can rely on some aggregation. For example, in cutting the price of strawberries, they might calculate the effect on the dollar sales of all other fruits combined and multiply it times the average dollar contribution margin per dollar sales of fruit.

Selecting loss leaders

In some cases, it can even pay to price a complementary product as a *loss leader*, that is, below its variable cost in order to attract customers to the remaining product line. The pricing of some products has a very strong effect on a customer's choice of which store to patronize. If customers purchase many other products once they are in the store, sales of those products increase the adjusted contribution margin of the product that attracts buyers to the store. Consequently, it may be quite sensible to price that product so low that it has a negative unadjusted contribution margin because the adjusted contribution margin for its sales is still quite high.

Loss leaders are common in grocery pricing. Supermarkets regularly take losses on a few advertised items in order to attract buyers to their stores because those buyers will then purchase the remainder of their needs at profitable prices. White bread, eggs, flour, and at least one brand of peanut butter are common candidates for pricing as loss leaders. There are two reasons why some products make good loss leaders.[2]

- First, it is impossible for a typical shopper to remember more than a small portion of the prices at various stores. Comparison shopping on an item-by-item basis is impossible. Most buyers remember the prices of only a few of the items they buy and use those prices to infer the general levels of prices at different stores. The prices that consumers are most likely to remember are those of the products they purchase most frequently. Consequently, frequently purchased products often make good loss leaders.

■ Second, different segments of shoppers not only have different price sensitivities but also purchase different combinations of products. For example, because families with children buy more food, they are generally more price sensitive in deciding where to shop. Moreover, their grocery purchases include large amounts of fruit punch, certain brands of peanut butter, and white bread for sandwiches. By pricing one or more of those products as loss leaders, a store can become more price competitive for patronage by large families without cutting its profits on grocery purchases by other customers. As this example illustrates, products purchased primarily by a price-sensitive segment of buyers often make good loss leaders.

The best loss leaders are those that meet both of these criteria: They are purchased frequently and primarily by price-sensitive shoppers.

Product-line interactions noticeably affect a firm's pricing in relation to competitors with narrower product lines. Supermarkets can profitably offer more loss leaders and larger discounts than can convenience stores because the former have more complementary products to sell to the additional customers that a loss leader attracts.

Similarly, retailers who offer a broad product line tend to price the high end of the line higher and the low end lower than retailers with a narrow line. The former can afford to lose sales at the high end because they offer a lower price product to which many customers will switch rather than go elsewhere. Moreover, because they have a higher-end product that draws the less price-sensitive shoppers, they can profitably use the low-end product to draw more price-sensitive shoppers to the store. Consequently, the range of prices within a single broad line may actually exceed the range across stores that specialize in fewer brands.[3]

PRICING AND PROMOTION

Promotion is a firm's effort to inform buyers and persuade them to perceive a product more favorably. Effective pricing complements the most salient forms of promotion: advertising and personal selling. In more subtle forms of sales promotion, price itself often becomes the promotional tool. Recognizing this close association between pricing and promotion, managers who price effectively make their pricing decisions in close consultation and coordination with their advertising agencies and sales management. In this section, we discuss the considerations that need to be taken into account.

Pricing and advertising

The coordination of pricing and advertising is important because advertising can affect how buyers respond to price differences. How it affects price sensitivity, however, has long been debated by both researchers and managers. At one time, nearly everyone accepted the bromide that advertising artificially differentiates otherwise similar products in the minds of easily manipulated consumers, thus reducing their price sensitivity through a spurious value effect. Fortunately, research in the last few decades has given us a much less jaundiced view of advertising's effect on consumers. Advertising is simply communication; its effect depends on the nature of the message communicated.

Most experts agree that advertising increases price sensitivity when it focuses on price explicitly. Grocery ads let shoppers know the prices charged for selected items before they choose where to shop; mail-order discounters advertise their prices to let buyers know just how much they can save by giving up the obvious advantages of dealing with a full-service retailer (see Exhibit 10.1). Being more aware of their alternatives, buyers are more price sensitive (the substitution effect) when deciding where to shop.[4] Companies using a penetration strategy use advertising to assert the claim that they offer equal value at a lower cost, thus undermining the unique value effect. Such advertising often makes explicit arguments (for example, "Why pay more?") to convince buyers that price should be the most important consideration in their purchase decision. If a firm enjoys a price advantage, it obviously pays to make buyers more sensitive to that aspect of the purchase decision.

In contrast, advertising specifically designed to minimize price sensitivity is certainly quite common. The advertising campaigns for Bayer to convince buyers that "All aspirin is not alike," and for Q-Tips that "A swab by any other name is not the same" are clearly intended to reduce buyers' price sensitivity by enhancing the perception that these products are better than those of the competition (the unique value effect). Hammermill's ads for its photocopier paper seek to reduce price sensitivity by reminding buyers that the cost of paper is just a small part of the total cost of the end product (the end-benefit effect). Johnnie Walker's ad for Black Label Scotch speaks directly to the price-quality effect: "When you are dealing with something quite extraordinary, price somehow seems irrelevant or even irreverent. Indeed, for those who appreciate fine Scotch, Johnnie Walker Black is priceless." One study of *individual* purchase decisions supports the contention that even "feel good" advertising, without a specific message,

Exhibit 10.1

Discounter's Price Advertising

can reduce individual price sensitivity.[5] In another study of individual purchase decisions, advertising appeared to increase price sensitivity except at very high levels of advertising exposure, when price sensitivity falls back to the level associated with no advertising.[6]

Regardless of the effect of advertising on the price sensitivity of individual purchasers, marketers are interested in effect on an aggregate level. On this question, the research results are quite consistent, at least for frequently purchased consumer products that dominate the studies; advertising increases the sales volume gain associated with a lower price. In technical terms, advertising appears to increase the price elasticity of market demand for a product.[7] Exhibit 10.2 illustrates this effect in a test market experiment for a frequently purchased convenience food. When price

EXHIBIT 10.2

Percentage Changes in Sales Due to Price Increases: The Effect of Advertising

	Advertising	
Price Change	Low	High
$0.50 to $0.60	–21%	–29%
$0.60 to $0.70	–19%	–33%

Source: Gerald Eskin, "A Case for Test Market Experiments," *Journal of Advertising Research,* 15 (April 1975), 27.

was raised in locations exposed to a low level of advertising, sales declined substantially less than they did when price was increased in locations exposed to about 70 percent more advertising.

How can the effect of advertising on the price sensitivity of market demand differ from its effect on individual purchase decisions? The answer is that advertising changes the composition of a product's demand by attracting new customers. Advertising may not increase the price sensitivity of any individual buyers but, as it increases sales, it apparently also increases the volume gains associated with a *reduction* in price and the volume losses associated with an *increase* in price. The implication is that buyers who are relatively more advertising sensitive are also relatively more price sensitive. The index of sales levels in Exhibit 10.3 illustrates this relationship for three different consumer packaged goods. Using the low price–low advertising sales level as a base, the index indicates that a high level of advertising raised sales by 80.7 percent for product A, by 52.5 percent for product B, and by 79.4 percent for product C. The index also indicates, however, that a price increase caused a much greater percentage loss of sales where the sales level was already inflated by advertising. For example, 22 percent of product A's sales were lost following a price increase where advertising was high, but only 3 percent were lost following the same price increase where advertising was low.[8]

The implication of this research for coordinating advertising and pricing is that a low price will increase sales more when coupled with a high level of advertising. From a different perspective, it indicates that advertising

EXHIBIT 10.3

Sales Under Different Price and Advertising Levels

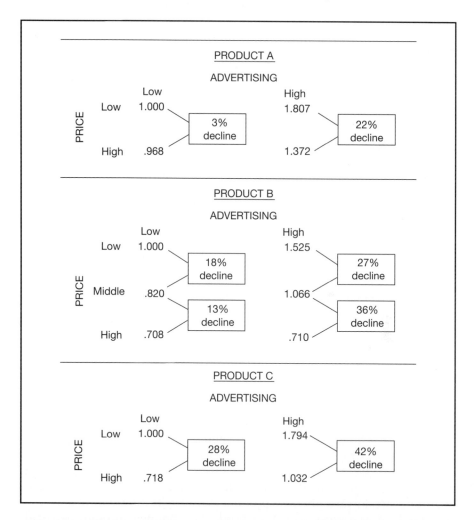

Index = Actual unit sales divided by unit sales in the low price–low advertising condition.

Source: Gerald Eskin and Penny Baron, "Effects of Price and Advertising in Test Market Experiments," *Journal of Marketing Research*, 14 (November 1977), 503.

is more effective when price is set low than when it is set high. Consequently, low prices should be matched with high advertising, when developing strategies for different times and locations. Two notes of caution, however, are in order.

First, research on price and advertising has focused on frequently purchased products in mature product categories. Given that researchers have not examined the interactions between price and advertising for durable goods, services, or products that are genuine innovations, inferences from the current state of research should be taken as only suggestive for those categories. More work is needed to establish or disprove the broader generality of these results.

Second, the conclusion that price elasticity is greater when advertising is high and that advertising is more effective when price is low, applies to a particular brand. *It is not valid for crossbrand comparisons.* For example, it would be entirely incorrect to infer that intensely advertised brands in a category have higher price elasticities than less advertised brands because more than the level of advertising changes when different brands are compared. Highly advertised brands are usually also brands that are highly differentiated and, therefore, have more to communicate than do brands that advertise little. The differentiation value of an intensely advertised brand may make consumers less sensitive to its price than to the price of a generic brand despite its higher advertising. One cannot draw valid inferences about relative price sensitivities and advertising levels among different products.

Pricing and personal selling

For most industrial products and for many large consumer durables as well, the major thrust of promotional effort is not advertising but personal selling. The extent of personal selling can vary from a minimally trained person who writes up orders to technically trained experts who spend days or weeks analyzing a customer's needs and explaining how a product could satisfy them. Selecting the right amount of sales effort is an important step toward pricing a product to realize its full profit potential.

Looking at a cross section of products promoted through personal selling, one can readily classify marketing strategies along a continuum between low price–low effort and high price–high effort. But it is a mistake to believe that any point on such a continuum represents a viable choice for any particular product. Products that are relatively generic in their features, or that are differentiated in ways obvious to a buyer, appropriately adopt low-effort strategies because there is little that a more intense selling effort could communicate. By keeping selling costs low, the seller can offer low prices to attract buyers who wish to spend a minimal amount on a basic product. Products with unique features, however, can realize differentiation values in their prices only to the extent that buyers understand those features. Consequently, such products require a higher level of sales effort to justify their higher prices to buyers.

Unfortunately, firms sometimes develop superior products and then attempt to use price rather than promotion to develop the market. Such a strategy is predictably ineffective. Consider, for example, the experience of Dewey and Almy Company with its two-part lithographic printing blanket.[9] The product was vastly superior to competing blankets in its durability, quality of impression, and ease of replacement. To introduce the product, Dewey and Almy chose distributors, usually not a source of strong selling efforts. To give buyers an incentive to adopt the product, however, Dewey and Almy priced it the same as that of competing blankets on a square foot basis, representing a substantial saving to printers because of the blanket's durability and other advantages.

The problem with Dewey and Almy's strategy was that its product's advantages were not obvious from simple observation. To appreciate them, printers first had to use the blanket—and use it properly. Thus Dewey and Almy's low price looked like a bargain only to printers who already knew of the product's advantages and would have been willing to pay more. It did not serve as an incentive for nonusers to try the product since they did not yet know the features that made the product worth much more than its price.

To develop the market for a product with superior but not obvious advantages, a company needs a sales effort that communicates its product's benefits and then assures that the buyer realizes those benefits at the time of initial use. Dewey and Almy, in fact, successfully used a high promotion strategy in its test market. Unfortunately, the company did not follow up with a strong selling effort in actual commercialization. As a result, the blanket suffered a slow rate of acceptance initially, which enabled established competitors to develop copies that captured a substantial share of the market.

The lesson is clear. A low price in relation to product value is no bargain unless buyers can appreciate that value, and a high price in relation to the competition is no deterrent if a strong sales effort can communicate that the product is worth the price. Market penetration on price alone makes sense only when a product's value is already known to buyers. That is usually the case only for established products that buyers have used in the past, products whose unique features are obvious from inspection, and products that offer only the minimal product features that buyers expect it to have. No firm can charge a price that reflects superior aspects of its product, or charge a price less than that amount, and gain rapid market penetration, unless it can first communicate to buyers the true value that the product offers.

A skilled sales force, in addition to explaining a product's features and use, can also provide important augmentations that reduce price sensitivity. A sales expert who understands how a product is used can often identify ways to save buyers money. Sometimes changes in buyers' manufacturing procedures will make the product perform better; sometimes a better ordering system will reduce buyers' inventory needs. When buyers see that skilled sales personnel can save them money, most are willing to share those savings by showing some loyalty in future competition for their business.[10]

Setting the promotional budget

In setting a promotional budget for either advertising or personal selling, coordination with pricing is essential.[11] An important factor in deciding the level of promotional spending is the dollar contribution in the price. The greater the profit contribution, the greater the reward for making each additional sale. Consequently, products with higher dollar profit contributions per sale normally justify greater promotional expenditures than those with lower contributions. The rationale is that when a product generates a greater contribution per sale, a firm can justify spending more on promotion to make difficult sales that require extra effort. When the dollar profit contribution is low, however, the additional sales generated by an intense promotional effort are less likely to be worth the cost.

Unfortunately, we frequently encounter companies that determine advertising and sales-support budgets using wasteful and ineffective criteria. A common method is to allocate promotional funding to those brands that "need more" to achieve their sales objectives. The effect of this is to give more promotional spending to weak brands and less to strong brands. Brands that cannot meet their sales objectives are generally weak because competition offers an equal or better value; brands exceeding their sales objectives are generally strong because they offer an exceptional value to their purchasers. Consequently, more money thrown at weak brands is likely to generate few initial sales with low repeat purchases, whereas money spent to promote the advantages of strong brands is likely to generate a much greater increase in both initial and repeat sales. Don't advertise your weaknesses; advertise your strengths.

In general, giving product managers promotional budgets is not recommended. Rather, they should be required to use profitably whatever they spend on promotion. The criteria for any change, positive or negative, in promotional expenditures should be that the expenditure at least pays for itself. As discussed in Chapter 3, any promotional expenditure adds to profitability when it increases sales volume by more than

$$\frac{\text{Change in promotional expenditure}}{\text{Contribution margin (per unit)}}$$

PRICE AS A PROMOTIONAL TOOL

In some cases, price is more than an adjunct to a promotional campaign; it is an integral part of it. Some companies use high prices to enhance the perception of quality. This strategy is most popular for consumables such as premium chocolates (for example, Godiva) and alcoholic beverages (for example, Chivas Regal), but it can be used to promote durable goods as well. Curtis Mathes, for example, boasts that it sells "the world's most expensive television," as part of a campaign to persuade buyers that it also sells the best. Other companies maintain stable prices to complement the images of their products. De Beers, the marketing agent for most gem quality diamonds, has long recognized the importance of price stability to the image of its product. De Beers promotes its diamonds as gifts that will symbolize forever the purchaser's love for the recipient. Part of that perception is not just that "a diamond lasts forever," but that its value will too. Consequently, De Beers buys and holds uncut diamonds to keep prices from declining during periods of temporary excess supply and actively counters speculative price increases until it is certain that they can be sustained in the long run. Although these tactics have sometimes required huge financial investments, they have succeeded in creating the expectation among buyers that a diamond's value will never decline.[12]

Occasionally, a seller may even price a product too low as part of a promotional campaign. When new movies premiere in Los Angeles and New York, the theaters charge standard ticket prices knowing they could fill the theaters at higher prices. They apparently believe that the resulting long lines for tickets (no advance purchases are allowed) generate publicity worth more than the price premium they could charge for the first few weeks. Similarly, developers of multiphase condominium projects will sometimes price the first phase low to make it sell very quickly. The developers hope this tactic will prompt other buyers to commit quickly to purchase units in the later phases. Most promotional pricing, however, is not designed to generate publicity. It is intended to induce buyers to try a frequently purchased product.

For consumer products, price "dealing" has become the most popular form of promotion, increasing from about half as much as advertising budgets in 1980 to over twice as much in 1992. Unlike promotion of regular prices, deals are discounts off the "regular" price. They may take the form of (1) *specially marked packages* that offer a temporarily low price or an extra quantity at the same price, (2) *coupons*, (3) *rebates*, or (4) *trade* (wholesale price) *discounts* that retailers may or may not pass on to the end consumer. The rest of this section concerns the use and abuse of each of these tactics.

Pricing tactics to induce trial

One of the most important strategic uses of pricing, especially when the product is new, is to obtain trial. A buyer's first purchase represents more than just another sale; it is an opportunity to educate him or her about the product's attributes.[13] Since only people who are familiar with a product can become loyal repeat purchasers, inducing potential buyers to make their first purchase is a critical step in building sales. Although new products need to build sales quickly, even companies marketing established products face the problem that some educated buyers leave the market, some switch to other brands, and some simply forget what they have learned. Consequently, to maintain a fixed market share, manufacturers must regularly obtain trial by new buyers.

One way to accomplish this is to offer the product in a form that minimizes the initial outlay required to try it. Packaged goods manufacturers sometimes introduce products in small, trial sizes. They have found that many people who would be unwilling to lay out $2.50 to try a 10-ounce regular package will spend $0.25 for a 1-ounce trial package. When marketing some industrial products, companies reduce the initial outlay required for sampling by offering leases. For example, companies introducing new software programs for mainframe computers find business customers reluctant to spend $50,000 on a program that may not work as well as promised. They are more willing to lease the software for $3,000 a month until they find out how well it really works.

A common tactic for inducing trial of repeat-purchase products is a promotional price *deal*. It makes sense for a firm to cut its price, even to an unprofitable level, for a first-time buyer because the firm benefits from a first purchase by much more than the revenue from that sale. A buyer who likes the brand becomes a repeat purchaser at its regular price, thereby beginning a stream of future income for the seller. The price deal is an investment in future sales.

Price deals normally take one of four forms: trial offers, coupons, rebates, or free samples. To understand why manufacturers use these methods rather than simply cut the explicit prices of their products, one needs to understand the objectives of the dealing firm.

■ First, the manufacturer wants the promotional price cut to benefit the end customer, not to add to the margin of a distributor. If the company simply cuts its wholesale price by the amount of the desired retail price cut, it cannot be sure that the wholesaler or retailer will pass along the savings.

■ Second, the manufacturer wants the end consumer to perceive the price cut as a special, exceptional offer in order to minimize the perception that the product may be of lower quality because it is offered at a lower price.

■ Third, the manufacturer wants to direct the price cut to first-time buyers and minimize the extent to which repeat buyers can take advantage of it to make multiple purchases.

An explicit price cut usually fails to achieve these objectives, whereas one of the four common dealing tactics often can.

Trial offers are simple price cuts that the seller makes clear are temporary. Although trial offers are the cheapest way to offer a price promotion, the trick to making them successful is ensuring that the temporary wholesale price cut to the trade actually gets passed through to the end consumer and that the end consumer actually perceives the lower price as a special deal. Usually these two objectives are accomplished with special packaging (see Exhibit 10.4). When the package says in banner print "20¢ Off Regular Price" or "Special $1.99," consumer pressure compels the retailer to pass on the promised savings. And consumers are unlikely to interpret the low price as a signal of low quality when it reflects a discount that is clearly temporary. Sometimes, a trial offer can also meet the third objective, excluding repeat buyers. Magazines, for example, offer discounted trial subscriptions at rates unavailable to current subscribers. For most products, however, separating new from repeat purchasers is not easy. This is not a major problem for new products, since almost all of their buyers are first-time purchasers. Consequently, trial offers are used most often for products that are new to a market.

Coupons meet all three of the objectives effectively, which explains their extreme popularity as a method of dealing.[14] Not only does the consumer receive the discount while seeing clearly that the regular price is higher, the coupon also limits the number of discounted purchases that repeat buyers can make. Moreover, coupons can often be distributed in ways that increase the probability that only first-time users will redeem them. For example, coupons for automatic dishwasher detergent are placed inside new dishwashers, and coupons for disposable diapers are mailed to new parents.[15] Finally, a coupon makes buyers aware of a deal even when the product is not yet stocked in the store where they shop. Their desire to redeem the coupons can then pressure the store into placing an order.[16]

Coupons do have their drawbacks. Because they are inconvenient, coupon redemption rates are low among families in some demographic groups (those with high incomes or with both spouses working).[17] Moreover, the manufacturer's cost of coupons greatly exceeds the amount of the discount that the consumer receives. In addition to the cost of printing and distributing coupons, retailers must be paid for handling them (at

---

EXHIBIT 10.4

Manufacturer Pricing of a Trial Offer

Courtesy of First Brands Corporation.

---

least $0.08), and clearing-houses must be paid for redeeming them (usually $0.02). Finally, a high rate of fraudulent redemption, 20 percent on average but as much as 80 percent in some cases, adds to their cost.[18] Nevertheless, the number of coupons issued attests to the fact that they are often worth these costs. By 1992, the number issued by manufacturers alone had grown to 310 billion with an average face value of $0.59.[19]

Rebates have grown popular in recent years as a substitute for couponing. Rebates can meet all three objectives of dealing, but they have the disadvantage of being more costly to the consumer. The average value of a coupon in 1982 was $0.279. Few people would invest the time and postage to claim a rebate of the same value. Consequently, rebates are effective only when the dollar amount of the discount is large. Companies that sell multiple products, however, can often overcome this problem by requiring the purchase of a number of different products to claim a single large rebate. For example, Richardson-Merrill offered a $2 rebate during the winter of 1980 to consumers who bought any four of its ten cold remedies. In addition to meeting all three of a manufacturer's objectives in dealing, the advantages of rebates are as follows:

- They avoid the problem of coupon counterfeiting and fraudulent redemption by retailers.
- They enable the firm to limit the offer to one per family, thus controlling the benefit to repeat purchasers.
- They often involve lower administrative costs than couponing, particularly when they cover multiple products.
- They enable the firm to develop a mailing list of deal-prone consumers that can be used for future promotions.
- Many consumers buy a product because of the rebate, but then fail to redeem it.[20]

The most effective and most costly deal is the *free sample*. A much larger percentage of consumers will use a free sample than will redeem a coupon, enabling the manufacturer to induce trial far more quickly and with broader coverage of the various demographic groups. For example, when Lever Brothers introduced its Sunlight dishwashing detergent, it used free samples to gain trial in 70 percent of all households. In contrast, a typical coupon or rebate offer is redeemed by only about 5 percent of the targeted households. Nevertheless, the high cost of free samples makes them a profitable promotional tactic only for products that are very frequently repeat purchased, such as soaps or cigarettes, or those with very high contribution margins, such as computer software.[21]

Defensive dealing

Over the past two decades, most consumer markets have moved from growth to maturity. Companies with strong brand images and profitable market shares should have recognized the need to change from growth-oriented to value-preserving strategies, as described in Chapter 10. Instead, many companies have offered larger and more frequent deals to sustain sales growth. Both researchers and managers have begun to suspect that such chronic dealing undermines consumer loyalties and increases marketing costs. Moreover, when the dealing is often financed at the expense of advertising, the short-term boost to sales is often more than balanced by a long-term loss in brand equity.[22]

Although dealing is still a useful tactic for new brand introductions in mature markets, it does not, in general, make sense for established brands to meet the price deals of new competitors. There are three reasons for this: First, only part of an established brand's buyers will actually respond to a dealing firm's inducements to try its brand. Unfortunately, the firm defending an established brand does not know who among its buyers are potentially disloyal. It must offer them all the defensive price cut in order to neutralize a competitor's deal. This puts the defending brand at a cost disadvantage if the dealing competitor has a smaller market share. Consider the case where the dealing brand has a 10 percent market share and the defending brand has a 90 percent market share, 5 percent of which is disloyal when presented with a deal. The dealing brand must offer the deal on two sales it would have made anyway in order to induce the switch of each additional sale from the established brand. This is because its current market share is twice the additional market share that it can induce to try its brand. In comparison, the defending firm must offer a defensive deal on seventeen sales that it would have made anyway in order to prevent disloyal buyers from trying the competing brand. This is because the loyal market share of the defending firm is seventeen times the share that it would lose if it did not meet the deal. Consequently, the defending firm must give up 8.5 times as much revenue to neutralize a deal as the dealing firm gives up to offer it.

Second, when a product's costs are primarily incremental and avoidable, firms can offer deals on small-share brands at little cost until customers respond to the deal and try the product. The defending firm, however, must bear the cost of a defensive deal each time it offers the deal to retain buyers' loyalty. Consequently, to the extent that costs are incremental and avoidable, a firm marketing a new brand can repeatedly offer attractive deals at little cost until it succeeds, whereas the established firm bears significant cost in repeatedly defending against it.

Third, as mentioned above, frequent dealing can tarnish a brand's image, thus reducing consumers' loyalty. Unless the established brand was already positioned as an economy product, the firm may have difficulty reestablishing its regular price without losing some previously loyal buyers.

Because of these disadvantages, dealing is generally much more effective for new brands or for those with small market shares to induce trial than for established brands trying to prevent it. Established brands should not simply ignore such threats; they should use other marketing instruments with which they have a greater advantage. In the beer industry, for example, Heileman, Stroh, and Pabst found couponing an effective marketing tool for entering new geographical markets where their beers were unknown. But Anheuser-Busch and Miller, brewers of the most popular national brands, wisely chose not to respond with deals of their own. Instead, they recognized that they could defend market share more cost effectively by increasing their advertising and distribution efforts because they enjoyed superior economies of scale in those activities.[23]

Defensive deals are occasionally advisable. Because costs in some markets are overwhelmingly fixed, a new firm offering a promotional deal on a new brand bears costs comparable to those of the defending firm, even if it makes no sales. In many markets, a premium image has so little effect on price sensitivity that the defending firm need not worry about cheapening it. In the airline industry, for example, costs are overwhelmingly fixed and buyers select flights more for convenience and service than for image. As a result, established firms on many routes successfully defend their markets by matching the promotional fares of new entrants.

Defensive dealing may also prove useful as a temporary segmentation technique during recessions. Coupon redemption rates increase during recessions and decline during recoveries.[24] In the chapter on price segmentation, we discuss how coupons offer one way to separate the price-sensitive segment for discounting. Often this can be done very cost effectively by printing a coupon or rebate certificate on the package for use by consumers willing to take the time to redeem them. Since the price-sensitive segment grows during recessions, these deals can maintain the brand loyalty of customers who are temporarily more price sensitive, without undercutting margins to all customers. Prices can then be increased more easily after the recession simply by dropping the deal.

Trade dealing

Manufacturers who distribute their products through independent retailers often complement their promotional or defensive pricing with *trade deals*. Traditionally, trade deals were temporary discounts to retailers from a product's regular wholesale price. Beginning in the 1970s, however, manufacturers began using the term to disguise what were actually nothing more than permanent price cuts. They did so in response to three changes in the economy.

First, after being stung by the imposition of price controls in 1970, manufacturers tried to protect themselves against such surprises by setting inflated wholesale prices which they would regularly discount. Later in the decade, constant trade deals were used to solve another problem: declining sales volume due to chronic recessions and competition from generic and house brands. Firms with slow-selling brands camouflaged wholesale price cuts as trade deals because (1) the cuts were then less visible to competitors who might otherwise retaliate, and (2) the cuts were more easily adjusted to reflect the precariousness of a brand's position in different stores and geographical areas.

In the 1980s, large retailers gained substantially more power to extract larger discounts from manufacturers than their smaller rivals. Since giving such discounts would be a blatant violation of the Robinson-Patman Act restrictions on price discrimination, manufacturers offered trade deals that these chains, with their substantial warehousing and distribution capacity, could benefit from disproportionately.

In contrast to such recent practices, the traditional trade deal is a temporary cut in the wholesale price to achieve a specific short-run goal. One such goal is to purchase retailers' favors during a promotional campaign. A packaged-food manufacturer may offer a trade deal in return for a grocery retailer's agreement to feature the product in its newspaper advertising or to display the product at a particularly prominent location with special on-site advertising. Special displays for soft drinks, for example, have been known to increase sales by a factor of six. For new brands that initially have low sales rates and therefore high holding costs for retailers, a discount is often necessary before retailers will allocate any shelf space at all to the product.

Manufacturers also offer trade deals on products that they produce seasonally in order to induce retailers to stock up at the time of production. Canned foods, such as salmon, peaches, and some vegetables, are packed by manufacturers at one time of the year and then must be stored at significant cost for sales in the off season. If retailers are willing to stock up during the production season in return for a discount less than the manufacturer's cost of holding inventory, such trade deals are a profitable tactic. Retailers are often willing to take advantage of such deals because (1) their inventory holding costs are sometimes lower than those of manufacturers since they fully utilize their storage space by purchasing different products on deal in different seasons, and (2) they can often induce consumers to stock up as well by passing on part of the trade deal as a price promotion of their own.[25]

Occasionally, leading manufacturers also use trade dealing as a defense against the introduction of competing brands. If a temporary trade deal prompts retailers and consumers to load up with inventories of the leading brand, they will be more reluctant to take on still more inventories of a new brand.

Sometimes, however, increased inventory holding by retailers results in an unintended and undesirable effect of dealing. If a manufacturer offers retailers a trade deal to discount and advertise a product for one week, they may order more of the product than they can actually sell that week, enabling them to reduce their purchases in later weeks at the regular wholesale price. In fact, retailers are notorious for effectively converting manufacturers' trial offers and periodic sales into trade deals by ordering more than they can sell during the period of the retail price cut. This "forward buying" unnecessarily raises distribution cost for both retailers and distributors by 1 to 2 percent of sales.

Top management must also be wary of the effect that trade dealing has on incentives for product managers. Trade deals, like price promotions, are sometimes used to meet short-term goals that arguably are not in the firm's long-run interest. When brand managers are rewarded for meeting sales quotas, they may use quick end-of-quarter trade promotions to reach their goals. Although the resulting stocking up by retailers depresses later sales at higher prices, that may be of little concern to some brand managers who may hope to be promoted before the effects of overdealing catch up with them. The money for these trade deals is often diverted from the advertising budget. Although advertising has less of a short-term effect on sales than a trade deal, it probably has a much larger impact on long-term brand equity with consumers. Moreover, as discussed below, the demand "pull" from manufacturer's advertising reduces retailer's power to set prices and dictate terms. Such short-run thinking is probably not typical in most firms, but it is sufficiently widespread to cause experts in industry, academe, and government to express alarm.[26]

PRICING AND DISTRIBUTION

The way a product is distributed distinctly affects the way it can be priced. A product's distribution affects

- Other products with which it is compared
- Image consumers have of it
- Ability to differentiate it through augmentation
- Ability to segment its market

Since all of these factors are considerations in formulating a pricing strategy, distribution and pricing need to be thoughtfully coordinated.

Selecting an appropriate channel

One important consideration when choosing a channel of distribution is its effect on the product's price level. Consider the following examples:

> When the U.S. Time Company developed its inexpensive line of Timex watches, the established channel of distribution was jewelry stores. That was an appropriate channel for watches that competed with one another on their claims of accuracy, the beauty of their designs, and their heirloom qualities. The jewelry stores offered skilled personnel to demonstrate those attributes and the appropriate environment in which to contemplate an expensive purchase. The Timex, however, was not a great timepiece; its attractive attribute was its low price. The sales and service of a jewelry store could do little to improve the perception of its inherent value, but the markups that jewelers expected could have seriously crimped its price advantage. Consequently, the company distributed through drug and department stores which, although they offered little service, generated maximum visibility while adding relatively little to the product's cost.

> Lenox makes fine-quality china dishes and figurines that carry premium prices. Since the major attributes of china are apparent before

purchase and it requires no postpurchase service, Lenox could offer the same physical product through practically any retail channel. But Lenox limits its distribution to high-quality department, jewelry, and specialty stores. The reason is that fine china is a prestige product, displayed for guests or given as gifts. Its image would be tarnished if it were available in stores that lacked luxurious displays and discounted its price.[27]

For a product that attracts buyers with a low price, the goal is to obtain low-cost distribution. For a product that attracts buyers with its superior attributes despite a high price, the goal is to obtain distribution that complements those attributes and makes them salient.

When a product's differentiation value stems from its augmentation, it is risky to rely completely on independent distribution. Not only must the manufacturer worry that the product is augmented appropriately, it must also worry that the augmentations might be used to sell competitors' products, eliminating its product's competitive advantage. Thus companies that rely heavily on augmentation develop distribution channels over which they can exercise at least some control. For example,

> Companies that manufacture high-priced cosmetics have a unique distribution system. They distribute in high-quality department stores, but they do not sell their products to those stores. Instead, they rent display space and staff it with their own sales representatives. They do so because much of the differentiation value of their products stems from augmentation. Each company's representative is trained as a cosmetologist to help a woman select cosmetics appropriate for her and to teach her how to use them most effectively. At the same time, the cosmetologist makes the connection between the customer's enhanced beauty and the particular brand of cosmetics that is sold.
>
> Caterpillar Tractor is legendary for the quality of its exclusive dealer network. Cat selects its dealers carefully and treats them royally in order to instill a feeling that they are part of a family of Caterpillar employees. This is because Caterpillar's reputation for reliability enables it to charge a substantial price premium. Although that reputation stems in part from the high quality of the physical product, it could be quickly destroyed if a dealer is not quick to come to a customer's aid when inevitable breakdowns occur. Caterpillar dealers, however, view a breakdown as a potential blight on their family name and will go to unusual extremes to correct it. Such commitment is well worth the extra cost to Caterpillar of maintaining its exclusive distribution network.[28]

The control and loyalty that these manufacturers enjoy are more costly than dealing with completely independent distribution channels, but the cost is justified when augmentations that occur in the channel add substantial value.

When companies use different pricing strategies for different versions of their products, they need to coordinate those strategies with different distribution channels. Despite the success of L'Eggs pantyhose in super-markets, Hanes continues to sell higher-quality, higher-priced hosiery through department stores. John M. Smythe, a Chicago furniture retailer, sells high-priced brands in attractive stores staffed with decorating consultants and low-priced brands in warehouse stores under a different name. Pitney Bowes continues to sell the bulk of its office equipment through its sales force but uses direct mail to sell its lowest priced scales and postage meters to small buyers. In each of these cases, low-priced products are appropriately distributed through low-cost channels that preserve their price advantage, whereas higher-priced products justify the higher cost of distribution methods that can enhance perceptions of the product's differentiating attributes.

Maintaining minimum resale prices

Although manufacturers can always state a suggested retail price for their products, they cannot legally insist that retailers charge that price. Under U.S. antitrust laws, independent resellers must be left free to charge any price they wish. A manufacturer cannot legally refuse to deal with those who do charge another price. Unfortunately, there are times when it is in the interest of some retailers to charge prices lower or higher than a manufacturer would like. Consequently, an important part of pricing through independent channels of distribution is the management of relations with resellers to influence, while not dictating, their pricing decisions.

Maintaining a minimum resale price can be essential for the success of products whose perceived value depends not only on the product itself, but also on related services offered by the retailer. The time spent by a computer store demonstrating the equipment and helping the customer select the most appropriate software strongly influences both the likelihood that customers will buy and ultimately be satisfied with their purchases. Similarly, most audiophiles will buy stereo speakers only if a retailer offers the service of a listening room, where the sounds of different speakers can be compared. Many first-time purchasers of food processors buy them only after seeing them demonstrated in a department store. Even though high-service retailers require higher margins to cover the higher incremental costs of these services, manufacturers eagerly solicit such retailers to carry their brands, knowing that the high levels of service they offer encourage far more sales than their higher prices discourage.

Unfortunately for manufacturers, retailers have an incentive to provide such services only as long as customers who use the services buy the product from them. If shoppers can see a product demonstrated and learn how to use it from a high-service retailer but purchase it from a low-service retailer at a discount price, the high-service retailer loses. Ultimately if enough potential customers go to the discounters, high-service retailers either stop promoting the brand or stop carrying it altogether. The value of the product declines and sales suffer.[29]

To avoid this, manufacturers of such products would like to set minimum resale prices, ensuring each reseller a large enough margin to support services that enhance the product's value. Before 1976, manufacturers could legally set minimum resale prices in any state that passed a fair trade law endorsing the practice.[30] Unfortunately, federal law no longer condones this practice, nor does it condone manufacturers' attempts to enforce resale prices on their own by cutting off supplies to discounters.[31]

There are other ways to overcome this problem, although not completely. Manufacturers can select the retailers with whom they will deal, as long as one criterion is not the prices they charge. Thus a computer retailer can refuse to supply a mail-order distributor by establishing a policy that its retailers must have display areas to demonstrate the equipment or a service department to repair it. Unfortunately, retailers who do meet those criteria often buy extra stock that they resell to discounters who do not. And discounters who are cut off from supplies often file antitrust suits claiming that their pricing and not their failure to meet certain other criteria was the real reason they were excluded.[32]

Alternatively, some manufacturers simply charge wholesale prices that leave low-service retailers with too little margin to discount. Then they pay the high-service retailers generous promotional allowances for specific services such as product displays. They may also supply free training for retailers' salespeople and give them financial incentive payments for each sale. Of course, these alternatives are administratively more costly, and they run the risk that some retailers will collect payments without providing the services that the manufacturer expects. However, they are the only alternatives when resale prices cannot be practically or legally enforced.

Limiting maximum resale prices

Manufacturers can usually distribute their products much more cheaply through independent retailers than they can directly. A clothing retailer, for example, can distribute the products of many manufacturers at a much lower cost than would be possible if each manufacturer tried to operate its own stores. Moreover, buyers are better served when they enjoy the wide assortment that an independent retailer can offer. Balancing these advantages, however, is a potentially significant disadvantage of using independent distribution. Independent distributors sometimes charge excessive resale prices that can make a manufacturer's product less competitive and therefore less profitable.[33] In most markets, competition among retailers limits their ability to overprice. In a few markets, however, the potential for overpricing is great enough to justify special contracts that minimize the problem. In extreme cases, it may even justify vertical integration of manufacturing and retailing within a single firm.

To see why overpricing occurs, consider the hypothetical example in Exhibit 10.5. An independent retailer currently charges $1.00 for a product she buys wholesale from the manufacturer for $0.70. She incurs an additional incremental cost of $0.05 to sell it. Thus her unit profit contribution is $0.25. The manufacturer, who set the wholesale price of $0.70, incurs an incremental manufacturing cost of $0.25. Thus, its unit profit contribution is

---

EXHIBIT 10.5

Incentives for Overpricing by the Channel

	Total	Per Unit(s)
Independent Retailer's Revenue and Costs		
Sales revenue (price)	$10,000	$1.00
Incremental product cost	7,000	0.70
Other incremental cost	500	0.05
Profit contribution	2,500	0.25
Manufacturer's Revenue and Costs		
Sales revenue (price)	$7,000	$0.70
Incremental cost	2,500	0.25
Profit contribution	4,500	0.45

Breakeven Sales Changes
5% Price increase by retailer

$$\frac{-0.05}{0.25 + 0.05} = -16.7\%$$

5% Price cut by retailer

$$\frac{-(-0.05)}{0.25 + (-0.05)} = 25.0\%$$

5% Price increase by integrated retailer-manufacturer

$$\frac{-0.05}{0.70 + 0.05} = -7.7\%$$

$0.45. What is the retailer's incentive to raise or lower the price, and how does it affect the manufacturer?

Chapter 2 illustrated the breakeven sales change needed to maintain profit following a price change. Applying that equation to this example, the retailer would profit from a 5 percent price increase if sales fell by an amount less than 16.7 percent. She would have to increase sales by more than 25 percent, however, to justify a 5 percent price cut. If the retailer believed that sales would decline by only 10 percent following a 5 percent price increase, she could raise the price and (assuming an initial sales rate of 10,000 units per month) increase her profits by $200.00.

Note, however, how the retailer's 5 percent price premium would affect the manufacturer. The manufacturer sells the retailer 1,000 fewer units each month. At a profit contribution of $0.45 per unit, the manufacturer would lose $450 in profit each month, or $250 more than the retailer gained, as a result of the price increase. Consequently, if the retailer and manufacturer were one integrated firm, they would not raise price at all. In fact, the integrated firm's breakeven sales change from a 5 percent price increase would be only 7.7 percent, which could actually justify a price reduction.

The independent retailer has the incentive to price higher than would an integrated retailer-manufacturer, because for the independent retailer the entire wholesale price is an incremental cost of doing business. Thus she sees her profit contribution as being only $0.25 per unit, or 25 percent of the initial selling price. Since much of the wholesale price goes to cover the manufacturer's fixed costs and profit, costs not incremental for pricing, in order to set price to maximize the joint profit from retailing and manufacturing the manufacturer calculates the profit contribution at $0.70 per unit ($1.00 − 0.05 − 0.25), or 70 percent of the initial selling price. It would therefore judge price cuts as much more attractive and price increases as much less attractive, given the same expected changes in sales.

It can clearly pay a manufacturer to recognize that retailers may have an incentive to price too high and to take steps to alleviate it. The easiest solution is to encourage competition among retailers, thus limiting their ability to charge excessive margins. The evidence is quite strong that a "pull strategy" of heavy brand advertising is the key to maximizing retail competition and minimizing retail margins. Exhibit 10.6 illustrates how dramatic these effects can be. Advertising increases retail competition, thus reducing retailer margins for all brands, but especially for the leading brands in each category. These relationships have been confirmed by other studies across many product categories.[34]

Unfortunately for manufacturers, not all distribution channels are competitive. In fact, manufacturers sometimes deliberately limit competition among those who sell their products. Automobile companies limit the number of dealers in a geographical area so that each dealer has enough

Exhibit 10.6

Typical Effects of Brand Advertising on Retail Margins

	Average Manufacturer Price	Average Retail Price	Average Retail Margin
Leading Brands			
With heavy advertising	$3.00	$3.95	24%
With light advertising	2.35	4.20	44%
Difference			−20%
Other Brands			
With heavy advertising	$1.70	$2.93	42%
With light advertising	1.96	4.00	51%
Difference			−9%

Source: Robert Steiner, as reported in Mark Albion, *Advertising's Hidden Effects: Manufacturers' Advertising and Retail Pricing* (Boston: Auburn House, 1983), p. 50. Auburn House is an imprint of Greenwood Publishing Group, Inc., Westport, CT. Reprinted with permission.

sales volume to justify carrying an adequate inventory of cars. Coca-Cola grants only one local bottler the exclusive right to sell in a particular territory. This ensures that a bottler who promotes the brand in an area and maintains high standards of quality will be able to capture the benefits from doing so. Unfortunately from the manufacturer's perspective, the limited competition also makes it easier for these retailers to raise prices too high.

Overcoming this problem is difficult when the distribution network is entirely independent. The most straightforward solution—that of a contract between the manufacturer and distributors specifying a maximum resale price—has consistently been found unacceptable under U.S. antitrust laws. However, there are other ways that manufacturers can hold down resale prices. For prepackaged products, manufacturers can limit resale prices by printing on the package a suggested retail price large enough that the retailer cannot easily cover it with a higher-price sticker. They can also advertise the suggested price, leading consumers to complain when retailers try to charge more. Unfortunately, these are all less than ideal solutions for many of the products affected by this problem.

The most common method of limiting resale prices is by minimum sales provisions. Many companies, selling everything from fast foods and gasoline to commercial security systems and water purification equipment, require resellers to sign franchise agreements. These agreements commonly include minimum sales quotas specified as a percentage of the average sales for a typical franchise or as a percentage of the estimated market potential in a particular location. Such contracts cannot legally dictate a specific resale price. Franchisees who set prices too high, however, cannot achieve their minimum sales quotas and can lose their franchises. Short of withdrawing a franchise, there are other ways that manufacturers can enforce minimum sales quotas. The auto manufacturers exert leverage over their dealers by offering joint advertising programs, preference in receiving models in short supply, and other special considerations only to those dealers who maintain sales levels commensurate with the sales potential in their areas.

SUMMARY

The process of pricing is in many ways unique, its end result being part of a larger marketing effort. Consequently, attempts to price independently of other elements in the marketing mix—the product, its promotion, and its distribution—are unlikely to be effective. Management must understand the interactions between pricing and the other elements of marketing in order to fashion a coordinated marketing strategy.

The product, probably more than any other element, determines the viability of a price. With all its augmentations, the product determines relative value, indicating the levels at which price can skim, penetrate, and remain neutral in a market. A product's effect on others in the firm's product line requires adjustments to ensure that price maximizes total profit, not only the profit from the individual product being priced. Flanking brands, to meet price competition from slightly differentiated brands or to preclude competition from new brands, plays an important role in maximizing the effectiveness of price competition.

Promotion influences pricing through its effect on price sensitivity. Advertisements can bring to the buyers' attention information that may make price less important in their purchase decisions. Conversely, advertisements can provide information that makes buyers more aware of their alternatives and encourages them to focus on price as an important attribute of choice. Even advertising that does not directly attempt to influence price sensitivity apparently increases it, at least for consumer nondurables. Personal selling, on the other hand, generally reduces price sensitivity by enabling buyers to appreciate the differentiating attributes of unfamiliar brands and by facilitating augmentation.

Price itself is often an effective promotional tool. A high price can signal superior quality, a stable price can signal stability of value, and the excess demand created by a low price can draw attention to a product. A low price deal can induce buyers to try a product once and in doing so, educate them about attributes that will prompt them to make future purchases at the regular price. A trade deal can induce retailers to advertise a product, promote it with a special in-store display, or purchase additional quantities for their inventories.

Finally, the choice of a distribution channel should complement a product's pricing. Products priced high to reflect their unique attributes or to ensure exclusivity need channels that will communicate the products' worth. Products designed to sell on the appeal of their relatively low prices need channels that will make consumers aware of their existence but add minimally to their cost. When companies practice segmented pricing, they may need different channels to complement the variations in their pricing to different segments.

Whenever the distribution channel is independent, a manufacturer must also consider how resellers' pricing influences the ultimate attractiveness of the product to consumers. If discounters can price the product too low to cover the cost of educational and promotional services, competing retailers will stop providing those services and the product's sales will suffer. Alternatively, retailers may have an incentive to price the product too high at the expense of volume and the manufacturer's profits. The manufacturer can minimize this effect by distributing through many competing retailers and by making consumers aware of a suggested retail price. The firm can also increase competition among retailers by advertising its brand name or can sell through dealers who agree to minimum sales levels that limit their ability to overprice. When managers responsible for pricing and those responsible for other elements in the marketing mix recognize these interactions, they can coordinate their activities to produce more effective marketing strategies.

NOTES

1. Rockney G. Walters, "Assessing the Impact of Retail Price Promotions on Product Substitution, Complementarity Purchase, and Interstore Sales Displacement," *Journal of Marketing*, 55 (April 1991), 17–28.

2. See Thomas Nagle and Kenneth Novak, "The Roles of Segmentation and Awareness in Explaining Variations in Price Markups," in *Issues in Pricing: Theory and Research*, ed. Timothy M. Devinney (Lexington, Mass.: D. C. Heath, 1988), pp. 313–332.

3. Steven M. Shugan, "Pricing When Different Outlets Offer Different Assortments of Brands," in *Issues in Pricing: Theory and Research*, ed. Timothy M. Devinney (Lexington, Mass.: D. C. Heath, 1988), pp. 289–311.

4. For empirical evidence, see Amihai Glazer, "Advertising, Information, and Prices—A Case Study," *Economic Inquiry*, 19 (October 1981), 661–71.

5. Lakshman Krishnamurti and S. P. Raj, "The Effect of Advertising on Consumer Price Sensitivity," *Journal of Marketing Research*, 22 (May 1985), 119–29.

6. Vinay Kanetkar, Charles B. Weinberg, and Doyle L. Weiss, "Price Sensitivity and Television Advertising Exposure: Some Empirical Findings," *Marketing Science* 11, no. 4 (Fall 1992), 359–71.

7. Lee Benham, "The Effect of Advertising on the Price of Eyeglasses," *Journal of Law and Economics*, 15 (October 1972), 337–52; Gerald Eskin, "A Case for Test Market Experiments," *Journal of Advertising Research*, 15 (April 1975), 27–33; V. Kanti Prasad and L. Winston Ring, "Measuring Sales Effects of Some Marketing Mix Variables and Their Interactions," *Journal of Marketing Research*, 13 (November 1976), 391–96; Gerald Eskin and Penny Barron, "Effects of Price and Advertising in Test Market Experiments," *Journal of Marketing Research*, 14 (November 1977), 495–508; Dick Wittink, "Advertising Increases Sensitivity to Price," *Journal of Advertising Research*, 17 (April 1977), 39–42.

8. Eskin, "A Case for Test Market Experiments."

9. See "Dewey and Almy Chemical Division: Pricing the Polyfibron Blanket," HBS Case No. 9-506-084, Rev. 4/71 (Boston: Harvard Business School, 1961).

10. See Somerby Dowst, "How Top Industrial Salespeople Serve Customers," *Industrial Marketing*, 66 (November 1981), 88–95.

11. See David A. Aaker and John G. Meyers, *Advertising Management* (Englewood Cliffs, N.J.: Prentice Hall, Inc., 1975), chapter 3; W. Semlow, "How Many Salesmen Do You Need?" *Harvard Business Review*, 38 (May–June 1959), 126–32; Charles Beswick and David Cravens, "A Multistage Decision Model for Salesforce Management," *Journal of Marketing Research*, 14 (May 1977), 135–44.

12. See Paul Gibson, "De Beers: Can a Cartel Be Forever?" *Forbes*, May 28, 1979, p. 45; John R. Emshwiller, and Neil Behrmann, "How De Beers Revived World Diamond Cartel After Zaire's Pullout," *Wall Street Journal*, July 7, 1983, pp. 1, 12.

13. Of course, this is only true to the extent that a brand actually has differentiating attributes that a buyer can learn by sampling. House brands and generic groceries, for example, do not have price promotions precisely because they lack differentiating attributes that buyers could learn enough about through sampling. Their appeal is their price.

14. See Russell Bowman, *Couponing and Rebates: Profit on the Dotted Line* (New York: Lebhar-Friedman Books, 1980), pp. 2–3.

15. Researchers are experimenting with systems that automatically issue coupons right in the supermarket checkout line to purchasers of competing products. In one such experiment, Dole issued coupons for its Fruit 'N Juice Bars to everyone who purchased Weight Watchers Treats or Jello Pudding Pops. Not only did Dole avoid giving unnecessary discounts to repeat purchasers, it also benefitted from an unusually high redemption rate, approximately 20 percent. "Coupons While You Wait," *Sales and Marketing Management*, November 12, 1984, p. 41.

16. See William Nigut Sr., "Is the Boom in Cents-Off Couponing Going to Burst?" *Advertising Age*, December 15, 1980, pp. 41–44.

17. William Massy and Ronald Frank, "Short-term Price and Dealing Effects in Selected Market Segments," *Journal of Marketing Research*, 2 (May 1965), 175–85; David Montgomery, "Consumer Characteristics Associated with Dealing: An Empirical Example," *Journal of Marketing Research*, 8 (February 1971), 118–20; Robert Blattberg and others, "Identifying the Deal Prone Segment," *Journal of Marketing Research*, 15 (August 1978), 369–77.

18. "Coupon Scams Are Clipping Companies," *Business Week*, June 15, 1992, pp. 110–11.

19. Scott Hume, "Coupons Set Record, but Pace Slows," *Advertising Age*, 64 (February 1, 1993), p. 25; Elliot Zweibach, "Coupon Redemptions Increase 10%," *Supermarket News*, 42 (October 12, 1992), 4.

20. See Toni Mack, "Rebate Madness," *Forbes*, February 13, 1984, pp. 76–77.

21. Software suppliers for mainframe computers sell systems for tens of thousands of dollars. They can produce copies, however, for only a few hundred dollars. To enable potential buyers to learn the value of these systems, they sometimes offer free samples of the software, but with a built-in subroutine that destroys the program after a limited time.

22. Charles Hinkle, "The Strategy of Price Deals," *Harvard Business Review*, 43 (July–August 1965), 75–85; C. A. Scott, "The Effects of Trial and Incentives on Repeat Purchase Behavior," *Journal of Marketing Research*, 13 (August 1976), 263–69; Joe Dodson, Alice Tybout, and Brian Sternthal, "Impact of Deals and Deal Retraction on Brand Switching," *Journal of Marketing Research*, 15 (February 1978), 72–81; John Philip Jones, "The Double Jeopardy of Sales Promotions," *Harvard Business Review*, September–October 1990, p. 146; David A. Aaker, *Managing Brand Equity* (New York: The Free Press, 1992).

23. Robert Reed, "Beer Couponing Foams to the Top," *Advertising Age*, February 21, 1983, pp. 10, 71.

24. Scott Hume, "Coupons Set Record, but Pace Slows," *Advertising Age*, 64 (February 1, 1993), p. 25; Zweibach, "Coupon Redemptions Increase 10%."

25. Even when retailers do not receive manufacturer trade deals, they may still offer deals to get consumers to stock up on certain items. This can pay if it reduces a retailer's inventory cost by more than the cost of the deal. See Robert C. Blattberg, Gary D. Eppen, and Joshua Lieberman, "A Theoretical and Empirical Evaluation of Price Deals for Consumer Nondurables," *Journal of Marketing*, 45 (Winter 1981), 116–29.

26. Monci Jo Williams, "The No-Win Game of Price Promotion," *Fortune*, July 11, 1983, pp. 93–102; Robert D. Buzzell, John A. Quelch, and Walter J. Salmon, "The Costly Bargain of Trade Promotion," *Harvard Business Review*, March–April 1990, pp. 141–49; Jakki J. Mohr and George S. Low, "Escaping the Catch-22 of Trade Promotion Spending," *Marketing Management*, vol. 2, no. 2 (1993), pp. 31–39.

27. "Rings on Her Fingers, China on Her Table," *Forbes*, February 20, 1978, pp. 76, 81; and Claudia Ricci, "Discounters, Alleging Price-Fixing, Are Fighting Cuts in Their Supplies," *Wall Street Journal*, June 21, 1983, p. 35.

28. Harlan S. Byrne, "A Leaping Caterpillar Is a Wondrous Thing, Even Its Rivals Agree," *Wall Street Journal*, April 19, 1976, pp. 1, 18; and Peters and Waterman, *In Search of Excellence* (New York: Harper & Row, 1982), pp. 171–72.

29. Lester Telser, "Why Manufacturers Want Fair Trade," *Journal of Law Economics*, 3 (October 1960), 86–104.

30. Contracts stipulating minimum resale prices are still enforceable in many other industrialized countries.

31. In December 1980, Cuisinart was fined a quarter of a million dollars for threatening to cut off retailers who discounted the Cuisinart food processor below its suggested resale price. In 1984, the Supreme Court upheld a $10 million judgment against Monsanto for cutting off a distributor (Spray Rite) who discounted Monsanto's herbicides.

32. See Ricci, "Discounters, Alleging Price-Fixing, Are Fighting Cuts in Their Supplies," pp. 35, 41.

33. Fritz Machlup and Martha Taber, "Bilateral Monopoly, Successive Monopoly, and Vertical Integration," *Economica*, 27 (May 1960), 101–19; Steven M. Shugan, and Abel P. Jeuland, "Competitive Behavior in Distribution Systems," in *Issues in Pricing: Theory and Research*, ed., Timothy Devinney (Lexington, Mass.: D. C. Heath, 1988).

34. Robert L. Steiner, "Does Advertising Lower Consumer Prices?" *Journal of Marketing*, 37 (October 1973), 19–26; Paul W. Farris, and Mark S. Albion, "The Impact of Advertising on the Price of Consumer Products," *Journal of Marketing*, 44 (Summer 1980), 17–35; Paul W. Farris, "Advertising's Link with Retail Price Competition," *Harvard Business Review*, 59, no. 1 (January–February 1981), pp. 40, 42, 44. Mark S. Albion, *Advertising's Hidden Effects: Manufacturers' Advertising and Retail Pricing* (Boston: Auburn House, 1983), pp. 185, 199–200.

COMPETITIVE ADVANTAGES

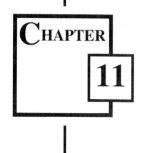

CHAPTER

11

ESTABLISHING FOUNDATIONS FOR MORE PROFITABLE PRICING

Previous chapters discussed differences among firms that affect the profitability of different pricing strategies. When discussing costs, we saw how a firm could profit despite relatively low prices because the product represented incremental business that did not need to cover nonincremental fixed costs. When discussing price sensitivity, we saw how the unique value effect of distinctive product attributes could induce buyers to pay a price premium. When discussing competition, we saw how a low-cost position could enable a company to pursue opportunistic pricing. We also saw how a product with attributes uniquely appealing to some market segment could facilitate skim pricing, whereas a product that could be produced at lower cost than competing products could facilitate penetration pricing. These differences among companies, enabling some to implement profitable pricing strategies that others cannot employ, are those companies' competitive advantages. They determine just how profitable even the most effective pricing strategy can be.

Effective pricing fully exploits a product's competitive advantages. Although fraudulent or deceptive pricing may enable an unscrupulous company to profit for a short time, sustainable profits are possible only so long as a company can serve at least one segment of buyers better and/or cheaper than its competitors. There are two types of competitive advantages that can ensure profit in even a highly competitive environment: those that produce lower costs and those that produce a differentiated product offering.

A firm that can produce an equal-quality product at lower cost can profit by capturing sales through opportunistic pricing. Later, it can maintain sales as a cooperative price leader or, occasionally, as a predatory enforcer. As long as a company can sustain its cost advantage, its profits are protected by its competitors' inability to profit by undercutting those prices. A differentiated product offering enables a company to profit as long as the cost of producing that differentiation does not exceed what buyers are willing to pay. The company can sustain profitability in a competitive environment as long as the price does not exceed the value of the product's differentiation. This chapter explains how companies develop the cost and product advantages that provide the foundation for a profitable pricing strategy.[1]

COMPETITIVE COST ADVANTAGES

Controlling costs is an ongoing activity in any successful company. It must be a continuing process because everyone involved with the company has a vested interest in seeing certain costs go up. Employees would like to see their departments increase in personnel or their expense accounts receive less scrutiny. Suppliers think that their service justifies a slightly higher price and that buyers should be more accommodating about scheduling deliveries and holding inventories. Fortunately, even though some employees or suppliers may want the company to let some particular cost rise, they realize that if the company concedes to all such desires, its viability would be threatened. Consequently, cost control is accepted as long as it is perceived that denial is suffered equitably.

It is rare, however, that cost control alone can generate competitive cost advantages for very long. Although tight-fistedness might produce a temporary cost advantage, the advantage will soon be lost due to decreases in employee morale and supplier goodwill or to competitors' imitation. Sustainable cost advantages are realized not by constant belt tightening, but by the efficient use of resources.

Internal cost efficiencies

There are three different ways that a company can reduce its unit costs through the efficient organization of its internal operations: exploitation of economies of scope, scale, and experience.

Economies of Scope   *Scope* refers to the breadth of a firm's product portfolio. Many firms sell multiple products. The goal of product planning is to compile a synergistic portfolio of products. One important source of synergy, receiving growing attention among marketing practitioners, is the economies that result when different products share a common set of costs. A firm that carefully selects the scope of its product portfolio to maximize shared costs can cut its incremental costs below those of competitors with less efficient portfolios.[2]

Consider, for example, the economies of scope that service stations such as Mobil and Arco gain through their on-site minimarts. This shared-cost strategy was pioneered by 7-Eleven during the mid-1970s in response to consumers' increased price sensitivity at the pumps. Adding a small convenience store on existing property requires no more labor or rent than operating the service station alone. The same cashier who rings up gasoline sales can ring up sales of beverages, junk food, and cigarettes. Therefore, labor costs—as well as some lesser costs for land, building, and utilities— are not incremental to ancillary sales.[3]

Airlines have captured similar advantages by diversifying into products that share costs. United Airlines trains flight crews for the military, and Delta Airlines services planes for smaller competitors—both airlines use employees and facilities already established to serve their own needs. American Airlines has also been creative. It established a subsidiary— American Airlines Telemarketing Services—that shares the cost of its telephone reservation system. American contracts to do telephone sales, surveys, fund raising, and other telemarketing activities at nonpeak hours, when the airline's phones and operators would be otherwise underutilized. American's rates are both highly competitive and profitable because the incremental cost of providing the service is so low.[4]

Developing a new product that can share current costs is more difficult than selecting from products that already exist. Dun & Bradstreet was very successful in developing a new product to generate incremental revenue from its costly credit report database. It learned the types and quantities of products particular companies sought from the credit requests they received about them. It recognized that this information would be valuable to other potential suppliers of those companies. Thus was born a new product, called Dun's Market Identifiers, which shared all the same research but served an entirely different need.

The trick to exploiting economies of scope is to find products that share a common set of costs. The more costs that the products can share, the greater the synergy from expanding the scope of a product portfolio. Economies of scope are sometimes limited by a loss in employee efficiency when a firm becomes less specialized, but they are usually limited only by management's entrepreneurial ability to identify products that could share a common set of costs.

Economies of Scale   *Scale* refers to the size of a firm as measured by its long-run, sustainable rate of output. In almost every activity, from purchasing to manufacturing to promotion and distribution, costs tend to decline as output increases. The reasons for economies of scale are numerous:

- A larger scale enables individual employees to work on more highly specialized tasks, increasing their proficiency and reducing the time lost changing tasks.
- Incremental fixed costs, such as those involved in product design, are lower per unit when they can be spread over more units.
- More efficient production processes (for example, assembly lines) are practical only when employed on a large scale.
- Larger sizes of capital equipment can often be built for less than a proportional increase in cost.[5]

Examples of scale economies abound. The British Textile Council noted that output per employee leaped 167 percent when the average run of rayon cloth increased from 3,800 to 31,000 yards. The Council's explanation was as follows:

> When staff at all levels can concentrate on the production of a very limited number of products, the smallest details can receive attention and be brought to near perfection . . . which would be wildly uneconomic in normal circumstances [but] can be justified if the volume of production is sufficiently great.[6]

Another notable example of scale economies is the automobile industry, where unit output and profitability are consistently correlated. The huge fixed costs in that industry yield a significant advantage to any company that can spread those costs over more units.[7]

Two distinct aspects of scale economies need to be distinguished when formulating pricing strategy—size and extent. These two aspects of scale economies are illustrated graphically in Exhibits 11.1 and 11.2. The *size* of scale economies refers to the percentage difference in unit cost between a small- and large-scale firm. The *extent* of scale economies refers to the minimum market share required to become the low-cost producer. Exhibit 11.3, adapted from a study of twelve American industries, shows scale economies of various sizes and extents. Note that although the size of scale economies for Portland cement is overwhelming, it can be fully exploited with a market share of only 1.7 percent. In contrast, the size of scale economies in refrigerators is only one-fourth that for cement, but the market share necessary to fully exploit these economies is a rather large 14.1 percent.[8]

Unexploited economies of scale offer a risky but potentially rewarding opportunity to establish and maintain a competitive cost advantage. In 1903, Henry Ford recognized that no one had yet fully exploited the scale economies from mass production of automobiles. He showed that by producing on a much larger scale he could profitably sell cars at prices far

EXHIBIT 11.1

Scale Economies of Different Size

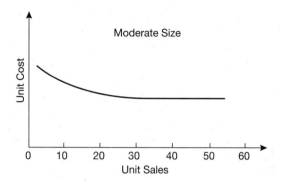

Moderate Size

Unit Cost

Unit Sales

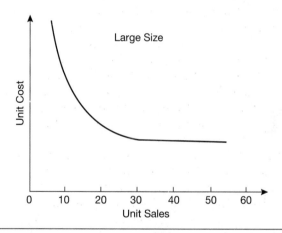

Large Size

Unit Cost

Unit Sales

below his competitors' costs. The strategy involved substantial risk, however, since it depended on a managerial analysis of price sensitivity that
could not be tested before going into production. Ford risked a fortune on
his belief that tens of thousands of people would buy his standardized
black Model T's, lured by the lower price that economies of scale would
permit him to charge. If Ford's guess about the number of price-sensitive
buyers had been wrong, he could not have achieved the large volumes, and
therefore the low unit costs, that enabled him to profit despite the low price
that his standardized product could command. Such a guess is not always
profitable, as Texas Instruments learned in 1983 after it cut the price of its
home computer in a grab for increased scale economies. Unfortunately,

Exhibit 11.2

Scale Economies of Different Extent

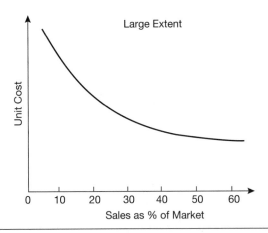

during the innovation stage, the home computer market proved insufficiently price sensitive to produce the volumes required. Texas Instruments' resulting losses forced its ultimate withdrawal from the market. In sharp contrast, increased demand together with heightened price sensitivity associated with the movement from growth into maturity, have provided the market conditions required to fuel Compaq's move to become the low-cost producer in the home computer market of the mid-1990s.

Cost advantages from scale economies are often particularly attractive because, under the right conditions, they can be sustained indefinitely. The key to sustaining scale economies is *limit-entry pricing*. A limit-entry price is

Exhibit 11.3

Estimated Values of the Minimum Efficient Scale, 1965

Industry	Minimum Efficient Scale	% Cost Disadvantage of Small Scale Operation*	% Market Share Required to Fully Exploit Economies
Beer brewing	4.5 million (31 U.S. gallon) barrels per year capacity	5.0	3.5
Cigarettes	36 billion cigarettes per year; 2,275 employees	2.2	6.6
Cotton and synthetic broad-woven fabrics	37.5 million square yards per year; 600 employees in modern integrated plants	7.6	0.2
Paints	10 million U.S. gallons per year; 450 employees	4.4	1.4
Petroleum refining	200,000 (42 U.S. gallon) barrels per day crude oil processing capacity	4.8	1.9
Nonrubber shoes	1 million pairs per year; 250 employees on single shift operation	1.5	0.2
Glass bottles	133,000 short tons per year; 1,000 employees	11.0	1.5
Portland cement	7 million (376 pound) barrels per year capacity	26.0	1.7
Integrated steel	4 million short tons per year capacity	11.0	1.6
Antifriction bearings	800 employees	8.0	1.4
Refrigerators	800,000 units per year	6.5	14.1
Automobile storage batteries	1 million units per year; 300 employees	4.6	1.9

*Assumes operation at one-third minimum efficient scale.

Source: Reprinted by permission of the publishers from THE ECONOMICS OF MULTI-PLANT OPERATION: AN INTERNATIONAL COMPARISONS STUDY by Frederic M. Scherer, Alan Beckenstein, Erich Kaufer, Dennis R. Murphy and Francine Bougeon-Massen, Cambridge, MA.: Harvard University Press, Copyright © 1975 by the President and Fellows of Harvard College.

one set low enough to discourage new entrants and smaller competitors from duplicating the company's cost advantage. Whether such pricing makes sense depends upon how low one must go to discourage competition. That depends on the size and extent of the scale economies. Once established companies have achieved scale economies of large size, a new entrant can be cost competitive only if it can quickly gain enough sales volume to also operate at an efficient scale. A new firm cannot afford to let the market gradually learn about its product if a low scale of production forces it to bear significantly higher unit costs. Consequently, where scale economies create a significant cost disadvantage for firms with a small share of a market, new entrants must promote aggressively in order to grow quickly. The higher start-up costs of plant operation and promotion at a small scale provide some degree of competitive protection for companies with an established cost advantage.

The value of such an advantage depends not just on the size of scale economies but also on their extent.[9] If a single company must have more than half of a potential market to achieve the low costs of scale economies, the first company to achieve that scale should be able to limit entry even with a high price. A new entrant would have to price low enough to bring forth all remaining market potential, and to take some sales from the established firm as well, before it could achieve the same scale economies as the established firm. Such a marketing effort would no doubt involve large promotional expenditures and a substantial period of operation at less than efficient scale. On the other hand, if economies of scale are of limited extent, enabling a single company to achieve low costs with only 5 percent of the market, an established firm will be forced to set a very low limit-entry price before it could convince a new entrant not to compete. A new entrant might reasonably believe that it could capture 5 percent of a market quickly and cheaply.[10]

In some markets, frequent technological change by a large-scale producer increases the extent of market share required by a new entrant, thus raising the limit price that the large-scale producer can charge without inviting entry. For example, Intel frequently changes the technology of its microprocessor chips as part of a continuing effort to improve speed and performance. Given Intel's large share, it can recapture the additional fixed investment in rather quickly. Its small-share competitors, however, require more time to recapture their fixed investments. The more frequently Intel changes its technology, the greater the minimum share required to recapture fixed investments between each change. Some firms have been accused of withholding new technologies until after competitors have made large investments in old ones.

Economies of scale are often a good source of cost savings and an effective competitive deterrent, but there is a downside risk. Management must be careful when attempting to exploit economies of scale by adopting more capital-intensive techniques. Usually those same techniques not only lower the cost of production when operating at full capacity but also raise the cost of operating far below capacity. In highly cyclical industries (for example, steel, construction, automobiles), the scale economies that some technologies produce at high volumes can be more than overwhelmed by the diseconomies they produce if a recession forces the company to contract.

Economies of Experience   *Experience economies* are reductions in cost that come with increases in the accumulated volume of output, as distinguished from scale economies which depend upon the current volume of output. An old firm and a new one may have an equal volume of output in a certain year, each enjoying the same economies of scale. But the older firm, having accumulated more volume from past years of operation, may enjoy lower costs due to greater economies of experience. Experience-cost economies result from learning by doing: The more a company produces, the more it learns how to do so efficiently. For example, in one early study of airplane assembly, the second plane produced took approximately 4,000 labor hours, but the eighth took only 2,600 hours due to learning on the part of employees.

Experience-cost economies do not continually accrue at such a rapid rate. As volume accumulates, costs decline at a decreasing rate, as illustrated by the experience curve shown in Exhibit 11.4. Fortunately, the decrease is surprisingly predictable. In most cases, experience economies generate an equal percentage reduction in unit cost for each doubling of accumulated volume. Thus, if costs decline by 20 percent when accumulated volume increases from 10 to 20 units, they will decline by another 20 percent when volume increases from 20 to 40 units, and decline by the same percentage when volume increases from 40 to 80, 80 to 160, 160 to 320, 320 to 640, and so on.[11]

The existence in manufacturing industries of an experience curve for labor (called a *learning curve*) had been observed by engineers and economists since at least the 1950s.[12] The idea, however, did not begin to influence marketing strategy until further developed and promoted by the Boston Consulting Group (BCG).[13] BCG argued that experience-cost economies affect not just labor costs but also capital, administration, research, and marketing costs. BCG consultants argued that experience effects are not limited to high-technology manufacturing but apply as well to services and simple consumables (for example, margarine and beer).

More important, BCG asserted that experience effects call for an entirely new and daring pricing strategy to establish a sustainable cost advantage. The typical strategy of passively following experience-cost declines with price reductions fails to recognize the opportunities that experience effects engender. A company enjoying experience effects should project its

EXHIBIT 11.4

A Typical Experience Curve

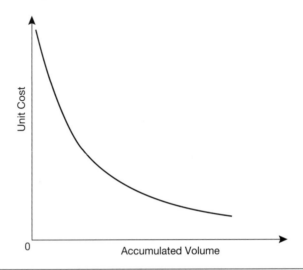

future cost declines and cut its prices in anticipation of those declines, even though such prices may not cover current production costs. Such pricing on the experience curve will enable a company to capture a dominant market share, increase its accumulated volume, and reduce its costs more rapidly than competitors. Moreover, once a company establishes a significant experience-cost advantage over its less quick-footed rivals, it can use that advantage to meet any competitive price, thus maintaining its volume lead and sustaining the advantage indefinitely.

To support their claim that experience effects are of overwhelming and universal importance in pricing, BCG consultants marshalled considerable evidence that costs or prices decline as industries accumulate volume and that firms with dominant market shares are more profitable than their smaller competitors. They were able to cite the notable success of an early client, Texas Instruments, which used pricing on the experience curve to grow rapidly and profitably throughout the 1960s and 1970s. Soon experience curves became somewhat of a fad, touted by most consultants and adopted widely in practice.[14] Like most fads, however, the strategy was often oversold and frequently misused.

The safe and effective use of experience-curve pricing requires thoughtful analysis and judicious application, lest one buy market share with low prices but never collect the future cost savings and anticipated profits. Pricing on the experience curve can be quite profitable under some circumstances, but can fail to pay off for any of the following reasons:

Buyers may not be sufficiently price sensitive. The most damning argument against experience curve pricing is the notable success of many high-priced firms. Caterpillar dominated the earth-moving equipment market, not by cutting price to buy market share but by supplying services. It is highly unlikely that its competitors could have changed history by cutting their prices more diligently. Buyers whose businesses depend on the reliability, service, and support of earth-moving equipment are just not sufficiently price sensitive for such a strategy to work. Instead, they must be courted with service, even if the service requires a premium price. Unless buyers are primarily price sensitive, pricing on the experience curve will not buy a firm enough additional volume to justify the price reductions.

Value added may be too small to justify price cutting. Even if buyers are fairly price sensitive and experience effects are large, a firm may still be unable to cut price adequately if its value added is only a small share of the price. Experience economies apply only to costs resulting from a firm's own production processes, not to costs accounted for by raw materials purchased externally. Thus a firm whose gross margin (value added) accounts for just 20 percent of the product's final price must expect a 25 percent reduction in operating costs to justify even a 5 percent reduction in price. Even with large experience effects, such a price cut does not usually generate the required volume to produce an equal reduction in cost.

Competitors may not be cooperative. Pricing on the experience curve to achieve a dominant share assumes that one's competitors will allow it to happen. Before the idea of experience curves became widely known, competitors may have thought that any firm that cut its price below cost would not stay in business very long. Now more knowledgeable competitors, realizing the risk of falling behind in the race for volume, may meet every price cut to maintain their shares. If they do, a battle for market share may ensue from which all firms will emerge as losers.

Experience may not be proprietary. Even when the knowledge gained from accumulated volume lowers one's costs, it will not increase one's profits unless that knowledge can be kept confidential. Otherwise, competitors will also learn how to quickly drive prices down to reflect the cost savings, leaving no reward for the experience curve pricer. For example, if the knowledge gained from accumulated volume is a cost-saving change in product design, competitors will learn about it as soon as the new design reaches the market. When the knowledge involves a cost-saving production process, competitors have ways of finding out about it. In highly competitive, high-technology markets, companies often hire competitors' key employees to learn of technological advances and occasionally even resort to espionage to steal competitors' proprietary information. Consequently, unless cost-saving information is known by only a few trusted employees, is patentable, or requires a long lead time to copy, competition may keep the cost savings from ever being converted into profits.

Experience may be shared among products. Cost savings do not actually result from the accumulation of production experience with a product, but rather with a production activity. If many products involve the same production activity, then being the market-share leader in only one of them may not ensure a cost advantage. Apple Computer clearly got a volume jump on all competitors in the personal computer market, but it would have been suicidal for Apple to price on the experience curve. The activities involved in producing personal computers are the same as those involved in producing many other high-technology, microprocessor-based products. Before Apple's competitors had ever sold a personal computer, many had accumulated experience in the necessary production activities to enter with equally low costs.

Experience may not be caused by total production volume. Perhaps the most dangerous misconception of pricing on the experience curve is the idea that accumulated volume causes cost declines when, in fact, the accumulated volume may simply be correlated with cost changes that have another cause. Consider, for example, a company that in past years consistently cut its costs by 15 percent with each doubling of volume. If it continued at its present production rate, it would double its volume again over the next year, cutting its costs again by 15 percent. What happens if this company slashes its prices, thus doubling its sales rate, in order to double its accumulated volume in just six months? The answer, according to advocates of experience curve pricing, is that 15 percent cost reduction will be reached six months sooner. But will it? It will only if production volume is really the cause of experience-cost savings. What if the cause of cost savings is the experience of a firm's R&D department, which in the past coincidentally accumulated research insights at about the same rate that the company accumulated production volume? Then doubling the production rate through price cutting without doubling the research budget would cut in half the anticipated cost savings to just 7.5 percent. Or what if the cause of cost savings is the skill that individual production employees accumulate over time? Then doubling the production rate through price cutting would actually increase unit costs because the firm would have to hire new, inexperienced employees to run a second shift or staff a second production facility.

Clearly, it is not enough to know that one has experience effects; one must also know their cause in order to develop appropriate strategy to exploit them. Sometimes price cutting to build volume more rapidly will produce a sustainable cost advantage, but not always. The firm whose cost economies come from R&D would do better maintaining its price and doubling its research budget than it would cutting its price and doubling its production rate. The firm whose cost economies come from the experience accumulated by individual employees would do better investing in fringe benefits that reduce employee turnover than it would investing in price cuts to buy market share.

Finally, even when experience effects exist, they are not always worth considering. In mature industries, where firms have already accumulated substantial volume, the rate of cost decline becomes so slow as to become irrelevant. In industries facing the prospect of radical technological change, there is little value in fighting to become the volume leader in a technology that will soon become obsolete. Pricing on the experience curve can be a successful strategy for achieving a cost advantage in some cases, but it is not the universal key to profitable pricing that it was once promoted to be.

External cost efficiencies

In addition to internal cost efficiencies, a company can also gain a cost advantage through the careful selection and management of its external relations with customers and suppliers. It can do so by organizing its marketing activities to exploit economies of focus and its purchasing activities to exploit economies of integration.

Economies of Buyer Focus   A company can often gain significant economies by focusing its marketing on one or two products or market segments. One obvious savings is in promotion and selling costs. For example, some suppliers to the automobile industry have essentially no specialized sales forces; their managements negotiate annual contracts with as few as one automobile company for all of their sales. This close working relationship gives them not only lower selling costs, but also a better understanding of how to meet their customers' needs.

Exploiting economies of focus is often essential for the small company whose larger rivals are in a position to exploit and sustain cost advantages from greater scope, scale, or experience. The success of Crown Cork and Seal's focus strategy illustrates the point.[15] After years of unsuccessfully competing with larger rivals, Crown recognized an opportunity to achieve cost advantages of focus equal to or greater than the economies of scope, scale, and experience that its rivals enjoyed. It withdrew from a wide variety of packaging markets and focused all of its resources on two segments: cans for hard-to-hold beverages (soda and beer) and aerosol cans.

Crown's focus enabled it to reduce costs and to service its buyers better in the process. By concentrating on a limited market it developed product improvements (pull tops and two-piece cans) that were highly valued by its customers. Crown built highly efficient production facilities, optimally designed to produce narrow product lines.[16] By locating plants in highly concentrated markets it reduced transportation costs while providing quicker and more reliable service for its customers. Crown remained a small company compared with its rivals, but Crown's economies of focus produced a return on sales that substantially exceeded the return of its larger, more diversified rivals.

Focus is not always a strategy for small market-share companies. The size and growth of a focused company are limited only by the size and growth of its targeted market. If that segment grows quickly, the targeted company enjoys the inside track to grow with it. In its earliest years, McDonald's was among the most focused of all restaurant chains. The key to the company's early success was mastery of a very limited product line (primarily hamburgers and fries) to serve a very specific segment (suburban families). With such a narrow focus, McDonald's was able to master every detail of the business, perfecting every item (even a special potato for its french fries) and developing a formula for achieving such quality at minimum cost. Since McDonald's was meeting the needs of a rapidly growing market segment, its own rapid growth proved quite consistent with focused marketing. Only later, as the growth of suburban families slowed and competition for the hamburger-and-fries segment intensified, did McDonald's broaden its focus to sustain its own growth.

Focus is a strategy that can produce both low costs and a sound basis for product differentiation, although it does entail the risk of tying one's fortunes to a single market. The Pullman company, for example, profited handsomely from its focus on serving rail passengers, but suffered when its only market was devastated by the development of air travel and interstate highways. The risk of focus is one that a small competitor must bear when it competes with larger rivals that enjoy cost advantages from diversity, size, and accumulated knowledge.

Economies of Logistical Integration   Companies worldwide are leveraging economies that are available through improved coordination of their operations with those of their suppliers and their channels of distribution.[17] Improved coordination of deliveries can minimize the cost of inventories, better coordination of specifications can minimize the need for further fabrication of a supplier's product, and better coordination of the pricing decision itself can make a company and its suppliers more price competitive and more profitable.

In its efforts to match the lower costs of Japanese competitors, General Motors is leading U.S. industry in attempting to integrate scheduling and manufacturing specifications with its own operations. In the manufacturing plants for General Motors' Saturn automobile line, suppliers remain in direct communication with the plant and with Saturn's engineering department. A computer link-up gives each supplier up-to-the-minute information on the plant's projected needs and current inventories. Any difficulties with a supplier's product or suggestions for cost-saving changes can be dealt with immediately through a computer consultation. If the manufacturing and engineering departments concur with the supplier, adjustments in a supplier's product can be made immediately to improve the Saturn's performance or reduce its cost.

Similar economies can also be achieved at the other end of the logistics chain during distribution. Differences in distributional efficiency can significantly affect a company's overall cost advantage. The high cost of holding inventories contrasted with the low cost of deregulated transportation has enabled many companies to reduce their distribution costs by centralizing their inventories. The money saved from reducing capital tied up in decentralized inventories now more than compensates for the greater cost of quick delivery by truck and air freight.

The greatest savings have come from changing the product itself to facilitate efficient distribution. Most automobile manufacturers hold down inventory costs by offering standardized option packages, a strategy pioneered by the Japanese. Apple Computer is now reducing its costs similarly by streamlining its Macintosh product line from six families down to four. One supplier of telephones redesigned its product to maintain product variety without bearing the corresponding cost of inventories. The company has standardized the internal mechanisms of its various telephones and ships them to retailers without the outer shells that distinguish styles. The retailers then attach covers to the internal assemblies as needed. This distribution method enabled the company to reduce inventories of internal mechanisms for itself and for its retailers without reducing the number of styles it offers.[18] Wal-Mart is the acknowledged leader in leveraging the economies of logistical integration. Its mastery of distribution and inventory management from raw materials to point of sale has enabled it to decrease costs while increasing profit margins.

Efficiency in Transfer Pricing   All the companies in a chain of production—the suppliers of raw materials, those who make parts, those who do assembly, and those who market the product to the final purchaser—benefit when the entire chain operates efficiently. Inefficient operation by any one member of the chain drives up the price to the end purchaser, thus reducing sales for all the members. Unfortunately, one of the most frequently unrecognized and generally misunderstood sources of inefficiency involves the way independent companies and independent divisions of the same company set the prices of products that pass between them. This problem, known as *transfer pricing*, represents one of the most common reasons why independent companies and divisions are sometimes less price competitive and profitable than their vertically integrated competitors.

Exhibit 11.5 illustrates this often overlooked opportunity. Independent Manufacturing, Inc., sells its product for $2.00 per unit in a highly competitive market. To manufacture the product, it buys different parts from two suppliers, Alpha and Beta, at a total cost per unit of $1.20. The parts purchased from Alpha cost $0.30 and those from Beta cost $0.90.

Independent Manufacturing conducts a pricing analysis to determine whether any changes in its pricing might be justified. It determines that its contribution margin (price – variable cost) is $0.60, or 30 percent of its

---

Exhibit 11.5

Inefficiencies in Transfer Pricing

	Current Price, Costs, Sales	10% Price Cut, 30% Sales Increase	Change
Independent Manufacturing, Inc.			
Current unit sales	1,000,000	1,300,000	
Price	$2.00	$1.80	
Variable materials cost	$1.20	$1.20	
Variable labor cost	$0.20	$0.20	
Fixed cost	$0.40	$0.31	
Contribution margin	$0.60	$0.40	
% CM	30%	22%	
Annual pretax profit	$200,000	$120,000	($80,000)
Alpha Parts Inc.			
Current unit sales	1,000,000	1,300,000	
Price	$0.30	$0.30	
Variable cost	$0.05	$0.05	
Fixed cost	$0.20	$0.15	
Contribution margin	$0.25	$0.25	
Annual pretax profit	$50,000	$125,000	$75,000
Beta Parts Inc.			
Current unit sales	1,000,000	1,300,000	
Price	$0.90	$0.90	
Variable cost	$0.35	$0.35	
Fixed cost	$0.40	$0.31	
Contribution margin	$0.55	$0.55	
Annual pretax profit	$150,000	$315,000	$165,000

price.[19] It then calculates the effect of a 10 percent price change in either direction. For a 10 percent price cut to be profitable, Independent must gain at least 50 percent more sales:

$$\frac{0.10}{0.30-0.10}=50\%$$

For a 10 percent price increase to be profitable, Independent can afford to forgo no more than 25 percent of its sales:

$$\frac{-0.10}{0.30+0.10}=-25\%$$

Independent's managers conclude that there is no way that they can possibly gain from a price cut, since their sales will surely not increase by more than 50 percent. On the other hand, they are intrigued by the possibility of a price increase. They feel sure that the inevitable decline would be far less than 25 percent if they could get their major competitors to follow them in the increase.

As Independent's management considers how to communicate to the industry the desirability of a general price increase, one of its major competitors, Integrated Manufacturing, Inc., announces its own 10 percent price *cut*. Independent's management is stunned. How could Integrated possibly justify such a move? Integrated's product is technically identical to Independent's, involving all the same parts and production processes, and Integrated is a company with a market share equal to Independent's. The only difference between the two companies is that Integrated recently began manufacturing its own parts.

That difference, however, is crucial to this story (see Exhibit 11.6). Assume that Integrated currently has all the same costs of producing parts as Independent's suppliers, Alpha and Beta, and expects to earn a profit from those operations. It also has the same costs of assembling those parts ($0.20 incremental labor plus $0.40 fixed per unit). Moreover, Integrated enjoys no additional economies of logistical integration. Despite these similarities, the two companies have radically different cost structures which respond quite differently to changes in volume and which cause the two companies to evaluate price changes quite differently. Integrated has no variable materials cost corresponding to Independent's variable materials cost of $1.20 per unit. Instead, it incurs additional fixed costs of $0.60 per unit ($0.20 + $0.40) and incremental variable costs of only $0.40 per unit ($0.05 + $0.35). This difference in cost structure between Integrated (high fixed and low variable) and Independent (low fixed and high variable)

EXHIBIT 11.6

Efficiency From Cost Integration

	Current Price, Costs, Sales	10% Price Cut, 30% Sales Increase	Change
Integrated Manufacturing, Inc.			
Current unit sales	1,000,000	1,300,000	
Price	$2.00	$1.80	
Variable materials cost	None	None	
Variable labor cost ($0.20 + $0.05 + $0.35)	$0.60	$0.60	
Fixed cost ($0.40 + $0.20 + $0.40)	$1.00	$0.77	
Contribution margin	$1.40	$1.20	
%	70%	67%	
Annual pretax profit	$400,000	$560,000	$160,000

gives Integrated a much higher contribution margin per unit than Independent's margin. For Integrated, $1.40, or 70 percent of each additional sale, contributes to bottom-line profits. For Independent, only $0.60, or 30 percent of each additional sale, falls to the bottom line. Integrated's break-even calculations for a 10 percent price change are, therefore, quite different. For a 10 percent price cut to be profitable, Integrated has to gain only 16.7 percent more sales:

$$\frac{0.10}{0.70 - 0.10} = 16.7\%$$

But for a 10 percent price increase to pay off, Integrated could afford to forgo no more than 12.5 percent of its sales:

$$\frac{-0.10}{0.70 + 0.10} = -12.5\%$$

It is easy to see why Integrated is more attracted to price cuts and more averse to price increases than is Independent. For Integrated, sales must grow by only 16.7 percent to make a price cut profitable, compared with 50 percent for Independent. Similarly, Integrated could afford to lose no more than 12.5 percent of sales (compared with as much as 25 percent for Independent) and still profit from a price increase. How can it be that two identical sets of costs result in such extremely different calculations? The answer is that Independent, like most manufacturers, pays its suppliers on a price-per-unit basis. That price must include enough revenue to cover the suppliers' fixed costs and a reasonable profit if Independent expects those suppliers to remain viable in the long run. Consequently, Alpha's and Beta's fixed costs and profit become variable costs of sales for Independent. Such incrementalizing of nonincremental costs makes Independent much less cost competitive than Integrated, which earns more than twice as much additional profit on each unit it sells.

Independent's cost disadvantage is a disadvantage to its suppliers as well. Independent calculates that it requires a 50 percent sales increase to make a 10 percent price cut profitable. Independent, therefore, correctly rejects a 10 percent price cut that would increase sales by 30 percent. With current sales of 1 million units, such a price cut would cause Independent's profit to decline by $80,000. Note, however, that the additional sales volume would add $240,000 ($75,000 + $165,000) to the profits of Independent's suppliers, provided that they produce the increased output with no more fixed costs. They would earn much more than Independent would lose by cutting price. It is clear why Integrated sees a 10 percent price cut as profitable when Independent does not. As its own supplier, Integrated captures the additional profits that accrue within the entire value chain (Alpha, $75,000; Beta, $165,000) as a result of increases in volume.[20]

Once Independent recognizes the problem, what alternatives does it have, short of taking the radical step of merging with its suppliers? One alternative is for Independent to pay its suppliers' fixed costs in a lump-sum payment, perhaps even retaining ownership of the assets while negotiating low supply prices that cover only incremental costs and a reasonable return. The lump-sum payment is then a fixed cost for Independent, and its contribution margin on added sales rises by the reduction in its incremental supply cost. General Motors does this with auto parts suppliers, bearing the fixed cost of a part's design and paying the supplier for all fixed costs of retooling and set up. Similarly, World Book buys and owns the presses that R. R. Donnelley & Sons uses to print World Book's encyclopedias. In these cases, the negotiated price per unit need cover only the supplier's variable costs and profit. As a result, General Motors and World Book earn more on each additional sale and so have a greater incentive to make marketing decisions, including pricing decisions, that build volume.

A second alternative is to negotiate a high price for initial purchases that cover the fixed costs, with a lower price for all additional quantities that cover only incremental costs and profit. Sears Roebuck sometimes uses this system with suppliers of its house brand products. Since the lower supply price is the incremental cost of additional sales, Sears can profitably price its products lower to generate more volume. In Independent Manufacturing's case, it might negotiate an agreement with Alpha and Beta that guarantees enough purchases at $0.30 and $0.90, respectively, to cover their fixed costs, after which the price would fall to $0.10 and $0.50, respectively.

Both of these systems for paying suppliers avoid incrementalizing fixed costs, but they do not avoid the problem of incrementalizing the suppliers' profits. They work well only when the suppliers' profits account for a small portion of the total price suppliers receive. Lump-sum payments could be paid to suppliers to cover negotiated profit as well as fixed costs. This is risky, however, since profit per unit remains the suppliers' incentive to maintain on-time delivery of acceptable quality merchandise. Consequently, when a supplier has low fixed costs but can still demand a high profit because of little competition, a third alternative is often used. The purchaser may agree to pay the supplier a small fee to cover incremental expenses and an additional negotiated percentage of whatever profit contribution is earned from final sales.

It is noteworthy that most companies do not use these methods to compensate suppliers or to establish prices for sales between independent divisions. Instead, they negotiate arm's-length contracts at fixed prices or let prevailing market prices determine transfer prices. One reason is that it is unusual to find a significant portion of costs which remain truly fixed for large changes in sales. In most cases, the bulk of costs that accountants label fixed are actually semifixed; additional costs would have to be incurred for suppliers to substantially increase their sales, making those costs incremental. One notable case where costs are substantially fixed is in the semiconductor industry. The overwhelming cost of semiconductors is the fixed cost of product development, not the variable or semifixed costs of production. Consequently, integrated manufacturers of products using semiconductors have often had a significant cost advantage. Bowmar, the company that pioneered the hand-held calculator, was ultimately driven from the market precisely because it was not cost competitive with more integrated suppliers and failed to negotiate contracts that avoided the incrementalization of their fixed costs of product development.

Companies that buy computer software to sell as part of their products should note that software, too, is a high fixed-cost product that often represents a substantial portion of the cost of computer-aided equipment. Independent software development houses that price on a per-unit basis should note this as well. By forcing their customers to incrementalize the fixed costs and profit of software development, they will ultimately find that their buyers are not cost competitive with companies that either write their own software or that have different pricing arrangements with their suppliers.

Temporary cost advantages

Cost reductions from cost economies and efficiencies are the most desirable sources of cost advantage for two reasons: (1) Cost savings from economies are generally somewhat sustainable once achieved, and (2) cost savings from economies can be achieved without adversely affecting relations with employees or suppliers or undermining product quality. In fact, they often enable a company to differentiate in ways that actually increase the product's value to customers. Mobil customers may be attracted not only by its low prices but also the availability of beverages, junk food, and cigarettes in its on-site minimarts. Crown Cork and Seal's buyers benefited as much from the quick delivery from Crown's nearby plants as Crown benefited from lower shipping costs.

Although our discussions have focused on ways of achieving sustainable cost economies, one should not underestimate the value of seeking cost reductions that are not sustainable. The benefits from one-time savings often make possible strategic moves that produce more sustainable advantages later on. The labor-cost advantage that the United Auto Workers granted Chrysler Corporation as part of its financial bailout enabled the company to price more aggressively than would otherwise have been possible. Although that advantage was eventually eliminated in later contracts, Chrysler is undoubtedly more profitable today because of that past advantage. The company now enjoys economies of scale because, in those earlier years of recovery, it could price to restore its market share and thereby prove the quality of its new line of cars.

One also must not underestimate the value of cost-quality trade-offs made with careful consideration of buyers preferences. Some buyers simply do not value certain aspects of product differentiation enough to justify their cost and may willingly forgo some product attributes in order to get a lower price. Liggett and Myers launched its most profitable new product in decades when it introduced generic cigarettes. Some smokers eagerly gave up costly flavorings, advertised images, and fancy packaging to save a few dollars a carton. Discount airlines likewise found that a large segment of travelers would gladly forgo such amenities as meals, baggage handling, and leg room in return for lower ticket prices. Any reduction in quality that buyers willingly accept for a price reduction less than the company's cost saving is a trade-off that adds to a company's profitability and to its competitive position.

COMPETITIVE PRODUCT ADVANTAGES

When a product offers buyers nothing more than its competition, the purchase decision tends to focus on price alone. An undifferentiated product leaves the most important determinant of price sensitivity—the unique value effect—working against the seller. Unless one or more of the other determinants is very favorable (that is, buyers do not know of the substitutes, the expenditure is too small to consider, or they are locked in by complementary expenditures), the resulting price sensitivity creates the potential for intense price competition. Even if cooperation can be maintained to minimize downward pressure on prices, there is little opportunity for growth beyond the growth in total market demand. There is also the constant threat of additional entry by smaller competitors whose interests will not be consistent with cooperative pricing. The kinds of cost advantages discussed can partially shield profits from competitive price cutting but cannot eliminate the threat itself. The key to disarming the threat is to minimize buyers' price sensitivity through differentiation.

Product superiority

One way to achieve differentiation is through constant innovation. Some companies—Procter & Gamble, Johnson & Johnson, 3M, Du Pont, Pfizer Pharmaceuticals—seem to possess an uncanny ability to maintain profitable prices by offering a constant stream of new and improved products, one step ahead of the competition. The advantages of product uniqueness are not limited to companies that can develop patentable products in costly research facilities. Even in the most mundane markets, a few companies differentiate their products in ways that enable them to achieve premium prices.

Loctite Corporation, a small company just a few years ago, has been particularly successful in making small product changes with big effects on pricing. After six weeks of interviewing product users, it reintroduced a new and improved version of its existing industrial adhesive under the name Quick Metal. Designed to keep broken equipment running until replacement parts arrive, Loctite targeted maintenance engineers who had authorization to purchase whatever they needed to repair broken equipment quickly. The new product was essentially the old one but reformulated as a gel (to make it less messy) and repackaged in a tube (to make it easier to apply). Because of the high value of those simple improvements to users, Quick Metal became a runaway success in spite of a price premium of nearly 100 percent.[21]

The key to offering a differentiated product is a clear understanding of the buyers—their product needs, the support they require, and their preferred ways of purchasing. Even when product differentiation is made possible by new technologies, one must first understand buyers' problems in order to recognize how technology might solve them.

North Face (skiing), Cannondale (biking), and Marmont (mountain climbing) are all examples of companies whose success is built on knowledge of the people their products serve and the problems they encounter.

Almost any good company has the technical ability to develop product lines such as these companies offer; but few have the necessary understanding of the *needs* that the products are designed to satisfy. These companies cater to the unmet needs of outdoor enthusiasts. Practically everything they sell offers something that the competition does not: extra zippers for easy ventilation, Y-joint sleeves that allow arms to be raised freely without pulling up the jacket, and hoods with cutaway sides for better peripheral vision. Those additional features are worth a lot to their customers when they are facing the elements far from a warm cabin, biking 100 miles, or making an ascent up a sheer cliff.

Product augmentation

Are some products just inherently undifferentiable? In his classic article, "Marketing Success Through Differentiation of Anything," Theodore Levitt makes a compelling case that any product can, in principle, be distinguished from the commodity mass.[22] The key is recognizing that what buyers purchase is more than just the physical product or particular service exchanged. They buy an entire package—including the ease of purchase, terms of credit, reliability of delivery, pleasantness of personal interactions, fairness in handling complaints, and so on—that is called the *augmented product*. Even when the physical product or service is immutable, the augmented product is invariably differentiable.

Consider Premier Industrial Corporation, whose maintenance division sells a variety of nuts, bolts, lubricants, welding supplies, and other products that people think of as commodities. But these products are not sold or priced as commodities by Premier. When Premier sells oil for heavy-duty truck engines, the buyer can send a sample to the company in a Premier-supplied mailing cannister and get a free computer analysis that aids in engine maintenance. At the Indianapolis 500 race, Premier sets up a complete parts shop that not only builds goodwill with influential mechanics and designers, but also lets them see the quality of Premier's products under adverse conditions. What Premier does not do is cut price in this or any of its other divisions. By augmenting its common products to make them uncommon values, it does not have to.[23]

Some companies are able to charge premium prices even when their products are technically inferior because their superior augmentations overcome those deficiencies. Although WordPerfect software may not offer the seamless integration that Microsoft's products possess under Windows® their outstanding on-line help and customer support help them to maintain market share in a market dominated by Microsoft Word. To find opportunities for successful augmentation, one must look beyond the obvious. As Levitt states,

> Differentiation is not limited to giving the consumer what he
> expects. . . . When a securities brokerage firm includes with its cus-
> tomers' monthly statements a current balance sheet for each customer
> and an analysis of sources and disposition of funds, that firm has aug-
> mented its product beyond what was required or expected by the
> buyer. When a manufacturer of health and beauty aids offers ware-
> house management advice and training programs for the employees of
> its distributors, that company too has augmented its product beyond
> what was required or expected by the buyer.[24]

Similar augmentations have successfully differentiated fertilizer, air
freight, vinyl latex, and, more recently, financial services—all products
usually thought of as inherently the same across sellers. Successful augmentations have also enhanced the inherent differences in household
kitchen appliances (augmented with cooking classes and magazines),
breakfast cereals (augmented with games printed on the box), and retail
outlets (augmented with uniquely appealing displays or exceptional service). Given the opportunity to augment, any firm selling any product can
offer buyers something extra that will limit price sensitivity or increase differentiation value. Finding that something extra is not easy. It usually requires a total commitment by the entire organization. There is much
evidence that such a commitment can produce a profitable augmented
product, even where the physical product is at best minimally differentiable.[25]

Sustaining product advantages

Unfortunately, product advantages are sometimes short-lived. When
a soap company enhances its detergent with a lemon scent, a paper company packages tissues in designer boxes, or a clothing company makes
skirts in a new style, competitors imitate the successful improvements
within a short time. Unless a company has a unique ability to bring forth a
constant stream of such improvements, it often provides little basis for sustained profitability. Some product improvements produce competitive advantages that can be sustained, enabling a company to skim a small market
indefinitely or to set prices that are high in dollar terms but are neutral or
penetrating when compared with economic value. There are a number of
reasons why the first company to improve its product offering may enjoy a
first-mover advantage that is sustainable against competitive imitation.

Known Supplier   When a product's differentiation involves an attribute
that consumers cannot easily observe without first buying the product
(such as reliability, cleaning power, or taste), it gains a sustainable competitive advantage as the known supplier. Recall from Chapter 4 that an important determinant of interbrand price sensitivity is the buyer's ability to

compare competing brands with ones already known to do the job well (the difficult comparison effect). When comparison among brands is easy, any imitator who offers even a small price discount can be attractive to a large market segment. Why pay more for what is obviously the same thing? When comparison is difficult, imitators must offer a substantial discount to induce buyers to learn that their products are comparable. Hence the first mover with a new differentiation can often sustain its position in spite of a price premium. That premium, however, can be no greater than the cost for buyers to confirm the claims of competitors.

Buyers' Investments   When a company's product requires that buyers make investments such as in employee training or complementary products, buyers will be reluctant to switch suppliers if it means making those investments again. They will accept a price premium as long as the total premium they spend on the original brand is less than the value of sunk investments (the switching cost effect). Although Microsoft promoted the superior value of its spreadsheet and data-base software (Excel and Access), most users of Lotus (Lotus 1-2-3) and Borland (Dbase) products remained loyal to their older packages giving Lotus & Borland time to incorporate the improvements. Although buyers acknowledge the improved performance of the Microsoft packages, the value of that performance did not exceed the sunk investment they made learning their old packages, nor the required investment to learn new ones.

Channel Preemption   The more brands that distributors and retailers carry, the greater their inventory, stocking, and purchasing costs. Like consumers, they will try the first brand simply because it is unique, hoping that it will attract new customers. They are reluctant, however, to carry me-too brands, unless they receive a larger margin to compensate for their trouble. That raises costs for imitators, reducing their ability to undercut the first mover's prices.

Scarce Resource Preemption   The first mover enjoys the first pick of scarce resources. As spring waters became popular, the first movers could buy or lease those springs with the best water and the easiest access. Similarly, the first pay TV channels contracted for the best reruns. And, as discount airlines began to proliferate following deregulation, the first movers got the best choices of available gates at airports.

Niche Marketing   Many products are differentiated to appeal only to a small niche in the marketplace. The product advantage of serving a niche is often sustainable because of economies of scale, even when the extent of those economies is small in relation to the total market. The market may just not be large enough to support many companies serving those same small segments.

Image   Finally, the first mover's innovativeness often gives its name a certain cachet with buyers that competitors find difficult to imitate, even when they can imitate the product itself. Because the best auto mechanics all bought Snap-On brand tools when there was no other brand of comparable quality, ownership of Snap-On tools has become a standard by which many garages now judge a mechanic's competence. Even when competitors can easily imitate a first-mover's product, images are difficult to duplicate. Moreover, the imitator's lack of image cannot easily be overcome by price cutting without further undermining buyers' perceptions of their quality (the price-quality effect). Part of what differentiates Perrier from other spring waters is precisely its image as an expensive indulgence.

SUMMARY

The techniques of effective pricing described in this book can only attempt to ensure that a company fully exploits its competitive advantages. How profitable effective pricing is depends upon the competitive advantages that a company enjoys. Competitive advantages are of two general types: cost advantages and product advantages.

Cost advantages may be either internal or external. Internal economies of scope, scale, or experience, and external economies of focus or logistical integration enable a company to produce some products at a lower cost than the competition. The coordination of pricing with suppliers, although not actually economizing resources, can improve the efficiency of pricing by avoiding the incrementalization of a supplier's nonincremental fixed costs and profit. Any of these strategies can generate cost advantages that are, at least in the short run, sustainable. Even cost advantages that are not sustainable, however, can generate temporary savings that are often the key to building more sustainable cost or product advantages later on.

Product advantages can partially insulate a company's pricing from that of its competitors. The most visible and certainly most sustainable product advantages stem from major improvements that are patentable. Some companies spend substantial sums on highly efficient research laboratories, gaining as their reward a constant stream of products that are always a step ahead of the competition. But product advantages are not limited only to companies with substantial resources, and those of considerable value are often technically very simple. The key to finding such advantages is a clear understanding of buyers' needs. Simple changes in packaging or product design, when they meet real consumer needs, often allow companies to earn significant price premiums.

Even when a product's physical attributes are not readily differentiable, opportunities to develop product advantages remain. The augmented product that customers buy is more than the particular product or service exchanged. It includes all sorts of ancillary services and intangible relationships that make buying the same product from one company less difficult, less risky, or more pleasant than buying from a competitor. Superior augmentation of the same basic product can add substantial value in the eyes of consumers, leading them to pay willingly what are often considerable price premiums.

Unfortunately, unless product advantages are patentable, they are sometimes short-lived. Competitors can observe product advantages and quickly copy them. Imitation by competitors does not always cut short the advantages to the innovator. The first company to improve its product offering often enjoys a first-mover advantage even after other companies have copied the product innovation. This is usually the case when competing products are difficult to compare: when buyers must make sunk investments to use a particular company's product, when the innovator can preempt the best channels of distribution or a scarce resource, when the innovator serves a niche that is not large enough to support multiple competitors, or when purchasing the product generally recognized as best is important to the customer's image.

NOTES

1. In *Competitive Advantage* (New York: The Free Press, 1985), Michael Porter offers a detailed procedure for analyzing a company's internal and external activities to create and sustain competitive advantages.

2. For an insightful discussion of the increasing importance of economies of scope in manufacturing, see Joel D. Goldhar and Mariann Jelinek, "Plan for Economies of Scope," *Harvard Business Review*, 61 (November–December 1983), p. 141–48.

3. Shawn Tully, "Look Who's a Champ of Gasoline Marketing," *Fortune*, November 1, 1982, pp. 149–54.

4. "Now Airlines Are Diversifying by Sticking to What They Know Best," *Business Week*, May 7, 1984, pp. 70, 72.

5. In process industries (for example, aluminum smelting, petroleum refining), engineers use the two-thirds rule: Any facility can be built with twice the capacity for only a two-thirds increase in cost.

6. As quoted by Frederic Scherer, *Industrial Market Structure and Economic Performance* (Boston: Houghton Mifflin, 1980), p. 82.

7. See "Why Detroit Can't Cut Prices," *Business Week*, March 1, 1982, pp. 110–11.

8. F. M. Scherer and others, *The Economies of Multiplant Operations* (Cambridge, Mass.: Harvard University Press, 1975), pp. 80, 94.

9. The ideal case for limit pricing, called a *natural monopoly*, occurs where the extent of scale economies is not exhausted even when the firm has 100 percent of the market.

10. The fact that economies of scale are to a small extent relative to the total indus-
    try does not mean, however, that they cannot be exploited for a sustainable
    competitive advantage. What is relevant is not their size and extent relative to
    industry sales, but their size and extent relative to the sales in a particular
    market. Although some industries consist of one large market in which all
    competitors compete for the patronage of all buyers, most industries are an
    aggregation of smaller, somewhat independent market segments. Two factors
    usually determine the existence and size of such submarkets: location and
    product differentiation. Grocery retailing is one example of a large industry
    with many locationally distinct submarkets. A single grocery in a small town
    may satisfy enough of the potential in that market to preclude the entry of
    any other competition.

11. This is called a *double-log function* because it appears as a straight line when
    both volume and costs are graphed on a log scale.

12. Harold Asher, *Cost Quantity Relationships in the Airframe Industry*, Rand
    Corporation Report, Santa Monica, Calif., 1956; R. W. Cooper and A. Charnes,
    "Silhouette Functions of Short-Run Cost Behavior," *Quarterly Journal of
    Economics*, 68 (February 1954), 131–50; Warner Z. Hirsch, "Manufacturing
    Progress Functions," *Review of Economics and Statistics*, 34 (May 1952), 143–55;
    Armen Alchian, "Costs and Output," in *The Allocation of Economic Resources:
    Essays in Honor of B. F. Huley*, ed. Moses Abramovitz and others (San Jose,
    Calif.: Stanford University Press, 1959), pp. 22–40; T. D. Wright, "Factors
    Affecting the Cost of Airplanes," *Journal of Aeronautical Science*, 3 (February
    1936), 122–28.

13. Bruce D. Henderson, *Perspectives on Experience* (Boston: The Boston Consulting
    Group, 1970); Bruce D. Henderson and Alan J. Zukon, "Pricing Strategy: How
    to Improve It (The Experience Curve)," in *Handbook of Business Problem Solving*,
    ed. Kenneth J. Albert (New York: McGraw-Hill, 1980). See also Bruce Robinson
    and Chet Lakiani, "Dynamic Price Models for New Product Planning,"
    Management Science, 21 (June 1975), 1113–22; and Robert Dolan and Abel
    Jeuland, "Experience Curves and Dynamic Demand Models: Implications for
    Optimal Pricing Strategies," *Journal of Marketing*, 45 (Winter 1981), 52–73.

14. See "Selling Business a Theory of Economics," *Business Week*, September 8,
    1973, pp. 85–89; and Michael Porter, "Experience Curve," in Manager's
    Journal, *Wall Street Journal*, October 22, 1979, p. 30. Among those firms often
    cited as practitioners of experience-curve pricing are Black and Decker,
    Briggs and Stratton, Emerson Electric, Du Pont, 3M, and most firms in the
    semiconductor industry.

15. Raymond Corey, "Key Options in Market Selection and Product Planning,"
    Harvard Business Review, 53 (September–October 1975), 119–28.

16. See Wickham Skinner, "The Focused Factory," *Harvard Business Review*, 52
    (May–June 1974), 113.

17. See Roy D. Shapiro, "Get Leverage from Logistics," *Harvard Business Review*, 62
    (May–June 1984), 119–26; and Graham Sharman, "The Rediscovery of
    Logistics," *Harvard Business Review*, 62 (September–October 1984), 71–79.

18. Sharman, "The Rediscovery of Logistics," p. 75.

19. $CM = \$2.00 - \$1.20 - 0.20 = \$0.60$
    $\%CM = \$0.60/\$2.00 \times 100 = 30\%$

20. An integrated company does not automatically gain this advantage. If separate divisions of a company operate as independent profit centers setting transfer prices equal to market prices, they will also price too high to maximize their joint profits. To overcome the problem while remaining independent, they need to adopt one of the solutions suggested for independent companies.

21. Bill Abrams, "Consumer-Product Techniques Help Loctite Sell to Industry," *Wall Street Journal*, April 2, 1981, p. 27.

22. Theodore Levitt, "Marketing Success Through Differentiation—of Anything," *Harvard Business Review*, 58 (January–February 1980), 83–91.

23. Susan Fraker, "Making a Mint in Nuts and Bolts," *Fortune*, August 22, 1983, pp. 131–34.

24. Levitt, "Marketing Success Through Differentiation," p. 87. See also, for additional illustrations, Theodore Levitt, *The Marketing Mode* (New York: McGraw-Hill, 1969), pp. 1–27; R. Karl van Leer, "Industrial Marketing with a Flair," *Harvard Business Review*, 54 (November–December, 1976), 117–24.

25. See Thomas J. Peters and Robert H. Waterman, Jr., *In Search of Excellence* (New York: Harper and Row, 1982).

PRICING PSYCHOLOGY

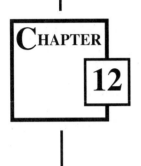

MODELS OF PURCHASE BEHAVIOR

This chapter is coauthored by Professor Gerald Smith of Boston College with Dr. Thomas Nagle.

As previous chapters have shown, customers' responses to prices are based on much more than rational calculation. First, a customer's response is determined not only by evaluation of the product and its price, but also by perception of the entire purchase situation. Thus, one aspect of pricing strategy is the presentation of prices in ways that will influence those perceptions to the seller's benefit. For example, in discussing product-line pricing, we saw that the addition of a new product to the top (or bottom) of a product line can influence a buyer's perception of the costliness of other products in that line. In discussing promotional pricing, we saw how it is important to offer promotional price cuts as special deals with the aid of special packaging, coupons, and rebates to ensure that buyers accurately perceive the discount prices as bargains.

Moreover, when buyers do perceive prices and purchase situations accurately, they often do not evaluate them perfectly rationally. This is not to say that buyers commonly process prices irrationally, but rather that they conserve their time and mental capacity by using imperfect, but convenient, decision rules.[1] A marketer who understands those decision rules can often present products in ways that lead buyers to evaluate them more favorably. Most pricing experts would agree, however, that we still have much to learn about the mental processes governing a buyer's response to price.

Fortunately, the psychology of price perception and evaluation is currently the subject of interesting and valuable research. In recent years, research has moved beyond the simple recognition that consumers do not always evaluate prices with calculating rationality toward understanding why and how consumers behave differently. In this chapter, we consider the implications of that research for the pricing strategist. The general topics to be discussed are:

- Perception of price differences
- Formulation of reference prices
- Mental "framing" of prices
- Pricing of probabilistic goods

PERCEPTION OF PRICE DIFFERENCES

Perception of percentage differences

If consumers were perfectly rational in their responses to price differences, the same absolute price difference would always generate the same behavioral response. Anecdotal and experimental evidence indicates that consumers' behavioral responses are not the same. Consider how you would respond in each of the following situations.[2]

Scenario A: You are a purchasing agent for a large organization. You have ordered for your own use a new electric typewriter with special features, which will cost $1,000. A friend discovers that the identical typewriter is available from another vendor for $600. Would you cancel the current order and switch to the other vendor? (Assume that cancelling the current order and initiating a new one will take one of the purchasing clerks who works for you about one-half day. Assume that there are no other costs such as loss of good will or delay in delivery.)

Scenario B: You have ordered a new word processor with special features, which will cost $20,000. Your purchasing department discovers that the identical word processor is available from another vendor for $19,600. Would you cancel the current order and switch to the other vendor? (Assume that cancelling the current order and initiating a new one will take a purchasing clerk one-half day and that there are no other costs such as loss of good will or delay in delivery.)

Since in both scenarios the amount that could be saved is $400, a purely rational purchaser would make the same decision in either case. In fact, most people see these two situations quite differently. When these questions were asked of business executives who are presumably more rational than the typical purchaser, 89 percent were willing to switch vendors in version A, but only 52 percent were willing to do so in version B. The reason for this difference is that $400 seems like a much larger price difference for a $1,000 purchase than for a $20,000 purchase. The results were even more striking when less sophisticated purchasers were asked a similar question regarding the opportunity to save $5 on a calculator. If a calculator cost $15, 68 percent of respondents were willing to drive to another store to save $5; but if it cost $125, only 29 percent of the respondents were willing to do so.[3]

This tendency of buyers to evaluate price differences relative to the level of the base price is known as the *Weber-Fechner Law*. This law suggests that buyers perceive price differences in proportional terms, rather than in absolute terms. For example, buyers in scenario A perceive the price difference between the two typewriters to be 40 percent, whereas buyers in scenario B perceive the price difference to be just 2 percent, even though the absolute difference in both scenarios is $400. According to Weber-Fechner, in order for the price difference in scenario B to be perceived as equivalent to the price difference in scenario A, the price of the competing vendor's word processor in scenario B would have to be $12,000 (that is, 40 percent less than the higher-priced brand at $20,000).

An important implication of Weber-Fechner is that the perception of a price change depends on the percentage, not the absolute difference, and that there are thresholds above and below a product's price at which price changes are noticed or ignored.[4] A series of smaller price increases below the upper threshold is more successful than one large increase. Conversely, buyers respond more to one large price cut below the lower threshold than to a series of smaller, successive discounts. For example, one full-service brokerage house raised its commissions approximately every six months over a three-year period with little resistance from customers. Seeing this success, its competitor tried to match these increases in one large step and encountered intense criticism. Researchers are now beginning to develop general theories to determine how these factors interact to result in purchase decisions. We discuss these below under Influence of Framing on Price Perceptions.

Perception of odd endings

A second factor commonly believed to influence buyers' perceptions of a price difference is the use of odd numbers—$1.99, $19.95, or $5,995, rather than round numbers like $2.00, $20.00, and $6,000. The belief is that buyers perceive the odd-number prices as significantly lower than the slightly higher round numbers that they approximate. To see why this might be the case, look at the two pairs of prices below and quickly answer the question, For which pair of prices is the lower price *more* of a bargain?

First pair	$0.89	$0.75
Second pair	$0.93	$0.79

Most people see the lower price as more of a bargain in the second pair of prices. They do so despite the fact that the difference is the same in both pairs, and the difference is a greater percentage of the price in the first pair. The apparent reason is that most people, attempting to avoid the effort to calculate the difference, simply compare the columns of prices from left to right. They notice that in the first pair, seven is just one less than eight, and in the second pair, seven is two less than nine. Consequently, they conclude that the price difference is greater in the second pair than in the first. Only if the first digits in the first column were the same would they have looked closely at the next column in making a price comparison.

The hypothesis that people process prices from left to right has received some confirmation in laboratory experiments.[5] But do people use this time-saving decision rule when comparing prices in real purchase situations, thus making odd pricing an important tactic to consider? The evidence is mixed. Two studies of odd price endings, one using data on catalog sales and the other on sales of fashion products, found no consistent effect.[6] Data collected on the pricing of grocery items however, indicate that cutting prices to an odd number just below a round one produces a substantially greater effect. Exhibit 12.1, showing the increases in sales when popular brands of margarine were discounted and advertised as weekly specials, illustrates the substantially greater effect of cutting the price to a number ending in 9.

What can we conclude about odd pricing? The effect seems to vary across purchase situations from none to quite significant. At this time, we do not know exactly why this variation occurs. One possible explanation is

---

EXHIBIT 12.1

Effect of Advertised Odd-Price Endings on Sales of Margarine

	Price/lb. ($)	Unit Sales
Parkay Brand		
Regular price	0.83	2,817
Discount price	0.63	8,283 (+194%)
Odd discount price	0.59	14,567 (+406%)
Imperial Brand		
Regular price	0.89	5,521
Discount price	0.71	9,120 (+65%)
Odd discount price	0.69	17,814 (+222%)

Source: Kenneth Wisniewski, and Robert Blattberg, Center for Research in Marketing, University of Chicago. Used by permission.

that odd pricing is effective only for products that are purchased quickly, such as grocery items, and not for products for which buyers take the time to contemplate the decision. It also may be that consumers have learned to associate odd endings with discount prices, and thus they simply draw more attention to the price. In fact, companies that price below round numbers are generally trying to present a low-price image, whereas those that try to present a higher-quality image carefully avoid this pricing tactic. At present, this would seem to be a prudent rule of thumb.

FORMULATION OF REFERENCE PRICES

Economists and market researchers have generally focused on the trade-off that buyers make between the utility they get and the price they pay for a product. A more recent theory, called *transaction utility theory*, suggests that buyers are motivated by more than just the "acquisition utility" associated with obtaining and using a product.[7] They are also motivated by the "transaction utility" associated with the difference between the price actually paid and what the buyer considers a reasonable or fair price for the product, called the *reference price*. This concept has already been discussed in previous chapters. For example, we recommended setting the initial list price of an innovation high relative to actual value in order to establish a high reference price in buyers' minds. We also discussed how adding a high-priced version to a product line can raise the reference price by which other products in the line are judged. And we discussed how the overuse of dealing can depreciate buyers' perceptions of the reference price for some branded products. Clearly, the reference price concept is extremely important in pricing. To use the concept in formulating strategy, it is useful to understand how a buyer's reference is determined and what factors influence that determination.

Three major categories of information influence buyers' reference prices. All three are partially under a marketing manager's control. They are (1) the *current prices* to which the buyer is exposed, (2) the *recalled prices* which the buyer remembers from past exposures, and (3) the *context* within which the price is offered.[8]

Current price influences

Product-Line Pricing   A marketer can influence the reference price by influencing the prices to which a buyer is currently exposed. In Chapter 10, we discussed how this is done as part of product line pricing. By adding a higher-priced product to the top of a line, the buyer's reference price increases, making the remaining products in the line appear somewhat less expensive. In one study, subjects were asked to choose among different models of microwave ovens. Half of the subjects were asked to choose between two models (Emerson and Panasonic); the other half where asked to choose from among three models (Emerson, Panasonic I, and Panasonic II) (see Exhibit 12.2). Although 13 percent of the subjects were drawn to the top-end model, the largest impact from adding that model was on sales of the Panasonic I, which gained 17 additional share points as a result of becoming the mid-priced brand.[9] The implications of product-line pricing are clear. Adding a premium product to the product line may not necessarily result in overwhelming sales of the premium product itself. It does, however, enhance buyers' perceptions of lower-priced products in the product line and influences low-end buyers to trade up to higher-priced models.

The implications for competitive price positioning are equally compelling. For instance, low-end sellers should be just as concerned with competitive entry at premium-price positions as they are with threats from potential discount competitors. Why? Because the addition of new premium products raises buyers' reference prices, making mid-price positions more acceptable. Indeed, buyers may now become suspicious of the quality of low-end products. They may reason that they cannot afford premium-priced models, but are not willing to risk getting poor quality at the low end. They, thus opt for mid-priced products instead.

EXHIBIT 12.2

Reference Price Effects of a High-End Product

Microwave Oven Model	Choice (%)	
	Group 1 (n = 60)	Group 2 (n = 60)
Panasonic II (1.1 cubic feet; regular price $199.99; sale price 10% off)	–	13
Panasonic I (0.8 cubic feet; regular price $179.99; sale price 35% off)	43	60
Emerson (0.5 cubic feet; regular price $109.99; sale price 35% off)	57	27

Source: Itamar Simonson, and Amos Tversky, "Choice in Context: Tradeoff Contrast and Extremeness Aversion," *Journal of Marketing Research*, 29 (August 1992), 281–95.

Suggested Frames of Reference   Another way marketers can influence reference prices is by suggesting frames of reference. For example, reference
prices can be raised by stating a manufacturer's suggested price, a higher
price charged previously—(Was $999, NOW $799)—or a higher price
charged by competitors—Their Price $999, OUR PRICE $799. The advertisement in Exhibit 12.3 attempts to raise reference prices used to evaluate the
company's $245 radar detector by suggesting a comparative frame of refer-
ence. It encourages U.S. buyers to consider what a good deal they are receiving relative to Japanese buyers, who value the product so much they
are willing to pay $715 for it.

Recent research has shown that advertisements containing suggested
frames of reference are more effective in influencing purchase decisions of
consumer durable products (video cameras) than those that do not. This
was shown to be particularly true for less knowledgeable buyers who relied more on price to make buying decisions.[10] Other researchers similarly
have found that providing buyers with a suggested reference point enhances perceptions of value and savings, even if the advertised reference
point is exaggerated.[11] Although buyers may discount or question the credibility of such claims, their perceptions and behaviors nonetheless are favorably influenced.[12]

Order Effects   All prices a buyer observes do not influence the reference
price equally; their relative impact depends on the order in which they are
presented. The order effect was discovered in a study conducted in the
mid-1960s.[13] Two groups of experimental subjects were shown the same
sets of prices for a number of products in eight product classes. One group
was shown the prices in descending order (from highest to lowest); the
other group was shown them in ascending order (from lowest to highest).
Then each subject was asked to evaluate the degree to which an individual
product in each product class was priced high or low. From those judgments, the researchers calculated average reference prices for each product.
Exhibit 12.4 shows the results.[14] Subjects who saw the prices in descending
order formed higher reference prices than those who saw them in ascending order, even though both groups saw the same set of prices before making judgments. When forming their reference prices, buyers apparently
give greater weight to the first prices they see in a range.

These results clearly have important implications for marketing management. In personal selling, they imply that the salesperson should begin
by first showing customers products above their price range, even if the
customers will ultimately look at cheaper products as well. This tactic,
known as top-down selling, is common in sales of products as diverse as
automobiles, luggage, and real estate. Direct-mail catalogs take advantage
of this effect by displaying similar products in the order of most to least expensive (see Exhibit 12.5). Within a retail store, the order effect has implica-

Courtesy of Cincinnati Microwave.

EXHIBIT 12.4

Order Effects on Reference Prices of Subjects Shown a Range
of Prices for Each Product

Product	Reference Prices When Range of Prices Shown in	
	Ascending Order ($)	Descending Order ($)
Electric shaver	20.18	24.00
Aftershave lotion	2.28	3.56
Dress shirt	4.85	6.69
Sport coat	39.85	44.64
Hair spray	1.02	1.41
Hair dryer	21.91	21.91
Dress shoes	15.89	17.83
Blouse	7.37	9.27

Source: Albert J. Della Bitta, and Kent Monroe, "The Influence of Adaptation
Levels on Subjective Price Perceptions," in *Advances in Consumer Research,* 1973
Proceedings of the Association for Consumer Research, vol. 1, eds. Peter Wright and
Scott Ward (Urbana, Ill.: ACR, 1974), p. 364.

EXHIBIT 12.5

Exploiting Order Effects in a Direct-Mail Catalog

Page Number of Product	Short-Sleeve Pullover ($)	Pair of Shorts ($)
2	27	32
4	26	24
7	22	
10	20	
16		24
18	18	
19		22
20	20*	
20	13	
31	13–15	
32		15–20
64	10	

*Heavy-weight rugby shirt.
Source: JCPenney's *Big Men's Catalog (Spring & Summer 1985).*

tions for product display. It implies, for example, that a grocery store may sell more low-priced (but high-margin) house brands by *not* putting them at eye level where they would be the first to catch the customer's attention. Rather, it may be preferable to have consumers see more expensive brands first and then look to the house brands.

Past price influences

A buyer's reference price is also influenced by recall of prices seen in the past. One recent study found that buyers of coffee were strongly affected by discrepancies between observed prices at point of purchase and a reference price, which was determined primarily by past prices and corrections for market trends.[15] Past prices have important implications for pricing new products. Many marketing theorists have argued that new products should be priced low to induce trial and thus build a market of repeat purchasers, after which price can be raised. But if the low initial price lowers buyers' reference prices, it may actually adversely affect some repeat sales. This is precisely the result that some researchers have found.[16]

Exhibit 12.6 compares unit sales for five new brands in two sets of stores. During an introductory period, the experimental stores sold the product at a low price without any indication that this was a temporary promotional price; the control stores sold it at the regular price. During a post-introductory period, both sets of stores charged the regular price. In all five cases, despite the fact that initial sales were greater in the experimental stores, sales during the post-introductory period were lower in the experimental stores than in the control stores. Moreover, total sales for the introductory and post-introductory periods combined were greater in the control stores than in the experimental stores where the low price initially stimulated demand. In an individual-level study, subjects were shown different pairs of three types of prices: the regular price, the sale price, and the manufacturer's suggested list price. These researchers found that showing subjects the sale price significantly reduced buyers' perceptions of the product's ordinary price. Moreover, presenting the sale price in combination with the regular price or manufacturer's suggested list price did little to persuade them that the ordinary price was, in fact, higher. This effect was particularly pronounced for male consumers, who were more skeptical and consistently underestimated the product's true ordinary price.[17] These studies demonstrate the importance of dealing tactics such as coupons, rebates, and special packages that minimize this effect by clearly establishing a product's regular price and offering lower prices only as special discounts. Otherwise, initially low promotional prices can establish low reference prices for judging the value of later purchases.

The price last paid has a particularly strong influence on the reference price because it is more likely to be recalled than past prices that were ob-

Exhibit 12.6

Effect of Initial Selling Price on Subsequent Sales

Product	Store Type*	Weekly Average Unit Sales	
		Introductory	Post-Introductory
Mouthwash	Experimental	300	365
	Control	270	375
Toothpaste	Experimental	1,280	1,010
	Control	860	1,050
Aluminum foil	Experimental	4,110	3,275
	Control	2,950	3,395
Light bulbs	Experimental	7,350	5,270
	Control	5,100	5,285
Cookies	Experimental	21,925	22,590
	Control	21,725	23,225

*Experimental stores began with a low price which was raised to the regular price in the post-introductory period. Control stores charged the regular price in all periods.

Source: Albert J. Della Bitta, and Kent Monroe, "The Influence of Adaptation Levels on Subjective Price Perceptions," in *Advances in Consumer Research*, 1973 Proceedings of the Association for Consumer Research, vol. 1, eds. Peter Wright and Scott Ward (Urbana, Ill.: ACR, 1974), pp. 359–69. The data in the original article by Doob and others, "Effect of Initial Selling Price," were presented in graphic form only.

served but not paid. This influence has a number of important marketing implications. First, numerous small price increases for frequently purchased items are more likely to be accepted than are infrequent large increases, since buyers' purchases after each small increase will raise their reference price before they encounter the next increase. For the same reason, resistance to price increases for infrequently purchased durable goods is likely to be especially great. Although the price of an automobile may increase no more rapidly than the price of food over four years, the buyer who has not bought a car in four years will approach the purchase with an outdated reference price. The reaction to seeing the result of four years' inflation all at once is what auto dealers call "sticker shock."

Past prices for a product other than the price last paid also have some effect on reference prices. It is claimed that older people may react more negatively to current prices because they can recall much lower ones from the past. Moreover, buyers may raise their reference prices for a product without being exposed to its price at all, simply because they have observed that the prices of other, similar products have been rising. Because every consumer's past experience and recall ability are unique, marketers should not look for a single reference price for their products. They should instead try to understand and influence the distribution of reference prices that consumers hold.

Purchase context influences

Although past prices influence buyers' reference points, recent empirical research has stressed that reference prices are actually more forward looking than previously supposed. One study found that consumers' reference prices were mostly influenced by current price information and by underlying price trends, which they projected to formulate "expected prices."[18] One skill of personal selling is to develop the purchase context in a way that makes the price seem fair or reasonable. For example, encyclopedia salespeople often break down the cost to a monthly payment and point out that "It's less than you probably spend for _____," filling the blank with something that should be less important to you than your child's education. Chevrolet advertised: "This Cavalier costs less a day than a burger, large fries and a shake—[just] $6.23 a day." But buyers' reference prices are influenced not only by what they think they should be willing to pay in the purchase context, but also by what they think sellers should reasonably charge. One way buyers infer fairness is to assess what it costs sellers to deliver the product. Consider the following scenario:

> You are lying on the beach on a hot day. All you have to drink is ice water. For the last hour you have been thinking about how much you would enjoy a nice cold bottle of your favorite beer. A companion gets up to make a phone call and offers to bring back a beer. He says that the beer might be expensive and asks the maximum price you are willing to pay. If the price is higher, he will not buy it. What price do you tell him if (1) the only nearby place where beer is sold is a fancy resort hotel, or (2) the only nearby place is a small, run-down grocery store?[19]

People surveyed differed dramatically in their responses. The median price stated for a beer from the fancy hotel was $2.65, and that from the run-down grocery was $1.50. Note that the person consuming the beer would not enter the establishment but would drink it on the beach. A rational consumer would, therefore, have been willing to pay the same amount in either case. However, people have reference prices that are influenced by where the product is sold. Most people questioned in this survey were willing to be thirsty rather than be "ripped off" by the grocery store.

One may go to great expense to determine what buyers' reference prices are; in most categories this is probably unnecessary. For frequently purchased products such as groceries, researchers have found that actual market prices are a reasonable surrogate of consumers' internal reference prices, because these buyers adapt relatively quickly to new price information.[20] For infrequently purchased products, however, identifying and managing reference prices may dramatically improve the effectiveness of a pricing strategy.

INFLUENCE OF FRAMING ON PRICE PERCEPTIONS

An emerging stream of research, called prospect theory, integrates the psychology of reference points with the economic theory of consumer choice.[21] Prospect theory challenges the economic theory that people evaluate purchases by comparing the positive utility of having a good with the negative utility of its price. Instead, prospect theory argues that people evaluate purchases in terms of gains or losses, relative to a reference point. According to prospect theory, because gains and losses are valued differently, marketers can influence purchase decisions by framing as either potential gains or losses.[22] To illustrate this effect, ask yourself from which of the two gasoline stations described below would you prefer to buy gasoline:

> Station A: Sells gasoline for $1.30 per gallon, and gives a $0.10 discount if the buyer pays with cash.

> Station B: Sells gasoline for $1.20 per gallon, and charges a $0.10 surcharge if the buyer pays with a credit card.

Of course, the economic cost of buying gasoline from either station is identical. Yet, most people psychologically prefer to buy from station A. Why? Because the perceived cost of purchasing from station A (with a discount) is less than purchasing from station B (with a surcharge).

Prospect theory can be characterized by the peculiarly shaped value function shown in Exhibit 12.7 This is similar in concept to economic theory's utility function, which represents levels of utility associated with levels of actual product consumption. Utility, or value, in prospect theory, however, is associated not with actual levels of consumption but with anticipated *changes* in well-being. The buyer's state of well-being at the time of a decision is characterized as the buyer's reference point, represented as the center point on Exhibit 12.7. The buyer then assesses prospective decision outcomes, called *prospects*, by first mentally categorizing them as either gains or losses relative to the reference point. For example, consumers automatically view income tax refunds as a welcome gain at the end of the tax year, relative to their normal flow of income or current level of savings. On the other hand, imposing an increase in income tax withholding during the year is quickly considered a loss relative to consumers' normal monthly after-tax income. Prospect theory differs from economic theory in describing how consumers weigh such gains and losses in making decisions.

EXHIBIT 12.7

Value Function of Prospect Theory

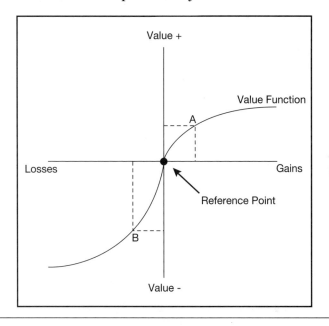

Economic theory predicts that gains and losses of equal size are valued the same, whereas prospect theory predicts that they are valued quite differently.

According to prospect theory, buyers judge a loss as more painful than they judge the gain of an equal amount as pleasurable. This theory is illustrated by the steeper slope of the value function in the negative quadrant of Exhibit 12.7, resulting in a larger negative value at point B than the positive value at point A. In addition, there are diminishing returns to both gains and losses. Increasingly larger gains are incrementally less pleasurable, (and smaller gains are almost as pleasurable as slightly larger gains) and increasingly larger losses are incrementally less painful (and smaller losses are almost as painful as slightly larger losses)

The value of prospect theory to marketers is that it may better predict how consumers actually behave, rather than how they ought to behave. To illustrate with the gasoline example above, economic theory would predict that buyers should be indifferent to buying gasoline from either station A or station B, but prospect theory predicts that buyers will prefer station A because of the way it has framed its price. Station A wisely suggests a higher regular price ($1.30) as an implicit reference point for buyers and then rewards buyers who pay cash with a discount, that is, a gain relative to the reference point. But station B unknowingly turns buyers away by framing its price differently. It establishes a lower regular price ($1.20) as a reference point and then penalizes buyers who use credit cards with a perceived loss.

How can managers use prospect theory to frame purchase decisions? There are three ways: (1) They can frame buyers' reference points by affecting perceptions of what buyers perceive as their status quo, called the *endowment effect*; (2) they can specifically frame decision outcomes in terms of gains or losses; and (3) they can frame multiple gains or losses as bundles that increase their perceived value.

Framing buyers' reference points: the endowment effect

Previously in the chapter, we cited studies that give evidence that marketers can influence reference points by eliciting comparisons to suggested list prices, competitors' prices, or other market prices. Prospect theory adds another dimension to this research, noting that because losses loom larger than gains, it is more painful to consumers' to give up an asset than it is pleasurable to obtain it. As a result, buyers are biased in favor of retaining the status quo. The *endowment effect* describes this reluctance of people to part with assets that belong to their endowment.[23]

A series of experiments at Cornell University illustrates the endowment effect.[24] A group of student subjects participated in a market experiment. Half of the subjects received tokens to be used as cash; the other half received Cornell coffee mugs, which sold for $6.00 at the bookstore. Buyers were paired with sellers into markets of one buyer and one seller each. Buyers then bid for the coffee mug and sellers countered, if they desired to sell. Of 22 mugs initially distributed, only 9 percent (2 mugs) were actually exchanged. The median price at which mug owners were willing to sell ($5.25) was much higher than the median price that cash holders were willing to pay ($2.75). Why were sellers so reluctant to sell and buyers relatively unwilling to buy? Because those given mugs and those given cash were each reluctant to part with their initially endowed asset.

Several important implications follow from the endowment effect. First, it should be easier to sell something if its price can be presented as an opportunity forgone rather than as an outright loss.[25] The reason for this is that out-of-pocket costs, which are viewed as losses of assets already owned, seem more painful than opportunity costs, which are viewed as potential gains forgone. In the early 1990s some banks offered buyers an option of paying a $5.00 per month service charge for a checking account or of keeping a minimum balance of $1,500 and paying nothing. At the time, interest rates on bank savings accounts were about 5.8 percent (compounded monthly). Most people preferred the free checking if they could afford the minimum balance, even though this cost them more. At 5.8 percent interest, these buyers were willing to forgo $7.25 in monthly interest income to avoid the pain of paying $5.00 out-of-pocket costs.

Although these examples involve adjusting the payment mechanism, the same effect on the buyer's perception of a price can be accomplished through advertising. Every spring, advertisers promote cars, home improvements, and other assets as products to be bought with an income tax refund. According to prospect theory, if these advertisers presented the product as something worth buying on its own merit rather than as something worth buying with the refund, the price would more likely be processed as an out-of-pocket cost rather than as an opportunity cost (a reduction in the refund) and would be deemed more painful.

A second implication for pricing, clearly supported by actual practice, is that price differences for the same product should always be presented as discounts from the higher price rather than as premiums over the lower price. Universities commonly state their tuitions as the highest amount they charge and then discount them through scholarships based on financial need. Imagine the outcry if universities stated tuitions as the amount the typical student actually pays. Those students paying higher rates because their families have high incomes would realize that they are actually being assessed premiums on the basis of their ability to pay. Similarly, hotels generally state their room rates as the highest they charge during peak demand periods and then discount those rates most of the time. If the explicit base price is seen as the starting point, buyers paying a higher price will view their failure to qualify for a discount as a gain denied. They will find that less objectionable than being charged a premium, which they would view as an explicit loss.

A third implication for pricing is that it is often better to decouple product acquisition and payment by first endowing buyers with the product. If buyers can be persuaded to take the product home, they will adjust their reference point to include the newly acquired asset. They will then be reluctant to return the product when payment is due, since this will require that they incur a loss. This is a frequent tactic of buy-now, pay-later plans. During holidays, for example, retailers frequently offer installment plans that delay payment for 90 days, so that buyers can integrate the new purchases into their reference points. Health clubs, fitness centers, and weight loss clinics offer an initial trial membership either free or at nominal rates. At the end of the trial period, customers have integrated the new services, benefits, and instructional relationships into their reference point, making it difficult to reject appeals to continue on with the program at regular rates. Some sweepstakes carefully describe the chances of winning in terms that suggest the buyer may have already won—a pseudo-endowment effect. Publisher's Clearinghouse, for example, addresses individuals who receive their direct-mail promotion as finalists and warns that that individual is about to lose $10 million if he or she fails to return the winning number by a certain date.

Framing gains and losses

A frequent advertising strategy used to market high-quality brands is framing the purchase, not in terms of the advantage of buying the high-quality brand (a gain), but in terms of the loss associated with *not* buying it. For example, American Express has long sustained a leading position in traveler's check sales by framing the advantage of easily available refunds that minimize the risk involved in traveling in a strange location and not being able to get a quick and easy refund from a less well known competitor. Two research studies found that appeals stressing the negative consequences of *not* performing specific health-related tests were more persuasive than appeals emphasizing the positive consequences.[26]

A more recent study of a mainstream consumer durables product—video cameras—suggests that framing effectiveness may depend on the nature of the product category. This study found that positive framing is more effective on buyers of video cameras.[27] The authors suggest that one reason for this is that video cameras *enhance* one's utility and usually evoke primarily positive thoughts and outcomes. Similarly, perfumes, fashions, collectibles, gourmet foods, and wines usually enhance one's utility. Negative frames in these product contexts would be so surprising, and distasteful, that buyers would likely reject the advertising and the product. Other product categories, however, *preserve* one's utility and usually cause buyers to think in terms of negative thoughts and potential outcomes. These product categories might include aspirin, home security systems, insurance, and mouthwash.[28] Framing potential losses is more likely to be effective in these product environments because buyers are often concerned with negative consequences.

Framing multiple gains or losses

Gains and losses have a diminishing effect as they grow larger. This third principle of framing of price states that each additional amount of gain, or loss, has a smaller effect on utility than the equal amount preceding it. Consequently, winning $100 is not ten times as pleasurable as winning $10, and losing $100 is not ten times as painful as losing $10.

This principle has important implications for framing multiple gains or losses which usually involve *bundling* or *unbundling* separate products, prices, or payments in ways that enhance buyers' perceived change in utility. There are four helpful pricing tactics using this principle: (1) unbundle gains, (2) bundle losses, (3) bundle smaller losses with larger gains, and (4) unbundle smaller gains from larger losses.[29]

Unbundle Gains Buyers perceive their utility to be more positively affected if multiple gains are offered separately. This bonus principle is frequently used by direct marketers to make an offer so appealing that buyers feel compelled to act. For example, instead of simply offering a discount for new subscribers, a sports magazine can make the purchase more appealing by offering an added benefit, such as a special video of sports highlights.

Bundle Losses   Buyers perceive their utility to be less negatively affected if multiple losses are bundled together. For example, it is easier to induce someone to buy a car stereo at the time of a car purchase than to make the same sale separately. The additional $250 for the stereo does not seem as daunting when added to the $20,000 price of the car, due to the diminishing returns associated with losses. Similarly, sellers of consumer durables often persuade buyers to buy extended warranty plans at the time of product purchase. A $100 plan seems little more painful when added to the price of a $700 television set and certainly much less painful than if the expenditure is considered alone.

Bundle Smaller Losses with Larger Gains   Buyers who perceive the price as simply reducing a large gain that has already been subject to diminishing returns find it less painful than if they see the price as a loss that stands alone. For example, National Lighting Systems, Inc., offers consulting services to corporations and institutions to update their electrical and lighting fixtures to achieve health benefits and energy cost efficiencies. Rather than charge clients daily consulting rates, they instead estimate the total savings the client will realize over a 5-year period and charge the client a portion of the savings. Similarly, it is well known that people are more likely to purchase savings bonds and insurance through payroll deductions. Paying for these by slightly reducing a large gain is much more palatable than incurring the cost outright.

Unbundle Smaller Gains from Larger Losses   This pricing tactic is called the *silver lining principle*. Buyers perceive their utility to be less negatively affected if a smaller gain is unbundled from a larger loss, rather than merely reducing the amount of the loss. The automobile industry of the 1980s relied heavily on price rebates to stimulate sales. Why not simply discount the price instead? One answer is that discounts lower buyers' reference prices. But prospect theory also suggests that buyers may actually perceive a greater change in utility by receiving a separate payment. Since separate gains are valued more highly than reduced losses, rebates become a silver lining benefit associated with a larger expenditure.

Anyone who thinks only in terms of objective economic values will find these principles far-fetched. One might argue that the buyers in these cases could easily think of the transactions as entirely different combinations of gains and losses, implying completely different behavior. That is precisely the point that prospect theorists make. There are different ways to frame the same transactions, and each way implies somewhat different behavior. Being aware of this, marketers can sometimes reduce the pain of higher prices by influencing the way they are framed. Researchers have presented survey subjects with many objectively identical problems, changing only the form of presentation. They have found that by influencing the structuring of the gains and losses, they can consistently change people's choices.

PRICING PROBABILISTIC GOODS

Many product attributes are probabilistic. Parts and equipment have probabilistic failure rates. Investments have probabilities of increasing or decreasing in value. Insurance involves the probability of actually incurring an insured loss. Similarly, fire and burglar alarm systems, air bags, service contracts, and prophylactic medications are all intended to reduce probabilistic losses. An important question for pricing is how purchasers weigh such attributes in determining what they are willing to pay for them.

How much more valuable is a photocopier that breaks down half as frequently? Traditionally, pricers have evaluated probabilistic attributes by calculating their expected value. Thus, if the probability of a photocopier breaking down within a month is 10 percent, and if the cost of repair and disruption is $300, the expected value of reducing that probability by half is $(0.1 \times \$300) \times 0.5$, or $15 per month. Unfortunately, consumers rarely evaluate probabilities in such a straightforward way. To avoid basing pricing strategies on erroneous relative values, pricers of products with probabilistic attributes must consider how consumers' valuations are likely to differ from expected valuations.

Researchers who study probabilistic choices have long observed that people are risk-averse when considering gains; they will choose a sure thing (say $50) over a risky gamble with the same or slightly higher expected value (51 percent chance of winning $100; 49 percent chance of winning nothing). But most probabilistic products (for example, insurance, safety devices) involve reducing the uncertainty of a loss, not a gain. Unfortunately for sellers of those products, people are more naturally inclined to risk a loss than to pay even the expected value of avoiding it.[30] Consequently, if given the choice between a 20 percent chance of losing $100 or the certainty of losing $20, most people gamble. This observation appears true even for purchasers whom one might expect to make thoughtful decisions. One research study with industrial purchasing agents found that those who framed purchase decisions in positive terms chose safer purchase options associated with higher prices, whereas those who framed in negative terms chose riskier contracts associated with lower prices.[31]

For this reason, the marketing of products designed to reduce losses often requires a hard sell to induce potential purchasers to disregard their

natural inclinations. Apparently, the hard sell can work. Years of promotion by the insurance industry has convinced many people to view insurance as more than just the choice between a certain loss (the insurance
premium) and the chance of a larger loss. The term *insurance* implies social
virtues such as concern for one's family, good citizenship, and financial
prudence. Insurance companies also have portrayed insurance as a way to
protect the future, which is, of course, brighter than the present. If people
think of insurance as something they buy to protect future gains rather
than to protect against losses, the decision is shifted into the domain of
gains where buyers are typically risk-averse and willing to choose the certainty that insurance provides.[32]

The shift from risk aversion when the probabilities involve gains to
risk preference when the probabilities involve losses is just one of many
quirks that psychologists have discovered in studying probabilistic choice.
Another is people's tendency to ignore, or at least discount, losses of low
probability, even though the expected value of the loss may be high. At the
extreme, people tend to treat very small probability losses as if they were
zero. Thus, they underestimate the value of reducing small probability
losses. Exhibit 12.8 illustrates this tendency. Participants in a laboratory experiment had the option of insuring against five risks of different probability and magnitude. They clearly preferred to insure against the higher
probability losses, even though the low probability losses were of a correspondingly greater size, making the expected value of each loss the same,
$495.[33]

EXHIBIT 12.8

Effect of Loss Probabilities on Insurance Purchases

Probability of Loss	Magnitude of Loss ($)	Insurance Premium ($)	Persons Insuring (%)
0.002	247,500	500	33
0.01	49,500	500	45
0.05	9,900	500	52
0.10	4,950	500	49
0.25	1,980	500	73

Source: Paul Slovic, and others, "Preference for Insuring Against Probable Small
Losses: Implications for the Theory and Practice of Insurance," *Journal of Risk and
Insurance*, 44 (1977), 237–58.

One way for marketers to circumvent this problem is illustrated in a study of attitudes toward seat belt use. Most people correctly believe that the chance of having a serious accident during any one automobile trip is extremely small. Therefore, they treat the chance of a serious accident as zero. Consequently, the value of seat belts does not seem worth the bother of buckling up. One group of psychologists discovered, however, that attitudes toward seat belts could be changed significantly, simply by presenting the consumer with probabilities they could conceptualize. Instead of describing the serious accident rate as the probability of a debilitating accident in a single trip (1 in 100,000), they described it as the probability of having such an accident over a 50-year lifetime (1 in 3). With the accident rate presented that way, approximately four times as many people (39 percent) indicated that the information would cause them to use their seat belts more frequently.[34] This same technique could be quite useful in raising the value that buyers place on other types of safety devices, service contracts, or insurance.

Researchers have found that at the other probability extreme, people typically value certainty or the perception of it much more highly than less certain alternatives. Thus, a new drug that unquestionably eliminates the probability of catching the flu would be valued much more highly than one that was "only" 99 percent effective. Again, an adroit marketer can influence the buyer's perception. A flu vaccine would be considered less valuable when presented as being effective 50 percent of the time than when presented as being completely effective in preventing one type of virus that accounts for 50 percent of all flu infections.[35]

SUMMARY

Current research on consumer psychology has many interesting and valuable implications for pricing. For some time, marketers have been aware that consumers do not always evaluate prices with calculating rationality. We are now beginning to learn why and how consumers behave differently, thus enabling us to take account of more psychological factors when implementing pricing strategy. In addition to the psychological aspects of pricing discussed in previous chapters, this chapter describes the implications of continuing research in four general areas: the perception of price differences, the formulation of reference prices, the mental framing of prices, and the effects of uncertainty.

Although much research on these topics is still ongoing and the implications remain controversial, we can offer some tentative conclusions.

- ■ Consumers' purchasing behavior is influenced not simply by the absolute difference in prices but by the difference relative to the base price.

- In some cases, but apparently not all, consumers perceive price differences as larger when the lower price ends in an odd number just below a round one.

- Consumers evaluate actual prices relative to reference prices, which are price levels that they would consider fair or appropriate. Reference prices are influenced by other prices that the consumer sees concurrently or has seen in the past. They are also influenced by the purchase context.

- Consumers seem to evaluate prices differently depending upon how they are framed in terms of gains and losses. They seem to judge losses as more painful than they judge equal gains as pleasurable. Both gains and losses also seem to be subject to diminishing effects as the total amount of each increases.

- When products involve probabilistic elements, the value of those elements to consumers often differs significantly from their true expected values. Consumers tend to be risk-averse when considering gains, but will prefer to bear a risk when considering losses. They tend to discount very small probabilities, and they place high value on certainty or at least the perception of it. Their estimates of true probabilities are also biased by their recent exposure to occurrences of the probabilistic events.

NOTES

1. The term *rational* is not used here in the popular sense of "logical" but in the economist's sense of "evaluating fully and completely." The consumer behavior discussed in this chapter results from what Herbert Simon has labeled "bounded rationality," which he argues results from the fact that "[t]he capacity of the human mind for formulating and solving complex problems is very small compared with the size of the problems whose solution is required for objectively rational behavior. . . ." See his *Models of Man* (New York: John Wiley, 1959).

2. This example comes from a study by J. Edward Russo and Paul Schoemaker and is discussed in more detail in their book J. Edward Russo and Paul J. H. Schoemaker, *Decision Traps: The ten barriers to brilliant decision making & how to overcome them*. New York: Doubleday, 1989. See also Richard Thaler, "Toward a Positive Theory of Consumer Choice," *Journal of Economic Behavior and Organization*, 1 (1980), 39–60, for discussion and examples of this pricing phenomenon.

3. Daniel Kahneman and Amos Tversky, "Choices, Values, and Frames," *American Psychologist*, 39, no. 4 (April 1984), 341–50.

4. Kent B. Monroe and Susan M. Petroshius, "Buyers' Perceptions of Price: An Update of the Evidence," in *Perspectives in Consumer Behavior*, 3rd ed., eds. H. Kassarjian and T. S. Robertson (Glenview, IL: Scott-Foresman, 1981), pp. 43–55.

5. Zarrel V. Lambert, "Perceived Prices as Related to Odd and Even Price Endings," *Journal of Retailing*, 51 (Fall 1975), 13–22; Robert M. Schindler and Alan R. Wiman, "Consumer Recall of Odd and Even Prices," working paper, Northeastern University, 1983; Robert M. Schindler, "Consumer Recognition of Increase in Odd and Even Prices," in *Advances in Consumer Research*, 11, ed. T. C. Kinnear (Association for Consumer Research, 1983), pp. 459–62.

6. Eli Ginzberg, "Customary Prices," *American Economic Review*, 26 (1936), 296.

7. Richard Thaler, "Mental Accounting and Consumer Choice," *Marketing Science*, 4, no. 3 (Summer 1985), 199–214.

8. Nonyelu Nwokoye, "Subjective Judgments of Price: the Effects of Price Parameters on Adaptation Levels," Proceedings, Fall Educators' Conference (Chicago: American Marketing Association, 1975).

9. Itamar Simonson, and Amos Tversky, "Choice in Context: Tradeoff Contrast and Extremeness Aversion," *Journal of Marketing Research*, 29 (August 1992), 281–95.

10. Gerald E. Smith, "Prior Knowledge and the Effectiveness of Message Frames in Advertising," unpublished dissertation, Boston University, 1992.

11. Joel E. Urbany, William O. Bearden, and Dan C. Weilbaker, "The Effect of Plausible and Exaggerated Reference Prices on Consumer Perceptions and Price Search," *Journal of Consumer Research*, 15 (June 1988), 95–110.

12. See Eric N. Berkowitz and John R. Walton, "Contextual Influences on Consumer Price Responses: An Experimental Analysis," *Journal of Marketing Research*, 17 (August 1980), 349–58; Albert J. Della Bitta, Kent B. Monroe, and John M. McGinnis, "Consumer Perceptions of Comparative Price Advertisements," *Journal of Marketing Research*, 18 (November 1981), 416–27; Cynthia Fraser, Robert E. Hite, and Paul L. Sauer, "Increasing Contributions in Solicitation Campaigns: The Use of Large and Small Anchorpoints," *Journal of Consumer Research*, 15 (September 1988), 284–87; Mary F. Mobley, William O. Bearden, and Jesse E. Teel, "An Investigation of Individual Responses to Tensile Price Claims," *Journal of Consumer Research*, 15 (September 1988), 273–79; James G. Barnes, "Factors Influencing Consumer Reaction to Retail Newspaper Sale Advertising," Proceedings, Fall Educators' Conference (Chicago: American Marketing Association, 1975), pp. 471–77; Edward A. Blair, and E. Laird Landon, Jr., "The Effects of Reference Prices in Retail Advertisements," *Journal of Marketing*, 45, no. 2 (Spring 1981), 61–69; John Liefeld, and Louise A. Heslop, "Reference Prices and Deception in Newspaper Advertising," *Journal of Consumer Research*, 11 (March 1985), 868–76. See also Robert E. Wilkes, "Consumer Usage of Base Price Information," *Journal of Retailing*, 48 (Winter 1972), 72–85; Sadrudin A. Ahmed and Gary M. Gulas, "Consumers' Perception of Manufacturers' Suggested List Price," *Psychological Reports*, 50 (1982), 507–18; Murphy A. Sewall and Michael H. Goldstein, "The Comparative Advertising Controversy: Consumer Perceptions of Catalog Showroom Reference Prices," *Journal of Marketing*, 43 (Summer 1979), 85–92.

13. Albert J. Della Bitta, and Kent B. Monroe, "The Influence of Adaptation Levels on Subjective Price Perceptions," in *Advances in Consumer Research*, 1973 Proceedings of the Association for Consumer Research, vol. 1, eds. Peter Wright and Scott Ward (Urbana, Ill.: ACR, 1974), pp. 359–69.

14. Prices shown to these subjects ranged from moderate to high, given typical prices at the time of the study. The authors also did this study with two other subjects, showing them prices that ranged from low to moderate. The study was not as successful; in two of the eight cases, the ascending price exceeded the descending price and, in one case, the two prices were equal. The remaining five cases were consistent with those in Exhibit 12.4.

15. Russell S. Winer, "A Reference Price Model of Brand Choice for Frequently Purchased Products," *Journal of Consumer Research*, 13 (September 1986), 250–56.

16. A. Doob and others, "Effect of Initial Selling Price on Subsequent Sales," *Journal of Personality and Social Psychology*, 11 (1969), 345–50.

17. John Liefeld, and Louise A. Heslop, "Reference Prices and Deception in Newspaper Advertising," *Journal of Consumer Research*, 11 (March 1985), 868–76.

18. Robert Jacobson, and Carl Obermiller, "The Formation of Expected Future Price: A Reference Price for Forward-Looking Consumers," *Journal of Consumer Research*, 16 (March 1990), 420–32.

19. Richard Thaler, "Mental Accounting and Consumer Choice," *Marketing Science*, 4 (Summer 1985), 199–214.

20. Joel E. Urbany and Peter R. Dickson, "Consumer Normal Price Estimation: Market Versus Personal Standards," *Journal of Consumer Research*, 18 (June 1991), 45–51.

21. Daniel Kahneman and Amos Tversky, "Prospect Theory: An Analysis of Decision Under Risk," *Econometrica*, 47 (March 1979), 263–91; Daniel Kahneman and Amos Tversky, "The Psychology of Preferences," *Scientific American*, 246 (January 1982), 162–70; Daniel Kahneman, and Amos Tversky "Choices, Values, and Frames," *American Psychologist*, 39, no. 4 (April 1984), 341–50; Amos Tversky and Daniel Kahneman, "The Framing of Decisions and the Psychology of Choice," in *New Directions for Methodology of Social and Behavioral Science: Question Framing and Response Consistency*, ed. R. Hogarth, no. 11 (San Francisco: Jossey-Bass, March 1982); Amos Tversky and Daniel Kahneman, "Advances in Prospect Theory: Cumulative Representation of Uncertainty," *Journal of Risk and Uncertainty* (1992).

22. The marketing implications of this theory, including its extension to decision making in nonprobabilistic situations, have been developed primarily by Richard Thaler in "Toward a Positive Theory of Consumer Choice," *Journal of Economic Behavior and Organization*, 1 (1980), 39–60; and in "Mental Accounting and Consumer Choice," pp. 199–214.

23. Kahneman and Tversky, "Choices, Values, and Frames."

24. Daniel Kahneman, Jack L. Knetsch, and Richard H. Thaler, "The Endowment Effect, Loss Aversion, and Status Quo Bias," *Journal of Economic Perspectives*, 5, no. 1 (Winter 1991), 193–206.

25. See Richard Thaler, "Toward a Positive Theory of Consumer Choice," *Journal of Economic Behavior and Organization*, 1 (1980), 39–60; and Amos Tversky and Daniel Kahneman, "The Framing of Decisions and the Psychology of Choice," *Science*, 211 (1981), 453–58.

322   Pricing Psychology

26. Beth E. Meyerowitz and Shelly Chaiken, "The Effect of Message Framing on Breast Self-Examination Attitudes, Intentions, and Behavior," *Journal of Personality and Social Psychology*, 52, no. 3 (1987), 500–510; Durairaj Maheswaran and Joan Meyers-Levy, "The Influence of Message Framing and Issue Involvement," *Journal of Marketing Research*, 27 (August 1990), 361–67.

27. Gerald E. Smith and Meera Venkatraman, "Framing Pain or Pleasure: The Influence of Framing in Enjoyable Product Categories," unpublished working paper, Boston College, 1993; Maheswaran and Meyers-Levy, also found positive frames more effective for buyers with low levels of involvement in the product category. See also Irwin P. Levin and Gary J. Gaeth, "How Consumers Are Affected by the Framing of Attribute Information Before and After Consuming the Product," *Journal of Consumer Research*, 15 (December 1988), 374–78.

28. This logic is similar to logic by Barbara E. Kahn and Robert J. Meyer, "Consumer Multiattribute Judgments Under Attribute-Weight Uncertainty," *Journal of Consumer Research*, 17, no. 4 (March 1991), 508–22, dealing with utility-enhancing versus utility-preserving product attributes.

29. This discussion expands on the seminal work by Thaler, "Mental Accounting and Consumer Choice."

30. See, for examples and references, Kahneman and Tversky, "Choices, Values, and Frames," pp. 341–50; and Amos Tversky and Daniel Kahneman, "Advances in Prospect Theory: Cumulative Representation of Uncertainty," *Journal of Risk and Uncertainty* (1992).

31. Christopher P. Puto, Wesley E. Patton III, and Ronald H. King, "Risk-Handling Strategies in Industrial Vendor Selection Decisions," *Journal of Marketing* 49 (1985), 89–98; see also his "The Framing of Buying Decisions," *Journal of Consumer Research*, 14 (December 1987), 301–15; and William J. Qualls and Christopher P. Puto, "Organizational Climate and Decision Framing: An Integrated Approach to Analyzing Buying Decisions," *Journal of Marketing Research*, 26 (May 1989), 179–92.

32. J. C. Hershey, and Paul Schoemaker, "Risk Taking and Problem Context in the Domain of Losses: An Expected-Utility Analysis," *Journal of Risk and Insurance*, 47 (1980), 111–32.

33. Paul Slovic and others, "Preference for Insuring Against Probable Small Losses: Implications for the Theory and Practice of Insurance," *Journal of Risk and Insurance*, 44 (1977), 237–58.

34. See Paul Slovic, Baruch Fischhoff, and Sarah Lichtenstein, "Accident Probabilities and Seat Belt Usage: A Psychological Perspective," *Accident Analysis and Prevention*, 10 (1978), 281–85.

35. Paul Slovic, Baruch Fischhoff, and Sarah Lichtenstein, "Response Mode, Framing, and Information-Processing Effects in Risk Assessment," in *New Directions for Methodology of Social and Behavioral Science: Question Framing and Response Consistency*, ed. Robin Hogarth (San Francisco: Jossey-Bass, 1982), pp. 21–36.

MEASURING PRICE SENSITIVITY

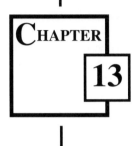
RESEARCH TECHNIQUES TO SUPPLEMENT JUDGMENT

Numerical estimates of customer price sensitivity can sometimes substantially improve the effectiveness of pricing. Some efforts to estimate price sensitivity, however, mislead management into making poor pricing decisions. It is not always possible to make reasonably accurate estimates, but there are always research firms willing to produce a number for a willing buyer. Managers who uncritically buy such estimates and use them to make pricing decisions often regret those decisions at a later time. Even the best estimate is no substitute for a thorough understanding of one's buyers, an understanding based on the kind of managerial analysis of price sensitivity described in Chapter 4. Without such knowledge one cannot develop tactics for segmented pricing, or discover product augmentations or promotional themes to influence the importance of price in the purchase decision. Managers who try to substitute a single number for a more complete understanding of their buyers' purchase motivations are likely to miss many profitable opportunities.

When managers critically evaluate numerical estimates of price sensitivity and use them to supplement, not to replace, information they have gained from studying buyers' purchase motivations, the estimates are often well worth the investment. There are numerous methodologies for estimating price sensitivity. Each method offers some particular advantages over the others, so the choice is not arbitrary. One must think carefully about the appropriate procedure for any particular product before beginning research.

TYPES OF MEASUREMENT PROCEDURES

Procedures for estimating price sensitivity differ on two major dimensions: the conditions of measurement and the variable being measured. Exhibit 13.1 classifies the various procedures according to these two dimensions.

The conditions of measurement range from a completely uncontrolled to a highly controlled research environment. When making uncontrolled measurements, researchers are only observers. They measure what people actually do, or say they would do, in a situation not of their making. For example, marketing researchers might collect data on consumer purchases of laundry detergent in a grocery store, but the prices and other variables that influence those purchases are beyond their control. In contrast, when making controlled measurements, researchers manipulate the important variables that influence consumer behavior to more precisely observe their effect. Researchers conducting an experimentally controlled study of price sensitivity for a laundry detergent would select the prices as well as the advertising and shelf placement of various brands in order to make the data more useful. Researchers might attempt to gain even more control by conducting a laboratory experiment in a simulated store and carefully selecting the individuals whose purchases would be recorded. Participants for the experiment could be chosen to represent various demographic variables (such as race, sex, income, and family size) in proportions equal to those of the product's actual market or to represent a particular group (such as mothers with children) to whom the product was intended to appeal. Controlled research produces more accurate estimates of the effects of

---

EXHIBIT 13.1

Techniques for Measuring Price Sensitivity

Variable Measured	Conditions of Measurement	
	Uncontrolled	Experimentally Controlled
Actual purchases	Aggregate sales data Store audit data Consumer panel data	In-store experiments Laboratory purchase experiments
Preferences and intentions	Direct questioning Buy-response surveys	Simulated purchase surveys Trade-off (conjoint) analysis

the controlled variables on price sensitivity. Unfortunately, collecting controlled data is also more costly and time-consuming.

The dependent variable measured for estimating price sensitivity is either actual purchases or purchase preferences and intentions. Actual purchase studies measure behavior, whereas preference-intention studies measure the choices that people claim they would make in a hypothetical purchase situation. Since the ultimate goal of the research is to estimate how people respond to price changes in actual purchase situations, research that measures actual behavior is generally more desirable. Unfortunately, it is also more costly, time-consuming, and sometimes impractical.

Managers selecting among the various research techniques for measuring price sensitivity face some difficult choices. The following summary of research techniques is intended to help them make those choices correctly.

Uncontrolled studies of actual purchases

One way to estimate price sensitivity is to analyze past sales data. Unfortunately, estimates of price sensitivity are needed most when setting prices for new products and when considering changing the prices of established products to new levels. In those cases, there is no directly comparable data on past sales from which to make estimates. Sometimes researchers will infer the price sensitivity of a new product from past sales data of a product that is similar from the buyer's perspective. At other times, researchers will try to infer the likely effect of a large price change from consumers' past responses to small changes. Although either technique may be of some value when there are no practical alternatives, the results of such studies do not warrant much confidence.

Generally, past sales data are valuable only for evaluating the effects of a proposed price change that is similar to one made for the same product in the past. For example, a company might regularly offer promotional specials during certain seasons of the year. Examining the effect of those specials in the past can be highly useful in forecasting the effect that similar price promotions will have in the future. Even then, however, changes in (1) the number of brands on the market, (2) how recently competitors offered price promotions, (3) the amount and effectiveness of advertising by each brand, and (4) general economic conditions can undermine the comparability of a current price cut with past cuts of similar magnitude. Moreover, past price changes are often accompanied by changes in advertising expenditures, sales support, or promotional displays, making it difficult to sort out the effect of price from the effects of those other variables.

There are three types of past sales data from which a marketing researcher might attempt to estimate price sensitivity: (1) *aggregate sales data*—aggregate sales reports for a brand from a company's own records or from a sales-monitoring service, (2) *panel data*—individual purchase reports from members of a consumer panel, and (3) *store audit data*—sales data for an individual retail outlet.

Aggregate Sales Data   Sales data collected as part of a company's regular operation are cheap and available for all products that have prior sales histories. Unfortunately, these data are normally collected only quarterly or monthly. Moreover, unless the company sells directly to the end user, its sales data reflect shipments to retailers, not actual retail sales during the period. Good estimates of actual retail sales are available for some products from companies that survey retail stores (for example, A. C. Neilsen[1]), but the data are reported only bimonthly. Consequently, it takes a long time to accumulate enough observations on sales from which to make estimates. The longer the period of data collection, the more likely it is that factors other than price will cause changes in sales levels, making the data from different time periods less comparable. For some of those factors such as product reformulations, changes in consumer tastes, changes in distribution, there is simply no way to take out the effect. For others, such as recessions or changes in the level of advertising, the researcher can statistically control the estimation process to take out their effects, but to do so requires an even longer series of data. That can lead to a "Catch 22" dilemma: More time to accumulate more data lets still more things change requiring still more data.

Another problem with aggregate sales data is that it is aggregated. Aggregate sales is the sum of sales in many different retail outlets. In any given week, some stores will charge higher prices than will others. Over time, the same store will put the product on sale for a week and then return its price to the regular level. These price variations influence sales and, therefore, could provide useful information about price sensitivity. Unfortunately, data that aggregate sales for all stores over a number of weeks conceal these price differences. Given the aggregation in the data, the researcher is forced to explain sales variations by looking at only the average retail price across stores and throughout the time period. Since the average of prices has much less variation than actual prices at individual stores in particular weeks, the data are much less useful than are data on individual purchase prices.

Moreover, for marketers of business-to-business products, demand for their products is driven by demand for their customers' products. Here, estimates of price sensitivity based on the company's previous sales, price, advertising, or other promotional expenditures will often miss the most important determinant of demand—the customers' sales in those downstream markets for which data may be difficult to obtain. Still, aggregate sales data should not be totally disregarded when one is attempting to understand price sensitivities, although no conclusions can be drawn from simple statistical analysis alone. A manager who can bring to the data some strong judgmental beliefs about how certain events have affected sales may gain, by combining those beliefs with the data, some useful insight that would elude the statistician who relies on the data alone.[2]

Panel Data   Fortunately, for some products, there are better sources of purchase data than aggregate sales data. A number of marketing research companies collect individual purchase data from panels of a few thousand households. Each household keeps a daily record of all brands purchased and prices paid. Since products are purchased daily, the data for each household must be aggregated to produce a series on weekly or biweekly purchases. Such data have a number of advantages.

1.   One can accumulate observations more quickly with weekly panel data than with bimonthly or quarterly sales data, reducing the problem that other factors may change and reduce the comparability of the data.

2.   One can observe the actual price paid, rather than an average of the retail prices that different stores charge, and one can identify sales that were made with coupons that reduce the regular price.[3] This produces much more price variation in the data, making the effects of price changes easier to detect.

3.   One can get data on the sales and prices of competing products (provided someone in the panel bought them) as well as on sales of one's own product.

4.   One can correlate price sensitivity with various demographic classifications of consumers and possibly identify opportunities for segmentation.[4]

One drawback of panel data is that it may not be adequately representative of the market as a whole. Of all households invited to join a panel, fewer than 5 percent accept the offer and accurately record their purchases. There is reason to suspect, therefore, that panel members are a biased sample of the population. Moreover, just the fact that panel members must record their purchases tends to make them more price aware, and thus more price sensitive. This problem increases the longer a household participates in a panel. Fortunately, a few research companies have developed panels that do not require consumers to record their purchases.[5] Instead, purchases are recorded automatically by in-store scanners whenever panel members identify themselves in the store's checkout line. This vastly simplifies panel membership, increasing the panel participation rate to over 70 percent and attenuating the problem of heightened price awareness.

Unfortunately, consumer panel data exist for a small percentage of products, generally consumer packaged goods sold in supermarkets. For such products, however, estimates of price sensitivities are possible.[6] The superiority of panel data estimates over those from aggregate sales data is due to the availability of more observations from a shorter and more comparable time period.

Store Audit Data   An alternate source of actual sales data comes from auditing prices and sales at individual retail stores. New technologies have made accurate weekly sales and price data available at reasonable cost. Any store that uses scanners can generate such data as part of its normal operations. The weekly frequency of scanner data makes it vastly superior to aggregate sales data. Although it lacks the corresponding demographics of consumer panel data, it also costs substantially less. Scanner data have become a major new source of information on the price sensitivity of consumer packaged goods.[7]

Analyzing Historical Data   Analysis of historical sales data usually involves application of linear regression analysis (see Exhibit 13.2). This statistical technique attempts to show how much of the historical variation in a product's sales can be explained by each of the explanatory variables, including price, that the researcher includes in the analysis. One should not expect, however, that the researcher will necessarily succeed in identifying the effect of price with such an analysis. If there has been little historical variation in a product's price, then no statistical technique applied to its sales data can reveal the effect of price changes. Moreover, if every time price was changed some other variable such as advertising was also changed, the best one can do is discover the joint effect of such a simultaneous change on sales. The researcher will not be able to isolate the portion of the effect accounted for by price alone.

Furthermore, one must be careful to recognize the limits of a successful analysis of historical data. To estimate a regression equation, the researcher must assume a mathematical form for the relationship between price and sales. To the extent that the assumed form incorrectly specifies the relationship, estimates of price sensitivity may be misleading. Moreover, the researcher's estimate of price sensitivity is valid only over the range of price and advertising levels used to estimate it. There is no reason to believe that the same relationship would necessarily apply to price changes outside that range. Finally, regardless of how well an estimated regression equation fits past data, its value in predicting the effect of future price changes rests on the assumption that the future is like the past. The more other factors change, the less the past can predict the future.

Despite these limitations, if a researcher has a lot of historical data with enough price variation in it, useful estimates of price sensitivity are possible. Exhibit 13.3 describes one of the first uses of regression analysis to estimate price sensitivity from panel data.

Exhibit 13.2

Analysis of Uncontrolled Sales Data Using Linear Regression

Analysis of sales data—whether from company records, a consumer panel, or an individual store—usually begins with an attempt to estimate a regression equation. Sales or market share is the dependent variable to be explained, and price is one of the explanatory variables. One should try to include as many other explanatory variables (for example, advertising levels, the prices of competing products) as possible if they have changed during the period of data collection. When analyzing panel data, it is common to include lagged market share as an explanatory variable. Although the form of the regression equation will vary depending upon the type of data and the researcher's judgment about the general form of the relationship, the following are typical forms with which one might begin an analysis.

$$\text{Unit sales} = a + b_1 \text{ price} + b_2 \text{ advertising} + e$$

$$\text{Market share} = a + b_1 \text{ lagged market share} + b_2 \text{ price} + e$$

The purpose of the regression analysis is to estimate the coefficients—a, b_1, and b_2—which reveal the relationship between changes in the explanatory variables and changes in sales or market share. In the first equation, for example, b_1 would be an estimate of the change in unit sales for a one-unit change in price. With that information, and knowledge of the product's current price and unit sales, one could easily calculate the product's price elasticity of demand.

When data are available on the prices and advertising levels of competing brands, the estimation can be vastly improved by replacing price (or any other variable) with relative measures in the equations above. For example, instead of using the simple dollar value of price as an explanatory variable, one might use either (1) the price for this brand divided by the average price for all brands, or (2) the difference between the price for this brand and the average for all brands. The results of a regression analysis can also be improved by adding variables that might influence sales (for example, growth in GNP or population, the time of year) and by controlling for the common statistical problems to which this type of data is subject.

For a brief introduction to regression analysis, see Thomas C. Kinnear and James R. Taylor, *Marketing Research: An Applied Approach,* 4th ed. (New York: McGraw-Hill, 1991), pp. 626–628; or Mark L. Bereson and David M. Levine, *Basic Business Statistics: Concepts and Application* (Englewood Cliffs, N.J.: Prentice Hall, 1992), Chapter 16.

EXHIBIT 13.3

Measuring Price Sensitivity for Orange Juice and Coffee: Regression Analysis of Panel Data

The Market Research Corporation of America (MRCA) operates a national consumer panel that is the source of data for this study. From this panel, MRCA provides monthly estimates of market share and price by brand for a number of frequently purchased consumer goods, including the ones analyzed in this study. The sample period for this study is 36 months. A condition of using these data is that individual brands not be identified in publication. They include, however, the following:

For frozen orange juice: Minute Maid, Birds Eye, Donald Duck, Snow Crop, Libby's, and Whole Sun

For regular coffee: Chase and Sanborn, Eight O'Clock, Folger's, Maxwell House, and Hills Brothers

For instant coffee: Borden's, Chase and Sanborn, Folger's, and Maxwell House

Letters are used to identify the brands, but not in the order given.

The following tables contain estimates of the following market-share regression for each brand:

$$MS_i = a + b_1 \text{ lagged } MS_i + b_2 \text{ price} + e$$

The dependent variable, *MS*, is the market share of brand *i*. The two independent variables are the market share lagged one month and the price variable. The price variable is the difference between the dollar price of brand *i* and the average price in the product class. (The article also includes comparable estimates using for the price variable the dollar price of brand *i* divided by the average price in the product class.) Following each regression are the price elasticities implied by the regression estimates.

Frozen Orange Juice Regressions

					Implied Elasticity	
Brand	a	b_1	b_2	R	Short Run	Long Run
A	.10754	.5247	–.01755	.8107	2.00	4.21
		(.1126)	(.004026)			
B	.03253	.7932	–.008946	.8627	1.78	8.61
		(.09568)	(.003886)			
C	.04659	.4662	–.01009	.8540	2.49	4.67
		(.1254)	(.002907)			
D	.02285	.4252	–.008890	.7585	3.11	5.41
		(.1472)	(.003248)			
E	.02785	.5337	–.01757	.7449	3.35	7.18
		(.1234)	(.004664)			
F	.01353	.2343	–.008510	.8915	3.23	4.21
		(.1198)	(.001482)			

Regular Coffee Regressions

Brand	a	b_1	b_2	R	Implied Elasticity Short Run	Implied Elasticity Long Run
A	.1111	.2833 (.129)	−.004758 (.00106)	.6965	2.32	3.27
B	.0349	.3204 (.101)	−.001976 (.000314)	.8956	4.60	6.76
C	.0234	.8116 (.0981)	−.000542 (.000987)	.8256	.21	1.13
D	.0709	.1674 (.143)	−.003135 (.000612)	.8057	4.23	4.85
E	.0768	.4158 (.105)	−.001833 (.000371)	.9242	1.63	2.59

Instant Coffee Regressions

Brand	a	b_1	b_2	R	Implied Elasticity Short Run	Implied Elasticity Long Run
A	.1806	.5642 (.100)	−.004809 (.00151)	.7955	.47	1.11
B	.0821	.7651 (.0928)	−.005812 (.00180)	.8733	2.62	10.28
C	.0228	.3663 (.150)	−.001339 (.000554)	.5664	3.05	4.24
D	.0388	.7852 (.0916)	−.001690 (.000733)	.9228	1.03	5.00

Source: Reprinted, by permission, from Lester G. Telser, "The Demand for Branded Goods as Estimated from Consumer Panel Data," *Review of Economics and Statistics*, 4 (August 1962), 300–24.

Experimentally controlled studies of actual purchases

A researcher might attempt to estimate price sensitivity by generating experimental purchase data. Such data may come from pricing experiments conducted in a store without the buyers' knowledge or from pricing experiments conducted in a laboratory. Since the researcher controls the experiment, price variations can be created as desired to generate results while holding constant other marketing variables, such as advertising levels and in-store displays, that often change with price variations in uncontrolled sales data. The researcher can examine the effect of a number of different prices quickly and either (1) exclude many unwanted external effects in the laboratory experiment or (2) establish a control in the in-store experiment that will take account of them. Moreover, all this can be done while still *providing* buyers with purchase decisions that are reasonably comparable to those they make in normal conditions. As a result, experimental research provides fairly reliable estimates of price sensitivity.

In-store Purchase Experiments   An in-store purchase experiment relies on actual purchase data collected when buyers are unaware they are participating in an experiment. Although the term *in-store* reflects the fact that most such experiments are conducted in supermarkets, the principles of in-store experimentation are equally applicable to any natural purchase environment. Such experiments are actually easier to conduct for products sold through mail order catalogs than for those sold in retail stores. The researcher simply selects a subset of the mailing list to receive catalogs with experimental prices that differ from those in the regular catalog. Even in direct sales to business, one can sometimes select a representative sample of customers from one sales area, offer them an experimental price, and monitor the difference between sales to those buyers and to those in other regions where sales are at the regular price.

The simplest design for an in-store pricing experiment involves monitoring sales at the historical price to obtain a base level of sales and then initiating a price change to see how sales change from that base level. In practice this is a very common experimental design that can yield useful information; however, it fails to exploit one of the major advantages of experimentation: the ability to control for external factors. Without such control, the researcher is forced to make the tenuous assumption that any sales change from the base level resulted from the price change alone, not from changes in other factors.

Fortunately, the addition of an experimental control store (or mail sample or sales territory) can reduce this problem substantially. To establish such a control, the researcher finds a second store in which sales tend to vary over the base period in the same way that they vary in the first store, indicating that factors other than price influence both stores' sales in the same way. The researcher then changes price only in the first store, but continues to monitor sales in both stores. Any change in sales in the control store indicates to the researcher that some factor other than price is also causing a change in sales. To adjust the results, the researcher subtracts from the sales in the experimental store an amount equal to the change in sales in the control store before determining the effect of the price change alone.[8]

One of the greatest benefits of in-store experimentation is the ability to test for interactions between price and other marketing variables that, in historical data, tend to change together. For example, Exhibit 13.4 describes a successful experiment that allowed the researcher to identify not only the effects of price and advertising levels alone, but also their interactions. Unfortunately, the cost of such experimentation is very high because each

---

Exhibit 13.4

Measuring Price Sensitivity for a New Food Product: An In-
store Experiment

A new convenience food for use as a snack or a nutritionally balanced meal
substitute was being contemplated for national introduction. Information
was sought concerning possible differential responses to several aspects of
the introductory marketing plan, the most important of which were variations in price and level of advertising expenditure.

A controlled store test was conducted for six months in four test markets. Three levels of price were tested: a base price below 50 cents, a price
10 cents above the base, and a price 20 cents above it. A sample of 30
stores within each of the test cities was split into three matched panels of
10 stores. Each of these matched panels received one of the three price
treatments. Variations in advertising expenditures were tested across the
four cities, with two cities receiving a low weight plan and two receiving a
high weight plan.

The following table shows the effects of price and advertising on purchase volume in this experiment. Purchase volume is measured by an
index set at 100 in the base price, low advertising stores. (A value of, say,
125, means that sales were 25% higher, a value of 75 means that sales
were 25% lower.)

Advertising

Price	Low	High	Average Over Both Advertising Levels
Base level	100	150	125
Plus 10¢	79	106	93
Plus 20¢	64	71	68
Average over all prices	81	109	

Source: Abridged and reprinted, by permission, from Gerald Eskin, "A Case for
Test Market Experiments," *Journal of Advertising Research*, 15 (April 1975), 27–33.

---

additional factor studied requires the inclusion of more stores. The experiment with the greatest amount of information, called a *full factorial design*,
would require enough stores to match every level tested for each marketing variable with every level of the other variables. Usually, therefore, the
researcher is forced to use a less-than-perfect experiment, called a *fractional
factorial design*, that sacrifices some precision (generally, an understanding
of interactions) in order to reduce the number of stores required.[9]

Although there are many articles that illustrate the successful application of in-store experimentation to estimate price sensitivity, the greatest

impediment to using in-store experiments is the high cost of monitoring sales, analyzing the data, and securing the cooperation of retailers.[10] Although in theory this is an inexpensive experiment because as few as two stores for one week could comprise a test, accurate tests require many stores and last for months. A large number of stores is necessary to reduce the problem of an external factor influencing just one store and to obtain a representative sample of consumers whose behavior can reasonably be generalized to the market as a whole. It is often necessary to set a long time period for an in-store test in order to get past the short-run inventory effect on price sensitivity that initially masks the long-term effect. Consequently, a good in-store experiment is very expensive. When, for example, Quaker Oats conducted an in-store experiment that focused on the effect of price alone, the study required 120 stores and ran for three months. Such a study can easily cost several million dollars.[11]

In addition to the financial and time cost of in-store experiments, there are other drawbacks. There is the potential loss of consumer goodwill when some buyers are charged prices above normal. On the other hand, charging prices below normal can become too costly when the product is a large-expenditure durable good such as an automobile or a piece of industrial equipment. An in-store test also involves the very real risk of being discovered by a competitor. If the product is new, a company may not wish to give its competitors an advance look. Moreover, when competitors find out about a test market, they often take steps, such as special promotions or advertising in selected areas, to contaminate the results.[12] Thus, although in-store experiments have the potential for yielding very high quality estimates, market researchers are more often forced to use alternatives. The closest of those alternatives is a laboratory purchase experiment.

Laboratory Purchase Experiments   *Laboratory purchase experiments* attempt to duplicate the realism of in-store experimentation without the high cost and exposure to competitors. A typical laboratory experiment takes place in a research facility at a shopping mall. Interviewers intercept potential participants who are walking by and screen them to select only those who are users of the product category being researched. Based on information from a short pretest questionnaire, the researchers can control the proportion of participants in each demographic classification (sex, age, race, income, family size) to ensure that the experimental population is representative of the actual population of buyers. If members of some demographic categories cannot be found in adequate numbers in the mall, telephone interviews may be used to contact such people and offer them an incentive to come and participate in the experiment.

The laboratory researcher can control who participates and can quickly manipulate prices and other elements in the purchase environment (such as shelf location and advertising) all at a single location. Moreover, the researcher can almost entirely eliminate external factors (such as changes in competitors' prices, stockouts of competing products, or differences among stores) that may contaminate the results of an in-store test. Participants exposed to different prices see exactly the same display at the same location in the laboratory experiment. Even effects associated with the time of day can be controlled by constantly changing prices for each new participant in the experiment. Thus, if testing three different price levels, approximately one-third of the consumers who take the test at any hour can be exposed to each price level. This ability to control the experiment so closely enables the researcher to draw inferences from far fewer purchases in much less time than would be possible with an in-store experiment.

Laboratory research facilities vary greatly depending upon the sophistication of the research organization and the budget of the client company. The simplest facilities may consist of an interviewing room with a display of products from a single product category. The price for each brand is clearly marked, and the participant is invited to make a purchase. In theory, since the consumer is actually making a purchase, or can choose not to buy at all, the purchase decision in a simple laboratory experiment is the same one that the consumer would make shopping in an actual retail store.

In practice, however, that conclusion may not be true. The problem lies with the artificiality of a simple laboratory environment. First, a single display in a laboratory encourages the consumer to give the purchase decision much more attention than would be typical in an actual shopping situation. Research indicates that most grocery shoppers do not even look at most prices when actually shopping in a supermarket. In a laboratory, however, consumers do not want to appear careless. They are, therefore, much more likely to note and respond to price differences. Second, when consumers know they are being watched, they may act as they feel they should rather than as they would in real life. Thus some consumers may buy the low-priced brand just to appear to be smart shoppers, or the high-priced brand so as not to appear stingy. They may also buy something from the category out of a feeling of obligation to the researcher who gave them the money, even though they would not buy from that category in a store.

To overcome these limitations, a few research companies offer highly sophisticated laboratory research facilities. The most elaborate facilities attempt to duplicate as closely as possible the actual conditions under which consumers buy the product. These facilities contain complete simulated stores the size of small convenience stores. Before entering the simulated store, consumers may view reruns of television programs within which are embedded television commercials for the research product or may read magazines within which are print advertisements for the product. When consumers finally enter the store, they are invited to do all their shopping, purchasing whatever they want, just as they would on a regular shopping trip. They do not know what products or what product categories are subjects of the research. They use their own money to make their purchases. Their reward for participation is a substantial discount off their total when they check out at the cashier. Exhibit 13.5 describes such a laboratory experiment.

Even the best laboratory experiment is somewhat artificial, introducing some bias into the results. Still, companies that do this research argue convincingly that the problem of bias is not as great as the problems of in-store experimentation and that they can accurately adjust the results of their laboratory experiments, based on their past experience with similar product categories, to take out the effects of any biases inherent in the experimental process.[13] Moreover, one cannot argue with the economics. The cost of even the most sophisticated laboratory experiment is only a small fraction of the cost of in-store testing. As a result, the leading marketers of consumer packaged goods and small appliances rely extensively on this research technique when making pricing decisions.

EXHIBIT 13.5

Measuring Price Sensitivity for a Computerized Clock Radio: A Laboratory Purchase Study

A major Japanese electronics manufacturer was interested in assessing how different advertising and pricing strategies would affect market demand for a new multi-function product (a combination digital clock, AM/FM radio, and cassette player with built-in memory calendar-date book). In addition to being a high-quality clock radio, the product enjoyed several unique features. The clock alarm could activate either a buzzer, the radio itself, or a cassette tape. (A demonstration tape played the old tune "When the red, red robin comes bob, bob, bobbing along. . . . Get up, you sleepy head. . . . Get up, get out of bed.") Another unique feature was the computer memory which permitted the user to program up to 500 key dates and/or times. With this system the user could peek ahead in a given month or week to see key dates coming up, and/or wait until the morning of the date when the preprogrammed information would appear on a small screen.

The key questions asked by the manufacturer were twofold. First, how should the product be positioned in television advertising, as an advanced clock radio or as a tabletop time management computer? Second, should the product be priced at $59 to attract a large share of the high-volume radio's market; at $79 to compete with high-quality AM/FM radio-cassette players; or at $99 to signal the product's uniqueness and skim the segment that valued those unique features most highly? To address this problem, the manufacturer contracted with Yankelovich, Clancy, Shulman (now Yankelovich Partners) to conduct a laboratory purchase experiment.

In each of four markets, 300 prospective buyers (men and women, age eighteen and over) were randomly recruited. They were invited to the company's laboratory facilities for the apparent purpose of previewing a new television program and seeing new home electronic products. The design for the study was very simple. Each participant was randomly assigned to a treatment group for exposure to one of the two possible positionings and three possible prices. Thus, at each location 6 groups (2 x 3) of 50 participants each were exposed to a different positioning/price combination.

The groups were first exposed to a new half-hour television program in which was embedded advertising for the new product, for competitive products, and for control products. Following this, participants were invited into an adjoining simulated electronics store where they had the opportunity to see the new product along with many competitive products, priced as they would be at local stores. They could ask questions of store salespeople and read available literature about the products.

All products in the store were for sale at a 30 percent discount off the listed price. Approximately 40 percent of all participants actually made a purchase. The nonbuyers were asked a set of questions to estimate what they would have purchased if they had made a purchase.

The results of the study showed significant effects of both positioning and price on demand. Overall, 14 percent of all prospective purchasers were buyers of the new product. Demand varied with positioning and price in the following way:

Percentage of Purchasers Under Different Conditions

Price	Advanced Clock Radio (%)	Time Management Computer (%)
$59	25	20
79	19	11
99	8	1

Source: Provided by Yankelovich, Clancy, & Shulman (now Yankelovich Partners), a marketing research, modeling, and consulting firm in Westport, Conn. (Although this description is based on an actual study, some details have been masked to maintain confidentiality.)

Uncontrolled studies of preferences and intentions

The most common research technique for directly estimating price sensitivity is the survey of brand preferences or purchase intentions. There are a number of reasons why companies prefer to measure preferences or intentions, rather than actual purchases.

1.   Survey data cost much less than purchase data to collect.

2.   Survey data can be measured for large durable goods, such as automobiles or photocopiers, for which in-store or laboratory experiments at various prices are impractical.

3.   Survey data can be collected even before a product is designed, when the information is most valuable in directing product development.

4.   The results can be collected quickly.

Unfortunately, the problem with survey research is that many consumers do not give answers to survey questions that are a reliable guide to their actual purchase behavior. This is especially true for questions regarding price. In order to solve this problem, some research companies cross-validate the results of one survey with the results of another, often using slightly different methods of data collection and questioning. For example, a firm might collect data using personal interviews and validate the results by telephoning a different group of respondents and asking the same set of questions. The closer the results are from the two samples and methods, the more valid and accurate the final results.

Direct Questioning   Very early in the development of survey techniques for marketing, researchers learned that it was futile to ask consumers outright what they would be willing to pay for a product. Direct questioning sometimes elicits bargaining behavior, with consumers stating a lower price than they would actually pay. Other times, it elicits a desire to please the researcher or to not appear stingy, prompting consumers to state a higher price than they would actually pay. Frequently, it simply elicits a cursory answer that consumers would change were they to give the question the same thought as an actual purchase decision. Consequently, uncontrolled direct questioning as a research technique to estimate price sensitivity should never be accepted as a valid methodology. The results of such studies are at best useless and are potentially highly misleading.

Buy-Response Surveys   A slight variant of the direct question survey involves showing consumers a product at a preselected price and asking if they would purchase at that price. Surprisingly, although directly asking consumers what they would pay usually yields meaningless answers, asking them if they would buy at a preselected price yields answers that are at least plausible. When the answers given by different consumers for different price levels are aggregated, they produce what looks like a demand curve for market share, sometimes called a *purchase probability curve* (Exhibit 13.6). Presumably, questioning willingness to buy generates better responses simply because it is structured more like an actual purchase decision than is an open-ended question about what the consumer would pay. The consumer has no opportunity to bargain with the researcher.[14]

Exhibit 13.6

A Simple Buy-Response Study: Opportunity for a Higher Price

A software firm developed a product for law firms that would easily produce high-quality legal documents and would manage document storage and billing of time for both small and large offices. The original estimates of price were $500 per unit. Chadwick Martin Bailey, Inc., conducted a national study to measure price sensitivity for the product. They began the process by conducting extensive exploratory research, including focus groups and semistructured interviews. This phase of the research initially indicated that prices in the range of $6,000 might be perfectly acceptable to a large segment of attorneys. A random sample of 603 attorneys was contacted by telephone and asked for the likelihood of purchase at either $2,000, $4,000, $6,000, or $8,000, yielding about 150 responses per price point. Probability of purchase was measured using a 0–10 likelihood of purchase scale, and all responses in the 8–10 range were used as a basis for assessing price sensitivity. At $2,000, 49 percent of the firms would have bought the package. Demand was found to be very inelastic for higher prices, as shown in Figure A. Movement from $4,000 to $8,000 in price made little difference in the proportion of law firms willing to buy the product, but produced large differences in revenue from sales, as shown in Figure B.

FIGURE A

Purchase Probability Curve

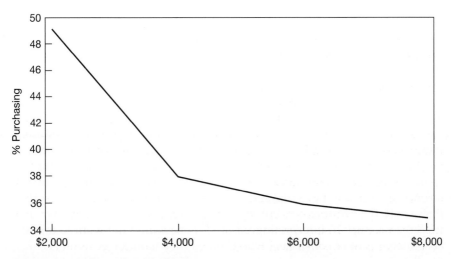

Source: Chadwick Martin Bailey, Inc.

FIGURE B

Total Revenue Estimates

Source: Chadwick Martin Bailey, Inc.

This study was provided by Chadwick Martin Bailey, Inc., a planning and market research firm located in Boston, Massachusetts.

One cannot, however, treat buy-response data as directly comparable to or directly predictive of the sales that would actually occur at the corresponding prices in a store. Most problematic is the fact that consumers' answers to the question depend on their recollection of the actual prices of competing products. To the extent that they overestimate or underestimate competing prices, they will misjudge their willingness to buy. Even with this form of the question, some consumers will still want to please the researcher, or will fear appearing stingy, and so will falsely claim a willingness to buy the brand over competing brands regardless of the price.

Nevertheless, such research is useful (1) as a preliminary study to identify a range of acceptable prices for a new product and (2) to identify changes in price sensitivity at different points in time or place, assuming that the biases which affect these studies remain the same and so do not affect the observed change. For example, recall that in Chapter 4 (Exhibit 4.4), we saw a buy-response survey for a new food product that showed no difference in consumers' willingness to buy at different prices when they knew only the product concept, but a significant difference after they had tried the product. In interpreting the study, one would not want to take the absolute percent of consumers who claimed they would buy as an accurate prediction of the percent who would actually buy at the different prices.

However, differences in the stated probability of purchase before and after trial may reliably predict the change in price sensitivity caused by the product trial.

Intention measurement is also sometimes used successfully to predict actual purchases when researchers have past experience with which they can adjust for the bias in subjects' stated intentions. Typically, purchase intentions are measured by asking people to indicate which of the following best describes their likelihood of purchase:

Definitely would buy
Probably would buy
Might/might not buy
Probably would not buy
Definitely would not buy

The leading survey research firms have asked such questions to millions of buyers for thousands of products. Consequently, they are able to develop adjustments that reflect the average bias in these answers for various product classes. Thus, an experienced researcher might expect that only 80 percent of people answering "definitely would buy," 50 percent answering "probably would buy," 25 percent answering "might/might not buy," and 10 percent answering "probably would not buy" will actually purchase.

Attribute Positioning Another method for evaluating price sensitivity is to include price as one of the attributes describing a product or a purchase situation. Consumers rate the importance of each attribute using a variety of scaling techniques. Those scales can be a 1 to 5 or a 1 to 10 importance rating or simply an evaluation of the percent of respondents mentioning the attribute as being important.[15] This approach is problematic because responses tend to be "off hand" and overly positive, due to reasons mentioned in the previous section.

Exhibit 13.7 lists the results of a traditional attribute-based study to determine the importance of various store attributes for grocery shoppers (the data in this example have been disguised). Note that *quality of produce, variety, meat department*, and *low prices* top the list of attributes that respondents claim are most important to them in selecting a store. However, when these responses are correlated with consumers' evaluations of ratings for "their favorite grocery store," price becomes less important and other features, mostly associated with convenience, now top the list. These results provide much deeper insights into why consumers actually choose a grocery store; in this case because the store is conveniently close to their home.[16]

Exhibit 13.7

Traditional Attribute-Importance Study

Attribute Importance

Attribute	Importance
Quality of Produce	28.24
Variety	26.11
Meat Department	25.93
Low Prices	22.67
Store Cleanliness	18.22
Convenience	17.84
Friendliness of Staff	17.34
Location	17.12
Layout	13.29
Hours	12.99

Correlation Analysis of Independent Variables

Dependent Variable: Rating for Grocery Stores

Attribute	Correlation
Minutes from Home	−.8347
Location	.8199
Fast Check Out Lines	.7437
Quality of Produce	.6843
Low Prices	.6201
Friendliness of Staff	.4213
Variety	.4213
Hours	.4080
Meat Department	.3911
Store Cleanliness	.3562
Convenience	.3489
Layout	.3360

Source: Hamlin Harkins, Ltd., a market research firm located in San Jose, California.

Experimentally controlled studies of preferences and intentions

To solve some of the problems of bias and extraneous factors when measuring preferences and intentions, researchers try to exercise some control over the purchase situation presented to respondents.

The questions must be designed to make the survey respondents consider the questions in the same way they would consider an actual purchase decision. The extent to which that can ever be fully accomplished is still an open question, but marketing researchers, recognizing the potential value of accurate survey information, are certainly trying.

Simulated Purchase Survey   Many researchers argue that the best way to get consumers to think about a survey question and to respond as they would in a purchase situation is to simulate the purchase environment as closely as possible when asking the survey questions. In the usual version of such a simulation, the researcher asks the consumers to imagine that they are on a shopping trip and desire to make a purchase from a particular product class. Then the researcher shows the consumers pictorial representations, descriptions, or actual samples of brands along with prices and asks the consumers to choose among them given various prices. Since actual products need not be used, this technique enables one to test product concepts before they are actually developed into products, thus enabling the firm to better focus its product development resources.

The primary difference between such a simulated purchase survey and a laboratory purchase experiment is that participants only imagine that they are purchasing the product, and so do not get to keep their choices.[17] The simulated purchase is a widely used form of pricing research that overcomes two important drawbacks of other types of surveys. Since it is structured as a choice among alternative brands, a consumer's thought process should more closely approximate the process actually used when making a purchase. And, since consumers have no way of knowing which brand is the one of interest to the researcher, they cannot easily think of the choice as a bargaining position or as a way to please the researcher. Thus, simulated purchase surveys sometimes predict price sensitivity reasonably well.

Exhibit 13.8 compares the results of some simulated purchase experiments with the results of in-store purchase experiments using the same price differences. It shows that a simulated purchase survey was accurate in predicting in-store price sensitivity for colas, but was poor in predicting price sensitivity for ground coffee.[18] To explain the difference, the researcher noted that studies on price awareness have found that consumers generally take careful note of cola prices, but not of coffee prices, when they are actually buying those products. Consequently, the high level of awareness generated by a simulated purchase experiment is more realistic of the actual purchase environment for colas than for coffees. Other validation studies have produced similarly mixed results.[19]

Given the fact that simulated purchase experiments are not consistently reliable, they should be used with caution and accepted only when the results are supported by actual purchase data or other types of tests. If, for example, a company wants to estimate the price sensitivity of a product

Exhibit 13.8

In-Store Versus Simulated Purchase Measures of Price Elasticity

	In-Store	Simulated Purchase
Colas		
Royal Crown	-2.67	-2.36
Coke Test I	-4.77	-5.23
Coke Test II	-6.73	-5.71
Ground coffee		
Hills Brothers	-0.08	-7.13
Maxwell House	-5.02	-8.92
Chase & Sanborn	-1.31	-5.59

The price changes in this study were Royal Crown, -11.2%; Coke Test I, -15.1%; Coke Test II, -25.8%; Hills Brothers, +6.0%; Maxwell House, -4.8%; and Chase & Sanborn, +11.9%.

These elasticities are ratios of the % change in quantity divided by the % change in price.

Source: Adapted from John R. Nevin, "Laboratory Experiments for Estimating Consumer Demand," *Journal of Marketing Research,* 11 (August 1974), 261–68, by permission of the American Marketing Association.

sold nationally, the cost of hundreds of in-store experiments throughout the country would be prohibitive. Consequently, it might use simulated purchase experiments to reduce the cost. If the company conducted both an in-store and simulated shopping experiment in a few locations and found them reasonably consistent, it could confidently use a simulated purchase survey to cover the remaining locations and to conduct future research on that product class. Even if the simulated purchase experiment showed a tendency to be biased but the amount of the bias was the same at different times and locations, simulated purchase surveys could still be used successfully after the results have been adjusted by the amount of that previously identified bias.

Trade-off Analysis   A measurement technique, called trade-off (or conjoint) analysis, has become popular for measuring price sensitivity as well as sensitivity to other product attributes.[20] The particular strength of trade-off analysis is its ability to disaggregate a product's price into the values consumers attach to each attribute. Consequently, trade-off analysis can help a company identify the differentiation value of unique product attributes and, more importantly, design new products that include only those attributes that consumers are willing to pay for. Currently, trade-off analysis aids in the design of a range of products from automobiles and office equipment to household cleaners and vacation packages.

   The basic data for trade-off analysis are consumers' answers to questions that reveal not their purchase intentions, but rather the underlying preferences that guide their purchases. The researcher collects such data by asking respondents to make choices between pairs of fully described products or between different levels of just two product attributes. The data are usually collected with a questionnaire, but can be collected with a personal computer.

   After obtaining a consumer's preferences for a number of product or attribute pairs, the researcher then manipulates the data to identify the value (utility) that each consumer attaches to each product attribute and the relative importance that each attribute plays in the consumer's purchase decision.[21] With that data, the researcher can predict at what prices the consumer would purchase products containing various combinations of attributes, including combinations that do not currently exist in the marketplace. With similar data from a number of consumers who are representative of a market, the researcher can develop a model to predict the share of a market that would prefer any particular brand over others at any particular price. Since the researcher has collected data that reveal underlying preferences, consumers' preferences can be predicted even for levels of price and other attributes not specifically asked about in the questionnaire, providing the attributes are continuously measurable and bounded by the levels that were asked about in the survey. Exhibit 13.9 provides an example of such a process. Readers should note how the basic features were varied along

---

EXHIBIT 13.9

A Conjoint Study: New Hotel's Best Price and Attributes

The Greater Southern Development Authority of Western Australia commissioned a conjoint study into the feasibility of building a new resort hotel in the southwest region of their country. The objective of the study was twofold: (1) to verify whether the demand was adequate to justify the project and (2) to determine the optimal features that the hotel should offer. Important hotel attributes—*cost per night*, *site* (view), *town center* (nearness to town)—and feasible "levels" of those attributes were identified by reviewing current hotels and developer proposals for new hotels and by interviewing possible users of the proposed facility.

   Using these attribute levels, sixteen feasible hotel profiles were developed and consumer preferences for them were tested. Telephone interviews were used to identify tourists likely to visit the area. A questionnaire was mailed to 300 potential tourists who were asked to rate the sixteen alternative hotel configurations. Eighty-one percent of the questionnaires were returned and included in the analysis.

   Respondents rated the alternative configurations using an 11-point "likelihood of purchase" scale. Average scores for each attribute level were compared to determine their overall value in the purchasing decision. The initial results of the analysis included an evaluation of the importance of each attribute and the value or utility that each of the attribute levels had relative to one another. Those utility values were then interpreted relative to the utility of the price of the hotel room in order to develop a dollar (Australian) value for the nonmonetary attributes. Table A lists the results for the attributes reported here. Because of the high negative utility associated with higher price points, the data suggest the market is too price sensitive for a high-priced resort hotel.

Unfortunately, many analysts using conjoint data would stop at this point. In fact, Table A shows only the price sensitivity for a mythical "average" consumer who may be unlike any in the marketplace. Different consumers often have very different price sensitivities for various products and their attributes. To understand these differences, the data for this study were analyzed by applying cluster analysis to individual utilities. This analysis resulted in the identification of four customer segments, each with differing values for the product attributes (see Table B).

Only when the attribute values of the individual segments are evaluated can we find a segment of *active water seekers* for whom price is relatively unimportant. Once this segment was found, the data were analyzed to predict the market share that the "ideal" hotel could obtain for this segment. The results: A hotel on the beach and a short walk to the town center could capture a 16.4 percent market share at a price of A$80, with most of the potential customers coming from the *active water seekers* segment. The fact that most of the customers in this market would deem this hotel a poor value is irrelevant.

TABLE A

Importance, Utilities, and Value for Attribute Levels

Attribute and Levels	Importance	Utility	Value[a]
Cost per Night	56		
40[a]		1.86	
60		0.28	
80		-0.45	
100		-1.99	
Site	6		
View		-0.01	$-0.16
Harbor		-0.19	-2.96
Mountains		-0.07	-1.09
Beach		0.25	3.89
Town Center	7		
Short Walk		0.05	$0.78
5 Minutes		0.21	3.27
20 Minutes		-0.26	-4.05

[a] Values are in Australian dollars.

TABLE B

Attribute Importance and Utilities for Different Segments

Attribute and Levels	Convenience Seekers		Basics Seekers		Active Water Seekers		Passive Viewers	
	Impor-tance	Utility	Impor-tance	Utility	Impor-tance	Utility	Impor-tance	Utility
Cost per Night	31		73		14		41	
40[a]		0.87		3.14		0.09		1.44
60		0.35		0.89		−0.05		0.64
80		0.15		−1.15		0.23		−0.12
100		−1.27		−3.89		−0.09		−2.17
Site	16		3		29		14	
View		0.16		−0.04		−0.35		0.19
Harbor		0.01		−0.10		0.22		0.31
Mountains		0.37		0.07		−0.30		0.31
Beach		0.28		0.14		0.30		0.47
Town Center	18		1		3		9	
Short Walk		0.15		0.01		0.04		−0.03
5 Minutes		0.39		0.04		−0.02		0.26
20 Minutes		−0.74		−0.05		−0.02		−0.34

[a]Values are in Australian dollars.

Source: Chadwick Martin Bailey, Inc., a planning and market research firm located in Boston, Massachusetts. The results of this study were reported in complete form at the Second International Conference on Marketing and Development, Budapest, July 10–13, 1988, in a paper entitled "Regional Planning for Resort Hotels: A Conjoint Application" by John Martin and David Blackmore.

with price in order to develop a relationship between features and value, here termed "feature *utility.*" Segmentation in the sample of respondents is needed to understand how some individuals have higher values for some attributes than others. In this study, those segmented ratings were used as the basis for successfully predicting the probable market share for the new hotel, given careful analysis of how existing hotels matched the needs of different consumers. Failure to segment the respondents into high- and low-value groups often hides the true nature of price and value sensitivity in the population.

Of all methods to estimate price sensitivity from preferences or intentions, trade-off analysis promises the most useful information for strategy formulation. The researchers can do more than identify the price sensitivity of the market as a whole. They can identify customer segments with different price sensitivities and, to the extent that those differences result from differences in the economic value of product attributes, can also identify the specific product attributes that evoke the differences. Consequently, researchers can describe the combination of attributes that can most profitably skim or penetrate a market. The economic value of a product can also be identified even when the product is not yet developed. Moreover, trade-off analysis can do all this for thousands of different product variations for not much more than the cost of a simulated purchase survey to evaluate just one product.

As a result of these promised advantages, the use of trade-off analysis by both market research firms and internal research departments is growing rapidly. But the promises of trade-off analysis are only as good as its ability to predict actual purchase behavior. That ability is a question that remains unanswered. There are, however, a number of reasons why a prudent manager might suspect the reliability of this technique. Trade-off analysis clearly does not simulate the actual purchase environment. The consumer is encouraged to focus much more attention on individual product attributes than is likely in a natural purchase environment. Trade-off analysis does not lead the consumer through the same mental processes that occur in a purchase decision. When making an actual purchase, consumers make one holistic choice from an entire array of brands; they do not consciously determine all the trade-offs involved. Whether consumers can accurately introspect and report the weights that various product attributes have in making such a choice is an unknown at the foundation of trade-off analysis.

Because trade-off analysis measures underlying preferences, the researcher has the ability to check if an individual consumer's responses are consistent. Consumers who are not taking the survey seriously, or who are basically irrational in their choice processes, are then easily identified and excluded from the sample. Still, a subject may give logically consistent answers that do not truly reflect underlying preferences. Thus, even more comforting are three separate studies that show a high degree of consistency when subjects are asked to repeat a trade-off questionnaire a few days after having taken it initially.[22] Since the subjects are unlikely to remember exactly how they answered the questions in the earlier session, the consistency of the answers over time strongly suggests that they do accurately reflect true underlying preferences. More comforting yet is the result of a study showing that the exclusion from the questionnaire of some product attributes a subject might consider important does not bias the subject's responses concerning the trade-offs among the attributes that are included.[23]

With the support of these studies, trade-off analysis should continue to grow in popularity despite the lack of direct proof of its predictive ability. The detailed information that it offers is unique among research techniques, and alternative techniques have certainly not proven any more reliable. Although trade-off analysis is more costly than a simple survey, it also provides much more information. Given its relatively low cost and the fact that it has met at least some tests of reliability, it certainly warrants consideration when seeking to develop a product with features that can be priced most profitably.

USING MEASUREMENT TECHNIQUES APPROPRIATELY

Numerical estimates of price sensitivity can either benefit or harm the effectiveness of a pricing strategy, depending upon how management uses them. If managers better understand their buyers and use that knowledge to formulate judgments about buyers' price sensitivity in the manner discussed in Chapter 4, an attempt to measure price sensitivity can be very useful. It can give managers new, objective information that can either increase their confidence in their prior judgments or indicate that perhaps they need to study their buyers further. On the other hand, if managers try to use empirical estimates of price sensitivity as a substitute for knowledge of their customers' purchase motivations, attitudes, and incentives, the quality of their pricing decisions is likely to suffer.

The implication that somehow soft managerial judgments about buyers are actually more fundamental to successful pricing than are numerical estimates based on hard data may come as somewhat of a surprise. Managerial judgments are necessarily imprecise, while in contrast, an empirical estimate of price sensitivity is a definite, concise number that management can use for profit projections and planning. However, the fact that empirical estimates of price sensitivity are concise does not imply that they are accurate. The history of marketing research reveals that estimates of price sensitivity are frequently far off the mark. Managers' imprecise judgment could lead them to predict accurately that the sales change following a price change will be within some broad range, while a concise empirical estimate of price sensitivity predicts a sales change that proves totally misleading. Accuracy is a virtue in formulating pricing strategy; conciseness is only a convenience.

If one were forced to choose between estimating price sensitivity by informed judgment or by concise empirical estimation, judgment would be the better choice. No estimation technique can capture the full richness of the factors that enter a purchase decision. In fact, measurements of price sensitivity are concise precisely because they exclude all the factors that are not conveniently measurable. Some estimation techniques enable the researcher to calculate a confidence interval around a concise estimate, indicating a range within which can be claimed with some degree of certainty that the true estimate of price sensitivity lies. That range is frequently wider than the interval that a well-informed manager could specify with equal confidence simply from managerial judgment. Unfortunately, researchers often do not (or cannot) report such a range to indicate just how tenuous their estimates are. When they do, managers often ignore it. Consequently, managers deceive themselves into thinking that an estimate of price sensitivity based on hard data is as precise as it is concise.

Fortunately, a manager does not have to make the choice between judgment and empirical estimation. Used effectively, they are complementary, with the information from each improving the information that the other provides.

Using judgment for better measurement

Any study of price sensitivity should begin with the collection of information about buyers—who they are, why they buy, and how they make their purchase decisions—since those are the essential inputs in the formulation of judgment. At least initially, the information should come from open-ended, qualitative or exploratory research that enables managers to discover facts and formulate impressions other than those for which they may have been specifically looking.[24] In industrial markets, such research may consist of accompanying salespeople to observe the purchase process. After a sale, managers might follow up to ask how and why the purchase decision was made. In many cases, managers can interview important customers and intermediaries by telephone to gain their impressions about a variety of price and marketing issues.[25] In consumer markets, such research may consist of observing consumers discussing their purchase decisions in focus groups. Insights generated from such informal observation could then be confirmed with more formal research in the form of a survey administered to a larger number of buyers.

In addition, managers can learn much about their buyers from secondary sources of data. In industrial markets, the Census of Manufacturers, the Survey of Industrial Buying Power, and numerous other governmental and private sources[26] can tell sellers the types of businesses their buyers conduct and the share of the total market each accounts for, the average size of their purchases in major product classes, and their growth rates. In consumer markets, consumer panel surveys are widely available to tell managers the demographics of their buyers (income, family size, education, use of coupons) as well as those of their closest competitors. Other companies, such as SRI International, develop complete psychographic profiles of buyers that go beyond just demographics to delve into the innermost psychological motivations for purchase. These are relatively inexpensive sources of data from which management can form judgments about price sensitivity.

Having formed judgments about buyers based on qualitative impressions developed from observing them, a manager will often find it practical and cost effective to expand this understanding through original primary research which attempts to measure certain aspects of buyer behavior, such as price sensitivity. That attempt is far more likely to produce useful results to the extent that management already understands the way buyers make their purchase decisions and uses that information to help structure the attempt at measurement. There are a number of ways that managerial judgment can, and should, guide the measurement effort.

1.   For experimentally controlled data estimation, managerial judgment should determine the focus of the research on certain target demographic groups and provide guidance for generalizing from those groups to the population as a whole.

- ■   Management may know that 80 percent of its product's buyers are women who are employed full time. That information is important if the researcher plans to measure price sensitivity with an in-home survey or an experiment in a shopping center. On a typical day between 9:00 A.M. and 5:00 P.M., few of the experimental subjects at home or in the shopping center would be representative of that product's buyers. To get a representative sample, the researcher might need to conduct the in-home survey in the evenings or the experiment only during the lunch hour at locations near where many women work. He or she might also ask a prescreening question (Are you employed full time?).

- ■   If management also knows that different demographic groups buy the product in different quantities, that information can be used to scale the survey results differently for different subjects in the sample to reflect their relative impact on the product's actual sales.

2.   For historical data estimations, the intervention of informed managerial judgment into the analysis is even more essential, since the lack of any experimental control invariably results in data that are full of statistical problems. Managerial judgment should be used to reduce random error and solve statistical problems.

- ■   The effect of price changes tends to get overwhelmed in historical purchase data by the amount of sales variation caused by other factors, which may not be obvious to the researcher but may be to managers who know their buyers. For example, a researcher analyzing many years' worth of data on the sales of a frozen seafood product could substantially improve the estimation of price sensitivity if management pointed out that many buyers purchase the product as part of their religious observance of Lent, a Christian holiday that shows up at a different time every year. That one bit of information about why consumers buy would enable the researcher to eliminate a substantial amount of random variation in the data.

■ The researcher using historical data is also often confounded by the problem called *colinearity*, where different explanatory variables change together. Perhaps, at the same time that a firm offers a promotional price deal, it always offers retailers a trade deal in return for a special product display. Without additional input from management, the researcher cannot sort out the effect of the price deal from that of the display. If, however, management knows that buyers of the product are like those of another product that is sometimes sold on special displays without a price deal, the researcher could use sales data from that other product to solve the colinearity problem with this one. Alternatively, if managers are confident in making a judgment about the effectiveness of special displays (for example, that they account for between a third and a half of the total sales change), that information can likewise help the researcher to narrow an estimate of the effect of price on sales. [27]

3.   Managerial judgment should also be used to select the appropriate structure for an experiment or survey, and the appropriate specification of a statistical equation for analysis of historical data.

■ A manager who has studied buyers should know the length of the purchase cycle (time between purchases) and the extent of inventory holding, both of which will govern the necessary length of an experiment or the number of lagged variables to include when analyzing historical data. Failure to appropriately specify the purchase cycle could cause a researcher to grossly miscalculate price sensitivity by ignoring the longer term effects of a price change.

■ Management may have much experience indicating that an advertisement affects buyers differently when the advertisement focuses on price rather than on other product attributes. If so, the researcher should separate those types of advertising in an experiment or in historical data analysis. The researcher might also treat price advertising as having an effect that interacts with the level of price, and nonprice advertising as having an independent effect.

4.   For survey research, managerial judgment should guide the preparation of product descriptions, to ensure that they include the variables relevant to buyers and that they describe them with the appropriate connotations.

■ For an automobile survey, management can point out that the amount of time required to accelerate to 50 mph is an important attribute to include when describing a sportscar, but not when describing a family car.

■ For a survey on television sets, managers can point out that the word *knob* in a description will carry a connotation much different from the word *control*, which may influence buyers' perceptions about other attributes such as reliability and state-of-the-art technology.

The common failure to use this type of managerial input (or the failure of management to know buyers well enough to provide it) is no doubt one reason why research to measure price sensitivity is often disappointing.

When measurement embodies managerial judgment, it is much more likely to provide useful information. But even then, the results should never be taken uncritically. The first question to ask after any marketing research is "Why do the results look the way they do?" The measurement of price sensitivity is not an end result but a catalyst to learn more about one's buyers. If the results are inconsistent with prior expectations, one should consider how prior judgment might have been wrong. What factors may have been overlooked, or have been given too little weight, leading to the formulation of incorrect expectations about price sensitivity? One should also consider how bias might have been introduced into the measurement process. Perhaps the measurement technique heightened buyers' attention to price or the sample subjects were unrepresentative of the product's actual buyers. Regardless of the outcome of such evaluation, one can learn more about the product's buyers and the factors that determine their price sensitivity. Even when one concludes that the measurement technique biased the results, the bias reveals information (for example, that the low level of price sensitivity that management expected is substantially due to buyers' low attention to price in the natural purchase environment, or that a segment of people who do not regularly buy the firm's product has a different sensitivity to price).

Selecting the appropriate measurement technique

The choice among measurement techniques is not arbitrary. Each is more appropriate than another under certain circumstances. Information about one determinant of price sensitivity, the unique value effect, is most valuable when a company is developing new products or improving old ones. The value buyers place on differentiating attributes should determine which ones the final product will include. Clearly, since one cannot use historical data or a purchase experiment to test undeveloped products, one must turn to research on preferences/intentions that require only product descriptions or experimental prototypes. Given the lack of realism in such research and the fact that it often predicts actual price sensitivity rather poorly, one may be skeptical of its value in the product development process. Surveys of preferences and intentions yield poor predictions of actual price sensitivity partly because they fail to capture some important factors in the actual purchase environment, such as price awareness and knowledge of substitutes. At the time of product development, however, those are not factors about which management is concerned. Product development focuses on efforts to enhance the unique value effect. Even when survey research accurately measures only the effect of product attributes on price sensitivity, it is a useful tool for product development, although it may be inadequate for actually setting prices later on.

Once a product is developed, management would like to have measurements that capture as many of the different determinants of price sensitivity as possible. In-store or sophisticated laboratory purchase experiments are definitely the first choice for frequently purchased, low-cost products. With few exceptions, such products are bought by consumers who have low price awareness and give the purchase decision little attention. Consequently, surveys to estimate price sensitivity for such products focus much more attention on price in the purchase decision than would occur naturally, thus distorting the estimates. The cost of in-store experiments, however, may make them impractical for testing on a large scale. In that case, management might best do a few in-store experiments with matched simulated purchase surveys. If the amount of bias in the latter is stable, the survey could be used for further research and adjusted by the amount of the bias.

When the fully developed product is a high-cost durable such as a television set or a photocopier, an in-store experiment is generally impractical. A laboratory purchase experiment may be practical since experimental control permits inferences from fewer purchases but will be too costly for many products. Fortunately, high-value products are also products for which consumers naturally pay great attention to price. In fact, they may give all aspects of the purchase careful thought because it involves a large expenditure. Consequently, a simple laboratory experiment or a simulated purchase survey may be reasonably accurate in predicting price sensitivity for these types of products. Even a buy-response survey may be useful to identify the range of prices that potential customers might find acceptable for such products, although the exact estimates of sales at various prices should not be treated with much confidence.

Once a product has been on the market for a while, historical data become available. Such data are most useful when managers are willing to implement marketing decisions in ways that can increase the research value of the resulting sales data. For example, sales data become more useful if price changes are sometimes accompanied by a change in advertising and other times not, enabling marketing researchers to isolate their separate effects. A log of unusual events that cause distortions in the actual sales data (for instance, a strike by a competitor's truckers may be causing stockouts of his or her product and increased sales of yours) is also extremely useful when the time comes to adjust the historical data. Moreover, as managers talk with and observe buyers, they should keep questions in mind that would aid the researcher using historical data: What is the length of the purchase cycle? To what extent do buyers purchase extra for inventories when price is expected to rise in the future? Even if historical data are so filled with random variations that no conclusions can be drawn from them with confidence, they may still point toward possible relationships between price and sales or other marketing variables that would be worth examining with another research technique.

Summary

Numerical estimation of price sensitivity is no shortcut to knowing a product's buyers—who they are, how they buy, and why they make their purchase decisions. Numerical estimates are an important source of objective information that can supplement the more subjective observations that usually dominate managerial judgments about price sensitivity. As a supplement, they can substantially improve the accuracy of such judgments and the effectiveness of a firm's pricing.

Measurement techniques differ in the variables they measure and in the conditions of measurement. The variable measured may be either actual purchases or preferences and intentions. Since the ultimate goal of research is to predict customers' actual purchases, research based on actual purchase data is generally more reliable than research based on preferences and intentions. Unfortunately, collecting and analyzing actual-purchase data costs more, requires much more time, and is entirely impossible for products that are not yet fully developed and ready for sale. Consequently, most research on price sensitivity infers purchase behavior from questions potential customers answer about their preferences and intentions.

Pricing research studies range from those that are completely uncontrolled to those in which the experimenter controls almost completely the alternative products, their prices, and the information that the customer receives. Although research techniques that permit a high degree of experimental control are more costly than uncontrolled research, the added cost is usually worth it. Uncontrolled data on actual purchases are plagued by too little variation in prices and too many variables changing at once. Uncontrolled data on preferences and intentions are biased by people's untruthful responses and by their inability to recall competitive prices. In contrast, controlled in-store experiments and sophisticated laboratory purchase experiments often predict actual price sensitivity well. Even experiments using preferences and intentions seem to warrant confidence when they are highly controlled. In particular, tradeoff analysis is proving highly useful in predicting at least that portion of price sensitivity determined by the unique-value effect.

Regardless of the technique used to measure price sensitivity, it is important that managers not allow the estimate to become a substitute for managerial judgment. The low accuracy of many numerical estimates makes blind reliance on them very risky. They should always be compared with a manager's own expectations, based on his or her more general knowledge of buyers and their purchase motivations. When inconsistencies occur, the manager should reexamine both the measurement technique and the adequacy of his or her understanding of buyers. The quality of numerical estimates depends in large part on the quality of managerial judgment that guides the estimation process. Managers who know their buyers can get substantially better estimates of price sensitivity when they use that knowledge (1) to select a sample of consumers that accurately represents the product's market, (2) to identify and explain extraneous changes in sales that might camouflage an effect, (3) to provide information to sort out the effects of price from other variables that tend to change with it, (4) to identify an appropriate equation or experimental structure, and (5) to properly describe the product for survey research.

The appropriate technique for numerically estimating price sensitivity depends on the product's stage of development. When a product is still in the concept or prototype stage, research measuring preferences or intentions is the only option. Trade-off analysis is especially useful at this stage because it can identify the value of individual product attributes, thus helping to decide which combination of attributes will enable the firm to price the product most profitably. When a product is ready for the market, in-store or laboratory purchase experiments are more appropriate because they more realistically simulate the actual purchase environment. After a product has been on the market for a while, actual purchase data can be an inexpensive source of estimates, provided that management monitors sales frequently and makes some price changes independently of changes in other marketing variables. Even when actual purchase data cannot provide conclusive answers, they can suggest relationships that can then be measured more reliably with other techniques.

NOTES

1. A. C. Neilsen conducts a bimonthly product audit of retail sales and retailer inventories for many types of frequently purchased products, including foods, household products, health and beauty aids, tobacco products, photo-

graphic products, writing instruments, small electrical appliances, and some automotive products. The Neilsen audit is based on a probability sample of all types of stores in which the product might be sold.

2. Recent advances in Bayesian statistics now enable a researcher to quantify a manager's prior beliefs and to reestimate equations using them. Unfortunately, such a formal marriage of prior belief and data is complicated, requiring the special skills of researchers well trained in statistics. For the clearest explanation for practical application of Bayesian techniques, see Edward E. Leamer, *Specification Searches: Adhoc Inferences with Nonexperimental Data* (New York: Wiley, 1978).

3. Actually, the researcher observes only the price that the consumer reports having paid. There is some risk of erroneous reporting, which weakens the data but does not bias it. Fortunately, this problem is being solved by technologies that enable consumers to avoid the task of reporting.

4. See Ronald E. Frank and William Massy, "Market Segmentation and the Effectiveness of a Brand's Dealing Policies," *Journal of Business*, 38 (April 1965), 186–200; Terry Elrod and Russell S. Winer, "An Empirical Evaluation of Aggregation Approaches for Developing Market Segments," *Journal of Marketing*, 46 (Fall 1982), 65–74.

5. The companies are Information Resources Inc. (headquarters in Chicago) and Burke Marketing Research (headquarters in Cincinnati, Ohio).

6. Lester G. Telser, "The Demand for Branded Goods as Estimated from Consumer Panel Data," *Review of Economics and Statistics*, 4 (August 1962), 300–24; Avijit Ghosh, Scott A. Neslin, and Robert W. Shoemaker, "Are There Associations Between Price Elasticity and Brand Characteristics?" *1983 AMA Educators' Conference Proceedings* (Chicago, American Marketing Association, 1983); Frank and Massy, "Market Segmentation," pp. 186–200; Elrod and Winer, "An Empirical Evaluation of Aggregation Approaches," pp. 65–74.

7. See K. Wisniewski and R. C. Blattberg, "Response Function Estimation Using UPC Scanner Data," in *Advances and Practices of Marketing Science, 1983*, ed. F. Zufryden, pp. 300–11; and Kenneth Wisniewski, "Analytical Approaches to Demand Estimation," *1983 Proceedings of the Business and Economic Statistics Section, American Statistical Association* (Toronto: ASA, 1983), pp. 13–22.

8. In practice, of course, there are always some external factors that will affect only one store's sales, undermining the effectiveness of the control. For example, the control store may run out of a competing brand. One can reduce the distorting effect of such factors by increasing the number of both experimental and control stores, but at a corresponding increase in cost.

9. For guidance in the proper design of either a field or laboratory experiment, see Thomas Cook and Donald T. Campbell, "The Design and Conduct of Quasi-Experimental and True Experiments in Field Settings," in *Handbook of Industrial and Organizational Psychology*, ed. Marvin Dunnette (Chicago: Rand McNally, 1976), pp. 223–35.

10. William Applebaum and Richard Spears, "Controlled Experimentation in Marketing Research," *Journal of Marketing*, 14 (January 1950), 505–17; Edward Hawkins, "Methods of Estimating Demand," *Journal of Marketing*, 21 (April 1957), 430–34; William D. Barclay, "Factorial Design in a Pricing Experiment,"

Journal of Marketing Research, 6 (November 1969), 427–29; Sidney Bennet and J. B. Wilkinson, "Price-Quantity Relationship and Price Elasticity Under In-store Experimentation," *Journal of Business Research*, 2 (January 1974), 27–38; Gerald Eskin, "A Case for Test Marketing Experiments," *Journal of Advertising Research*, 15 (April 1975), 27–33; Gerald Eskin and Penny Baron, "Effect of Price and Advertising in Test Market Experiments," *Journal of Marketing Research*, 14 (November 1977), 499–508.

11. Barclay, "Factorial Design in a Pricing Experiment," p. 428.

12. Paul Solman and Thomas Friedman, *Life and Death in the Corporate Battlefield* (New York: Simon and Schuster, 1982), p. 24.

13. Each company develops its own adjustment factors, which are closely guarded trade secrets.

14. One might well argue that buy-response surveys should be included with the experimentally controlled studies since the researcher does exercise control over the price asked. That observation is correct. The reason that buy-response questioning is better than direct questioning is precisely because the researcher introduces a bit of control. Still, the amount of control that the researcher can exercise in these studies is slight. No attempt is made to control the respondents' perception of competitive prices, exposure to promotion, or demographics.

15. Henry Assael, *Consumer Behavior and Marketing Action*, 2nd ed. (Boston, Massachusetts: Kent Publishing, 1983).

16. Three sources providing excellent examples of attribute-based positioning techniques are: David A. Aaker and J. Gary Shansby, "Positioning Your Product," *Business Horizons* (May–June 1983), pp. 56–62; John A. Martilla and John C. James, "Importance Performance Analysis," *Journal of Marketing* (January 1977), pp. 77–79; Alvin C. Burns, "Generating Marketing Strategy Priorities Based on Relative Competitive Position," *The Journal of Consumer Marketing*, 3, no. 4 (Fall 1986) pp. 49–56.

17. D. Frank Jones, "A Survey Technique to Measure Demand Under Various Pricing Strategies," *Journal of Marketing*, 39 (July 1975), 75–77.

18. John R. Nevin, "Laboratory Experiments for Estimating Consumer Demand," *Journal of Marketing Research*, 11 (August 1974), 261–68.

19. Roy G. Stout, "Developing Data to Estimate Price-Quantity Relationships," *Journal of Marketing*, 33 (April 1969), 34–36; Andre Gabor, Clive W. J. Granger, and Anthony P. Sowter, "Real and Hypothetical Shop Situations in Market Research," *Journal of Marketing Research*, 7 (August 1970), 355–59.

20. The first article on trade-off analysis to appear in the marketing literature was Paul E. Green and Vithala R. Rao, "Conjoint Measurement for Quantifying Judgemental Data," *Journal of Marketing Research*, 8 (August 1971), 355–63. For a nontechnical discussion of applications specifically to pricing, see Patrick J. Robinson, "Applications of Conjoint Analysis to Pricing Problems," in *Market Measurement and Analysis*, ed. David B. Montgomery and Dick R. Wittink (Cambridge, Mass.: Marketing Science Institute, 1980), pp. 183–205.

21. The following articles describe data manipulation procedures for conjoint analysis: J. B. Kruskal, "Analysis of Factorial Experiments by Estimating

Monotone Transformations of the Data," *Journal of the Royal Statistical Society,* Series B (1965), pp. 251–63; Dove Peckelman and Subrata Sen, "Regression Versus Interpolation in Additive Conjoint Measurement," *1976 Association for Consumer Research Proceedings* (ACR, 1976), pp. 29–34; Phillip Cattin and Dick Wittink, "Further Beyond Conjoint Measurement: Toward Comparison of Methods," *1976 Association for Consumer Research Proceedings* (ARC, 1976), pp. 41–45.

22. Franklin Acito, "An Investigation of Some Data Collection Issues in Conjoint Measurement," in *1977 Proceedings American Marketing Association,* ed. B. A. Greenberg and D. N. Bellenger (Chicago: AMA, 1977), pp. 82–85; James McCullough and Roger Best, "Conjoint Measurement: Temporal Stability and Structural Reliability," *Journal of Marketing Research,* 16 (February 1979), 26–31; Madhav N. Segal, "Reliability of Conjoint Analysis: Contrasting Data Collection Procedure," *Journal of Marketing Research,* 19 (February 1982), 139–43.

23. McCullough and Best, "Conjoint Measurement," pp. 26–31.

24. Bobby J. Calder, "Focus Groups and the Nature of Qualitative Marketing Research," *Journal of Marketing Research,* 14 (August 1977), 353–64.

25. Johny K. Johansson and Ikujiro Nonaka, "Market Research the Japanese Way," *Harvard Business Review* (May/June, 1987).

26. The *Census of Manufacturers* is a publication of the U.S. Department of Commerce. For other federal sources, see the Commerce Department publication entitled *A Guide to Federal Data Sources on Manufacturing.* The "Survey of Industrial Buying Power" is published annually as an issue of *Sales and Marketing Management* magazine. Other useful sources of information about the demographics and motivations of buying firms can be obtained from the buying firms' trade associations (for example, Rubber Manufacturers Association, National Machine Tool Builders Association) and from privately operated industrial directory and research companies (for example, Predicasts, Inc., Dun & Bradstreet, Standard & Poors).

27. For the reader trained in classical statistics, these suggestions for adjusting the data with managerial judgment may seem unscientific. But it is important to keep in mind that the purpose of numerical measurement of price sensitivity is to derive useful estimates, not to objectively test a theory. If managers have strongly held beliefs, in light of which the historical record of sales could yield much better estimates, it is simply wasteful to ignore those beliefs simply because they may not be objective. See Edward E. Leamer, "Let's Take the Con out of Econometrics," *American Economic Review,* 73 (March 1983), 31–43.

THE LAW AND ETHICS

CHAPTER

14

DETERMINING THE CONSTRAINTS ON PRICING

This chapter is coauthored by Neil E. Graham, J.D., and Professor William E. Kovacic, J.D., of the George Mason University School of Law with Dr. Thomas Nagle.

When making pricing decisions, the strategist must consider not only what is profitable, but also what is legal and ethical.

Since 1890, the federal government has been committed to maintaining price competition through antitrust law. Three major acts of Congress, several modifications of those acts, and countless judicial decisions have shaped policies through which the government punishes firms, and sometimes individuals, who engage in pricing behavior it finds anticompetitive. Unfortunately, some of those policies are highly ambiguous; others are sometimes contradictory. All of them are subject to changes in judicial interpretation that can be applied retroactively.

Given the ambiguity in the law, developing pricing strategies without running afoul of the law is often a frustrating exercise in risk management. Beyond issues of legality, managers must also consider when pricing decisions are consistent with ethical norms. Although these decisions differ across individuals and social contexts, it is important for managers to resolve them in their minds before ethically ambiguous situations arise. This chapter offers a topology for exploring ethical issues as they relate to pricing and for implementing pricing strategies consistent with those standards.

THE LEGAL SANCTIONS

What does a firm risk if its pricing strategy violates the law? The most visible risk is a legal suit brought by the U.S. Department of Justice. Under the antitrust laws, the Justice Department as well as the Federal Trade

Commission (FTC) can petition a court to radically change the way a firm does business. For example, the government's attorneys sometimes ask that a firm be divided into separate parts, that it be forced to give competitors the right to use its patents, or that it be ordered to refrain from marketing tactics that its competitors may still continue to use. The chance, however, that the Justice Department will actually bring a suit against any particular firm is really quite small. The Antitrust Division has limited resources and selects cases largely for their value in establishing new legal precedents.

Although a few highly visible cases result in dismemberment or radical restrictions of the convicted firm, such severe remedies are extremely rare. Fines are more common. Over the past decade, Congress has raised the maximum Sherman Act fine for corporations to $10 million, and for individuals to $350,000.[1] Even larger fines may be imposed under an alternative statutory scheme established by Congress enabling the government to collect antitrust damages equal to double the harm suffered by victims of illegal conduct or double the gain realized by the defendant (the "double loss/double gain" provision).[2] Over the past decade Congress has also increased the maximum prison term to three years for individuals convicted of violating the Sherman Act. Fines and prison sentences may be imposed concurrently. Moreover, since 1987, all sentencing must be in accordance with guidelines established by the U.S. Sentencing Commission.[3] The base-level offense corresponds to a minimum recommended sentence of four to ten months' imprisonment.

Under these enhanced and overlapping statutory regimes, courts have imposed substantial fines and prison sentences.[4] The expansion of federal efforts to detect and prosecute "hard-core" offenses such as price-fixing has increased the probability that a case will be brought, and it is now much more likely that convicted antitrust defendants will serve time in prison.[5]

An even more serious threat posed by the antitrust laws stems not from federal suits but from private antitrust suits brought by a company's competitors or customers. Such cases are not only frequent but are also the most expensive to lose. In private antitrust suits, the plaintiff sues the defendant for actual damages plus attorney's fees. Then if the plaintiff wins, the law calls for tripling the actual amount of damages to determine what the defendant must pay. Since multimillion-dollar damage suits are the rule, and claims in the hundreds of millions are not uncommon, losing a private antitrust suit can seriously weaken and sometimes destroy a defendant company's financial condition.

A company can usually avoid liability by not using the types of pricing practices that the courts have found illegal in the past. However, a firm can nevertheless be forced to pay triple damages for having used a pricing practice that no one realized was illegal at the time. In general, firms can reduce these damages by maintaining rigorous internal antitrust compliance programs.

In addition to court suits, pricing practices are also subject to administrative review by the FTC. Such reviews are very much like legal proceedings. Their purpose, however, is not to punish past wrongdoing, but to make new law. For the most part, the FTC's remedies consist of commanding firms to discontinue specific practices. The FTC begins by investigating a suspicious practice. If that investigation reveals potential illegality, the FTC issues a complaint against the offending firm or firms, subpoenas records, calls witnesses, and holds a hearing. After the hearing, the five FTC commissioners vote on whether to issue an order to cease and desist from engaging in the questionable practice. That order may apply only to the individual firm against whom the complaint was filed, or it may apply generally to all firms engaging in the practice. The affected firms have sixty days to appeal the order to the U.S. Court of Appeals. If they do not appeal, or if they lose the appeal, the order becomes law. Violations are thereafter subject to fines of $10,000 per violation per day.

Although the FTC cannot itself impose punishments, the risk of such a proceeding should not be taken lightly. Information revealed in the hearing may lead the Justice Department, a competitor, or a customer to file an antitrust suit. The public announcement of a complaint alone can tarnish a firm's reputation, even if no order is issued. Moreover, the FTC's mandate to issue orders is very broad. It can order a firm to cease and desist from any business practice that it deems unfair, even though that practice would not be deemed anticompetitive in court.[6] Consequently, its power to restrain the ways a firm can conduct its business in the future is quite broad.

In recent years, state antitrust enforcement has assumed increasing importance.[7] The Sherman Act was passed when twenty-six states already had some form of antitrust prohibition, and Congress expressly intended federal enforcement to supplement and not supplant state efforts. For many years the states ceded leadership to the federal government. During the 1970s, however, following the states' solid successes in generating revenues from massive treble-damage class actions, state legislatures fortified the powers of their attorneys general to sue on behalf of people residing within their states. State attorneys general have used these enhanced powers to great effect.

To coordinate the growing enforcement efforts of state attorneys general across the country, the National Association of Attorneys General (NAAG) established a task force in 1983. Among other initiatives, the task force has been notably successful in a number of vertical price-fixing cases involving the retail electronics industry. In one case, after receiving complaints by retailers of Minolta cameras who had been terminated for failing to adhere to minimum retail prices, thirty-seven states brought suit on behalf of their consumer citizens against Minolta and its dealers, charging that they had conspired to fix minimum prices on Minolta cameras. A settlement was eventually reached whereby each purchaser could recover either $8 or $15 depending on the camera purchased. Nearly 70,000 consumers received refund checks, totaling nearly $1 million.[8] This and similar successes have ensured that the states will continue to be a significant "third leg" (along with the Justice Department and the FTC) in the antitrust enforcement triad.

Clearly, the legal risks in pricing are not trivial. When formulating strategy, the marketing manager would do well to keep them in mind. The remainder of this chapter explains, to the extent possible given the antitrust laws' ambiguities, what is and is not legal pricing behavior.[9] We focus first on the legislated law (the law as it is written) and then on the case law (the law as the courts interpret it). The reader should be forewarned, however, that new precedents are constantly expanding the law in some areas and narrowing its scope in others. Only an attorney who specializes in this area can accurately estimate the current probability that a particular pricing practice might be declared illegal, and the only final authority is the Supreme Court, which evaluates the legality of strategies only after the fact.

PRICING AND THE LAW: A BRIEF HISTORY

In the latter half of the nineteenth century, U.S. industry underwent a radical transformation. The rapid improvement in the U.S. transportation system converted the country from hundreds of small isolated markets with little competition among them into an integrated, national marketplace. Concurrently, technological innovations substantially increased economies of scale in major industries. As a result, big business began to form. In the process, it threatened the survival of many small, regional competitors and raised suspicions among an individualistic people who feared faceless concentrations of power. Indeed, as many smaller firms went bankrupt and others merged, monopolies or trusts came to dominate the markets for rail transportation, fuel oil, steel, sugar, matches, whiskey, and many other essentials of the day.

The trusts' key to growth and power was not necessarily limited to selling better products at lower prices. They sometimes used questionable tactics against both competitors and customers to maintain their dominant positions. When depressions struck in the mid-1870s and the 1880s, many people, particularly farmers, blamed the ensuing problems on the trusts, claiming that they extracted price concessions for what they bought while maintaining prices for what they sold. In 1888, one observer described the mood as one where "the public mind had begun to assume a state of apprehension, almost amounting to alarm, regarding the evil economic and social tendencies of these organizations. The social atmosphere seems to be surcharged with an indefinite, but almost inexpressible fear of trusts."[10]

Both political parties in the election of 1888 called for national legislation to limit the trusts. In 1890, Congress passed, and President Harrison signed, the first national antitrust law, the Sherman Act. This act is still the cornerstone of U.S. antitrust policy. As subsequently amended, the act declares that

Section I

Every contract, combination . . ., or conspiracy, in restraint of trade or commerce . . . is hereby declared to be illegal.

Section II

Every person who shall monopolize, or attempt to monopolize, or combine or conspire with any other person or persons to monopolize, any part of the trade or commerce of the several states, or with foreign nations,[11] shall be guilty of a felony. . . .

The Sherman Act was initially more a statement of political intent, designed to mollify public discontent, than a law. Congress surely did not mean that "every contract . . . in restraint of trade . . . is . . . illegal," since restraint is precisely the purpose of every contract. What Congress did mean it left for the courts to decide, and in the early years the courts decided that the law meant very little.[12] They ruled in favor of the defendents in six of the first seven cases that the Justice Department prosecuted under the Sherman Act.

The tide turned in 1901 when Theodore Roosevelt, a fiery critic of the trusts, became President. He convinced Congress to establish a separate antitrust division in the Justice Department and to provide additional funds for antitrust enforcement. He also appointed an attorney general who, unlike his predecessors, was enthusiastic about antitrust enforcement. In 1904, the federal government won its first big case, the *United States* v. *Northern Securities*, which stopped a merger designed to reduce price competition between two competing railroads.[13] In 1911, the government won major cases against both the Standard Oil and the tobacco trusts, substantially restricting their business practices.[14] These rulings proved that, in spite of its vagueness, the Sherman Act was not without teeth.

Supporters of antitrust were still not satisfied with the narrow interpretations of the act embodied in many of the courts' rulings. For example, in the *Standard Oil* case, the court ruled that the government would have to prove actual anticompetitive effects of a business practice in order to establish a Sherman Act violation, but by the time those effects could be proven, the damage would have been done. Moreover, the courts were reluctant to label as a violation any practice that historically had been widely used in an industry. As a result, Congress began work on two additional pieces of legislation designed to further restrain business practices of which it disapproved, especially pricing practices.

The first measure, the Federal Trade Commission Act (FTC Act), became law in September 1914. Essentially its intent was to establish a commission that would supply substance for the sentiments expressed in the Sherman Act. Section 5 of the FTC Act reads (in part): "The Commission is hereby empowered and directed to prevent persons, partnerships, or corporations . . . from using unfair methods of competition in commerce."

The legislative history of the act indicates, "(1) that the phrase 'unfair methods of competition' was deliberately left vague and open-ended, to depend on the Federal Trade Commission interpretation, and (2) that the new agency was to control monopolistic and other anticompetitive practices wherever they arose and whether full-blown or incipient."[15] The FTC Act circumvented the requirement under the Sherman Act to prove to a court that a practice had, in fact, already caused anticompetitive effects. The FTC could ban the use of any business practice simply because of suspicion that it was an unfair way to compete that might produce anticompetitive effects if continued.

The other antitrust law that Congress passed in 1914 was the Clayton Act. Unlike the other acts, it forbids specific business practices. Two sections restrict pricing practices. Section 2 forbids price discrimination under certain circumstances. Section 3 limits tying and bundling contracts that require buyers to purchase separate products from the same seller. In both cases, however, there is still room for interpretation, since the prohibitions apply only when the practices in question are found "to substantially lessen competition."

The Clayton Act was substantially strengthened in 1936 by the Robinson-Patman Act. In the 1930s, large chain stores, particularly grocery chains, began to displace the traditional independent retailers by offering consumers lower prices. The independents looked to Congress for some relief from the competition, claiming that the chains' lower retail prices stemmed from their ability to wrest lower wholesale prices from manufacturers.[16] In response, Congress passed the Robinson-Patman Act, which did the following in its major provisions:

- Deleted the exemption, which existed in the original Clayton Act, that allowed firms to price discriminate among buyers who purchased different quantities of a good
- Forbade price rebates to selected buyers in the form of fees for brokerage, handling, processing, or any other services when those same fees were not offered to all buyers equally
- Made it illegal for buyers (that is, the large chains) to solicit lower prices from manufacturers if those prices would be discriminatory under the amended Clayton Act

These laws are the three main pillars of antitrust enforcement. They have been amended a number of times by later acts. Some amendments have established exemptions of varying scope for special interest groups, such as farm cooperatives, insurance companies, and labor unions. In 1918, the Webb-Pomerene Act exempted export sales from Sherman Act restrictions on price-fixing. Other amendments strengthened the government's enforcement powers. The Wheeler-Lea Act of 1938 expanded the FTC's power to include control over unfair or deceptive acts or practices as well as the original unfair methods of competition. It also gave the FTC the explicit right to regulate advertising. The Trans-Alaska Oil Pipeline Act of 1973 contained a section (totally unrelated to the act's title) that empowered the FTC to prosecute firms under the antitrust laws and to seek legal injunctions halting business practices. If one were to read all the laws and all the amendments carefully, one would find them a very poor guide to the legality of pricing or any other business practices. For such a guide, one must examine the rulings of the courts and the FTC to understand how they interpret the laws.

THE CASE LAW

Judicial rulings in antitrust cases can establish two different types of precedents. When a court finds a business practice so inherently anticompetitive that no circumstances could ever justify it, it will declare the practice per se illegal. Thereafter, that court and all lower courts will (or should) refuse to consider any evidence except that relating to whether or not the defendant used the practice. If it was used, the defendant is guilty regardless of the circumstances. On the other hand, the court may declare that it cannot determine the legality of a practice without applying the *rule of reason*. In doing so, the court is announcing that it, and all lower courts, will (or should) consider the circumstances surrounding a practice before making a judgment about its legality in the case of any particular defendant. The surrounding circumstances that the court will consider, however, are only those relating to the competitive effects of the practice. With this distinction in mind, let us now examine the case law to determine how the courts are likely to rule on the legality of specific pricing practices that a firm might be accused of misusing.

Explicit agreements

The courts have been largely consistent in condemning agreements among firms that set the same price or that price according to the same formula. Such price-fixing has been regarded as per se illegal since the very first pricing case decided by the Supreme Court under the Sherman Act.[17] In that case, a group of railroads argued that their formation of an association to maintain railroad rates was not illegal because the rates set were reasonable. The majority rejected that idea out of hand, and later cases have generally upheld the per se illegality of price-fixing agreements.

The ultimate statement of this per se doctrine was delivered in 1940 in the Socony-Vacuum Oil Case.[18] Here the Court firmly rejected the argument that the agreement in question was justified because it was both reasonable and necessary for the health of the industry. To eliminate the cutthroat pricing that resulted from an oil glut during the Depression, the major oil companies agreed to buy the excess production of the small producers, who might have been most tempted to price opportunistically. Although prices were not directly fixed, the effect of this agreement among the majors was to limit price competition. In its decision, the Supreme Court stated forcefully,

> Ruinous competition, financial disaster, evils of price cutting, and the like appear throughout our history as ostensible justifications for price fixing. . . . [However,] Congress has not left with us the determination of whether or not particular price-fixing schemes are wise or unwise, healthy or destructive.

Thus, the argument that the agreement was strictly defensive and necessary for the health of the industry was deemed irrelevant.[19] Moreover, the Court went on to say that the failure of some firms to implement terms of the agreement, the success or failure of the agreement to control prices, and the amount of commerce actually affected were also irrelevant. The crime is the agreement, not the results.

Fortunately, since the late 1970s courts have shown some reluctance to apply the per se standard to restraints that appear to have offsetting procompetitive benefits. Aware that a hasty per se characterization may chill potentially procompetitive conduct, courts now make an initial cost-benefit analysis before applying the per se rule.

A turning point in this trend away from summary classification came with the *Broadcast Music, Inc. (BMI)* case.[20] In *BMI,* 4,000 authors and composers were granted nonexclusive rights to a trade association to license their musical compositions for a fee. Licensees were required to take a full license to an artist's entire repertoire, with fees based on the licensee's advertising revenues. One licensee, Columbia Broadcasting System, challenged the blanket licensing arrangement as illegal price-fixing. Conceding that a price-fixing agreement was "literally" at stake, the Court nevertheless refused to apply a quick per se characterization, stressing that the arrangement should first be examined to determine whether it was efficient. The Court found that the arrangement contained offsetting efficiencies that argued against application of a per se standard. The arrangement promoted the orderly operation of the market by reducing transaction costs among contracting parties. With a single blanket license covering all members of the trade association, a buyer of musical works would only have to negotiate with one entity for the right to use all products represented by the licensor rather than license with each composer separately. The arrangement also provided that individual copyright owners were free to sell compositions outside of the blanket license. Thus supply and output were not restricted.[21]

An overview of the Supreme Court's price-fixing jurisprudence from *Standard Oil* to *Socony* might yield the following principle: Agreements among competitors that raise, lower, or stabilize prices are per se unlawful, except when the restraint is truly ancillary to a procompetitive integration of the parties' economic activities, and except when cooperation is required to produce procompetitive efficiencies—such as synergies and economies of scale resulting from the pooling of new resources or from the creation of a new product—that offset the imposed restraints because of a reduction in transaction costs. The existence of integrative efficiencies distinguishes legitimate cooperation from naked cartel behavior among competitors and protects them from summary per se analysis.

The decline of the summary per se characterization of traditional price-fixing agreements has also affected other types of arrangements traditionally placed in the per se category. Historically, agreements among actual or potential competitors to divide or allocate markets, whether part of a price-fixing scheme or not, were held to be per se unlawful. Today, however, some lower courts have declined to apply the per se rule to horizontal market and customer allocations that are ancillary to a procompetitive intergation of the parties' economic activities.[22] Although it is still per se illegal to agree to share markets by type of customer, quota, or technological application, or to boycott or blacklist a competitor if the effect is to restrict that competitor's ability to compete, today only a narrow window remains through which the court will apply its per se presumption of illegality to concerted refusals to deal. Otherwise, the rule of reason is the touchstone of analysis.[23]

Resale Price Maintenance   Agreements between manufacturers and their distributors to set minimum resale prices have been per se unlawful since the *Dr. Miles* decision in 1911.[24] In that case, the Court reasoned that dealers should be free to set prices for goods that they own and that a restriction on competition imposed by a manufacturer in the distribution of its goods (a vertical restraint) is equivalent to a cartel among the distributors (a horizontal restraint), which is per se illegal under the Sherman Act.

Support for resale price maintenance (RPM) has waxed and waned over the years as various political constituencies have persuaded Congress to enact their economic preferences into law. When large supermarket chains began to undercut the prices of small retailers in the 1930s, Congress responded to the protests from the small "mom and pop" stores by amending the Sherman Act in 1937 to permit resale price maintenance in any state that condoned the practice.[25] The pendulum swung again in 1976, however, when, under pressure from consumer groups, Congress repealed the 1937 amendment. The most recent pendulum swing occurred during the first Reagan Administration, when the Justice Department urged the repeal of the Dr. Miles rule in the *Monsanto* case,[26] arguing that price maintenance often has procompetitive benefits that should exempt it from per se condemnation.

Although the per se status of RPM has in recent years been the subject of intense scrutiny, the Court has repeatedly reaffirmed that RPM is a per se violation of the Sherman Act.[27] Recent cases focus not on the reasonableness of the restraint but on the decisive question of classification: Is the restraint unilateral (permitted) or concerted (unlawful)? What are the proper boundaries of the per se category?

When there is no concerted action, there is no violation. Independent action by a manufacturer has long been recognized as immune from liability.[28] Because a manufacturer is free to establish unilaterally the prices at which it sells its products, courts have upheld consignment arrangements.[29] A manufacturer is also allowed to specify the services that distributors must provide in order to sell its product. By choosing only distributors who provide a high level of service, a manufacturer may indirectly limit price discounting.[30] And manufacturers may announce "suggested" resale prices and refuse to deal with retailers who do not adhere to those prices.[31]

But when a manufacturer terminates a distributor for price discounting after receiving complaints from another distributor, the courts have wrestled with the difficult question of when such conduct crosses the line into the impermissible "concerted" category. Does the communication between a disgruntled distributor and manufacturer become an unlawful "agreement" to fix prices? In *Business Electronics Corp.*,[32] the plaintiff-dealer was terminated by Sharp after it had repeatedly sold at prices below list and after a competing dealer had threatened to drop Sharp products. The complaining dealer claimed that it was less concerned about its competitor's price discounting than it was about the "free riding" on its own product promotion efforts.[33] The Court held that the per se label must be reserved for a very narrow class of cases. An agreement between a manufacturer and a distributor to terminate another distributor because of the latter's pricing practices, without any understanding as to the prices that will be charged by the remaining distributor or distributors, might constitute concerted action, but could not be characterized as concerted action to fix resale prices within the meaning of the per se rule, the court held. "[A] vertical restraint is not illegal per se unless it includes some agreement on price or price levels."[34]

Business Electronics leaves the per se status of resale price maintenance only nominally intact and decreases the likelihood that a terminated dealer can mount a successful attack against a manufacturer.[35] The Supreme Court is now skeptical that vertical agreements can be used to foster collusion among manufacturers or among retailers. And even if a terminated dealer is able to prove the existence of an agreement on price, the problem of showing antitrust injury may become an additional hurdle.[36]

Recent cases have also witnessed inroads on the application of the per se rule to maximum resale price maintenance. Although maximum RPM is per se unlawful,[37] the Supreme Court in 1990 accepted the view that a plaintiff cannot have antitrust injury from maximum resale price maintenance by a competitor and its supplier in the absence of predatory pricing.[38]

Some Permitted Agreements   In a few special cases, the courts do permit some types of explicit agreements that fix prices. In particular, the courts have allowed restrictions to maintain price consistency in organized markets. In *Chicago Board of Trade* v. *United States*, the Justice Department challenged a Board of Trade rule that members purchase or sell all commodities contracts at the last closing price during hours when the Board was closed. The Supreme Court threw out the case, agreeing with the defense's contention that the rule was in no way intended to prevent competition or to control price, but simply to maintain an orderly market.[39] As the *BMI* case illustrates, courts will also permit explicit price-fixing agreements when joint activity or close interdependence among competitors is required before a product can be marketed at all or when cooperation lowers transaction costs sufficiently to offset the reduction in output caused by the restraint.

Patent owners may also legally control the prices charged by their licensees within certain limits. In establishing what is known as the *G. E. Doctrine*, the Supreme Court stated,

> When the patentee licenses another to make and vend and retains the right to continue to make and vend on his own account, the price at which his license will sell will necessarily affect the price at which he can sell his own patented goods. It would seem entirely reasonable that he should say to the licensee, "Yes, you may make and sell articles under my patent but not so as to destroy the profit that I wish to obtain by making them and selling them myself."[40]

The Department of Justice has thus far failed in its stated goal of reversing the G. E. Doctrine, but it has managed to restrict its application. If a company licenses a patented machine, it may not set the price of the unpatented product of that machine, even if the machine has no other use except to make that product.[41] Furthermore, companies that own complementary patents that they cross-license to one another cannot fix prices for one another or for their licensees. The same applies if patent holders pool or combine patents in a joint venture.[42] Finally, the patent holder must be careful not "to issue substantially identical licenses to all members of the industry under the terms of which the industry is completely regimented, the production of competitive unpatented products suppressed, a class of distributors is squeezed out, and prices of unpatented products stabilized."[43]

Nonexplicit agreements

The Justice Department is understandably pleased when it uncovers explicit agreements in restraint of competition, because, except for the few special cases previously discussed, these are illegal per se. The Justice Department can thus avoid what the courts have labeled "the necessity for an incredibly complicated and prolonged economic investigation into the entire history of the industry . . . in an effort to determine at large whether a particular restraint has been unreasonable—an inquiry so often fruitless when undertaken."[44] Understandably, few businesspeople are foolish enough to make explicit agreements, or at least to leave evidence of them.[45] Instead, "competitors have an incentive to engage in all of the preliminary steps required to coordinate their pricing, but to stop just short of 'agreeing' on what to charge."[46]

At what point does such a nonexplicit understanding become an illegal agreement? Allegations of concerted action by competitors are often based on a pattern of uniform business conduct which courts refer to as *conscious parallelism*. The courts have held that parallel behavior alone is insufficient to prove conspiracy.[47] Other facts and circumstances, known as *plus factors*, must be combined with evidence of conscious parallelism to support an inference of concerted action.[48]

The most important plus factors are those that tend to show that business conduct would be in the parties' self-interest only if all acted in the same way (a rational motive test). This type of evidence has included artificial standardization of products, price increases in times of surplus, or pretextual reasons to explain behavior. However, when a defendant has legitimate business reasons for engaging independently in the challenged conduct, a court will require more direct evidence before inferring concerted action.[49]

Other important plus factors include evidence showing that the defendants had an opportunity to collude. Evidence of correspondence or secret meetings, especially when quickly followed by simultaneous, identical actions on the part of the alleged conspirators, is highly suggestive circumstantial evidence of agreement, at least when defendants are unable to offer plausible legitimate business justifications for their communications. Market phenomena that cannot be explained rationally except as the product of concerted action (for example, price uniformity over a long period of time not caused by a rise in the cost of a common input) have been held to be another plus factor.[50]

Courts also examine industry structure. Collusion is thought to be unlikely in settings in which there is a large number of sellers, entry barriers are low, the product is homogeneous, the buyer community is composed of a small number of sophisticated purchasers, and transactions are infrequent (the purchase of a new car as opposed to a last-minute purchase at the checkout counter of a supermarket).[51] A final plus factor is industry performance. The stability of market shares over time and high profit margins suggest industrywide tacit collusion.[52]

The watershed case setting standards for determining when parallel conduct crosses over into prohibited "agreement" is the *Matsushita* decision.[53] In *Matsushita*, the alleged conspiracy consisted of a scheme by Japanese suppliers of electronics equipment collectively to price below cost in the United States, to drive U.S. firms from the market, and later to raise prices to monopoly levels (a classic predatory pricing scheme).

The Court held that the evidence of conspiracy was insufficient for the case to go to the jury. Emphasizing that mistaken inferences of conspiracy could injure consumers by deterring firms from offering low prices— the very object the antitrust laws are meant to protect—the Court held that when a plaintiff relies on circumstantial evidence to establish concerted action, he or she must present evidence that "tends to exclude the possibility" that the alleged conspirators acted independently. . . . Conduct as consistent with permissible competition as with illegal conspiracy does not, standing alone, support an inference of antitrust conspiracy."

Matsushita is a defendant's decision. It instructs courts to dismiss claims that rest upon ambiguous, circumstantial evidence or that lack "economic rationality."[54] The full effect of the decision, however, will depend heavily on the economic preferences of the lower court judges who interpret it.[55]

The FTC has tried to extend the reach of the antitrust laws to cover parallel pricing conduct that falls short of collusion but that encourages oligopolistic practices by declaring such conduct an unfair method of competition under the FTC Act. Courts have decisively resisted this expansionary effort. In *Ethyl*,[56] the FTC charged that Du Pont, Ethyl, and two other producers of lead antiknock gasoline additives had engaged in unfair methods of competition by using prior announcements of price changes and other methods of signaling pricing intentions, even though there was no evidence of collusion or agreement. The U.S. Court of Appeals reversed the FTC's decision, finding that

> . . . Before business conduct in an oligopolistic industry may be labeled "unfair," . . . a minimum standard demands that, absent a tacit agreement, at least some indicia of oppressiveness must exist, such as (1) evidence of anticompetitive intent or purpose . . . or (2) the absence of an independent legitimate business reason for its conduct.[57]

The Court noted that the latter requirement is comparable to the need to identify plus factors before conscious parallelism is found conspiratorial in violation of the Sherman Act.[58] The court further observed that if the gas

producers had been unable to come forward with some independent business justification for their challenged practices, the FTC might have succeeded in its claim that the practices were unfair methods of competition.
But the Court found overwhelming evidence that each producer "adopted
its practice for legitimate business reasons."[59]

In general, parallel pricing and the tactics that maintain it are legally
acceptable if they are based on an independent business justification.
Although the FTC Act, unlike the Sherman Act, does not require proof of
an agreement to restrain trade, the courts have effectively narrowed the
FTC's jurisdiction to ban unfair methods of competition and have aligned
the two statutory schemes. Any hint of "agreement" will therefore be fatal
to parallel pricing practices under both the Sherman and FTC Acts. Short of
"agreement," however, there must be indicia of oppressiveness and an absence of an independent business reason for parallel pricing conduct before
a practice may be labeled "unfair" within the FTC Act.

Exchanges of Price Information   Trade associations frequently exchange
information on the availability of raw materials, join together to promote
their industry through institutional advertising, and exchange data on inventory and supply levels. When the exchange of data affects price, even
indirectly, antitrust is implicated.

The mere exchange of price information is not unlawful.[60] The competitive consequences of such exchanges depend on industry structure, the
nature of the information exchanged, and how the firms respond to the
data exchange. Because of the uncertain consequences of data dissemina-
tion activity, courts generally apply a rule of reason analysis.[61]

Early cases involving data exchange focused on the purpose of competitors in exchanging price information and prohibited such exchanges
only when they were intended to affect prices.[62] In one early case,[63] the
Court, finding no purpose to fix prices or otherwise restrain trade, upheld
an open exchange of statistical information of past prices and other data
which did not identify particular customers, even though the Court recognized that the effect of the exchange would be "to bring about uniformity
in prices through the operation of economic law."[64] The information was
also fully available to the public. Even though the defendant controlled 70
percent of total production, the Court stressed the importance of allowing
the free exchanges of information. No evidence of price stabilization (no effect) was found.[65] Four years later, the court upheld an exchange of price
information involving particular customers because, the Court found, the
exchange was not designed to fix prices but was rather intended to prevent
customer fraud.[66]

The touchstone of modern price exchange cases is not the "purpose and
effect" test but market structure. Borrowing heavily from economics for first
principles, courts have reasoned that the more concentrated a market, the
more predisposed it will be toward collusive stabilization of prices when

there is a price exchange. Conversely, the less concentrated a market, the more an exchange of price information can be procompetitive. The more market information is available to competitors, the greater the chance that allocative efficiency (sellers producing exactly what buyers want) will be enhanced.

The *Container Corp. of America* case[67] was the Court's first explicit recognition that market structure may affect price exchanges. The Justice Department challenged the activities of a group of eighteen firms that supplied 90 percent of the cardboard cartons sold in the United States. The carton suppliers regularly telephoned one another to verify claims of customers that a rival seller was offering a stated price. The Court found that the defendants had conspired to swap data on presale prices:

> Each defendant on receiving (a) request usually furnished data with the expectation that it would be furnished reciprocal information when it wanted it. That concerted action is of course sufficient to establish the combination or conspiracy.
>
> There was of course freedom to withdraw from the agreement. But the fact remains that when a defendant requested and received price information, it was affirming its willingness to furnish such information in return.

The Court accepted the theory that exchanges of price data tend toward impermissible price uniformity in oligopolistic markets, and it inferred anticompetitive conduct from market structure.[68]

Container appears to limit narrowly the circumstances under which price data may be shared by competitors.[69] It does not, however, hold that all such exchanges are illegal. The Court's current standard on exchanges of price information might be summarized as follows: The Court is likely to approve an exchange of *past* data in summary or aggregate form, when the data do not disclose individual transactions or customers, where (1) the market structure of the industry suggests that it is not highly concentrated, (2) there is no disclosure of present or future information, (3) the data are available to the public, and (4) there are no coercive mechanisms that pressure members to adhere to price schedules.[70] More generally, exchanges of price information may be upheld where the defendants can prove that there was a legitimate business reason for the exchange and that its purpose and effect were not to stabilize prices.[71]

Price discrimination

The Clayton Act proscribes some business practices explicitly. Section 2, as amended by the Robinson-Patman Act, deals with price discrimination and declares, in part, that

> It shall be unlawful for any person engaged in commerce . . . to discriminate in price between purchasers of *commodities of like grade and quality*

—where either or any of the purchasers involved in such discrimination are *in commerce,*

—where the effect of such discrimination may be *substantially to lessen competition* or tend to create a monopoly in any line of commerce, or to injure, destroy, or prevent competition with any person who either grants or knowingly receives the benefit of such discrimination, or with the customers of either of them. [Emphasis added.]

The interpretation of the Act turns essentially on the italicized points.

Commodities of Like Grade and Quality   The courts have interpreted the term *commodities of like grade and quality* rather narrowly. The term *commodities* means tangible goods; the act does not apply to discrimination in services.[72] Moreover, the courts have interpreted any tangible difference in the materials, workmanship, or design of the products as a difference in grade or quality. Thus, a manufacturer can safely sell a deluxe model, or a model adapted to a particular customer's requirements, at a premium price that more than reflects any additional cost of producing it.

The legal treatment of intangible differences, such as advertising and brand name, is only slightly less clear.[73] A problem arises when commodities are physically identical but are viewed by the public to be different due to variations in labelling and consumer preference. In a leading case, Borden sold chemically identical brand-name and private-label evaporated milk at different prices.[74] The FTC held that brand names and labels are not determinants of "grade and quality" and challenged the price discrimination. The U.S. Court of Appeals, accepting Borden's argument that because the Borden brand had achieved significant consumer preference and sold at a higher price than Borden's private-label brand, the two products were of a different "grade" and hence the price discrimination was outside the Robinson-Patman Act. The Supreme Court rejected Borden's claim that milk sold with the Borden label was a different product from the same milk sold with a private label and sent the case back to the appellate court to determine whether Borden's price difference had injured competition. In an ironic turn of events, after adopting an "injury test" based on the principle that no injury occurs if "a price differential between a premium and a non-premium brand reflects no more than a consumer preference for the premium brand,"[75] the appellate court ruled that Borden's price differential met this test and was therefore legal.

In Commerce   The term *in commerce* means that the Act applies only if the injured party is a business whose ability to compete is hindered by the discriminatory price. Thus one can always charge some consumers (for example, regular theater attendees) a higher price than other consumers (for example, student theater attendees), since consumers are not using the product in commerce.[76] But a food manufacturer may violate the Act by charging one retail store a higher wholesale price than it charges a competing retail store, since its buyers are in commerce.[77]

Levels of Competition   The phrase *substantially to lessen competition* is interpreted more broadly for some types of competition than for others. Price discrimination violates the law if it harms competition at either of two levels. *Primary-level* competition is between the firm that price discriminates and its own competitors. *Secondary-level* competition is between two firms that are customers of the firm that price discriminates (or are customers of a middleman who is, in turn, a customer of the price discriminating firm).

The courts do not want to discourage price-cutting at the primary level, even when it is discriminatory, unless competition is clearly harmed. The fact that competitors are harmed by a firm's discriminatory price cut, however, does not necessarily mean that competition is harmed.

Older primary-line court cases tended to interpret the Robinson-Patman Act as favoring the protection of competitors over competition.[78] When a local producer of frozen desert pies with a dominant share of the local market began to experience stiff price competition from national firms that were able to charge lower prices in certain markets because of their ability to charge higher prices elsewhere, the Court found impermissible price discrimination, even though there was a "deteriorating price structure" in the market during the period of competition.[79] The decision has been widely criticized as actually discouraging rather than encouraging price competition: If a national firm must lower prices in all markets in order to engage in competition in any one market, the firm may have to leave the market to a local monopolist.[80]

The analytical focus of the older court cases tended to determine whether a firm had predatory intent. Absent such intent, courts were inclined to uphold a discrimination in price. Thus, when Anheuser-Busch cut the price of beer it sold in St Louis below the price elsewhere, the Court ruled that the firm's price discrimination was not illegal because the price cut was a temporary attempt to build market share and was not intended to drive competitors out of business.[81] Similarly, a permanent discriminatory price cut to maintain market share in locations with growing competition was found acceptable.[82]

The more recent cases show the Court shifting its analytical focus away from the protection of competitors to the protection of competition. The current approach is to ask whether there is evidence that a price-discriminating competitor had predatory intent as determined by pricing behavior, and not merely subjective intent. Under this approach, Robinson-Patman is interpreted in a manner that is consistent with the Sherman Act.[83]

This convergence of goals of the Robinson-Patman and Sherman Acts is embodied in the Court's latest treatment of primary-line injury.[84] After

Brooke Group (hereafter Liggett, its more well-known former name) introduced a line of inexpensive generic cigarettes, Brown & Williamson (B &
W) countered with its own line of generics. A fierce price war ensued.
Liggett eventually filed suit against B & W, alleging that B & W was offering volume rebates to wholesalers which amounted to price discrimination
and predatory pricing. Liggett charged that B & W's pricing strategy was
part of a complex scheme to force Liggett to raise prices on its generics,
thus restraining the generic segment's growth and preserving B & W's
supracompetitive profits on *branded* cigarettes by means of oligopolistic
price coordination with other manufacturers.

The Court was unpersuaded by this argument. The conduct at issue
here, the Court noted, should receive the same analysis whether the claim
was brought under Robinson-Patman or the Sherman Act: "The essence of
the claim under either statute is the same: A business rival has priced its
products in an unfair manner with an object to eliminate or retard competition and thereby gain and exercise control over prices in the relevant market."[85] A plaintiff seeking to establish a claim under either statute must first
prove that the prices complained of are below an appropriate measure of
its rival's costs.[86] The second prerequisite to holding a competitor liable is
to show that the competitor has a reasonable prospect of recouping its investment in below-cost prices.[87]

The standards for determining competitive damage are much broader
when they are applied to secondary competition. Recall that the Robinson-
Patman Act was passed in response to complaints from small retailers that
larger competitors were securing lower wholesale prices. Recognizing that
Congress intended to grant some protection to those retailers, the courts
have been protective of small retailers' interests. For example, Morton Salt
granted up to a 15 percent discount to retailers who bought large quantities
of salt over a year. The FTC sued Morton, charging that the company was
illegally price discriminating. Morton contended, however, that since salt
represented a small portion of a grocery's sales, its discount could not substantially lessen competition between large and small stores. Morton also
noted that the FTC could produce no evidence thay any small retailer's
ability to compete was ever impaired. The Supreme Court ruled, however,
that the act's requirement that "the effect may be substantially to lessen
competition" does not require actual proof when applied to secondary
competition. Morton was guilty because, according to the Court, it was reasonable to assume that small retailers were harmed somewhat and could
be substantially injured if many food manufacturers discriminated as
Morton had.[88] Following this case, there has been a presumption that injury
to competition can be inferred from a substantial price difference alone (the
Morton Salt presumption).

The Morton Salt presumption proved decisive in a recent case.
Suppliers of products frequently market their goods both directly to retail-

ers and through wholesalers or distributors who resell to retailers. The latter may receive a lower price—a "functional discount"—than the price charged to direct-buying retailers. Although some discounts may be covered by the cost justification defense or by the meeting competition defense,[89] there is no blanket exemption under Robinson-Patman for all such discounts.

In *Hasbrouck*,[90] Texaco sold directly to plaintiff and other independent retailers at one price, but granted substantial discounts to two middlemen. Over a nine-year period, the middlemen flourished and many of the independent retailers went out of business. Hasbrouck filed suit, alleging price discrimination. Texaco defended by arguing that (1) there was no "discrimination in price" where the price differential was between purchasers at different levels of distribution (wholesalers and retailers), and (2) there was "no injury" to competition because any competitive advantage enjoyed by the competing retailers was the product of independent decisions by the wholesalers to pass on the discounts to those retailers. The Court disagreed and found Texaco liable. It held that (1) a plain reading of the statute shows that it prohibits differentials in prices offered to wholesalers and retailers. As to (2), the court acknowledged that a legitimate functional discount that constitutes a reimbursement for the buyer's actual marketing functions does not violate the act. In this case, however, the discount was "completely untethered to the supplier's savings or the wholesaler's costs."[91] Because there was no evidence that the functional discount available to Texaco's wholesale customers was "reasonable" and that those customers resold most of the discounted product directly to consumers, Texaco was unable to overcome the Morton Salt presumption that injury to competition can be inferred from a substantial price difference alone.[92]

How influential is the Robinson-Patman Act today? Despite the *Hasbrouck* decision, the Act is often viewed as misguided in light of modern antitrust theory[93] and as posing only a minor threat. The interest of the Justice Department and the FTC has waned considerably over the years.[94] Recent cases show the Court analogizing primary-line injury cases to predatory pricing schemes which, in the wake of *Matsushita*, are considered inherently implausible.[95] And whatever strength the Act had by way of private enforcement has been reduced by a decision that made recovery of damages by private litigants exceptionally difficult.[96]

Legal Defenses Even when a firm's pricing is found discriminatory and harmful to competition, the Clayton Act offers two legal defenses. The first, known as the *cost justification defense*, states that "nothing herein contained shall prevent [price] differentials which make only due allowances for differences in the cost of manufacture, sale or delivery. . . ." The burden of proving the cost defense falls, however, on the defendant. The price-discriminating firm must show that it carefully studied its costs before arriving at a price differential and that the differential is no greater than the difference in the full cost (including a reasonable allocation of the fixed cost) of serving different classes of buyers.

Even then, the court must be convinced that the buyer classifications are reasonable. American Can lost a private suit brought by one of its buyers, Bruce's Juices, although it showed that the cost of serving Bruce's was higher than the cost of serving larger juice companies. The problem arose because American Can set a single discount price for sales to large juice companies, even though the cost of delivery to any one plant of those companies might be as high as the cost of delivery to a smaller firm. Thus, the court ruled, American Can's price differentials were "tainted with the inherent vice of too broad averaging.[97]

The other way that a firm may justify a discriminatory price is with the *meeting competition defense*, which states that "nothing herein contained shall prevent a seller rebutting the prima facie case thus made by showing that his lower price . . . was made to meet an equally low price of a competitor, or the services or facilities furnished by a competitor." Much to the chagrin of the FTC, the courts have refused to weaken this defense. In a case against Standard Oil of Indiana, the FTC ruled that even though Standard Oil cut its price only to meet the price of competitors, "the potentially injurious effect of a seller's price reduction upon competition at lower levels" outweighed the "beneficial effect in permitting the seller to meet competition on its own level." The Supreme Court rejected the FTC's argument, declaring that meeting competition is an absolute defense.[98]

The FTC has also tried another approach to undermine this defense. It has argued that a firm meeting a competitor's lower price must verify its exact amount and prove that the competitive price was actually offered. The courts, however, recognizing that companies cannot legally or practically discuss price with their competitors, have generally rejected this argument. For example, when A&P informed Borden that its quotation to supply milk was "not even in the ballpark" but would not tell Borden exactly what the competitors' prices were, Borden substantially reduced its bid and won the business. The Supreme Court held that Borden had acted in good faith based on the limited information available to it.[99]

Tie-in sales and requirements contracts

The Clayton Act also limits a seller's ability to require that, as a condition of purchasing one product, customers must buy other products exclusively from the seller. Section 3 states that

> . . . it shall be unlawful . . . to lease or make a sale or contract . . . for goods, wares, merchandise, machinery, supplies, or other commodities . . . on the condition . . . that the lessee or purchaser thereof shall not use or deal in the goods, wares, merchandise, machinery, supplies or other

commodities of a competitor . . . where the effect . . . may be to substantially lessen competition.

Although tying arrangements are classified as per se violations, the
test used to determine whether the per se rule should be applied to a particular arrangement is, in practice, similar to a rule of reason inquiry because a number of market-related inquiries must be conducted before the
per se rule is applied.

Early cases were less cautious in condemning tying arrangements.[100]
As courts began to see the procompetitive benefits of certain tying arrangements, the per se standard began to totter. Courts began to allow tie-ins
(usually by holding that there was a "single" product) if a firm could offer
a business justification for the arrangement. For example, a seller of an-
tenna systems who required purchasers to buy the complete system although several components could be sold separately was allowed to use
this arrangement. The Court held that the tie-in was necessary to assure the
proper functioning of the system and to protect the goodwill of the firm.[101]
Courts also began to allow franchisors to require franchisees to buy products from them that were essential to maintain quality or to preserve a market image. Thus, a court upheld McDonald's requirement that licensees
operate their restaurants on premises leased from McDonald's after examining evidence that such a requirement had enabled McDonald's to obtain
superior sites, assure quality and goodwill, and compile a successful track
record. Voluntary tie-ins were easily accepted.[102] Courts also began to look
favorably on firms that, through innovation, were able to maintain tie-ins
simply by staying ahead of their competitors.[103] Finally, tie-ins were increasingly upheld when an industry was in a developmental period and a
tie-in allowed a firm to maintain goodwill.

Over time these exceptions almost swallowed the per se rule, and
prompted a reexamination of the prohibition against tie-ins.[104] Today, the
per se label will not be applied until a court has examined a firm's market
power. Two modern cases illustrate current standards applicable to tying
arrangements.

In Hyde,[105] a hospital contracted with a firm of anesthesiologists to
provide all the hospital's anesthesiological services. An excluded anesthesi-
ologist charged the hospital with tying anesthesiological services to hospital services. The Supreme Court agreed. First, there were "two products"
and not a "functionally integrated package of services,"[106] as claimed by the
hospital. Consumers viewed hospital and anesthesiological services as distinct, and this was sufficient to prove two products. Second, the Court
found that the hospital had sufficient market power to raise prices above
competitive levels and was thus able to "coerce" consumers to purchase an
"unwanted product."[107] After Hyde, for a tying arrangement to be per se unlawful, the seller must have the requisite degree of economic power in the

tying product to produce an appreciable restraint in the market for the tied product. The seller can possess this power by virtue of market share, a patent, or its ability to offer a unique product. And coercion is now an independent prerequisite for application of the per se rule.[108]

The Supreme Court in *Kodak*[109] upheld claims that a manufacturer of copier equipment had unlawfully tied the sale of service for its machines to the sale of replacement parts. Independent service organizations (ISOs) that repaired Kodak equipment at below-dealer rates had complained that Kodak was forcing them out of business by selling its nongeneric replacement parts exclusively to buyers of Kodak equipment. In finding an illegal tie-in between services and parts, the Court rejected Kodak's argument that its lack of market power in copying machines precluded competitive harm because buyers could take service policies into account when bargaining with rival suppliers of original equipment. The ISOs advanced evidence showing that certain parts were available only from Kodak, that Kodak had control over the parts it did not manufacture, that Kodak pressured Kodak equipment owners from selling parts to ISOs, and that consumers switched to Kodak service even though they often preferred ISO service. The Court's focus on the realities of market imperfections may signal a shift away from the "Free-market" efficiency concerns that increasingly guided federal antitrust enforcement during the Reagan and Bush years.[110]

Predation

Chapter 5 introduced the concept of a predatory price, a price set so low that the firm harms its own profitability in an attempt to do greater harm to a competitor. The purpose of such behavior is either to discipline a competitor for competing too intensely or to drive it from the market and thus eliminate its competition entirely. The expectation is that, once the competition is reduced or eliminated, the price can be raised to a more profitable level and the cost of using predatory pricing can be recovered. The Sherman Act was meant to control such pricing by the trusts, which allegedly used predatory pricing to eliminate competitors who resisted mergers.[111]

Most cases of alleged predatory pricing involve selective price cuts in one geographical area where the predator faces more intense local competition. The predator's profitability in other locations is what gives it the superior financial strength to successfully pursue predatory pricing in one location. Even if such a selective regional price cut were profitable, it would still be illegal price discrimination under the Clayton Act if it substantially lessened competition.[112] In some cases, however, predatory pricing is alleged even in the absence of geographical price discrimination.

Recent predatory pricing decisions start from the premise that "predatory pricing schemes are rarely tried, and even more rarely successful."[113] Courts have reasoned that the odds are overwhelmingly stacked against successful price predation. A successful predatory firm must be able to maintain monopoly power for long enough to recoup its losses and harvest additional gain. Such sustained monopoly power may be difficult or impossible where market barriers are low and vigorous new firms can easily enter the market. Recognizing that the line between procompetitive price-cutting (which the antitrust laws are meant to encourage) and anti-competitive predatory pricing is often a fine one, courts have imposed greater evidentiary burdens on parties alleging predatory pricing schemes than they did in the past.

Between 1975 and 1986 courts placed a heavy emphasis on price-cost analysis in evaluating predatory pricing claims. Prices below reasonably anticipated marginal cost were deemed predatory, whereas prices at or above reasonably anticipated marginal cost were deemed nonpredatory. Because marginal cost was difficult to measure, average variable cost was used as its surrogate.[114] Since the *Matsushita* case,[115] courts have favored an analysis of market conditions as a way to short-circuit the cumbersome price-cost analysis, which has made antitrust cases among the most prolonged and expensive types of litigation. Typically courts determine whether a predatory scheme could succeed by examining the likelihood of cost recoupment and barriers to entry.

The unlikelihood of recoupment was a significant factor in *Matsushita*. There, Japanese electronics manufacturers were alleged to have engaged in a predatory pricing scheme over a period of twenty years. The Supreme Court found that even if the manufacturers could have raised prices to monopoly levels, they could not have expected to recoup the substantial losses incurred during the twenty-year period of alleged predation. In the absence of entry barriers, other firms could be expected to enter the market if prices rose to monopoly levels. The low probability that the alleged predators could ever recover their losses led the Court to dismiss the case.

Commentators predicted that *Matsushita* would pose an insuperable barrier to predatory pricing claims.[116] Although the success rate for plaintiffs has increased since the decision, the underlying strength of the defendants is shown by the low damage recoveries.[117] This trend is illustrated by *Brooke Group* (discussed previously in the discussion of the Robinson-Patman Act). In *Brooke Group*, a manufacturer of generic cigarettes (Liggett) alleged that a rival manufacturer (Brown & Williamson) had used below-cost pricing to subdue Liggett's efforts to sell generic cigarettes. The jury gave Liggett a trebled award of nearly $150 million. After reviewing the record, the court vacated the award,[118] and, on appeal, the Supreme Court agreed, emphasizing that Liggett had failed to show that Brown & Williamson could recoup its investment in below-cost pricing.[119] The modern trend in predatory pricing cases may be that courts will regard sophisticated, efficiency-oriented theories as sufficient to get a case before a jury, but inadequate to support large damage awards.[120]

ETHICAL CONSTRAINTS ON PRICING

"[P]erhaps no other area of managerial activity is more difficult to depict accurately, assess fairly, and prescribe realistically in terms of morality than the domain of price."[121] This oft-quoted assessment reflects the exceptional divergence of ethical opinions with respect to pricing. Even among writers sympathetic to the need for profit, some consider it unethical to charge different prices unless they reflect differences in costs, while others consider pricing unethical unless prices are set "equal or proportional to the benefit received."[122] Consequently, there is less written on ethics in pricing than on other marketing issues, and what is written tends to focus on the easy issues, like deception and price-fixing.[123] The tougher issues involve strategies and tactics for gaining profit.

This text is intended to help managers capture more of the value created by the products and services they sell in the profits they earn. In many cultures, and among many who promulgate ethical principles, such a goal is morally reprehensible. Although this opinion was once held by the majority, its popularity has generally declined over the last three centuries due to the success of capitalism and the failure of collectivism to deliver an improvement in material well-being. Still, many people, including many in business practice and education, believe that there are legitimate ethical constraints on maximizing profit through pricing.

It is important to clarify your own and your customers' understanding of those standards before ambiguous situations arise. The topology of ethical constraint in pricing illustrated in Exhibit 14.1 is a good place to start. Readers should determine where to draw the line concerning ethical constraint—for themselves and their industry—and determine as well how other people (family, neighbors, social groups) might view such decisions.

Most people would reject the idea of zero ethical constraint, where the seller can dictate the price and terms and force them on an unwilling buyer. Sale of "protection" by organized crime is universally condemned. The practice of forcing employees in a one-company town to buy from the "company store" is subject to only marginally less condemnation. Even when the government itself is the seller that is forcing people to purchase goods and services at a price (tax rate) it sets, people generally condemn the transaction unless they feel empowered to influence the terms. This level of ethical constraint was also used to condemn the "trusts" that, before the antitrust laws, sometimes used reprehensible tactics to drive lower-priced competitors out of business. By denying customers alternative products, they arguably forced them to buy theirs.

The first level of ethical constraint, embodied in all well-functioning, competitive market economies, requires that all transactions be voluntary. Early capitalist economies, and some of the most dynamic today (for in-

EXHIBIT 14.1

When Is a Price Ethical?

	Ethical Restraint	
Level	The Exchange Is Ethical When:	Implication/Proscription
(1)	the price is paid voluntarily	"Let the buyer beware."
(2)	. . . and based on equal information	No sales without full disclosure (used-car defects, risks of smoking).
(3)	. . . and not exploiting buyers' "essential needs"	No "excessive" profits on "essentials" such as life-saving pharmaceuticals.
(4)	. . . and justified by costs	No segmented pricing based on value. No excessive profits based on shortages, even for nonessential products.
(5)	. . . and provides equal access to goods regardless of one's ability to cover the cost.	No exchange for personal gain. Give as able and receive as needed.

stance, Hong Kong), condone any transaction that meets this criterion. The legal principle of caveat emptor, "Let the buyer beware," characterized nearly all economic transactions in the United States prior to the twentieth century. In such a market, people often make regrettable purchases (for example, expensive brand-name watches that turn out to be cheap substitutes, and stocks in overvalued companies). On the other hand, without the high legal costs associated with meeting licensing, branding, and disclosure requirements, new business opportunities abound even for the poor—making unemployment negligible.

The second level of ethical restraint imposes a more restrictive standard, condemning even voluntary transactions by those who would profit from unequal information about the exchange. Selling a used car without disclosing a known defect, concealing a known risk of using a product, or misrepresenting the benefits achievable from a product are prime examples of transactions that would be condemned by this ethical criterion. Thus, many would condemn selling land in Florida at inflated prices to unwary out-of-state buyers, or selling lottery tickets to the poor, since the seller could reasonably expect these potential buyers to be ignorant of, or unable to process, information needed to make an informed decision. Since sellers naturally know more about the features and benefits of products than most consumers do, they have an ethical duty to disclose what they know completely and accurately.[124]

Ethical level three imposes a still more stringent criterion: that sellers earn no more than a "fair" profit from sales of "necessities" for which buyers have only limited alternatives. This principle is often stated as follows: "No one should profit from other people's adversity." Thus even nominally capitalist societies sometimes impose rent controls on housing and price controls on pharmaceutical costs and physicians' fees. Even when this level of ethical constraint is not codified into law, people who espouse it condemn those who raise the price of ice during a power failure or the price of lumber following a hurricane, when the demand for these products soars.

Ethical level four extends the criteria of ethical level three to all products, even those with many substitutes and not usually thought of as necessities. Profit is morally justifiable only when it is the minimum necessary to induce companies and individuals to make decisions for the good of "less-advantaged" members of society.[125] Profit is ethically justifiable only as the price society must pay to induce suppliers of capital and skills to improve the well-being of those less fortunate. Profits from exploiting unique skills, great ideas, or exceptional efficiency (called *economic rents*) are morally suspect in this scenario unless it can be shown that everyone, or at least the most needy, benefits from allowing such profits to be earned, such as when a high-profit company nevertheless offers lower prices and better working conditions than its competitors. Profits from speculation (buying low and selling high) are clearly condemned as is segmented pricing (charging customers different prices to capture different levels of value), unless those prices actually reflect differences in cost.

Ethical level five, the most extreme constraint, is inconsistent with markets. In some "primitive" societies, everyone is obliged to share good fortune with those in the tribe who are less fortunate. "From each according to his ability, to each according to his need" is the espoused ethical premise of Marxist societies and even some respected moral philosophers. Those that have actually tried to put it into practice, however, have eventually recoiled at the brutality necessary to force essentially self-interested humans "to give according to their abilities" without reward. Within families and small, self-selected societies, however, this ethical principle can thrive. Within social and religious organizations, members often work together for their common good and share the results. Even within businesses, partnerships are established to share, within defined bounds, each other's good and bad fortune.

For each level of ethical constraint on economic exchange, one must determine the losses and gains, for both individuals and societies, that will result from the restriction. What effect does each level have on the material and social well-being of those who hold it as a standard? Should the same standards be applied in different contexts? For example, is your standard different for business markets than it is for consumer markets? Would your ethical standards change when selling in a foreign country where local competitors generally hold a higher or lower ethical standard than yours? In assessing the standards that friends, business associates, and political representatives apply, managers must ask themselves if their personal standards are the same for their business as well as for their personal conduct. For example, would they condemn an oil company for earning excess profits as a result of higher crude prices, yet themselves take excess profits on a house that had appreciated substantially in a hot real estate market? If so, are they hypocrites or is there some justification for holding individuals and firms to different standards?

Although we as the authors of this text certainly have our own beliefs about which of these ethical levels is practical and desirable in dealing with others, and would apply different standards in different contexts, we feel that neither we nor most of the people who claim to be experts on business ethics are qualified to make these decisions for someone else. Each individual must make his or her own decisions and live with the personal and social consequences.

SUMMARY

The development of strategies that do not violate the law is an important aspect of pricing. In addition to the risk of legal actions initiated by the government, a company can be sued by its competitors or its customers. If they can prove that the company's pricing violated an antitrust law, the company can be forced to pay triple damages, plus its own and its accusers' legal fees. A company's pricing is also subject to FTC complaints, which can harm its reputation and lead to serious restrictions on its future pricing tactics.

Unfortunately, which pricing tactics are illegal is not always clear. The laws themselves are vague. To discern what they mean, one must rely on the courts' interpretation of them in past cases. The courts have generally found explicit agreements to fix prices, whether among competitors or between a company and its distributors, as per se illegal. But courts today are more cautious in applying the per se label than they were in the past. They will more readily uphold an agreement affecting price if they determine that cooperation is required to produce procompetitive efficiencies that compensate for the restrictions in output caused by the agreement. Based on this rationale, courts have upheld agreements that lower overall transaction costs, help maintain order in organized markets, and create new products that would not otherwise exist.

In the case of alleged nonexplicit agreements, the courts have applied the rule of reason. The decision by different companies to make price changes in parallel is not automatically illegal. It is also not necessarily illegal for them to exchange information via a trade association, although such information may tend to stabilize prices. Both parallel pricing and the exchange of information can, however, be used with other evidence—called by the courts *plus factors*—to infer a secret agreement to fix prices. Plus factors that a court will consider include whether the parties had a rational motive or opportunity to collude and whether the structure of the industry is predisposed toward collusion. Based on these somewhat opaque variables, companies that find cooperative pricing in their interest must scrupulously avoid any communication that would imply an agreement to establish or continue such pricing.

Pricing identical commodities (not services) differently to different buyers can also be illegal if such price discrimination hinders competition. In general, the courts will not find such pricing illegal simply because it harms a competitor unless the competitor is smaller and financially weak. The courts are more likely to find price discrimination illegal when it harms one customer's ability to compete with another. Even in cases where a company has discriminated in price and the court finds that competition was harmed, it has two defenses. Price discrimination never violates the law if it is shown to have been entirely cost-justified or to have been done in good faith to meet a competitor's equally low price.

Contracts that tie purchases of one good with sales of another good are generally illegal when used as a pricing tactic, but courts are more willing to accept certain kinds of tie-ins today than they were in the past. Maintenance of good will and product quality are two common justifications for tying arrangements. Courts will also examine whether a firm has sufficient market power in the tying product to coerce purchases in the tied product. Similarly, the courts generally side with the defendant in cases of alleged predatory pricing. Claims of predatory pricing are almost never sustainable unless the predatory firm has priced below average cost, or unless market structure suggests that the predator would be *likely* to recoup its losses due to the presence of *high* entry barriers.

Finally, the FTC can find prices unfair or deceptive, even when they are not anticompetitive. The FTC has published guidelines for making price and value comparisons and for advertising prices designed to guide marketers in making pricing decisions.

NOTES

1. Antitrust Amendments Act of 1990, Pub. L. No. 101–588 (1990) (to be codified at 15 U.S.C. sections 1, 2).
2. 18 U.S.C. sections 3621–3624. This measure was adopted by the Criminal Fines Improvements Act of 1984, Pub. L. No. 98–596, 98 Stat. 3132, and reenacted as

the Criminal Fines Improvements Act of 1987, Pub. L. No. 100–185, 101 Stat. 1279. See also William E. Kovacic, "The Identification and Proof of Horizontal Agreements Under the Antitrust Laws," 38 *Antitrust Bulletin*, 11–12 (1993).

3.   The Guidelines only apply to bid-rigging, price-fixing, and market allocation agreements. 18 U.S.C.A. App. *Federal Sentencing Guidelines*, section 2R1.1 (1989 Supp.).

4.   See *United States* v. *Mobile Materials, Inc.*, 871 F.2d 902, 918 (10th Cir.), (individual was sentenced to three years' imprisonment and fined $100,000), Cert. denied, 493 U.S. 1043 (1989). Fines ranging from $1 million to $4 million are not uncommon. See *ABA Antitrust Section, Antitrust Law Developments*, 3rd ed. p. 597, footnote 368 (1992) (listing representative cases and fines imposed). Fines levied in the past tended to be much lighter. Until 1988, the maximum fine for corporations was only $1 million. The average fine for cases tried between 1975 and 1979 was $445,517. Imprisonment was rare and, when imposed, brief. Fifteen of the seventeen individuals sentenced to prison between 1975 and 1979 for antitrust violations served 90 days or less. Richard A. Posner, and Frank H. Easterbrook, *Antitrust: Cases, Economic Notes, and Other Materials*, 2nd ed. p. 320. (St. Paul, Minn.: West Publishing, Co., 1981).

5.   See *ABA Antitrust Section, Antitrust Law Developments*, 3rd ed. pp. 596–97 (1992).

6.   *FTC* v. *R. F. Keppel & Brothers*, 291 U.S. 304 (1934); *FTC* v. *Sperry & Hutchinson Co.*, 405 U.S. 233 (1972).

7.   The following discussion is partially based on the "State Enforcement" section of *ABA Antitrust Section, Antitrust Law Developments* 3rd ed. (1992), pp. 603–41. The reader is also referred to *ABA Antitrust Section, State Antitrust Practice and Statutes* (1990) for more detailed information.

8.   See *In re Minolta Camera Products Litigation*, 668 F.Supp. 456 (D.Md. 1987). Other prominent cases have involved Panasonic: *In re Panasonic Consumer Electronics Antitrust Litigation*, No. 89–CV 0368 (SWK) (S.D.N.Y. filed January 18, 1989) (charging Panasonic with establishing and enforcing a minimum price for its goods; settlement provided for refunds of up to $16 million to 600,000 purchasers); Mitsubishi Electronics, *Maryland ex rel Curran* v. *Mitsubishi Electronics of America*, Civ. No. S–91–815 (D.Md. filed March 27, 1991) (alleging that Mitsubishi attempted to set resale prices on all its products; the dealers were told that failure to maintain those prices could result in termination; the settlement required Mitsubishi to refund $7.95 million to consumers who purchased specific TVs during 1988); and Nintendo, *Nebraska* v. *Nintendo of Am., Inc.*, No. 91–CV 2498 (RWS) (S.D.N.Y. filed April 10, 1991) (charging Nintendo with conspiring to maintain prices; settlement provided that consumers were eligible for a $5 coupon).

The discussion above is based on *ABA Antitrust Section, Antitrust Law Developments*, 3rd ed. (1992), pp. 610–11.

9.   Although this review focuses on the legal constraints on pricing, the antitrust laws proscribe other business practices (for example, anticompetitive mergers) as well.

10.   Quoted in A. D. Neale and D. G. Goyder, *Antitrust Laws of the United States*, 3rd ed. (Cambridge: University of Cambridge, 1980), p. 15.

11. The Webb-Pomerene Act of 1918 and the Export Trading Company Act of 1982 provide substantial protection for agreements among direct rivals concerning export trade.

12. As the Supreme Court later noted, "Congress did not intend the text of the Sherman Act to delineate the full meaning of the statute or its application in concrete situations. The legislative history makes it perfectly clear that it expected the courts to give shape to the statute's broad mandate. . . ." *National Society of Professional Engineers* v. *United States*, 98 S.Ct. 1355 (1978).

13. *United States* v. *Northern Securities* [A *Railway* case], 193 U.S. 197 (1904).

14. *U.S.* v. *Standard Oil* 221 U.S. 1 (1911); *United States* v. *American Tobacco Co.*, 221 U.S. 106 (1911).

15. Stephanie W. Kanwit, *Federal Trade Commission* (Shepard's Regulatory Manual Series) (New York: McGraw-Hill, 1979), pp. 3.9–3.11.

16. A 1934 FTC investigation revealed that only 15 percent of the chains' price advantage was due to the lower wholesale prices they obtained. The remainder was due to the greater efficiency of their operations. Federal Trade Commission, *Final Report on the Chain Store Investigation* (Washington, D.C.: Government Printing Office, 1934).

17. *United States* v. *Trans-Missouri Freight*, 116 U.S. 290 (1897).

18. *United States* v. *Socony Vacuum Oil Co. Inc.*, 310 U.S. 150 (1940).

19. To see, however, how the courts can occasionally be guilty of blatant inconsistency when they believe that conditions warrant it, see *Appalachian Coals* v. *United States* 288 U.S. 344 (1933). In that case, decided during the depth of the Great Depression, the Supreme Court ruled that the coal companies could use a selling agency much like that of the oil companies. The court cited "the deplorable condition" of the industry as a relevant consideration in the decision. Later cases have shown this decision to be an anomaly.

20. *Broadcast Music, Inc.* v. *Columbia Broadcasting System*, 441 U.S. 1 (1979).

21. Id. at 20–23.

22. See, for example, *Polk Bros.* v. *Forest City Enters.*, 776 F.2d 185, 188 (7th Cir. 1985); *National Bancard Corp.* v. *VISA USA*, 779 F.2d 592, 601–602 (11th Cir.) (fixed-fee VISA assessments for processing VISA charges through its computerized network is part of a larger integrated, joint-venture type system that would not be available at all if the fee were not assessed), Cert. denied, 479 U.S. 923 (1986). See also *ABA Antitrust Section, Antitrust Law Developments*, 3rd ed. (1992), p. 77, footnote 437.

23. See *Northwest Wholesale Stationers, Inc.* v. *Pacific Stationery & Printing Co.*, 472 U.S. 284 (1985), (not all concerted horizontal refusals to deal are subject to per se condemnation); and *FTC* v. *Indiana Federation of Dentists*, 476 U.S. 447 (1986) (refusal by a group of dentists to forward X-rays to insurance companies should be reviewed under the rule of reason).

    The blurring of the distinction between per se and rule-of-reason analysis may have reached a terminal point. In *FTC* v. *Superior Court Trial Lawyers Association*, 493 U.S. 411 (1990), the Court shifted analysis away from a path that promised to lead to abandonment of the sharp historical dichotomy between rule of reason and per se offenses. The Court declined to apply a rule-of-reason standard to an agreement by a group of attorneys to refuse to accept cases involving indigent criminal defendants unless the District of Columbia government increased the fees for such cases. The opinion reasserted the dichotomy between per se and reasonableness inquiries.

See Gellhorn and Kovacic, "Anti-Competitive Forces May Stir Anew," *National Law Journal*, May 24, 1993, p. 19. See also *ABA Antitrust Section, Antitrust Law Developments*, 3rd ed. (1992), p. 84, for a general discussion of the cases noted above.

24. *Dr. Miles Medical Co.* v. *John D. Park & Sons Co.*, 220 U.S. 373 (1911).

25. The Miller-Tydings Amendment of 1937 to the Sherman Act exempted from illegality certain agreements fixing minimum or stipulated resale prices of branded commodities that were in free competition with commodities of the same general class produced by others. The exemption was applicable only in states that had statutes authorizing the agreements. For a discussion of this exemption, see *ABA Antitrust Section, Antitrust Law Developments*, 1st ed. (1975), pp. 9–14.

26. *Monsanto Co.* v. *Spray-Rite Serv. Corp.*, 465 U.S. 752 (1984).

27. See discussion in *ABA Antitrust Section, Antitrust Law Developments*, 3rd ed. (1992), p. 101, footnote 554.

28. *United States* v. *Colgate and Co.*, 250 U.S. 300 (1919).

29. The key cases in the consignment area are *United States* v. *General Electric Co.*, 272 U.S. 476 (1926); and *Simpson* v. *Union Oil Co.*, 377 U.S. 13 (1964).

In *General Electric*, the Court upheld RPM by a seller who retained title to its products and merely consigned them to agents for sale. In upholding the plan, the Court stated that "genuine contracts of agency" do not violate the Sherman Act because the owner of an article is not prohibited from "fixing the price by which his agents transfer the title directly from him to [a] consumer." 272 U.S. at 488 (1926).

In *Simpson*, the Court reached the opposite result, finding that Union Oil's system of consigning gasoline to independent dealers and fixing the prices at which the gasoline was to be sold to consumers had "no legitimate business purpose." 377 U.S. at 21 (1964). The nominal consignees possessed most of the indicia of ownership of the gasoline, the court held, including risk of loss. 377 U.S. 21 (1964).

Modern cases focus on the question of which party bears the greatest business risk. When most of the risk remains with the manufacturer, the consignee is more likely to be an agent, and the arrangement will be upheld. Courts have recognized that firms bearing the greatest risk in the marketplace should be permitted leeway in making pricing decisions.

See *ABA Antitrust Section, Antitrust Law Developments*, 3rd ed. (1992); and Sullivan and Harrison, *Understanding Antitrust and Its Economic Implications*, p. 151 (New York: Matthew Bender Co., 1988).

30. *United States* v. *Colgate and Co.*, 250 U.S. 300 (1919).

31. *United States* v. *Parke, Davis & Co.*, 362 U.S. 29, 44 (1960); and *Monsanto Co.* v. *Spray-Rite Serv. Corp.*, 465 U.S. 752, 761 (1984) (manufacturer can announce resale prices in advance, and distributors can independently decide to adhere to such prices).

The Law and Ethics

32. *Business Electronics Corp.* v. *Sharp Electronics Corp.*, 485 U.S. 717, 108 S. Ct. 1515 (1988).

33. The concept of "free riding" has been a staple of modern economic analysis of the law. An example from everyday experience illustrates the concept. When consumers decide to buy a product, they often go to a well-stocked show-room attended by courteous, well-informed salespeople to learn about the features of the various products available. Then, after ascertaining which product they want, they go to the nearest discount store, with none of the amenities of the first store, and buy the product at a greatly reduced price. "The second retailer here can take a free ride on the first—urging his customers to shop the first retailer and then come back to him for a bargain price made possible by his not bearing the expense of providing the elaborate pre-sale services furnished by the first retailer." Posner, *Economic Analysis of Law*, 4th ed. p. 295 (Boston: Little, Brown & Company, 1992).

34. 108 S.Ct. at 1518.

35. Congressional reaction to *Business Electronics* has been unfavorable. A measure introduced in the 101st Congress would have made an agreement between a manufacturer and a distributor to terminate another distributor a per se violation regardless of an agreement on prices or price levels. The bill failed to pass. See *ABA Antitrust Section, Antitrust Law Developments*, 3rd ed. (1992), p. 106, footnote 580.

36. Sullivan and Harrison, *Understanding Antitrust and Its Economic Implications* (New York: Mathew Bender, 1986), p. 158.

37. *Albrecht* v. *Herald Co.*, 390 U.S. 145 (1968).

38. *Atlantic Richfield Co.* v. *USA Petroleum Co.*, 495 U.S. 328, 110 S. Ct. 1884 (1990).

39. *Chicago Board of Trade* v. *United States*, 246 U.S. 231 (1918).

40. *United States* v. *General Electric*, 272 U.S. 476 (1926).

41. *United States* v. *General Electric* [The *Carbolay* case], 80 F.Supp. 989 (S.D.N.Y. 1948).

42. *United States* v. *Line Material*, 333 U.S. 287 (1948); *United States* v. *New Wrinkle* 342 U.S. 371 (1952).

43. *United States* v. *U.S. Gypsum* [The *Gypsum* case], 333 U.S. 364 (1948).

44. *Northern Pacific* v. *United States* 365 U.S. 1 (1958).

45. See J. Q. Lawyer, "How to Conspire to Fix Prices," *Harvard Business Review*, 41 (March–April 1963), 95–103.

46. Richard A. Posner, *Antitrust Law, An Economic Perspective* (Chicago: University of Chicago Press, 1976), p. 135.

47. *Theatre Enterprises* v. *Paramount Film Distributing Corp.*, 346 U.S. 537 (1954) ("circumstantial evidence of consciously parallel behavior may have made heavy inroads into the traditional judicial attitude toward conspiracy; but 'conscious parallelism' has not read conspiracy out of the Sherman Act entirely").

Two additional cases in the historical development of parallel conduct case law should be mentioned since they continue to be the focus of scholarly debate.

In *Interstate Circuit, Inc.* v. *United States*, 306 U.S. 208 (1939), the court held that uniform conduct among eight motion picture distributors was sufficient to infer conspiracy when combined with other factors, including the fact that all participants were aware of the actions of others, all had a strong motive to collude, and the defendants were unable to offer an explanation for their parallel behavior.

Similarly, in *American Tobacco Co.* v. *United States*, 328 U.S. 781 (1946), the court found conspiracy based on otherwise unexplained parallel conduct by three leading tobacco companies making up 90 percent of total U.S. cigarette production. Evidence showed that defendants held list prices absolutely identical for twenty years and raised prices in lockstep fashion, often on the same day, even during the Depression when their costs were declining. Defendants could offer no explanation for their conduct.

For further discussion of these and more recent cases, see *ABA Antitrust Section, Antitrust Law Developments*, (3rd ed. p. 5–6 1992).

48. Even when plus factors have been identified, however, courts recognize that there are gray areas that make the inference of conspiracy highly problematic. For example, firms may coordinate their behavior by doing little more than observing and anticipating the price moves of their rivals. In some industry environments, these efforts at coordination may yield competitive effects that mimic those of an express cartel agreement. Whether antitrust doctrine should proscribe interdependent coordination is a matter of longstanding debate.

See Kovacic, "The Identification and Proof of Horizontal Agreements Under the Antitrust Laws,," 38 *Antitrust Bulletin*, 5, 8 (1933).

49. This discussion is based on the discussion in *ABA Antitrust Section, Antitrust Law Developments*, 3rd ed. (1992), p. 9.

50. *Pevelry Dairy Co.* v. *United States*, 178 F.2d 363 (8th Cir. 1949) (proof that defendant dairy companies' prices had moved uniformly and almost simultaneously was insufficient to prove conspiracy when input prices for raw milk were set by federal regulation, union contracts established uniform labor costs, and local health ordinances standardized the dairies' products).

See Kovacic, "The Identification and Proof of Horizontal Agreements Under the Antitrust Laws," 38 *Antitrust Bulletin*, 5, 43 (1993).

51. See Clark, "Price-Fixing Without Collusion: An Antitrust Analysis of Facilitating Devices After Ethyl Corp.," *Wisconsin Law Review* (1983), 887, 894–99. See also *State of Arizona* v. *Standard Oil Company of California*, 906 F.2d 432 (9th Cir. 1990) ("parallel pricing alone may be all the proof that is required" to establish a Sherman Act violation "when a market is highly unconcentrated").

52. See *Estate of Le Baron* v. *Rohm & Haas Co.*, 441 F.2d 575 (9th Cir. 1971) ("evidence of high-profit margins is probative of the existence of a conspiracy").

The discussion above of plus factors is based on Kovacic, "The Identification and Proof of Horizontal Agreements Under the Antitrust Laws," 38 *Antitrust Bulletin*, 5, pp. 31–55 (1993).

53. *Matsushita Electric Industry Co.* v. *Zenith Radio Corp.*, 475 U.S. 574, 106 S. Ct. 1348 (1986).

54. DeSanti and Kovacic, "*Matsushita*: Its Construction and Application by the Lower Courts," 59 *Antitrust Law Journal* 609, 653 (1991):

As an exercise, it [*Matsushita*] urges a hard edged, early weeding out of claims that lack strong economic content or evidentiary support. As a statement of substantive doctrine, it displays a pervasive skepticism toward predatory pricing as a theory of liability.

55. DeSanti and Kovacic argue that by suggesting a congruency between "common sense" and economic theory, *Matsushita* invites judges to become amateur economists. One danger is that the case law may crystallize around a set of economic assumptions that may become outdated as economic thinking about antitrust progresses. Id. at 653. It is also clear that judges are influenced over time by changing views of what constitutes sound economic theory. See, for example, *Eastman Kodak* v. *Image Technical Services, Inc.*, 112 S.Ct. 2072 (1992) (relying extensively on recent academic scholarship concerning information theory).

56. *Ethyl Corp.*, 101 F.T.C. 425 (1983), vacated sub. nom. *E.I. Du Pont de Nemours & Co.* v. *FTC*, 729 F.2d 128 (2d Cir. 1984).

57. *E.I. Du Pont de Nemours & Co.* v. *FTC*, 729 F.2d at 139.

58. Id. at 139 n. 10 (citing *Naumkeag Theaters Co.* v. *New England Theaters, Inc.*, 345 F.2d 910, 911–12) (1st Cir.) cert. denied, 382 U.S. 906 (1965). See Kovacic, "The Identification and Proof of Horizontal Agreements Under the Antitrust Laws," 38 *Antitrust Bulletin*, 5, 78 (1993).

59. 729 F.2d at 140.

60. *Sugar Institute, Inc.* v. *United States*, 297 U.S. 553 (1936).

61. Justice Douglas suggested a per se rule of illegality in *United States* v. *Container Corp. of America*, 393 U.S. 333 (1969). But in two subsequent cases, *United States* v. *Citizens & Southern National Bank*, 422 U.S. 86 (1975); and *United States* v. *Gypsum Co.*, 438 U.S. 422 (1978), the Supreme Court rejected a per se approach: "[T]he exchange of price data and other information among competitors does not invariably have anticompetitive effects; indeed such practices can in certain cases increase economic efficiency and render markets more, rather than less, competitive." 438 U.S. at 441, n. 16. A rule-of-reason analysis is therefore applied to cases of interseller price communications.

62. The seminal "purpose and effect" case is *American Column and Lumber Co* v. *United States*, 257 U.S. 377 (1921).

63. *Maple Flooring Manufacturers Association* v. *United States*, 268 U.S. 563 (1925).

64. *Maple Flooring Manufacturers Association* v. *United States*, 268 U.S. 567 (1925).

65. *Maple Flooring Manufacturers Association* v. *United States*, 268 U.S. 563 (1925).

66. *Cement Manufacturers Protective Association* v. *United States*, 268 U.S. 588 (1925).

67. *United States* v. *Container Corp. of America*, 393 U.S. 333 (1969).

68. *Container* has been severely criticized for its economic analysis. As critics have noted, low market concentration and low entry barriers should have led the Court to conclude that exchanges of price information might have been pro-competitive. See L. Sullivan, *Handbook of the Law of Antitrust*, p. 272 (1977).

69. The exchange of price information is frequently prohibited in consent decrees settling horizontal price-fixing cases. The Department of Justice recently filed a civil complaint against twenty-two Savannah, Georgia, obstetricians/gyne-

cologists for price-fixing, stemming from the exchange of current and prospective fee information. A consent decree was filed with the complaint prohibiting the exchange of such information for ten years. *United States* v. *Burgstiner*, No. CV491–044 (S.D.Ga. filed February 7, 1991). See *ABA Antitrust Section, Antitrust Law Developments*, 3rd ed. (1992), p. 72, footnote 417, and cases cited therein.

70. See Sullivan and Harrison, *Understanding Antitrust and Its Economic Implication*, p. 98 (New York: Matthew Bender, 1986).

71. *ABA Antitrust Section, Antitrust Law Developments*, 3rd ed. (1992), p. 71.

72. When the provision of services involves the sale of commodities, courts focus on the "dominant nature of the transaction," with the sale of tangible items considered beyond the coverage of the Act if furnished incidentally. See *ABA Antitrust Section, Antitrust Law Developments*, 3rd ed. (1992), 410, and cases cited therein.

73. Advertising has generally been held not to be a commodity. See *ABA Antitrust Section, Antitrust Law Developments*, 3rd ed. (1992), p. 410, and cases cited therein.

74. *Borden Co.* v. *FTC*, 339 F.2d 133, 138 (5th Cir. 1964), *revised* 383 U.S. 637 (1966).

75. *Borden Co.* v. *FTC*, 381 F.2d 175, 181 (5th Cir. 1967).

76. Price discrimination among final consumers is precluded under the Civil Rights Act if the basis of the discrimination is the race, religion, or sex of the purchaser.

77. The manufacturer could, however, charge all retail stores one price and all restaurants a lower price for the same product, since the buyers receiving the lower price would not be directly competing with those receiving the higher price.

78. This was undoubtedly due to the Act's New Deal origins. The Robinson-Patman amendments were passed during a period in which the protection of small businesses was viewed as a valid independent antitrust concern. See F. Rowe, *Price Discrimination Under the Robinson-Patman Act*, pp. 22–23 (1962). For another excellent account of the origins of the Act, see Hansen, "Robinson-Patman Law: A Review and Analysis," 51 *Fordham Law Review*, pp. 1113, 1120–24 (1983) (noting that the Act was a product of the Great Depression: "[A]lthough some consumers viewed the increase in the number of chain stores at the expense of small corner stores as a competitive benefit, others viewed it as a threat to religious values, the ability of working people to buy food, and the quality of small-town life in general").

79. *Utah Pie Co.* v. *Continental Bakery Co.*, 386 U.S. 685, 701 (1967).

80. Bowman, "Restraint of Trade by the Supreme Court: The Utah Pie Case," *Yale Law Review*, p. 70 (1967).

81. *FTC* v. *Anheuser Busch, Inc.*, 363 U.S. 536 (1960).

82. *Balian Ice Cream Co.* v. *Arden Farms Co.*, 231 F.2d 356 (9th Cir. 1955).

83. A fuller discussion of predatory pricing is found later in the text under Predation. For a discussion of the historical conflict concerning the goals of the Robinson-Patman and Sherman Acts, see Sullivan and Harrison,

Understanding Antitrust and Its Economic Implications, p. 322–23 (New York: Matthew Bender, 1988).

84. *Brooke Group Ltd.* v. *Brown & Williamson Tobacco Corp.*, 61 U.S.L.W. 4699 (decided June 21, 1993). A more detailed discussion of *Brooke Group* is postponed until the discussion under Predation.

85. *Brooke Group Ltd.* v. *Brown & Williamson Tobacco Corp.*, 61 U.S.L.W. 4702 (decided June 21, 1993).

86. The court noted in *Brooke Group* that because the parties stipulated that the relevant measure of cost should be average variable cost, it need not resolve the conflict among the lower courts over the appropriate measure of cost.

87. *Brooke Group Ltd.* v. *Brown & Williamson Tobacco Corporation*, 61 U.S.L.W. 4703 (decided June 21, 1993).

88. *FTC* v. *Morton Salt*, 344 U.S. (1948).

89. See discussion under Legal Defenses below.

90. *Texaco Inc.* v. *Ricky Hasbrouck*, 496 U.S. 543, 110 S.Ct. 2535 (1990).

91. *Texaco Inc.* v. *Ricky Hasbrouck*, 496 U.S. 563, 110 S.Ct. 2535 (1990).

92. Justice Scalia, in a concurring opinion, criticized the majority for accepting the proposition that a functional discount would be acceptable practice even if it was "reasonable." Congress explicitly specified the exceptions to Robinson-Patman liability, Justice Scalia observed, and only Congress should say whether such discounts should be permissible. *Texaco Inc.* v. *Ricky Hasbrouck*, 496 U.S. 579, 110 S.Ct. 2535 (1990).

93. R. Posner, *The Robinson-Patman Act: Federal Regulation of Price Differences* (1976). Posner and others have noted that the actual influence of its prohibitions can be to *increase* prices and *decrease* output. The problem is that the Act was passed during the Depression and reflects a general distrust of competitive market forces that characterized that era. See also Rowe, *Price Discrimination Under The Robinson-Patman Act* (1962).

94. Hansen, "Robinson-Patman Law: A Review and Analysis," 51 *Fordham Law Review*, pp., 1174–82 1113 (1983).

95. See discussion of predatory pricing under Predation.

96. *J. Truett Payne Co.* v. *Chrysler Motors Corp.*, 451 U.S. 557 (1981) (A price discrimination causes "antitrust injury" only when the favored customer actually uses its advantage in a way that impairs the disfavored customer's ability to compete. If the favored customer simply pockets the price difference, the discrimination has not injured the plaintiff. The plaintiff must show that it lost customers or profits because the favored customer used the discount either to lower its resale prices or otherwise to solicit business). See *ABA Antitrust Section, Antitrust Law Developments*, 3rd ed. (1992), p. 449.

This section has benefited from the discussion in Sullivan and Harrison, *Understanding Antitrust And Its Economic Implications* (New York: Matthew Bender Co, 1988), p. 307.

97. *American Can* v. *Bruce's Juices*, 187 F.2nd 919, modifies 190 F.2d 38 (8 Cir. 1951); see also *United States* v. *Borden*, 370 U.S. 460 (1962).

98. *FTC* v. *Standard Oil of Indiana*, 340 U.S. 231 (1951).

99. *Borden* v. *FTC*, 339 F.2d 953 (7 Cir. 1964); (1979); see also *United States* v. *U.S. Gypsum*, 438 U.S. 422 (1978).

100. See *International Salt Co.* v. *United States*, 332 U.S. 12 (1947). Defendant International Salt leased its patented machines only on the condition that lessees purchase from it all the salt used in the machines. The court held that it was "unreasonable per se to foreclose competitors from any substantial market." 332 U.S. at 396. The court made note of the "limited monopoly," 332 U.S. at 395, held by International Salt but did not indicate that such a finding was necessary for applying the per se standard.

101. *United States* v. *Jerrold Electronics Corp.*, 187 F.Supp. 545 (E.D. Pa.), *aff'd per curiam*, 365 U.S. 567 (1961).

102. F. M. Scherer, *Industrial Market Structure and Economic Performance*, 3rd ed. (Chicago: Rand McNally, 1990), p. 568. Twenty years after a court ordered IBM to stop tying sales of punch cards to sales of its tabulating machines, the company still retained nearly 90 percent of the market. This shows that if a firm maintains a good reputation and offers a quality product, buyers may accept a tie-in voluntarily.

103. In 1979, an appeals court ruled that Kodak could develop unique cameras and films without telling its competitors in advance about the technology. The court ruled that the benefits of a technological tie between a new camera and its film are a legitimate reward for the innovator. *Berkey Photo* v. *Eastman Kodak*, 603 F.2nd 263 (2d Cir.), Cert. denied, 444 U.S. 1093 (1980).

104. Four of the concurring Justices in *Jefferson Parish Hospital* v. *Hyde*, 466 U.S. 2, 35–36 (1984), argued for abandoning the per se approach to tying. Justice O'Connor's opinion is noteworthy because it reflects an attempt to apply modern economic thought to tying. She questioned the "leverage" theory as a justification for barring tying (O'Connor, J., concurring).

105. *Jefferson Parish Hospital* v. *Hyde*, 466 U.S. 2 (1984).

106. Id. at 18–19.

107. Id. at 18.

108. See Sullivan and Harrison, *Understanding Antitrust and Its Economic Implications* (New York: Matthew Bender, 1988), p. 196.

109. *Eastman Kodak Company* v. *Image Technical Services, Inc., et al*, 112 S.Ct. 2072 (1992).

110. See Gellhorn and Kovacic, "Anti-Competitive Forces May Stir Anew," *National Law Journal*, May 24, 1993, p. 19.

111. See *Standard Oil*, 221 U.S. 1 (1911).

112. See *Moore* v. *Mead's Fine Bread*, 348 U.S. 115 (1954); *Maryland Baking* v. *FTC*, 243 F.2d 716, 718 (4th Cir. 1957).

113. *Matsushita Electric Industry Co.* v. *Zenith Radio Corp.*, 475 U.S. 574, 106 S.Ct. 1348, 1358 (1986).

114. The formula given in the text is the Areeda-Turner test, which stems from a 1975 article by Professors Areeda and Turner. Although one appeals court has recently observed that "the Areeda-Turner test is like the Venus de Milo:

it is much admired and often discussed, but rarely embraced," *McGahee* v. *Northern Propane Gas Co.*, 858 F.2nd 1487, 1495 (11th Cir. 1988), Cert. denied, 490 U.S. 1084 (1989), virtually all courts draw upon it to some extent by using a cost-based predatory pricing test. The law in the circuits varies, however, as to the appropriate cost standard. See *ABA Antitrust Section, Antitrust Law Developments*, 3rd ed. (1992), pp. 227–34, for a review of the standards used in the various circuits.

115. *Matsushita Electric Industry Co.* v. *Zenith Radio Corp.*, 475 U.S. 574, 106 S.Ct. 1348, 1358 (1986).

116. See Kovacic and Larson, "Predatory Pricing Safeguards in Telecommunications Regulation: Removing Impediments to Competition," 35 *St. Louis University Law Review*, pp. 28–29 (1990): "One commentator has concluded that nearly all predatory pricing claims decided from 1975 to 1986 could have been disposed of summarily for the defendant under the standards of *Matsushita*." See also Liebeler, "Whither Predatory Pricing? From Areeda and Turner to *Matsushita*," 61 *Notre Dame Law Review*, p. 1952 (1986).

117. See DeSanti and Kovacic, "*Matsushita*: Its Construction and Application by the Lower Courts," 59 *Antitrust Law Journal*, pp. 609, 644 (1991).

118. *Liggett Group, Inc.* v. *Brown & Williamson Tobacco Corp.*, 748 F.Supp. 344 (M.D.N.C. 1990), 964 F.2nd 335 (1992).

119. *Brooke Group Ltd.* v. *Brown & Williamson Tobacco Corp.*, 61 U.S.L.W. 4699 (decided June 21, 1993).

120. DeSanti and Kovacic, "*Matsushita*: Its Construction and Application by the Lower Courts," 59 *Antitrust Law Journal*, pp. 609, 651 (1991).

121. Clarence C. Walton, *Ethos and the Executive* (Englewood Cliffs, N. J.: Prentice Hall, 1969), p. 209.

122. William J. Kehoe, "Ethics, Price Fixing, and the Management of Price Strategy," in *Marketing Ethics: Guidelines for Managers*, eds. Gene R. Laczniak and Patrick E. Murphy (Lexington, Mass.: D. C. Heath, 1985), p. 72.

123. Kehoe, "Ethics, Price Fixing," p. 71.

124. Manuel G. Velasquez, *Business Ethics*, 3rd ed. (Englewood Cliffs, N.J.: Prentice Hall, 1992), pp. 282–83.

125. Tom L. Beaucamp and Normal E. Bowie, *Ethical Theory and Business*, 4th ed. (Englewood Cliffs, N.J.: Prentice Hall, 1993), pp. 697–98.

INDEXES

SUBJECT INDEX

A

Accounting depreciation formulas, 29
Accounting statements, misleading, 26-28
Activity-based costing, 15, 28
Advertising:
  discounter's, 242-43
  effect on retail margins, 263
  as a nonprice defense, 135
  price sensitivity and, 242-46
  to establish perceived end benefit, 88-89
  to raise reference price, 304-5
Aggregate sales data, estimating price,
  325-27
Agreement among competitors:
  explicit, 366-71
  nonexplicit, 371-74
Airlines industry, 18, 127-28, 171, 216-18,
  224, 271
Alcoa, 227-28
American Hospital Supply Company, 193
American West Airline, 127-28
Anheuser-Busch, 135-36
Antitrust laws, 360-66
Antitrust suits, private, 361-62
Apple, 10-11
AT&T, 113, 130, 133
Attribute-based study, 341-42
Augmented products, 258-59, 290-91
Avoidable costs, 18, 23-28
Avoiding the price trap, 198-99

B

Bell Telephone system, 216-27
Berkley Photo v. *Eastman Kodak Company*
  (1979), 229*n*
Bic Company, 134-35
Bidding (*see* Competitive bidding)
Block discounts, 221
Borden Co. v. *FTC* (1964), 375
Borden Milk, 375
Boston Consulting Group, 277-78
Brand managers, 256-57

Brand preferences, studies of, 324-25
  experimentally controlled, 342-49
  uncontrolled, 337-42
Breakeven analysis:
  baseline for, 54-55
  breakeven ratio, 38-41
  change in profit calculation, 48-50
  change in variable costs, 41-43
  chart development, 48-50, 61-63
  derivation of formula for, 58-60
  incremental fixed costs and, 43-46, 63-66
  non-incremental fixed costs and, 55-56
  price changes, 61-70
  reactive pricing, 46-48
  sales curves, 50-53
  sunk costs and, 55-56
  value-added, 227-28
British Textile Council, 272
Broadcast Music, Inc. v. *Columbia Broadcasting
  System* (1979), 367
Bundling, 180, 225-28, 314-16
Business Electronics Corp v. *Sharp Electronics
  Corp.* (1988), 369
Buyer adoption, 171-72
Buyer focus, economies of, 281-82
Buyer identification, segmenting by, 211-13
Buyers (*see* Industrial buyers; Price sensitiv-
  ity; Psychological aspects of pricing)
Buyers' investments, 293
Buying center, 192
Buy-response surveys, 338-41

C

Capacity costs, 216-17
Car rental companies, 222-23
Case law, 366-83
Caterpillar Tractor, 258, 279
Chadwick Martin Bailey, Inc., 324, 339-40,
  347
Channel:
  conflict, 262-64
  managing pricing within, 259-64

Channel (*cont.*)
  preemption, 293
  selection, 257-59
Chicago Board of Trade v. *United States* (1918),
    370
Chrysler Corporation, 127, 289
Clayton Antitrust Act of 1914, 228, 365-66,
    374-76, 378-81
Collusion, 372-73
Compensation, sales force, 191, 208-9
Competition (*see* Competitive cost
    advantages; Competitive product
    advantages; Competitor price behavior;
    Price competition)
Competition-driven pricing, 8-9
Competitive advantage, seeking, 130-32
Competitive analysis, 144
Competitive bidding:
  average opponent approach, 201-2
  government contract, 203
  preparing, 199-205
  qualitative analysis, 199-201
  specific opponent approach, 203-5
  winner's curse, 205
Competitive cost advantages, 270-89
  economies of buyer focus, 281-82
  economies of experience, 277-81
  economies of logistical integration, 282-83
  economies of scale, 271-77
  economies of scope, 270-71
  efficiency in transfer pricing, 283-88
  external cost efficiencies, 281-89
  internal cost efficiencies, 270-81
  temporary, 289
Competitive product advantages, 289-94
  product augmentation, 291-92
  product superiority, 290-91
  sustaining, 292-94
Competitive Strategy (Porter), 131
Competitor price behavior:
  anticipation of, 119-21
  establishing pricing policies, 121-23
  evaluation of, 124-26
  neutral pricing, and, 160-61
  opportunism, 128
  penetration pricing, and, 158-60
  profitable pricing, 118-23
  selectively communicate information,
    126-29
  skim pricing and, 153-58
Competitor pricing analysis, 123-26, 144
Complementary products:
  defined, 236
  as loss leaders, 240-41
  pricing, 238-40
Confrontations:
  avoiding, 133-34
  nonprice, 135-36
  retaliation, 133-34

selecting, 132-36
Conjoint analysis, 96, 344-49
Consolidation strategy in declining
    market,184-85
Consumer psychology (*see* Psychological
    aspects of pricing)
Contribution margin:
  adjustments for complementary products,
    238-40
  adjustments for substitute products,
    238-40
  calculation, 27
  percent, 31-33
  (*see also* Breakeven analysis, price
    changes)
Convenience buyers, 162
Copyrights, 155
Cost advantages (*see* Competitive cost
    advantages)
Cost-based pricing, 2-5
Cost leadership strategy, 173-77
Costs:
  average, 22, 28
  avoidable, 18, 23-28, 30-31
  breakeven analysis and (*see* Breakeven
    analysis, price changes)
  capacity, 216-17
  decline phase of products and, 182
  determining relevant cost, 18-28
  estimates of, problems with, 28-31
  fixed, 19
  historical, 30
  importance to pricing decision, 17-18
  incremental, 19-23
  non-incremental, 19
  opportunistic pricing and, 128-29
  opportunity, 29-30
  percent contribution margin and, 31-33
  relevant, 18-31
  resale value, 23
  semi-fixed, 19
  sunk, 18, 25
  variable, 19
Coupons, 251-52
Crown Cork and Seal, 281-82
Current prices, influences, 302-7
Customer-driven pricing, 7-8

D

Data collection, 142-43
Dealing, 250-57
  defensive, 253-55
  product trial, inducement of, 250-53
  trade, 255-57
De Beers, 249
Deceptive pricing, 383-84
Decline phase, pricing products, in, 182-85

Defensive pricing, 253-55
  (*see also* Breakeven analysis, reactive
    pricing; Nonprice defense; Value-
    added bundling)
Depreciation, 23, 29
Derived demand, 87
Development phase, pricing during, 168-72
Differential product strategy, 173-77
Differentiation value, 74-77, 107, 162
Difficult comparison effect, 81-83, 97
Direct questioning to estimate price
    sensitivity, 338
Discounts:
  block, 221
  order, 220-21
  quantity, segmenting by, 218-23
  selective, 128, 217-18
  step, 221
Distribution:
  marketing innovations through, 172
  maturity phase of products and, 181-82
  pricing strategy and, 257-64
Dun & Bradstreet, 271
Du Pont, 107-13

E

Eastman Kodak Company, 381
Eastman Kodak Company v. *Image Technical
    Services, Inc.* (1992), 381
Economics of price sensitivity, 100-101
Economic value analysis, 73-77, 96, 107-13
Economic value profile, 111-13
Economies:
  of buyer focus, 281-82
  of experience, 277-81
  of logistical integration, 282-83
  of scale, 271-77
  of scope, 270-71
Efficiencies, cost, 270-89
  external, 281-89
  internal, 270-81
  in transfer pricing, 283-88
Elasticity of demand, 53
Electric companies, 221-22
End-benefit effect, 87-89, 98
Endowment effect, 312-13
Established pricing policies, 121-23
Estimating price sensitivity (*see* Price
    sensitivity measurement)
Ethical constraints on pricing, 383-86
Excess capacity, 30, 147-48
Exclusive products, 83-84
Expenditure effect, 86-87, 98
Experience, economies of, 277-81
Experience curve, 277-81
Experimental design, 349-55
Experiments:

in-store purchase, 332-34
laboratory purchase, 334-37
Explicit agreements, 366-71
Exploratory research, 350
External cost efficiencies, 281-89

F

Fairness effect, 91-92, 99
Federal Trade Commission (FTC), 361-66
Federal Trade Commission Act of 1914,
    365-66
Federal Trade Commission v. *Morton Salt*
    (1948), 220
Firestone Tire and Rubber Company, 183-84
First-mover advantage, 292-94
Fixed costs, 19
Fixed-price policy, 122, 191
FOB (free on board), 214
Focus groups, 350
Focus strategy, 282
Ford, Henry, 272-73
Ford Motor Company, 5-7, 169, 194
Fractional factorial design, 333-34
Framing, price, 310-16
Free samples, 170, 253
Freight absorption, 214
FTC v. *Morton Salt* (1948), 378
Fuji, 134
Full factorial design, 333-34

G

Game Theory, 117-18
  negative-sum, 118
  positive-sum, 117-18
Gasoline stations, 237-38
G. E. Doctrine, 370
General Electric Company, 370
General Motors Corporation, 161, 194, 282-83
Gillette Corp., 134-35
Goodrich, B.F. , Company, The, 184
Goodyear Tire and Rubber Company, 184-85
Government contracts, 203
Greater Southern Development Authority,
    345-47
Growth phase, pricing in, 172-78

H

Hamlin Harkins, Ltd., 342
Harvesting strategy, 184
Heaton Peninsular v. *Eureka Specialty Co.*
    (1896) , 228*n*
Henry v. *A. B. Dick* (1912), 228*n*
Historical booking path, 218-19
Historical costs, 30
Historical sales data, 328-30, 351-55

I

Iacocca, Lee, 5-7
IBM Corporation, 83, 171, 196
Image, first-movers and, 294
Image products, 83-84
Impulse buying, 86
Income statements, 26-28
Incremental breakeven analysis, 37-38
Incremental costs:
    as avoidable costs, 18, 27-28, 30-31
    defined, 18-19
    fixed, breakeven sales with, 19
    fixed costs, 19
    reorganization of income statement and,
        26-27
    variable cost, 19
Industrial buyers:
    end-benefit effect and, 81-83
    evaluation alternative, 212-13
Inelastic demand, 100-101
Information, competitive:
    collection and evaluating, 124-26
    diffusion of, 123-29, 169
    price, 126-27
Innovations, pricing, 168-72
Installment plans, 313
In-store purchase experiments, 332-34
Insurance industry, 92, 317
Intel Corporation, 276
Intention measurements (*see* Purchase
    intentions, studies of)
Internal cost efficiencies, 270-81
International Business Machines Corporation
    v. *United States* (1936), 228n
Introduction phase, pricing in, 168-72
Inventory effect, 93-94, 99-100

J

Jones, Indiana, 132
Justice Department, 362-63

L

Laboratory purchase experiments, 334-37
Learning curve, 277-81
Leasing, 250
Legal considerations:
    antitrust laws, 360-66
    case law, 366-83
    deceptive pricing, 383-84
    explicit agreements, 366-71
    history of, 363-66
    nonexplicit agreements, 371-74
    predation, 381-83
    price discrimination, 374-79
    requirements contracts, 379-81
    sanctions, 361-63
    tie-in sales, 379-81

Legislative law, 363-66
Lenox Company, 257-58
Life cycle (*see* Product life cycle, pricing
    over)
LIFO (last-in, first-out), 24
Limit-entry pricing, 274-76
Linear regression, analysis of sales
    data using, 328-29
Line extensions, 181
Loctite Corporation, 290
Lodging industry, 211
Long-term goals, 116-17
Long-term relationships, developing, 197
Loss leaders, selection of, 240-41
Lotus 1-2-3, 81
Loyal buyers, 195-96

M

Managing competitive information, 123-29
Market-based pricing, 37-38
Market decline, pricing products in, 182-85
Market development phase, pricing products
    in, 168-72
Market growth phase, pricing products in,
    172-78
Marketing mix, pricing in, 235-65
    distribution and, 257-64
    personal selling, 246-48
    price as a promotional tool, 249-57
    product line and, 235-41
    promotion and, 241-49
Marketing plans, 119
Market introduction phase (*see* Market
    development phase)
Market maturity phase, pricing products in,
    178-82
Market Research Corporation of America
    (MRCA), 330-31
Market segmentation (*see* Segmented
    pricing)
Market share myth, 139-40
Marlboro cigarettes, 164
Matsushita, 372, 382
Matsushita Electric Industry Co. v. *Zenith Radio
    Corp.* (1986), 372
Maturity phase, pricing products in, 178-82,
    253-54
McDonald's Corporation, 282, 380
MCI Communications, Inc., 113
Measurements of price sensitivity (*see*
    Price sensitivity measurement)
Mental "framing" of prices, 310-16
Metering, segmenting by, 229-30
Michelin Tire Corporation, 184-85
Microsoft, 130, 174, 291, 293
Miller Brewing Company, 136
Minolta Cameras, 363
Model T, 169, 272-73

Morton Salt, 377-78
Motion Picture Patents Co. v. *Universal Film Mfg. Co.* (1917), 228*n*
Movie industry, 249

N

Negotiation strategies, 193-99
  avoiding price trap, 198-99
  with loyal buyers, 195-96
  with price buyers, 193-95
  with value buyers, 196-98
Neilson, A.C., Company, 326
Neutral pricing, 154, 160-61, 174
Nevin, John, 183
New products:
  pricing in development phase, 168-72
  pricing in growth phase, 172-78
Newspaper industry, 225-26
Niche marketing, 293
NIFO (next-in, first-out), 24
Nonexplicit agreements, 371-74
Nonprice defense, 135-36
Northwest Airline, 127-28

O

Objectives of pricing strategy, 9-12
Odd-ending prices, perception of, 300-302
Off-peak pricing, 147-52
Opportunistic pricing, 36-38
Opportunity costs, 29-30, 201
Optional bundling, 226-27
Order discounts, 220-21
Order effects, 304-7

P

Panel data, estimating price sensitivity from, 327-28
Past prices, influences, 307-9
Past sales data, estimating price sensitivity from, 325-28
Patents:
  legal considerations concerning, 370-71
  protection, 155
Peak-load pricing, 147-52, 215-17
Peak reversal, 217
Penetration pricing, 153, 158-60, 173-74
Perceived substitute effect, 78-79
Percentage contribution margin and, pricing strategy, 31-33
Percentage price differences, perception of, 299-300
Personal selling, pricing and, 246-48
Pharmaceuticals industry, 91-92
Philip Morris, 164-65
Planning a pricing strategy, 118-23
Polaroid, 154, 156

Predatory pricing, 113, 381-83
Preferences (*see* Brand preferences, studies of)
Premier Industrial Corporation, 130-31, 291
Prestige products, 83-86
Price buyers, 162, 193-95, 197
Price changes (*see* Breakeven analysis, price changes; Competitor price behavior; Price sensitivity)
Price competition, 115-40
  anticipation, 119-21
  difficult comparison effect and, 81-83, 97
  estimate pricing policies, 121-23
  evaluation of, 124-26
  factors influencing, 115-17
  importance of, 115-17
Price cutting (*see* Breakeven analysis, price changes; Competitor price behavior; Price sensitivity)
Price deals, 250-53
Price differences, perception of, 299-302
Price discrimination, 374-79
  (*see also* Segmented pricing)
Price elasticities:
  defined, 100-101
  generalizations about, 101-3
Price gouging, 24, 91
Price-induced sampling, 170-71
Price information, exchanges, 126-29, 373-74
Price negotiations, reason for, 190-91
Price perception (*see* Psychological aspects of pricing)
Price-quality effect, 83-86, 97-98
Price sensitivity:
  advertising and, 242-46
  derived demand, 87
  difficult comparison effect, 81-83, 97
  economics of, 100-101
  end-benefit effect, 87-89, 98
  estimating (*see* Price sensitivity measurement)
  expenditure effect, 86-87, 98
  fairness effect, 91-92, 99
  growth phase of products and, 176
  inventory effect, 93-94, 99-100
  managerial analysis of, 94-100
  measurement of (*see* Pricing strategy)
  price-quality effect, 83-86, 97-98
  pricing strategy and (*see* Pricing strategy)
  shared cost effect, 87, 89-91, 99
  substitute awareness effect, 78-79, 95-96
  switching cost effect, 80-81, 96-97
  total expenditure effect, 86-87
  unique value effect, 79-80, 96
Price sensitivity measurement, 323-56
  aggregate sales data, 325-27
  buy-response surveys, 338-41
  conjoint analysis, 344-49
  direct questioning, 338

Price sensitivity measurement (*cont.*)
  experimentally controlled studies of
    actual purchases, 331-37
  experimentally controlled studies of
    preferences and intentions, 342-49
  historical sales data, 328-30
  in-store purchase experiments, 332-34
  laboratory purchase experiments, 334-47
  panel data, 327-28
  past sales data, 325-28
  simulated purchase surveys, 343-44
  store audit data, 328
  tradeoff analysis, 344-49
  uncontrolled studies of actual purchases,
    325-30
  uncontrolled studies of preferences and
    intentions, 337-42
  use of techniques, 324-25, 349-55
Price trap, avoiding, 198-99
Pricing, ethical constraints on, 383-86
Pricing and the law (*see* Legal considerations)
Pricing environment, 9-14, 117-18
  negative sum game, 117-18
  positive sum game, 117-18
  (*See also* Competitor price behavior; Costs;
    Marketing mix, pricing in; Price
    sensitivity; Product life cycle, pricing
    over)
Pricing psychology (*see* Psychological
  aspects of pricing)
Pricing strategy, 141-52, 238-40
  competition and (*see* Competitor price
    behavior)
  complementary products, 238-40
  confrontations, 132-36
  economic value analysis and, 73-79, 96,
    107-13
  establishing policies, 121-23
  to induce trial, 250-53
  neutral pricing, 154, 160-61
  penetration pricing, 153, 158-60
  product-line interactions, 241
  retaliation, 134-35
  skim pricing, 153-58
  substitute products, 237-38
Pricing strategy development model, 9-12
Pricing tactics, 11-12
Primary level competition, 376
Probabilistic goods, pricing, 316-18
Procter & Gamble, 117
Product advantages, competitive (*see*
  Competitive product advantages)
Product augmentation, 258-59, 291-92
Product bundling, segmenting by, 11-12, 180,
  225-58
Product design, segmenting by, 223-25
Product differentiation, 79-80, 162, 289-94
Product economic value analysis, 73-79, 96,
  107-13

Product life cycle, pricing over, 122
  market decline phase, 182-85
  market development phase, 168-72
  market growth phase, 172-78, 196
  market maturity phase, 122, 178-82, 253-54
Product line:
  interactions, 241
  pricing strategy and, 235-41, 303-4
Product specialization, 177
Product superiority, 290-91
Product trial, inducement of, 250-53
Profit, calculation of change in, 26-28
Profitable pricing, 118-23
Profit contribution, 56
Promotion:
  price as adjunct to, 249-57
  price as integral part of, 241-57
Promotional budget, setting, 248-49
Prospect theory, 310-13
Psychological aspects of pricing, 298-319
  formulation of reference prices, 302-10
  mental "framing" of prices, 310-16
  past prices influences, 307-9
  perception of price differences, 299-302
  probabilistic goods, 316-18
  product lines and, 303-4
  purchase context influence, 309-10
Purchase intentions, studies of:
  experimentally controlled, 342-49
  uncontrolled, 337-42
Purchase location, segmenting by, 213-15
Purchase quantity, segmenting by, 218-23
Purchases, actual:
  experimentally controlled studies of,
    331-37
  uncontrolled studies of, 325-31

Q

Quantitative bidding analysis, 199-201
Questioning, direct, 338

R

Rebates, 93, 252-53
Recall of prices, 307-9
Reference prices:
  defined, 79
  formulation of, 302-10
Reference value, 74-77, 107
Regression analysis, 328-30
Relevant costs determining, 18-31
Replacement costs, 23-24
Requirements contracts, 379-81
Resale price maintenance, 368-70
Resale prices, 259-64
  limiting maximum, 260-64
  maintaining minimum, 259-60
Reservation price, 100
Retaliation by competitor, 133-34

Retrenchment strategy, 183-84
Robinson-Patman Act of 1936, 255, 365-66,
    374-78
Rohn and Haas Chemical, 225
Roosevelt, Theodore, 364
Rule of reason, 366

S

Sales force:
    compensation, 191, 208-9
    management, 123
Salespeople:
    incentives for, 208-9
    price by (*see* Negotiation strategies)
    segmenting by, 212-13
Sanctions, legal, 361-63
Saturn automobile, 282-83
Scale, economies of, 271-77
Scope, economies of, 270-71
Sears, 164-65
Secondary level competition, 376
Segmentation analysis, 144
Segmented pricing, 161-65, 210-32
    basis for, 231
    buyer identification and, 211-13
    importance of, 121, 230-31
    metering and, 229-30
    price discrimination, legal restrictions on,
        374-79
    product bundling and, 225-28
    product design and, 223-25
    purchase location and, 213-15
    purchase quantity and, 218-23
    tie-ins and, 228-30
    time of purchase and, 215-18
Selective discounts, 128, 217-18
Selective participation, 193-94
Semi-fixed costs, 19
Sequential skimming, 156-58
Shared cost effect, 87, 89-91, 99
Sherman Act of 1890, 361-62, 364-67, 373,
    376-77
Short-turn price sales goals, 116-17
Simulated purchase surveys, 343-44
Skim pricing (skimming), 153-58
Standard Oil, 364, 368, 379
Step discounts, 221
Sticker shock, 308
Store audit data, analysis of, 328
Strategic analysis, 143-45
Strategic objectives, 10
Strategy formulation, 9-11, 144-45
    (*see also* Pricing strategy)
Substitute awareness effect, 78-79, 95-96
Substitute products:
    defined, 236
    pricing, 237-38
Suggested retail prices, 259-60, 369

Sunk costs, 18
Supermarket industry, 226-27, 240-41
Supersaver fares, 218
Suppliers, 82-83
Survey research:
    attribute-based, 341-42
    buy-response, 338-41
    preferences and intentions, 353-55
    purchase intentions, 337-42
    simulated purchase, 343-44
Switching cost effect, 80-81, 96-97

T

Target marketing, 130-32
Target return pricing, 3-4
Temporary cost advantages, 289
Texaco, 378
Texaco Inc. v. *Ricky Hasbrouck* (1990), 378
Texas Instruments, 10, 273-74
Tie-in sales, 228-29, 379-81
Time of purchase, segmented pricing and,
    215-18
Time of purchase, segmenting by, 215-18
Timex watches, 257
Total expenditure effect, 86-87
Trade barriers, 214
Trade dealing, 255-57
Tradeoff analysis, 96, 344-49
Trans-Alaska Oil Pipeline Act, 366
Transfer pricing, 283-89
Trial, pricing tactics to induce, 250-53
Trial offers, 251
Two-part pricing, 222-23

U

Unbundling related products and services,
    180, 196, 314-16
Undifferentiated product, 75-77
Unique value effect, 79-80, 96
United Auto Workers, 289
United Shoe Machinery Corporation v. *United
    States* (1922), 228n
United States v. *American Can Company*
    (1949), 228
United States v. *Container Corp. of America*
    (1969), 374
United States v. *General Electric* (1926), 370
United States v. *Jerrold Electronics Co.* (1960),
    228
United States v. *Northern Securities* (1904), 364
United States v. *Socony Vacuum Oil Co. Inc.*
    (1940), 367
U.S. rail system, 230-31
U.S. Time Company, 257

V

Value-added bundling, 227-28
Value analysis (*see* Economic value analysis)
Value-based pricing, 4-5, 9, 191-92, 196-98

Value buyers, 162
Variable costs, 19
Volume discounts, 219-20
Volvo, 80

W

Wal-Mart, 129-30, 164-65, 174, 283
Wang Laboratories, 3
Wayne, John, 132

Webb-Pomerene Act of 1918, 366
Weber-Fechner Law, 300
Wheeler-Lea Act of 1938, 366

X

Xerox Corporation, 229-30

Y

Yankelovich Partners, 336-37
Yield management, 217-18

AUTHOR INDEX

A

Aaker, David A., 80n, 248n, 253n, 341n
Abramovitz, Moses (ed.), 277n
Abrams, Bill, 290n
Acito, Franklin, 348n
Ahmed, Sadrudin A., 304n
Albert, Kenneth J. (ed.), 277n
Albion, Mark S., 262n
Alcaly, Roger E., 86n
Alchian, Armen, 277n
Anderson, M.J., 175n
Applebaum, William, 334n
Asher, Harold, 277n
Assael, Henry, 341n

B

Bailey, Earl L., 101n
Barclay, William D., 334n
Barnes, James G., 304n
Barron, Penny, 244n, 245, 334n
Bass, Frank M., 169n
Bearden, William O., 304n
Beaucamp, Tom L., 385n
Beaujon, George J., 28n
Behrmann, Neil, 249n
Bellenger, D.N., 348n
Benham, Lee, 244n
Bennet, Sidney, 334n
Bereson, Mark L., 329
Berkowitz, Eric N., 304n
Best, Roger, 348n
Beswick, Charles, 248n
Blackmore, David, 347
Blair, Edward A., 304n
Blattberg, Robert, 251n, 256n, 301, 328n
Bohi, Douglas R., 81n
Bonoma, Thomas V., 192n
Borden, James P., 28n
Boring, R.A., 84n
Bowie, Normal E., 385n
Bowman, Russell, 251n, 376n
Broome, Charles, 85n

Burke Marketing Services, Inc., 85
Burns, Alvin C., 341n
Buzzell, Robert D. 257n
Byrne, Harlan S., 258n

C

Calder, Bobby J., 350n
Campbell, Donald T., 333n
Campbell, W.M., 205n
Capen, E.C., 205n
Carpenter, Gregory S., 169n
Cassady, Ralph, Jr., 228n
Cattin, Phillip, 345n
Chaiken, Shelly, 314n
Chakravarthi, Narasimhan, 212n
Charnes, A., 277n
Churchill, Neil, 24n
Clapp, R.V., 205n
Coe, Barbara, 14n
Cook, Thomas, 333n
Cooper, Arnold C., 176n
Cooper, Robin W., 28n, 277n
Corey, Raymond, 15n, 72n, 281n
Cravens, David, 248n

D

Day, George, 167n
Dean, Joel, 153n
Della Bitta, Albert J., 304n, 306, 308
Devinney, Timothy (ed.), 240n, 241n, 260n
Dhalla, Nariman K., 167n
Dickson, Peter R., 310n
Dixit, Avinash, 117n
Dodson, Joe, 253n
Dolan, Robert J., 14n, 200n, 219n, 277n
Doob, A., 307n
Dowst, Somerby, 248n
Dunnette, Marvin (ed.), 333n
Durairaj, Maheswaran, 314n

E

Easterbrook, Frank H., 361n
Emshwiller, John R., 249n

Enis, Ben, 85n
Eppen, Gary D., 225n, 256n
Eskin, Gerald, 244, 244n, 245, 246n, 333, 334n

F

Farris, Paul W., 262n
Fischhoff, Baruch, 318n
Fleming Associates, 14n
Flint, Jerry, 88n
Forbis, John L., 111n
Fraker, Susan, 291n
Frank, Ronald, 251n, 327n, 328n
Fraser, Cynthia, 304n
Friedman, Thomas, 334n
Fruhan, William E., 176n
Fuld, Leonard M., 126n

G

Gabor, Andre, 84n, 86n, 343n
Gaeth, Gary J., 314n
Gardner, David, 85n
Ghosh, Avijit, 101n, 102n, 328n
Gibson, Paul, 249n
Ginzberg, Eli, 301n
Glaxer, Amihai, 242n
Glover, Fred, 218n
Glover, Randy, 218n
Goldhar, Joel D., 271n
Goldstein, Michael H., 304n
Gonsior, M.H., 84n
Goyder, D.G., 364n
Graham, Neil E., 360-87
Granbois, Donald H., 78n
Granger, Clive, W.J., 84n, 86n, 343n
Green, Paul E., 344n
Greenberg, B.A., 348n
Gulas, Gary M., 304n

H

Haddock, Rafael, 85n
Hall, William, 177n, 179n
Hamermesh, R.G., 175n
Hanson, Ward A., 225n, 378n
Harmer, Richard, 162-63
Harris, J.T., 175n
Hawkins, Edward, 334n
Hayek, Frederick, 140n
Henderson, Bruce D., 277n
Henkoff, Ronald, 165n
Hershey, J.C., 317n
Heslop, Louise A., 304n, 307n
Hinkle, Charles, 253n
Hirsch, Warner Z., 277n
Hite, Robert E., 304n
Hogarth, Robin (ed.), 310n, 318n
Hume, Scott, 252n, 255n

I

Iacocca, Lee, 6-7

J

Jackson, Barbara B., 72n, 82n
Jacobson, Robert, 309n
Jacoby, Jacob, 85n
James, John C., 341n
Jelinek, Mariann, 271n
Jeuland, Abel P., 178n, 260n, 277n
Johansson, Johny K., 350n
Jones, D. Frank, 343n
Jones, John Philip, 253n

K

Kahn, Barbara E., 314n
Kahneman, Daniel, 91n, 92n, 300n, 310n, 312n, 316n
Kanetkar, Vinay, 244n
Kanwit, Stephanie W., 365n
Kaplan, Robert S., 27n, 28n
Kassarjian, H. (ed.), 300n
Kehoe, William J., 383n
Kessel, Reuben, 212n
Khumawata, Basheer M., 201n
King, Ronald H., 316n
Kinnear, Thomas C., 301n, 329
Knetsch, Jack L., 91n, 92n, 312n
Kosela, Rita, 117n
Kotler, Philip, 181n
Kottas, John F., 201n
Kovacic, William E., 360-87, 361n, 368n, 371n, 372n, 378n, 381n, 382n, 383n
Kreidberg, David, 189-209
Krishnamurthi, Lakshman, 101n, 242n
Kruskal, J.B., 345n

L

Laczniak, Gene R., 383n
Lakiani, Chet, 277n
Lambert, Zarrel V., 301n
Landon, E. Laird, Jr., 304n
Lawyer, J.Q., 371n
Leamer, Edward E., 327n, 352n
Leavitt, Harold, 84n
Levin, Irwin P., 314n
Levine, David M., 329
Levitt, Theodore, 167n, 171n, 181n, 291-92, 291n, 292n
Lichtenstein, Sarah, 318n
Lieberman, Joshua, 256n
Liefeld, John, 304n, 307n
Lorenzo, Joe, 218n

M

Machlup, Fritz, 260*n*
Mack, Toni, 253*n*
Maher, Philip, 172*n*
Marn, Michael, 192*n*
Martilla, John A., 341*n*
Martin, John, 347
Martin, R. Kipp, 225*n*
Massy, William, 251*n*, 327*n*, 328*n*
McCullough, James, 348*n*
McGinnis, John M., 304*n*
Mehta, Nitin T., 111*n*
Meyer, Robert J., 314*n*
Meyerowitz, Beth E., 314*n*
Meyers, John G., 248*n*
Meyers-Levey, Joan, 314*n*
Michaels, Ronald E., 169*n*
Milbank, Dana, 131*n*
Mobley, Mary F., 304*n*
Monroe, Kent B., 98*n*, 300*n*, 304*n*, 306, 308
Montgomery, David, 251*n*, 344*n* (ed.)
Moore, David J., 86*n*
Moran, William T., 101*n*
Morris, Betsy, 80*n*
Murphy, Patrick E., 383*n*

N

Nagle, Thomas, 115n, 240*n*
Nakamoto, Kent, 169*n*
Nalebuff, Barry, 117*n*
Neale, A.D., 364*n*
Neslin, Scott A., 101*n*, 102*n*, 328*n*
Nevin, John J., 184*n*
Nevin, John R., 343*n*, 344
Nigut, William, Sr., 251*n*
Nonaka, Ikujiro, 350*n*
Novak, Kenneth, 240*n*
Novak, William, 6-7
Nwokoye, Nonyelu, 302*n*

O

Obermiller, Carl, 309*n*
Ohmae, Kenishi, 117*n*
Olshavsky, Richard W., 78*n*, 86*n*, 169*n*
Olson, Jerry, 85*n*

P

Patton, Wesley E., III, 316*n*
Peckelman, Dove, 345*n*
Peters, Thomas J., 258*n*, 292*n*
Petroshius, Susan M., 300*n*
Porter, Michael E., 131, 132*n*, 168*n*, 173*n*, 179*n*, 270*n*, 278*n*
Posner, Richard A., 361*n*, 369*n*, 371*n*, 378*n*
Prasad, Kanti V., 244*n*

Primeaux, Walter J., Jr., 213*n*
Puto, Christopher P., 316*n*

Q

Qualls, William J., 169*n*, 316*n*
Quelch, John A., 257*n*

R

Raj, S.P., 101*n*, 242*n*
Rao, Vithala R., 85n, 344*n*
Reed, Robert, 254*n*
Ricci, Claudia, 258*n*, 260*n*
Ring, L. Winston, 244*n*
Robertson, T.S. (ed.), 300*n*
Robinson, Bruce, 277*n*
Robinson, Patrick J., 344*n*
Rogers, Everett M., 169*n*
Rosiella, Robert, 192n
Rowe, F., 376*n*
Russo, J. Edward, 82*n*, 299*n*

S

Salmon, Walter J., 257*n*
Sauer, Paul L., 304*n*
Saunier, Fredric, 198*n*
Scherer, Frederic M., 272*n*, 380*n*
Schindler, Robert M., 301*n*
Schmalensee, Richard, 160*n*
Schoemaker, Paul J. H., 101*n*, 102*n*, 169*n*, 299*n*, 317*n*, 328*n*
Schwadel, Francine, 125*n*
Scott, C.A., 253*n*
Segal, Madhav N., 348*n*
Semlow, W., 248*n*
Sen, Subrata, 345*n*
Sewall, Murphy A., 201*n* 304*n*
Shanklin, William L., 140*n*
Shansby, J. Gary, 80*n*, 341*n*
Shapiro, Benson P., 72*n*, 84*n*
Shapiro, Roy D., 282*n*
Sharman, Graham, 282*n*, 283*n*
Sherman, Stratford, 196*n*
Shugan, Steven M., 241*n*, 260*n*
Signhal, Vinod R., 28*n*
Simonson, Itamar, 303, 303*n*
Skinner, Wickham, 282*n*
Slovic, Paul, 317, 317*n*, 318*n*
Smallwood, John E., 167*n*
Smith, Edward, 85*n*
Smith, Gerald, 36-70, 298-319, 304*n*, 314*n*
Solman, Paul, 334*n*
Sowter, Anthony P., 343*n*
Spears, Richard, 334*n*
Stafford, James, 85*n*
Steiner, Robert L., 262*n*, 263
Sternthal, Brian, 253*n*

Stigler, George, 225*n*
Stocking, G.W., 225*n*
Stout, Roy G., 343*n*
Sullivan, L., 370*n*, 374*n*, 376*n*, 378*n*, 381*n*

T

Taber, Martha, 260*n*
Taylor, James R., 329
Teel, Jesse E., 304*n*
Telser, Lester, 101*n*, 102, 260*n*, 328*n*, 331
Thayler, Richard, 91*n*, 92*n*, 205*n*, 299*n*, 302*n*,
    309*n*, 310*n*, 312*n*, 314*n*
Tull, Donald, 84*n*
Tully, Shawn, 271*n*
Turney, Peter B.S., 28*n*
Tversky, Amos, 300*n*, 303, 303*n*, 310*n*, 312*n*,
    316*n*
Tybout, Alice, 253*n*

U

Udal, Jon G., 14*n*
Urbany, Joel E., 304n, 310*n*

V

van Leer, R. Karl, 292*n*
Velasquez, Manuel G., 385*n*
Venkatraman, Meera, 314*n*
Vilcassim, Naufel J., 212*n*

W

Walters, Rockney G., 236*n*
Walton, Clarence C., 383*n*
Walton, John R., 304*n*
Ward, Scott (ed.), 304*n*
Waterman, Robert H., 258*n*, 292*n*
Watkins, M.W., 225*n*
Weilbaker, Dan C., 304*n*
Weinberg, Charles B., 244*n*
Weiss, Doyle L., 244*n*
Whyte, William H., 169*n*
Wilkes, Robert E., 304*n*
Wilkinson, J.B., 334*n*
Willey, John, 298*n*
Williams, Monci Jo, 257*n*
Wiman, Alan R., 301*n*
Winer, Russell S., 307*n*
Wisniewski, Kenneth, 301, 328*n*
Wittink, Dick R., 212n, 244*n*, 344*n*, 345*n*
Wolf, Bob, 197, 197*n*
Woo, Carolyn Y., 176*n*
Wright, Peter (ed.), 304*n*
Wright, T.D., 277*n*

Y

Yankelovich Partners, 337
Yosper, Sonia, 167*n*

Z

Zukon, Alan J., 277*n*
Zweibach, Elliot, 252*n*, 255*n*